OUTER LIMITS

HOWARD HUGHES

OUTER LIMITS

THE FILMGOERS' GUIDE TO
THE GREAT SCIENCE-FICTION FILMS

I.B. TAURIS

LONDON · NEW YORK

3/17/15
WW
$19.50

Published in 2014 by I.B.Tauris & Co. Ltd

6 Salem Road, London W2 4BU
175 Fifth Avenue, New York NY 10010
www.ibtauris.com

Distributed in the United States and Canada
Exclusively by Palgrave Macmillan
175 Fifth Avenue, New York NY 10010

ISBN: 978 1 78076 166 4 (PB)
         978 1 78076 165 7 (HB)
         978 0 85773 475 4 (eBook)

A full CIP record for this book is available from the British Library
A full CIP record is available from the Library of Congress

Library of Congress Catalog Card Number: available

Typeset by Tetragon, London
Printed and bound by CPI Group (UK) Ltd, Croydon, CR0 4YY

MIX
Paper from
responsible sources
FSC
www.fsc.org   FSC® C013604

For Clara

CONTENTS

NOW AND THEN:
AN INTRODUCTION TO
SCIENCE-FICTION CINEMA

t all started in a galaxy far, far away. Well, the Odeon cinema in Chester actually, where I first saw *Star Wars* in the late 1970s. I can't remember how I found out about the film, whether it was from school friends or reading about it in the latest issue of *Look-in*, but I certainly remember the afternoon my mum took my sister and me to see it. Before the movie started, the enterprising cinema staff set the scene by projecting a starfield onto the darkened auditorium's ceiling. The cinema was transformed into a planetarium, the dim twinkling reaches of outer space, and the imperial starship that roared overhead in the film's opening sequence seemed to emerge from the inky blackness of another galaxy.

The 1970s were the golden age for cinema science fiction, the moment when the genre found its place in popular culture as fashionable and massive-grossing international entertainment. Although sci-fi had been popular from the flickering dawn of cinema, it rose to prominence in the postwar nuclear age and enjoyed great attention in the 1950s, as the global space race caught the public's imagination. The quantum leaps forward in special-effects technology, partially facilitated by Stanley Kubrick's Oscar-winning *2001: A Space Odyssey* in 1968, made the impossible possible, and by 1977 space travel and the galaxy's outer reaches could be depicted with something approaching realism, whether in the fantastical worlds of George Lucas's *Star Wars* or the alien visitations to our Earth in Steven Spielberg's *Close Encounters of the Third Kind*.

Science-fiction cinema has many varied forms. It has depicted life on Earth in the future, in the past, or now. It has portrayed life and warfare in space and on distant planets, and alien creatures beyond our imaginations (and sometimes beyond filmmakers' budgets). The creation of alien beasts and our concepts of them are one of the most interesting aspects of sci-fi. If we met them, what would our interplanetary neighbours look like? There have been many cinema manifestations of alien forms, from realistic depictions of humanoids and 'little green men' to scuttling tentacled fiends and bulbous-eyed oddballs with hydrocephalic heads. Some kill with disintegrating death rays, others tear their victims apart with claws, chomp them with hideous jaws or bodily envelop them, leaving behind only a pile of bones or a smoking patch of dust. Of course, anything 'invisible' – invisible ray, invisible ship, invisible alien – is cheaper to recreate for those more budget-conscious.

Keep Watching the Skies: The artwork for *Invaders from Mars* (1953) was typical 1950s alien-invasion fare.

One of the most popular subjects for science-fiction cinema is alien invasion of Earth in its many forms, from *The War of the Worlds* and *Independence Day* to *Mars Attacks!*, *Skyline*, *Earth vs. the Flying Saucers* and *Cloverfield*. There are various key thematic threads running through *Outer Limits: The Filmgoers' Guide to the Great Science-Fiction Films* – for example, time travel and future worlds – and chapters open out to look at how these subjects have been dealt with by different generations of filmmakers. I survey the most interesting and popular movies, with key films in each chapter used as launch pads to discuss lesser-known influences and follow-on derivatives, from Hollywood A-movies to B-movies worldwide.

SPATIAL RELATIONSHIPS

Despite their distracting, superficially fantastical trappings, many sci-fi films are really about human relationships – the space between us. Sci-fi is the film genre that has managed to do this more than any other. To take some random examples, *The Abyss*, *The Last Starfighter*, *Innerspace*, *Short Circuit*, *Avatar* and *Starman* are all really boy-meets-girl, or boy-reconciles-with-girl, or girl- (or boy-)meets-alien. The formation of surrogate families also features in such disparate sci-fis as *The Clone Wars*, *Night of the Comet* and *Race to Witch Mountain*. *Independence Day* even features a wedding, just before the Earth-versus-aliens showdown. Traditional stories are dressed up in special effects, so audiences think they're watching a sci-fi movie. But the only way the director or writer could get their love story made was to put a robot in it, or to set it thousands of leagues under the sea, on a spaceship, on a distant planet, or during an alien invasion.

For example, in John Carpenter's *Starman* (1984), the *Voyager 2* space probe is launched in 1977, offering greetings in 54 languages and an invitation to visit Earth. Several years later, an alien craft is shot down by the military in woodland near Chequamegon Bay, Wisconsin. Using a lock of hair and a photo album, a visiting alien being assimilates the form of Scott (Jeff Bridges), the recently deceased husband of Jenny Hayden (Karen Allen). The alien is on a scouting mission and has a noon rendezvous to be picked up in three days' time in a meteor indent known as the Barringer Crater in the Arizona desert. If 'Scott' doesn't make it, he'll die, so he and Jenny head off in her 1977 Ford Mustang. *Starman* is a road movie during which Jenny falls in love with the Starman. She doesn't want him to return home, so attached does she become to the living embodiment of her dead husband. In the fairy-tale finish, as army helicopters try to waylay the interstellar visitor, an orb-like spacecraft beams him up, amid a celestial aura that resembles falling snow. Charles Martin Smith was SETI (Search for Extraterrestrial Intelligence) investigator Mark Shermin, who allows the Starman to escape, and Richard Jaeckel was security chief George Fox, hot on Starman's trail. *Starman* is a charming film, with an eccentric, Best Actor-nominated performance from Bridges. Starman is endowed with special powers and performs a variety of 'miracles'. He makes a tree burst into flames, melts a crowbar, saves wounded Jenny from a car-crash inferno (he revives her with a kiss) and brings a shot deer back to life. Jenny is unable to have children and while they travel towards Arizona, they make love and she becomes pregnant. His healing and life-giving powers – and his designation as descendant from the heavens – add religious significance to this gentle fable, which is backed by some ethereal musical themes from Jack Nitzsche.

Sci-fi films are also sometimes sensual or sexual. Space heroes often sport sexy, revealing, tight-fitting clothing – think Flash Gordon's tights, or outfits donned by Barbarella, Æon Flux, Saint-Exmin and Seven of Nine. There have also been many space-set sexploitation movies, from Doris Wishman's *Nude on the Moon* (1960), the Kubrick-parodying *Kiss Me Quick* (1964) and *Flesh Gordon* (1974) and its sequel *Flesh Gordon meets the Cosmic Cheerleaders* (1990), to the bizarro, eclectically cast UK *Carry On*-meets-Corman sci-fi of *Zeta One* (1969; *The Love Factor*), starring Charles Hawtrey, James Robertson Justice, Brigitte Skay, Valerie Leon, Yutte Stensgaard, and Dawn Adams as Zeta. Sexuality is further highlighted by the shapes of some of the spacecraft and weaponry. Phallic space rockets were taken to a ridiculous degree in the parody *Flesh Gordon* and the rusting steel gonads of Shad's spacecraft in *Battle beyond the Stars* (1980).

UNDERWORLDS: THE ROUTES OF SCIENCE FICTION

Science fiction's founding fathers were the writers Jules Verne and H.G. Wells. Their imaginations explored where no man had gone before and they sent their protagonists there too. The influence of the two authors and those who followed in their wake – Isaac Asimov, Philip K. Dick, Arthur C. Clarke, Robert A. Heinlein, John Wyndham, Michael Crichton and Ray Bradbury – can still be felt today and resonates in modern science-fiction cinema. The descriptive élan of some sci-fi literature loses something in translation from page to screen, which occasionally leads to a 'literalisation' of complex imagery or emotions, though improvements in special effects have made this less prevalent.

In his most famous works, Verne looked at Earth's unseen worlds. His 1864 novel *Voyage au centre de la Terre* took his protagonists to the centre of the Earth and was followed in 1869 by *Vingt mille lieues sous les mers* (*Twenty Thousand Leagues under the Sea*). Georges Méliès's 21-minute film *Le Voyage dans la Lune* (1902; *A Trip to the Moon*) drew on Verne and Wells in its depiction of a rocket mission to the Moon. The rocket's splattered landing in the Man in the Moon's eye has become an iconic moment in early sci-fi cinema. *Voyage au centre de la Terre* was made into a nine-minute film in 1909, but the most famous version was Henry Levine's *Journey to the Center of the Earth* (1959). When Icelandic igneous rock is discovered in a volcano in the Mediterranean, Sir Oliver S. Lindenbrook (James Mason), a university professor of geology in 1880s Edinburgh, and his acolyte Alec McEwen (Pat Boone) embark on an expedition to the centre of the

Claws for Concern: What's waiting for us on the dark side of the Moon according to Arthur Hilton's *Cat-Women of the Moon* (1953). The superintelligent, telepathic cat women cause one visiting astronaut to note: 'You're too smart for me, baby, I like 'em stupid.'

Earth. In the volcanic mountains of Iceland, they set off on their journey downwards, where they discover crystal grottos, stalactite-bedecked caverns, towering mushrooms, a giant red-glowing volcanic lizard, a colony of Dimetrodons (fin-backed dinosaurs), the vast 'Ocean of the Underworld', whirlpools and the ancient ruins of the sea-swallowed civilisation of Atlantis, before being jettisoned to safety through a volcanic chimney via the erupting Italian volcano Stromboli. The other members of the expedition were Carla (Arlene Dahl), the widow of geologist Professor Göteborg (Professor Lindenbrook's competitor), Nordic muscleman Hans (Peter Ronson) and his beloved duck, Gertrude. Diane Baker played Jenny, Alec's lover back in Edinburgh, and Thayer David was the expedition's would-be saboteur, Count Saknussemm. Many of the exotic subterranean scenes were lensed in CinemaScope and DeLuxe Color in the Carlsbad Caverns National Park, New Mexico, as posters stated: 'A Fabulous World below the World'. These inner worlds were part fact, part fiction – the real centre of the earth, the inner core, is a solid ball of nickel and iron.

Variations on the underground-explorers theme include Kevin Connor's gloriously silly slice of Victoriana, *At the Earth's Core* (1976), based on a book by Edgar Rice Burroughs, with rock-jawed explorer Doug McClure, doddery doctor Peter Cushing, slinky Caroline Munro and rubbery flapping 'birdmen', the Mahars. Terrell O. Morse's low-budget *Unknown World* (1951; *To the Center of the Earth*) was a twist on Verne's story set in the post-nuclear age. Dr Morley (Victor Kilian), a prophet of doom and founder member of the 'Society to Save Civilisation', suggests burrowing into the ground to seek safe haven in the event of nuclear war. He assembles a team of five scientists, builds a moling craft called a Cyclotram and sets off via dormant volcano Mount Neleh. The project is financed by media tycoon's son Wright Thompson Jr. (Bruce Kellogg), on the condition that he can go along. Though the Cyclotram burrows deep below the Earth's surface, the film doesn't really go anywhere at all. The party encounter lakes, eyeless cave-fish, pearls, noxious gas and an expansive underwater world, with mountains, waterfalls, clouds, sand dunes and seas, which is suitable for human habitation. For their budget journey to the centre of the Earth (shot in Carlsbad Caverns), the party seem woefully underequipped, with miners' helmets with lamps attached, gas masks and anoraks. Kellogg is a charisma-free hero and his love interest, Dr Joan Lindsey (Marilyn Nash), gets all the best lines. When Wright asks her if she's ever been romanced, she notes: 'Not 900 miles below sea level.'

Eric Brevig's 2008 adaptation of *Journey to the Center of the Earth* was set in modern times and plays more like a Verne sequel. Geology professor Trevor Anderson (Brendan Fraser) and his nephew Sean (Josh Hucherson) trek to the Icelandic volcano Snæfell in search of Max Anderson (Trevor's brother, Sean's father), who vanished on an expedition to find the centre of the Earth in July 1997. Trevor is a Vernian, who believes that the author's work is fact. With help from vulcanologist's daughter Hannah Ásgeirsson (Anita Briem), they travel down a volcanic tube and discover a world of oceans, chasms, crystal caves, strangling vines, snapping, carnivorous plants, exotic animals, deserts, rivers, flying piranha, waterfalls and dinosaurs, which are rendered in eye-popping 3-D visuals. The heroes are jettisoned to safety out of Vesuvius, on a geyser powered by boiling lava. Funny facial expressions pass for acting and there's a fair dollop of sentiment, but once it gets going, the action doesn't let up and most of the film is an extended moment of jeopardy. There's lots of plummeting, as the story becomes a roller-coaster ride of 3-D effects when the adventurers speed through miles of caverns on a mining truck railway track. Brevig's movie predates James Cameron's *Avatar* (2009), but some of the 3-D effects are similar. At the Earth's core, there's a fantastical world with giant fossilised mushrooms, glowing, fluttering bluebirds, radiant in their bioluminescence (a visual effect which appeared extensively in *Avatar*), floating stepping-stone rock slabs, and a scene with delicate, drifting dandelion-clock spores that resemble *Avatar's* wood spirits. Brevig's movie plays OK on TV, but is much more thrilling in a theatre in 3-D. This popcorn adaptation is so knowingly post-modern that the heroes use Verne's novel as a guidebook.

Disney adapted Verne's undersea novel *20,000 Leagues under the Sea* (1954), with Kirk Douglas as Ned Land and James Mason as Captain Nemo, and there have been many explorations of 'undersea worlds', from Cameron's *The Abyss* (1989) back to *The Incredible Petrified World* (1957), a tale barely spun to feature length with undersea aquatic nature footage, including a lengthy duel between an octopus and a shark. Four explorers in a diving bell become trapped in labyrinthine Caribbean underwater caverns (shot at Colossal Cave, Tucson, Arizona) and encounter a crazy, marooned old hermit with a stick-on beard, who resembles Michael Palin's 'It's' man in *Monty Python's Flying Circus*. The ever-reliable John Carradine led the rescue mission.

INNER SPACES

Verne's fiction also inspired journeys not to outer but into 'inner space'. Richard Fleischer's *Fantastic Voyage* (1966) was a mind-bendingly original sci-fi trip. Defecting Czech scientist Jan Benes (Jean Del Val) is ambushed by 'the other side' and left in a coma with a blood clot in his brain. At Combined Miniature Deterrent Forces (CMDF), a crack team of scientists and their submarine *Proteus* are microscopically miniaturised and injected into Benes's bloodstream, to zap the clot with a laser. The crew of *Proteus* featured Stephen Boyd as Grant (communications officer and frogman war hero), Arthur Kennedy as 'top brain man' Dr Duval, Raquel Welch as his shapely assistant Cora Peterson, Donald Pleasence as medical chief Dr Michaels, and William Redfield as the sub's pilot Captain Bill Owens. The operation is overseen at the CMDF control room by General Carter (Edmond O'Brien) and Colonel Reid (Arthur O'Connell), where Benes's body lies in the operating theatre and a clock counts down the 60-minute duration of the miniaturisation process. CMDF is developing the miniaturisation of military hardware and Benes knows how to extend the shrink time, but someone is out to sabotage the mission.

Fantastic Voyage was an Oscar-winning special-effects spectacle from Twentieth Century-Fox in CinemaScope and DeLuxe Color, which took audiences 'where no one has been before'. It speculated that 'going to the Moon will soon be upon us and where the most incredible things are happening around us, someday, perhaps tomorrow, the futuristic events you are about to see can and will take place'. In vibrant settings the *Proteus* navigates the human body, through the bubbling veins, to the heart, lungs, the inner ear and finally the brain, where in the cobwebby matter, bursts of electric light (flashes of inspiration) illuminate Duval's destruction of the clot. Michaels and the *Proteus* are overpowered by defensive white corpuscles, and the crew escape via the optic nerve and are extracted from Benes's eye moments before they return to normal size. The film's big flaw is that Michaels and the *Proteus*, both of which are left inside Benes, would grow back to normal size too and tear the scientist apart. The lava lamp psychedelics have dated badly – who'd have thought the inside of the human body would have looked like a Pink Floyd concert? In fact astro-journeymen space-rockers the Floyd (whose song titles include 'Astronomy Domine', 'Interstellar Overdrive' and 'Set the Controls for the Heart of the Sun') played a live accompaniment to as-it-happened BBC coverage of the Apollo 11 Moon landing in July 1969, during an *Omnibus* edition called *What If It's Just Green Cheese?*

Inner Space: A journey into the human body in *Fantastic Voyage* (1966) sees the crew of miniature submarine *Proteus* navigating the interior of a defecting Czech scientist to zap a blood clot.

Joe Dante's *Innerspace* (1987) revisited *Fantastic Voyage* in a madcap 1980s hybrid of screwball comedy and special-effects-led sci-fi movie. Ex-test pilot Lieutenant Tuck Pendleton (Dennis Quaid) is part of a miniaturisation programme by researchers Vectorscope. He and his module are shrunk and are about to be injected into a rabbit, but an attack by rivals seeking the company's research results in Tuck's being accidentally injected into fretful hypochondriac Jack Putter (Martin Short), an assistant manager in a Safeway supermarket. As Tuck notes, a Vectorscope scientist 'tried to save my ass by injecting me into yours'. When Jack hears Tuck's voice in his head, he shrieks, 'Somebody help me! I'm possessed!' Tuck and Jack enlist Tuck's estranged lover, Lydia (Meg Ryan), a journalist, to restore Tuck to normal size. Tuck encourages hyperventilating hero Jack to be more forthright and dynamic, while Jack begins to fall in love with Lydia. The villains are led by Victor Scrimshaw (Kevin McCarthy) and include Dr Margaret Canker (Fiona Lewis), hitman Mr Igoe (Vernon Wells) – who has an impressive array of deadly attachments for his artificial hand – and Mexican heavy the Cowboy (Robert Picardo). Roger Corman regular Dick Miller popped up as a cab driver. The film made good use of San Francisco locations and Jerry Goldsmith's score. The special effects for the centrifugal miniaturisation of Tuck's capsule (which is blown into billions of molecules and then reforms a fraction of its size) and the 'innerspace' of Jack's body are a massive improvement on *Fantastic Voyage*. End titles inform us: 'Martin Short's Interiors produced by Industrial Light & Magic', for which they won an Oscar for Best Visual Effects, and *Innerspace* was the first major film to be released in the US on tape in the 'letterboxed' widescreen format. Tuck finally escapes from Jack via a massive sneeze, but the film is really about the reconciliation between Tuck and Lydia (who's expecting their baby) and Jack's transformation from hypochondriac jerk to two-fisted hero. As the film's multilayered tagline implied: 'Inside Jack Putter there's a hero trying to get out.'

WATCH THE SKY: DEEP IMPACTS

There are many unanswered questions about space. Is it just stars, planets and bits of rock and gas? Is there anybody (or anything) out there and do we need to fear it? Should we heed that 1950s advice and keep watching the skies, keep looking? When John Lennon wrote in his song 'Imagine' that above us there is only sky, was he thinking about the nonexistence of extraterrestrials? Probably not. He was most likely referring to the nonexistence of God, or a higher being (Lennon was an atheist). Religion featured prominently in 1950s sci-fi, a confrontation between science and religion. While fending off invading aliens, earthlings prayed to God for salvation. In the 1953 *The War of the Worlds*, for example, He answered their prayers. But did God create man, or man create God? Sci-fi is often filled with quasi-religious imagery (bright lights, spiritual experiences, unexplained miraculous phenomena) and features credo mantras of advice or understanding – 'Live long and prosper' and 'May the Force be with you'. The idea that the Force is spiritual adds gravitas to the original *Star Wars* trilogy, but this was dissipated in the sequels, with the introduction of the concept of midi-clorians, a biological, scientifically rational (but boring) explanation of the Force's power.

One thing that's definitely up in space is large chunks of space rock. If it's not being threatened by alien invaders, Earth's next biggest extraterrestrial nemeses are meteors and stars, in films such as Rudolph Maté's *When Worlds Collide* (1951). With its heavenly hosts on the soundtrack and biblical pronouncements, this was a sci-fi retelling of the Old Testament's Noah's Ark story. As the opening voice-over states: 'And God looked upon the Earth, and, behold, it was corrupt; for all flesh had corrupted His way upon the Earth.' Scientists on Earth discover that two new celestial bodies have appeared in space – the star Bellus will collide with Earth and the Earth-like planet Zyra will pass close by. The United Nations decides to build rockets to take a few colonists to Zyra to start a new civilisation at the very moment Earth is obliterated by Bellus. The US rocket is financed by a rich businessman, Sydney Stanton (John Hoyt). Zyra's proximity to Earth causes earthquakes and volcanic eruptions, bridges collapse, houses are reduced to burning rubble and New York is swept away by an impressive tidal wave. The rocket itself resembles a silver V-1 missile, which is launched on a mile-long track. The world is destroyed and the rocket – with its 44 passengers (chosen randomly by lottery) and a store of food and livestock – launches and lands successfully on Zyra. Dr Tony Drake (Peter Hansen), his fiancée Joyce Hendron (Barbara Rush) and David Randall (Richard Derr) are the film's love-triangle subplot. The colour special effects are excellent for the period, and when the survivors finally land on Zyra the bleak snowy alpine landscape gives way to lush greenery, woodland, mountains and lakes. In the distance, the new residents spot the ruins of an ancient civilisation, evidence that Zyra is indeed apt for colonisation.

Ronald Neame's *Meteor* (1979) played like an all-star TV movie. Dr Paul Bradley (Sean Connery) is the inventor of Project Hercules, an orbiting nuclear-deterrent satellite armed with 14 missiles. Natalie Wood played his astrophysicist love interest Tatiana Donskaya, an interpreter for Bradley's Russian opposite number, Dr Dobov (Brian Keith). When a comet crashes though an asteroid belt into meteor Orpheus, the explosion destroys the US's *Challenger II* probe and sends shards of rock Earthwards. One, five miles wide, causes particular concern, as its impact will be the equivalent of 2.5 million megatons of TNT. It will impact Earth on 7 December, but many smaller splinters crash-land beforehand, including one that smashes into Siberia, another that causes an avalanche in the Swiss Alps and one that triggers a tidal wave that washes away Hong Kong. New York is hit, too, destroying the US–Russian base of operations. While the survivors try to escape through subway tunnels, the Hudson River bursts its banks, resulting in a mudslide that causes particular strife for Connery's toupee. Statesmanlike Henry Fonda played the Roosevelt-like US president, and Karl Malden, Martin Landau and Trevor Howard also appeared, with Howard last cast as Sir Michael Hughes at Jodrell Bank observatory in Cheshire, England. Hercules and its Russian equivalent launch their missiles and destroy the meteor. From Connery's opening line ('Give me the horn'), the script is risible and only the scenes of devastation slaked 1970s audiences' appetite for destruction.

In Mimi Leder's *Deep Impact* (1998) a menace christened the Wolf-Biederman comet is on a collision course with Earth. At seven miles long, it's the size of New York City, and at 500 billion tons, it's bigger than Everest. Its existence is discovered by delving MN-NBC reporter Jenny Lerner (Téa Leoni), who thinks Ele is a woman having an affair with US President Tom Beck (Morgan Freeman). In fact, ELE is an Extinction Level Event. The government dispatch a rocket called the *Messiah*, commanded by Spurgeon 'Fish' Tanner (Robert Duvall), to destroy the comet with eight nuclear warheads, but it breaks the meteor in two. The first, smaller rock, one and a half miles wide, will hit in the Atlantic and cause a massive tidal wave, while the second, six-mile-wide chunk will hit western Canada and result in an ELE, including a massive dust cloud, the death of all plants in four weeks and animals in a matter of months. In the US a network of caverns in the limestone cliffs of Missouri is an ideal location for one million people to survive for two years. Two hundred thousand talented people automatically receive places in the Ark Caves. A further 800,000 are randomly selected by the Ark National Lottery, but no one over 50 is eligible. *Deep Impact* is superior sci-fi, packing a hefty emotional wallop in addition to delivering special-effects thrills. The human drama tells how the survivors will be chosen, how the authorities deal with the disaster scenario and the selflessness of the *Messiah*'s crew – they eventually pilot their craft with the remaining warheads into the second comet, so the Earth is only hit with a tidal wave. The wave claims many lives, but the water recedes and the final shot is of the White House under reconstruction. The scenes of civil unrest and panic are convincing, with roads clogged with traffic as the civilian population scrambles for high ground. Young astronomer Leo Biederman (Elijah Wood) marries Sarah (Leelee Sobieski) so she can accompany him on the Ark, but there's an administrative mix-up and her family is left behind. Jenny's estranged parents, Robin and Jason, are played by Vanessa Redgrave and Maximilian Schell. Morgan Freeman is very good in the prescient role of the black US president. In 1998 that seemed like science fiction too.

Another chunk of Earth-threatening astral debris hurtled into Paul Ziller's *Polar Storm* (2009). A fragment of comet Copernicus hits Alaska, knocking Earth off its axis and causing a global wave of energy and damage to the planet's electromagnetic field. The ensuing catastrophic polar reversal results in increased seismic activity, animals becoming confused, unnatural polar auroras, and plays havoc with everything from engines to pacemakers. Astrophysicist Dr James Mayfield (Jack Coleman) sees the danger and formulates a plan to sail a bomb-laden Russian submarine into the Mariana Trench. Set in the town of Lindenville, Washington State (but shot in Canada), the film bundles together sci-fi action with domestic strife and teenage angst, as three generations of Mayfields – James's wife Cynthia (Holly Dignard), son Shane (Tyler Johnston) and father General Mayfield (Terry David Mulligan) – strive to survive. The idea of a black US president (Roger Cross) was much more plausible in 2009.

LIVE LONG AND PROSPER

There's an odd contradiction in the generic definition 'science fiction'. Science is knowledge, knowledge as provable fact, while fiction is imagination. Its parameters are vast and unlimited, and account for the genre's continued popularity with filmgoers. Sci-fi films and franchises have been among the most profitable in cinema history. In addition to being a family-friendly genre, thereby maximising audiences, two of the most popular sci-fi subgenres are shoot-'em-up sci-fi action movies, such as *The Terminator*, *Aliens*, *Terminator 2: Judgment Day* and *Starship Troopers* and visceral sci-fi horrors, like *Alien*, *Alien Contamination* and *The Thing*, aimed at the late-teen and adult audience. Unlike some genres, such as musicals or Westerns, sci-fi has endured seasonal appeal and competition from other media and remains a resilient box-office magnet. Many sci-fi films have been the biggest worldwide grossers for their respective years: *2001: A Space Odyssey* (1968), *Star Wars* (1977), *Moonraker* (1979), *The Empire Strikes Back* (1980), *E.T. the Extra-Terrestrial* (1982), *Return of the Jedi* (1983), *Back to the Future* (1985), *Terminator 2: Judgment Day* (1991), *Jurassic Park* (1993), *Independence Day* (1996), *Armageddon* (1998), *The Phantom Menace* (1999) and *Avatar* (2009).

Lewis Gilbert's *Moonraker* (1979) is an interesting film, in that it was made at a time when sci-fi was massively popular, but it is also part of another huge-grossing franchise, the James Bond series. Though many of the Bond spy thrillers featured elements of science fiction (or even, as in 1967's *You Only Live Twice*, visited outer space), *Moonraker* was the one that took the series into orbit. Agent 007 James Bond (Roger Moore) is assigned to find out who's stolen the Moonraker space shuttle. The narrative moves from the Californian desert and the canals of Venice (which Bond navigates in his customised 'Bondola') to Brazil and eventually a space station. The plot is a reworking of *The Spy Who Loved Me* (1977), with space replacing underwater and shuttles replacing submarines. The villain is Hugo Drax (Michael Lonsdale) of Drax Industries and his henchmen include Chang (Toshirō Suga) and metal-toothed Jaws (Richard Kiel). Bond has the expected close encounters: Corrine Cléry is excellent but underused as Corrine Dufour, Drax's PA; Bond's principal love interest is Dr Holly Goodhead (Lois Chiles), a CIA operative; and there's *Barbarella*-inspired gravity-defying sexual intercourse ('I think he's attempting re-entry, sir!'). Drax plans Operation Orchid, to release a deadly nerve gas from 50 globes into Earth's atmosphere and then to found a new dynasty on the planet with his Noah's Ark of beautiful people. It was the most expensive of the series up to that point ($30 million), but the sci-fi trappings gave it added draw at the box office and guaranteed its enormous success. It took $203 million worldwide, making it by some margin the biggest grosser of the series until *GoldenEye* in 1995.

Of the many great films discussed in *Outer Limits*, I would highly recommend (in order of preference) *Star Wars*, *Mad Max 2*, *Invasion of the Body Snatchers* (1956), *2001: A Space Odyssey*, *Blade Runner*, *The Terminator*, *Planet of the Apes*, *The Thing* (1982), *Alien*, *Independence Day* and *Avatar* as classics of the genre. Definitive or near-definitive editions of all these films are available for home viewing, though many of them rely on spectacle best served by cinema screens. Among the second echelon, I would also propose *The Man Who Fell to Earth*, *Back to the Future*, *Return of the Jedi*, *The Day the Earth Stood Still* (1951), *Tarantula*, *The War of the Worlds* (1953), *RoboCop* and the original *Gojira* as rewarding sci-fi experiences.

Sci-fi may have given us some of the most financially successful and perennially popular films of all time, but also some of the worst. The gulf between 'best' and 'worst', while wholly subjective, is more apparent here than in any other film genre. With regards to special effects: when they're good they're very good, but when they are bad, you sometimes feel you could have done better yourself. Fredric Gadette's *This Is Not a Test* (1962) epitomises ultra-low-budget filmmaking and is by far the cheapest nuclear crisis movie ever made. Characters describe stuff we can't see, events happen off-screen as we focus on a small group of protagonists jeopardised by larger events beyond their (or our) control. Del Oro County, California, is in a 'yellow alert' state of emergency, as a nuclear air strike is imminent. At four in the morning, Deputy Sheriff Dan Colter sets up a desert roadblock to prevent entry to a city and the entire film follows the people he stops there, who argue and chat while attempting to convert the back of a Discount World truck into a fallout shelter. This un-gripping crisis is enacted by an ensemble cast of nobodies from the Ed Wood school of versatility – from barnstorming to comatose – including Seamon Glass, Thayer Roberts, Aubrey Martin, Mary Morlas, Don Spruance, Carol Kent, Alan Austin, Michael Greene and Ron Starr (as escaped murderer Clint Delany). The twist ending has the deputy, the one man who attempted to keep order throughout the entire story, trapped outside the bomb shelter as the missile strikes.

SPACE ODDITIES

My preferred brand of science fiction is the B-movie jungle of *Attack of the...* or *Invasion of the...*, the cult of budget monsters and mayhem, from the 1950s to the 1980s. In addition to the sci-fi classics listed above, I would also recommend the alien horrors of *Fiend without a Face* and *IT! The Terror from beyond Space*, or Roger Corman's *Not of This Earth* and *It Conquered the World*. Check out the colourful, vibrant sci-fi movies from Japan (such as *Invasion of the Astro-Monsters*, *Matango: Attack of the Mushroom People* and *Destroy All Monsters*) and Italy (*Planet of the Vampires* and *The Wild, Wild Planet*) and

The Clones
Are Coming:
Transmorphers
(2007) is one
of a new breed
of mockbusters,
which, in their DVD
packaging and
advertising, hope
to be confused for
more prestigious
productions.

bleak, corrosive, monochrome UK sci-fi, like *These Are the Damned* and *Quatermass 2*. Other cult delights include *I Married a Monster from Outer Space, Android, Trancers, Alien Contamination* and *Goke, Bodysnatcher from Hell*. For some reason, many low-budget sci-fi films are picked on by film critics and singled out as 'worst movies ever made'. There have been some awful sci-fi movies, it's true. Films such as *Santa Claus Conquers the Martians, Robot Monster, Plan 9 from Outer Space, The Creeping Terror, Teenagers from Outer Space* and *The Giant Claw* are far from the greatest contributions to world culture. They may be badly made, but they are entertaining (at least on first viewing), which is something many films with much bigger budgets, and often with lofty ambitions, are not. I'd rather watch the giant, clawed Venusian cucumber in *It Conquered the World* over Keanu Reeves in the leaden remake of *The Day the Earth Stood Still* any day. The cucumber has a wider range of facial expressions. The 1950s and 1960s were the heyday of 'bad' sci-fi, but it's heartening to write that slapdash, slipshod and shamelessly derivative sci-fi films are still being made today – these include a cash-in on Reeves's remake called *The Day the Earth Stopped* (2008), *I Am Omega* (2007) a rip-off of both *I Am Legend* and *The Ωmega Man*, *Transmorphers* (2007), which hoped to confuse itself with the *Transformers* reboot, and *AVH: Alien vs. Hunter* (2007), after *Alien vs. Predator*.

The future has been disappointing, with the world of tomorrow we were promised failing to materialise. Houses have looked the same for the last century and are not dissimilar to dwellings from many years ago – most of us aren't living in Plexiglas domes, hovering bubbles or subterranean bunkers. Construction materials have improved, but architectural designs remain largely traditional. However, the technology within our homes – phones, computers, TVs, interactive games consoles – is unrecognisable from the previous century. We may not have travelled into outer space, but we live in cyberspace. So, too, the technical capabilities of film special effects have improved drastically. Physical sets rarely exist in sci-fi for films shot using computer-generated landscapes, rather than models, miniatures and locations. The geeks have inherited the Earth (or at least the sci-fi movie industry) from the craftsmen.

Outer Limits is a tour of the sci-fi cinema universe, in all its fantastical, celestial glory, as the cinema screen becomes our window into other worlds. This genre's story traces developments in cinema from monochrome silents, through colour, CinemaScope and 3-D, to IMAX and HD 3-D. The story is also filled with a galaxy of stars, including directors James Cameron, Roger Corman, George Lucas, Steven Spielberg, Ishirō Honda, Ridley Scott, Jack Arnold and John Carpenter, as well as composers John Williams, James Horner and Jerry Goldsmith, whose visions have shaped the sights and sounds of sci-fi cinema. So come on a journey through time and space to infinity and beyond, a limitless expanse of stars, of faraway worlds beyond our Earthly concepts, to discover civilisations or unexplored distant planets, where no human eye has set foot.

HOWARD HUGHES

JUNE 2071

ACKNOWLEDGEMENTS

It's taken me approximately 18 of your Earth months to research and write *Outer Limits*. During that time many people have helped to ensure that this was a comprehensive survey of science-fiction cinema in all its varied forms.

Thanks to Philippa Brewster, my editor at I.B.Tauris, for her help and advice during the writing of *Outer Limits*. Thanks, too, to Stuart Weir, Paul Davighi and Cecile Rault at I.B.Tauris, and also to Bryan Karetnyk and Alex Billington at Tetragon, for their hard work on this project.

As always, Andy Hanratty has been invaluable in tracking down rare films, and he's located some of the most obscure sci-fi films discussed in this book – from *Robot Monster* to *The Green Slime*. My thanks also go to Gareth Jones, Mark Payne, Peter Jones, Charlie Adlard, Simon Hawkins, Alex Coe, Roger Brown, Richy Greenwell and Neil Burlingham, who pointed me in the right direction of titles I should include in the outer reaches of this book.

Thanks as ever for research, advice or ideas to Paul Duncan, Tom Betts, Lee Pfeifer and Dave Worrall at *Cinema Retro*, to William Connolly, Mike Eustace, Mike Oak, Jamie Russell, Belinda and Chris Skinner, Ann Jones, Kevin Wilkinson, Michael Roberts, Rhian Thomas, Team Zebra, Mum and Dad, and especially to Clara.

1

'DEATH TO THE MACHINES'

METROPOLIS (1927)

Director: Fritz Lang
Producer: Erich Pommer
Story: Thea von Harbou
Screenplay: Thea von Harbou and Fritz Lang
Directors of Photography: Karl Freund, Günther Rittau and Walter Ruttmann
Music: Gottfried Huppertz (1927; Ufa German premiere)
A Universum Film AG (Ufa) Production
Released by Parufamet
119 minutes

Alfred Abel (Joh Fredersen, master of Metropolis), Gustav Fröhlich (Freder, Joh's son), Rudolf Klein-Rogge (C.A. Rotwang, inventor), Fritz Rasp (the Thin Man, Joh's spy), Theodor Loos (Josaphat), Erwin Biswanger (worker No. 11811), Heinrich George (Grot, chief foreman of the Heart Machine), Brigitte Helm (Maria and Machine Man Maria), Hanns Leo Reich (Marinus), Fritz Alberti (creative human who conceives Babel), Georg John (worker who causes explosion of M-Machine)

❊　❊　❊

The first truly great work of science fiction cinema was *Metropolis*. In 1927 the silent era was almost at an end – the first talkie, *The Jazz Singer* was released that same year – when Fritz Lang directed his epic. Lang married actress and author Thea von Harbou in 1922. They divorced in 1933 (when she joined the Nazi Party and he fled the country), but during their marriage they collaborated on the script for *Metropolis*. Von Harbou's source novel, also called *Metropolis*, first appeared in the magazine *Das Illustrierte Blatt* in Frankfurt in 1925, and a book version was published shortly before the film's release.

The futuristic city of Metropolis is one of chasmic class divides. Below ground, workers toil in their subterranean city, ensuring the well-oiled wheels of Metropolis turn and its pistons pump. Above ground, the rich and privileged enjoy the luxurious delights of the Eternal Gardens or the bacchanalian 'entertainment district' of Yoshiwara. The master of Metropolis is Joh Fredersen (Alfred Abel). Freder (Gustav Fröhlich), his son, rejects his father's class when he encounters Maria (Brigitte Helm), a nanny to the workers' children. Fascinated by Maria's simple, pure beauty, Freder descends into the city's bowels to seek her out. He becomes a factory labourer, trading identities with worker No. 11811, and is eventually invited to a meeting in the 2,000-year-old catacombs below Metropolis. There he finds Maria preaching to the workers the legend of the Tower of Babel (an allegory of their toil for Joh in Metropolis) and assures them that the hour of their deliverance is at hand via a 'mediator'. Joh and inventor Rotwang spy on the workers and resolve to destroy the workers' faith in Maria. They substitute Maria with Rotwang's latest project – a robotic 'machine man'. As Joh instructs: 'I want you to visit those in the depths, in order to destroy the work of the woman in whose image you were created.' Their robot, the living image of Maria, sows discord among the workers, while the real Maria is locked away. But the inventor plans to destroy both the rich man and his son, as Rotwang has programmed Maria to obey only his will.

Metropolis was shot at Babelsberg Studios. It took 16 months to film, in 1925–26, with a cast of over 37,000, on gargantuan sets. At the equivalent of over $200 million, it is still both the most expensive silent film and the most expensive German film ever lensed. Brigitte Helm was excellently cast as both the serene Maria and her crazy-eyed evil twin, the 'Machine Man Maria', who inspires frenzied lust with her near-naked erotic dances for the rich sinners in Yoshiwara and incites the proletariat in the workers' city to destroy the machines. She says they are 'living food for the machines in Metropolis' which lubricate 'the machine joints with their own blood'. Fritz Rasp played Joh's shadowy spy, the Thin Man, but most influential was Rudolf Klein-Rogge (from Lang's *Dr Mabuse* films) as the madcap inventor, Rotwang, with his wild hair and artificial hand. His creation, the Machine Man, remains an iconic sci-fi creation. The sequence of the Machine Man coming to life, encircled in throbbing hoops of electronic energy, is among the most resonant in futurist cinema.

Metropolis's cityscape is a fantastical architectural creation. Some sources date the film's setting as around AD 2000, though this is not specified in the film. The art direction and set design was by Otto Hunte, Erich Kettelhut and Karl Vollbrecht, with sculptures by Walter Schultze-Mittendorf. The special-effects shots were conceived and staged by Ernst Kunstmann and Eugen Schüfftan (anglicised to Eugene Shuftan in the US). Schüfftan was the progenitor of the Schüfftan process, which comprised an angled composite shot that combined miniatures and background scenery, with actors in the foreground. The process was later overtaken by matte shots. In Metropolis, cars clog the broad streets and biplanes fly between the towering buildings. There are metro-train monorails and highways in the sky. Lang was inspired by his impression of the Manhattan skyline in October 1924, when he visited the US to observe Hollywood filmmaking techniques.

Metropolis is a living, breathing city, with a heart and lungs – the phalanx of workers is its lifeblood. The Machine Halls are vivid powerhouses of steel and steam. Rotwang's bubbling laboratory and Machine Man's rebirth as Maria influenced the equivalent scenes in Hollywood's sci-fi horror *Frankenstein* (1931). The catacombs are recreated in great detail, with burial chambers, skulls and skeletons, as is the grim statuary of the cathedral. The Eternal Gardens, an earthly Eden, is strewn with exotica – flora and fauna, graceful birds and ornate fountains – amongst which the rich elitists idly flit. The stylised look of the film displays the influence of German expressionism (as epitomised by *The Cabinet of Dr Caligari* [1920]), but is also a haunting vision of future science fiction from cinema now long past.

Lang's workers plot insurrection in the City of the Dead catacombs, while the indolent rich carry on regardless. The shuffling workers are drones, who advance rank on rank like automatons. They are replaced by the next shift, which piles into the city's vast elevators, ensuring the machines never sleep. There are also references to classical mythology and the Bible. In the cavernous machine halls, Freder imagines the M-Machine as the hideous, gaping-mouthed god Moloch, with the workers as sacrificial victims, while another scene recreates the construction of the Tower of Babel. The workers cry 'Death to the machines', storm the Machine Hall and overload the Heart Machine (in some prints called the Central Dynamo). The Vegas-style lights flicker out, industry comes to a standstill, escalators plummet and smash, and the workers' city is engulfed in a rushing flood of biblical proportions. Maria and Freder save the workers' children from the flood, eventually

Metropolis: German poster art for Fritz Lang's silent sci-fi epic speaks volumes for the film's stylised, futuristic production design.

taking them to the Club of the Sons. The workers seek out the 'witch' they think is respon-sible for their children's deaths and burn Robot Maria at the stake outside the cathedral, while Rotwang chases Maria through the cathedral, where the daredevil bell-swinging seems inspired by *The Hunchback of Notre-Dame*. Society's class divides are depicted straightforwardly and the story's mantra 'The mediator between head and hands must be the heart' is visualised in the denouement. A V-shaped phalanx of workers led by burly Grot (Heinrich George) approach the cathedral. The 'Mediator' (Freder) unites labour (Grot) with financial capital (Joh). Unlike Sergei Eisenstein's montages of worker revolution, Lang's film proffers peaceful resolution.

Metropolis bombed in Germany on its release early in 1927 and brought Ufa close to bankruptcy. It was saved by Alfred Hugenberg, one of Adolf Hitler's financial backers. Was Lang thinking about the political situation in Weimar Germany and the rise of Fascism when he made *Metropolis*? *Mein Kampf* was published shortly before Lang shot his film and the workers are galvanised by Robot Maria, a wild-eyed zealot with big ideas. When the Nazis came to power in Germany in 1933, Hitler and his henchmen invited Lang to be their propaganda filmmaker. Lang, worried about his ancestry (his mother had a Jewish background) headed for the US, via France and Britain, where he continued to make films, only returning to Germany at the end of his career in the late 1950s.

Metropolis exists in many different prints, of varying quality and length, some as short as 75 minutes. The best versions are the 119-minute German print (prepared by the Murnau Foundation in 2002) and a US public domain version, running 118 minutes. All that survives of Lang's masterpiece are 'incomplete original negatives' and 'copies of shortened and re-edited release prints'. The 119-minute version recreates the 1927 German film premiere version, via all available materials, 'based on the version in the Filmmuseum Munich and material preserved in the Bundesarchiv-Filmarchiv'. The images have been restored and additional intertitles describe what is still missing from the plot – this mainly includes the Thin Man keeping Freder under observation, Josaphat (Joh's assistant) and the workers. Gottfried Huppertz's original score was reconstructed and conducted by Berndt Heller, and performed by the Rundfunk-Sinfonieorchester Saarbrücken. The film is structured in three sections: the Prelude (until Maria is imprisoned by Rotwang), the Intermezzo (as Freder hallucinates that the Grim Reaper comes to life and 'Death descends upon the city') and the Furiosi (the film's finale, including the workers' revolt and the destruction of the city).

The US print anglicises several names (Joh becomes John, Josaphat Joseph) and is miss-ing several sequences, including athletes sprinting in a grand stadium and all reference to Joh's deceased wife Hel, who died giving birth to Freder. The US print begins with a quote from von Harbou, stating: 'This film is not of today or of the future. It tells of no place. It serves no tendency, party or class.' A 1984 reissue at 87 minutes included colour tints and a score by Giorgio Moroder (featuring songs by such artists as Freddie Mercury, Pat Benatar, Bonnie Tyler and Adam Ant). Footage from *Metropolis* also appeared in Queen's promo for their single 'Radio Ga Ga'. Following the discovery of an unexpurgated print, the monumental 2010 reconstruction of *Metropolis* has extended the film, with much footage previously thought lost, to 153 minutes.

Metropolis is the name of the city setting in *Superman*, and Lang's film inspired a Japanese anime, also called *Metropolis*, which was directed by Rintaro in 2001. The people of Metropolis celebrate the opening of the Ziggurat, a Tower of Babel that looms over the futuristic city, which is rumoured to harbour a powerful secret weapon or a military facility. President Boone rules the city, but the Marduk Party led by Duke Red covet power. Duke Red has renegade scientist Dr Laughton create a blonde robot woman, Tima. Detective Shunsaku Ban arrives from Japan in search of the doctor, who has international warrants standing for his arrest. With help from his nephew Kenichi and friendly robot bodyguard Pero, he scours the city. An attempted coup d'état by revolutionaries led by Atlas is suppressed by the Marduks, and Duke Red overthrows President Boone. Duke Red's son Rock tries to destroy Tima, but she survives and is revealed to be a powerful computer capable of destroying mankind with biological weapons. Rintaro's cityscapes and subterranea are a feast for the eyes, and the retro futuristic atmosphere is enhanced by a jazzy score, composed by Toshiyuki Nakura and performed by the Metropolitan Rhythm Kings, including Rintaro himself on bass clarinet. Also featured are jazz songs 'I Can't Stop Loving You' by Ray Charles and 'There'll Never Be Good-Bye – The Theme of Metropolis', sung by Minako 'Mooki' Obata.

Back in Hollywood in 1930, David Butler directed the ambitious *Just Imagine*, which recreated a Metropolis-like cityscape of New York circa 1980 – this footage later showed up in the *Buck Rogers* (1939) kids' matinée serial as the Hidden City. Almost a decade after *Metropolis*, William Cameron Menzies directed the British production *Things to Come* (1936). It was an adaptation of H.G. Wells's novel *The Shape of Things to Come*, which Wells himself adapted for the screen in collaboration with Lajos Bíró. The settings were designed by Vincent Korda (producer Alexander's brother), the special effects were directed by Ned Mann and photographed by Edward Cohen, and the costumes were attributed to John Armstrong, René Hubert and the Marchioness of Queensbury. The patriotic score by Arthur Bliss became the first ever film soundtrack to be released to the public on disk. The story of 'Everytown' begins at Christmas, 1940, after the outbreak of war, as Everytown is enduring aerial bombing (in scenes that pre-date the London Blitz of 1940–1). Via montages of marching troops, naval engagements, tank battles and aerial gas attacks, the war wears on, until the land is laid waste and in 1966 the enemy is defeated. Everytown is in ruins and its population live in rag-clothed deprivation, ravaged by 'wandering sickness', which has been dispersed by enemy planes. By 1970 this plague, having killed half the human race, ceases to spread thanks to the strict policy of shooting dead all carriers. Society is governed by a warlord known as the Chief or the Boss (Ralph Richardson), who rules the independent sovereign state. Resigned to brigandage, the populace wage war with the 'Hill Men'.

Eventually they are pacified when Wings over the World – a technologically advanced organisation that flies sleek bombers and is part of World Communications (whose HQ is in Basra) – intervene. Everytown is bombed with a 'gas of peace'. Wings over the World restore order and begin a new civilisation. By 2036, Everytown now resembles a partly subterranean Metropolis, where people wear togas, capes and tunics, and a 'space gun' has been developed to shoot explorers moonward. *Things to Come* is a film that exalts design – in the postwar period the engineers ('the last trustees of civilisation') have survived. In the future, we see massive mining operations, buildings constructed by goliath machines, industry and production lines, and the gigantic space gun, a massive-bore cannon that fires astronauts into orbit in a canister. But there is a section of society that doesn't want such a device to be used, or space explored, and they attempt to destroy the gun. Like *Metropolis*, print lengths vary considerably (from an original 130 minutes to 113 and 94) and *Things to Come* was not a success on initial release.

In contrast to the seriousness of Lang and Wells, *Radio Ranch* (1940) was one of the most unusual and popular sci-fi movies of the period. With his cowpoke friends, singing cowboy Gene Autry runs a Country and Western radio station from his 'Radio Ranch'. Scientists led by Professor Beetson (Frank Glendon) covet the radium deposits which they have located on Gene's land, which sits above the futuristic subterranean lost city of Mu. Radium-rich and 25,000 feet below the surface, the 'Scientific City of Murania' is ruled by Queen Tika (Dorothy Christy), while scheming chancellor Lord Argo (Wheeler Oakman) plots revolt against her. Gene is helped by his kiddie sidekicks Frankie Baxter (Frankie Darro) and his sister Betsy (Betsy King Ross, a 'World's Champion Trick Rider') and hindered by Oscar (Lester 'Smiley' Burnett) and Pete (William Moore) and their comedy relief. Gene has to keep finding ingenious ways to broadcast his show, otherwise he'll lose his radio contract. This results in several musical interludes – including performances of 'Uncle Noah's Ark' and 'Silver-Haired Daddy of Mine' – which are as deadly as the Muranians' Disintegrator Ray.

Radio Ranch was a 69-minute abridgement of Mascot Pictures' *The Phantom Empire* (1935), a 12-chapter serial co-directed by B. Reeves Eason and Otto Brewer. These serials, of which there are many examples, were much more representative of sci-fi during the pre-World War II period than *Metropolis* or *Things to Come*. They were aimed at the children's matinée crowd and offered up easy-to-follow, fast-and-furious action in bite-sized weekly episodes or 'chapters', each of which ended with a cliffhanging 'what happens next?' finale. *Radio Ranch* plays up the 'Western' story, while the 12-chapter serial highlights the futuristic sights of Murania, a cityscape that resembles Lang's Metropolis – a world underground, 'with cities, and people and everything'. 'Everything' includes boxy silver robots, marrow-shaped lithium ray guns, a radium gun that melts stone, elevators and TV monitors, wireless telephones, ground-to-air torpedoes, a Cavern of the Doomed, the electrocuting Chamber of Death, and the Radium Reviving Chamber. Some of the futuristic gadgetry is pretty simple. A robot operates the cave entrance (which resembles

Flash by Name: *Flash Gordon Conquers the Universe* (1940), the third of Larry 'Buster' Crabbe's three-serial stints for Universal as Flash Gordon, was 12 chapters of cliffhanging thrills.

a garage door) in Thunder Valley by cranking a bicycle chain. The Muranian Thunder Riders hurtle along on horseback wearing gas masks, capes and helmets, and in the finale the 'Disintegrating Atom-Smashing Ray' melts the city. *Radio Ranch* was also released as *Men with Steel Faces* (1940; *Couldn't Possibly Happen*) and abridged for syndicated TV in 1988 as *The Phantom Empire*.

Larry 'Buster' Crabbe's three-serial stint for Universal as Flash Gordon began with *Flash Gordon* (1936; 13 chapters) and continued with *Flash Gordon's Trip to Mars* (1938; 15 chapters) and *Flash Gordon Conquers the Universe* (1940; 12 chapters), which were based on Alex Raymond's comic strips. Crabbe played the intergalactic hero who battles pointy-bearded despot Emperor Ming the Merciless (Charles Middleton) on Planet Mongo, while saving Dale Arden (Jean Rogers) and Dr Zarkov (Frank Shannon). Richard Alexander played Arborian Prince Barin, Jack 'Tiny' Lipson played King Vultan of the Hawkmen and Priscilla Lawson was Ming's temptress daughter, Princess Aura. *Flash Gordon's Trip to Mars* reused most of the first serial's cast, but Carol Hughes replaced Rogers as Arden and Shirley Deane played Aura in the last instalment. The first two Flash serials were also released as abridged feature films, *Flash Gordon* (1936) and *Mars Attacks the World* (1938), and later in 1966 to TV as *Spaceship to the Unknown* and *Deadly Ray from Mars*, respectively. *Flash Gordon Conquers the Universe* was edited into two different TV features: *Peril from the Planet Mongo* and *Purple Death from Outer Space*.

Following his success as Flash Gordon, Crabbe also played the title role in *Buck Rogers* (1939; 12 chapters), based on Philip F. Nowlan's comic strip. After a crash in the polar regions in 1938, Lieutenant Buck Rogers (Crabbe) and his sidekick George 'Buddy' Wade (Jackie Moran) wake up 500 years later, to battle gangsters and racketeers led by Killer Kane (Anthony Warde). *Buck Rogers* was subsequently re-edited as the feature *Planet Outlaws* (1953) and as the TV movies *Destination Saturn* (1965) and *Buck Rogers* (1977). Such was the character's popularity that in the wake of *Star Wars* in 1977, *Buck Rogers* was revived on US TV from 1979–81 as the series *Buck Rogers in the 25th Century*, with Gil Gerard as Buck, Erin Gray as Colonel Wilma Deering, Henry Silva as Kane, and cute gold robot Twiki (played by Felix Silla and voiced by Mel Blanc). In the 1930s and 1940s, filmmakers and theatre proprietors designated sci-fi as children's fare, fine for Saturday matinée serials such as Republic's 12-chapter *King of the Rocket Men* (1949), but not for features and certainly not A-features. Since *Metropolis*, science fiction had moved – some would say regressed – from the realism of Lang and Wells to the comic-book serial adventures that endured throughout the 1930s to the end of the 1940s.

2

'REGARDED THIS EARTH WITH ENVIOUS EYES'

THE WAR OF THE WORLDS (1953)

Director: Byron Haskin
Story: H.G. Wells
Screenplay: Barré Lyndon
Director of Photography: George Barnes
Music: Leith Stevens
Technicolor
A Paramount Production
Released by Paramount Pictures
82 minutes

Gene Barry (Dr Clayton Forrester), Ann Robinson (Sylvia Van Buren), Les Tremayne (Major General Mann), Bob Cornthwaite (Dr Pryor), Sandro Giglio (Dr Bilderbeck), Lewis Martin (Pastor Dr Matthew Collins, Sylvia's uncle), William 'Bill' Phipps (Wash Perry), Paul Birch (Alonzo Hogue), Jack Kruschen (Salvatore), Vernon Rich (Marine Colonel Ralph Heffner), Ralph Dumke (Buck Monahan, mechanic), Walter Sande (Sheriff Bogany), Sir Cedric Hardwicke (narrator)

❋ ❋ ❋

The 1950s marked the beginning of a golden age for science-fiction cinema, during an era when filmmakers' imaginations created a box-office model staple that survives today. Although space exploration and colonisation were first to find an audience in the 1950s, it was alien invasions of Earth and 'creature features' that firmly established sci-fi as an authentic genre. Just as we explored space, so space came to explore us.

Author Herbert George (H.G.) Wells called *Metropolis* 'quite the silliest film', though his own brand of sci-fi was just as far-fetched. Wells's *The War of the Worlds* was first published as a novel in 1898. The story follows the first-person narrator, who witnesses a Martian invasion that envelops an area south-west of London.

War of the Worlds: Classic poster artwork for George Pal's adaptation of H.G. Wells's 1898 novel, which relocated the Martian invasion from Surrey and London in England to Pine Summit, California.

An alien cylinder, the first of several fired from a huge gun on Mars, lands on Horsell Common, north of Woking in Surrey. The Martians zap a peaceful deputation with a heat ray and then proceed in their tripod war machines north towards London, harvesting humans to extract their blood, killing the population with noxious 'black smoke' gas and laying waste to the landscape, which becomes shrouded in creeping tendrils. The narrator's brother witnesses the populace's stampede from London and a sea battle between a Martian tripod and ironclad battleship HMS *Thunder Child*. Wells's vivid descriptions remain powerful to readers today. In the book's opening paragraph Wells expertly establishes mood, as he outlines our extraterrestrial observers:

> This world was being watched keenly and closely by intelligences greater than man's and yet as mortal as his own [...] yet across the gulf of space [...] intellects vast and cool and unsympathetic, regarded this earth with envious eyes, and slowly and surely drew their plans against us.

Orson Welles and his *The Mercury Theatre on the Air* dramatised *The War of the Worlds* live for CBS Radio at 8 p.m. on Sunday, 30 October 1938. Their version cleverly interwove news reports of the Martians landing at Grovers Mill, New Jersey, and eyewitness reports with routine weather, news bulletins and musical interludes to create a sense of the alien invasion unfolding. So convincingly in fact that those tuning in late thought the transmission to be the actual news. Widespread panic resulted in people fleeing their homes with towels over their heads to protect them from the Martians' deadly gas, troops were put on standby, reports came in from real eyewitnesses who claimed to have seen more Martians landing and there were stampedes, praying and even an attempted suicide. In the sci-fi comedy *Spaced Invaders* (1990; *Martians!*), a rebroadcast of Welles's dramatisation on Halloween 50 years later attracts a bunch of curious aliens to Earth.

Producer George Pal rose to prominence at the beginning of the decade with sci-fi films such as *Destination Moon* (1950), and he produced Rudolph Maté's *When Worlds Collide* (1951). In the early 1950s, Pal embarked on recreating a Martian invasion of Earth on the big screen. In the rolling hills and woodland of Pine Summit, California, a meteor crash-lands and a scientist from Pacific Tech, Dr Clayton Forrester (Gene Barry), investigates. When he examines the superheated meteor, he discovers that it is radioactive. He also meets Sylvia Van Buren (Ann Robinson), a library science teacher from USC and an admirer of Clayton's work, and for this reason agrees to stick around in Linda Rosa until the meteor cools off. During the night the meteor opens and hatches an alien periscope, which proceeds to vaporise three locals who proffer peace. The site is besieged by sightseers and the US marines are called out, but soon three flying machines rise from the crater and the army's hardware is helpless against the aliens' dome-like protective force field and ray guns. Meteors have landed worldwide and global panic ensues as Europe, South America, Australia and Asia are overrun. An A-bomb dropped on the

Martians' landing site in the Puente Hills has no effect and Los Angeles is evacuated. As the machines level Los Angeles, their pilots begin to die. They are destroyed by the Earth's everyday micro-organisms that humans have a natural immunity to. As soon as they began to breathe our air, they begin to lose their battle.

The War of the Worlds is by far the most impressive 1950s alien-invasion movie and remained so until the 1970s. Paramount's Jesse Lasky had owned the film rights to Wells's novel since 1924. The setting was shifted from Victorian England to 1950s California, but there was a precedent for this. When Wells's story turned out to be a success, rip-offs appeared in other journals, relocating the invasion to their readerships' cities. The film version was shot for $2 million, $1.4 million of which went on the special effects. The film's trailer noted the film was two years in the making, with principal photography of the actors taking place from January to February 1952. Many of the film's 'exteriors' were filmed on sound stages at Paramount Studios, and the special effects were created by Paramount's effects department. On-location exteriors were filmed in the Simi Valley, California, in Florence and Phoenix, Arizona, and the city of Corona in California was used as 'Linda Rosa'. Filming locations in Los Angeles included the City Hall, Saint Brendan's Catholic Church, the US Government District Court Building and the First United Methodist Church.

Both *Destination Moon* and *When Worlds Collide* had won Oscars for their special effects, so Pal was the natural choice to tackle Wells's classic. The vivid comic-book cinematography was by George Barnes, who died in May 1953, before the film was released. The film's frantic, panic-inducing title sequence was cut to a dramatic, clashing cue from Leith Evans. The film opens with artistic depictions of planets in outer space – Pluto, Neptune, Uranus, Saturn, Jupiter and Mercury. These paintings were by Chesley Bonestell, who had worked on *Destination Moon* and *When Worlds Collide*. A stentorian voice-over from Sir Cedric Hardwicke tells us that Earth is being regarded from afar, as the inhabitants of dying planet Mars look for a new home.

In depicting 'The super-race from the Red Planet' (as the trailer calls them) Pal and his production team, including the Paramount Effects Department and artist Chesley Bonestell, pulled out all the stops. The Martian machines are both impressive and beautiful – a sleek sci-fi design classic. The craft were designed by Japanese-born Albert Nozaki and made from copper. They consisted of an arched flying wing, tipped with glowing green lights (which fire green laser beams) and a graceful, cobra-like neck and head, with a red eye that emits a blasting, sparkler heat ray. Unfortunately in spotless DVD prints, as the craft emerge from the glowing, smoking meteor impact, the many wires supporting the heavy scale models of the Martian ships are clearly visible. The screeching sound effects to these ray guns, and other electronic whirs and hums of the Martian soundscape throughout the film, are still being imitated in sci-fi cinema today. The craft are piloted by Martians with spindly arms and three long, thin fingers with sucker fingertips. The elongated, snake-like exploratory probe that investigates a ruined farmhouse has a tricolour seeing-eye head.

Clayton and Sylvia are menaced by the periscope probe (which Clayton beheads with an axe), and an *E.T.*-like pink alien with hunched shoulders and a three-coloured seeing eye reaches for Sylvia's shoulder – she screams and the creature rushes off in a rather comical way. For its original UK release in March 1953 *The War of the Worlds* was rated X. It is now rated PG on home video and DVD.

What is surprising is the accent placed on easy-option nuclear weapons and the religious aspect of the Earth–Martian conflict. The atom bomb deployed in the film is described as being ten times more powerful than anything previously used, the latest thing in nuclear fission. No special effects were needed for the bomb's conveyor, the Flying Wing Northrop YB-49. Impressive US air-force archive footage was used to depict the seven-man, eight-engined jet bomber. But the A-bomb fails – as Major General Mann (Les Tremayne) rants: 'Guns, tanks, bombs. They're like toys against them.' Early in the film, Sylvia's uncle, Pastor Collins (Lewis Martin), attempts to reason with the Martians and is zapped for his trouble. The Martians will overrun the world in six days, and Sylvia notes: 'The same number of days it took to create it.' She later takes refuge in a church – 'Praying for the one who loved me best to come and find me' – and refugees sing hymns and pray for miraculous 'divine intervention'. The Martian war machines begin to crash-land, their alien pilots dead. Bells ring out peals of celebration, as narrator Hardwicke intones: 'After all that men could do had failed, the Martians were destroyed and humanity was saved by the littlest things, which God in his wisdom had put upon this Earth.'

The War of the Worlds was released in the US in August 1953. The trailer announced: 'It's coming! The biggest story that could ever happen to our world, filling the screen with a mighty panorama of earth-shaking fury. Is there nothing that can stop the Martian death machines?' The Paramount Studios effects department won the 1953 Oscar for Special Effects. Pal's next movie for Paramount, a sequel to *Destination Moon* called *Conquest from Space* (1954), flopped and Pal left Paramount. He went to MGM and directed *tom thumb* (1958), which won an Academy Award for Best Special Effects, before returning to science fiction with *The Time Machine* (1960).

Taking Pal's lead, several other Technicolor sci-fi invasion movies were released in the wake of *The War of the Worlds* which often managed to disguise their slim budgets with ingenuity and vivid imagination. A master at this was Italy's Antonio Margheriti, whose *Battle of the Worlds* (1961) was influenced by Pal's adaptation. A British take on alien invasion was Steve Sekely's *The Day of the Triffids* (1962), based on John Wyndham's 1951 novel. Anyone who witnesses an intense meteor shower is blinded (this is most of the world's population), while those who survive have to evade towering Triffids: flesh-eating flowering plants that are on walkabout, seeking human prey. American Bill Masen (Howard Keel) awakens from an operation at Moorfields Eye Hospital, London, removes his bandages and discovers London in chaos. He wanders the city's streets filled with dazed, sightless victims and witnesses a packed passenger train crash into the buffers at Marylebone Station. With 12-year-old runaway schoolgirl Susan (Janine Faye), who can also see, he heads for Southampton, then by boat to France, through Paris and Toulon, and eventually to Alicante in Spain, where survivors are being evacuated by submarine. In a parallel storyline, marine biologists Tom and Karen Goodwin (Kieron Moore and Jeanette Scott) are trapped in a lighthouse off the coast of Cornwall, where they are menaced by the prowling plants and engage in risible, lovey-dovey small talk ('I was hoping we could get back to dissecting that stingray this evening'). Tom sprays the monsters with salt water, which dissolves the Triffids into green sludge.

The Day of the Triffids was shot in garish Eastmancolor and CinemaScope by Ted Moore on location in London, Spain and at Shepperton Studios. The film attempts to convey global panic and catastrophe on a grand scale via radio announcements and patchy special effects. A plane, its crew blinded, crashes into the docks and a passenger liner, the SS *Midland*, drifts aimlessly across the ocean, in moments that are eerie, hideous, but obviously cheaply staged. More effective is when the Triffids stalk Susan through a fog-shrouded wood, or a blinded doctor explains that meteors have burnt away his optic nerve, before throwing himself from a window. The real problem is the perambulating plants themselves. They resemble seven-foot hybrids of palm trees, asparagus and oversized snapdragons with wobbly tentacles, which emit a gurgling croak as they approach.

The Day of the Triffids: Steve Sekely's *The Day of the Triffids* (1962), based on John Wyndham's 1951 novel, saw humanity savaged by intergalactic shrubbery.

The special effects are attributed to Wally Veevers (later of *2001*) and this is schlocky sci-fi, Brit-style, with flashes of tasteful middle-class gore, as when Tom beheads a Triffid with a harpoon and when the Triffids' stung victims turn green. A BBC radio report announcing that the entire population of England is blind and that Triffids equipped with a deadly sting are roving the countryside helpfully advises: 'If you are blind: stay indoors.' The film's memorable opening scenes depict a nightwatchman (Ian Wilson) at the Royal Botanic Gardens savaged by a roving Triffid during the multicoloured meteor shower. At a Spanish villa, fugitives are besieged, so Bill electrifies the perimeter fence and deploys a fuel-truck hosepipe as an industrial strength flame-thrower, which results in a crisp salad, and lures the plants away, Pied Piper-style, with an ice cream van.

The Day of the Triffids' botanical barbarism was a missed opportunity, a mixed salad that's in need of some dressing. London was also menaced in the excellent TV spin-off, Gordon Flemyng's *Daleks – Invasion of Earth: 2150 A.D.* (1966), with Peter Cushing as Dr Who and a supporting cast including Bernard Cribbins, Ray Brooks, Andrew Kier, Jill Curzon and Roberta Tovey.

Edward L. Cahn's *Invasion of the Saucer Men* (1957; *Invasion of the Hell Creatures*) was a typical 1950s blend of comedy, horror and sci-fi, aimed at the teen and drive-in markets. It's also an American International Pictures (AIP) production that parodies AIP's own formula. A spacecraft lands in woodland near the sleepy town of Hicksburg. Two teenage lovers, Johnny (Steve Terrell) and Joan (Gloria Castillo), accidentally run over an alien and the thing's severed hand punctures their tyres. Local drunk Joe (impressionist Frank Gorshin, later the Riddler in the 1960s *Batman* TV series) sees the monsters as a way of making a quick buck. The air force tries a cover-up and inadvertently destroys the spacecraft, which they claim is a jet crash. The alien's severed hand, with its seeing-eye, menaces Johnny and Joan from the back seat of their car and a farmer's bull gores one of the aliens. The extraterrestrials drug their victims with alcohol, injected via spikes protruding from their claws. The adult authority figures are all disbelieving idiots who deem the teenagers' sightings of little green men pure fiction. Eventually the teenagers dispatch the aliens with bright car headlights. Created by Paul Blaisdell, the four-foot-high aliens, with their angry faces, clawed hands, bulbously veiny heads and boggly eyes, are the most memorable aspect of the film. The film's colourful US posters depicted an alien considerably taller than four feet carrying off a woman and flying saucers attacking a city, none of which appears in *Saucer Men*.

Perhaps the most infamous alien-invasion movie is Edward D. Wood Jr.'s *Plan 9 from Outer Space* (1958). Made with the working title *Grave Robbers from Outer Space*, it features alien invaders arriving in San Fernando, California, and implementing 'Plan 9': the resurrection of the dead. The ghouls will become the aliens' army to march on the world's capitals. Pretty soon the Los Angeles police and the army are investigating unexplained throbbing lights, creeping 'weirdies', murder victims who appear to have been 'savaged by a bobcat' and a strange odour emanating from the local cemetery. There are bizarre, jarring switches from daylight to night-time, often within the scene, with the graveyard cloaked in perpetual mist and night. The terrible flying saucer effects consist of customised plates on strings. There's a lack of adequate sets, often with curtains deployed instead of doors, for everything from an aircraft cockpit to the interior of Space Station 7. The narrative is bookended by two on-screen monologues by silver-haired, dinner-suited Criswell, a TV psychic, who intones, 'We are all interested in the future, for that is where you and I are going to spend the rest of our lives.' He claims the events of the film are based on 'sworn testimony'.

Police inspector Daniel Clay was played by ursine former wrestler 'The Swedish Angel' Tor Johnson, who garbled his dialogue into an unintelligible mash, but was convincing as a member of the lumbering zombie undead. LA cops – played by Paul Marco, Carl Anthony and Conrad Brooks – were leaden comedy relief. Gregory Walcott played pilot Jeff Trent and Mona McKinnon was his worrisome wife Paula. The alien ruler 'His Excellency' was played with fey disinterest by John 'Bunny' Breckinridge, and his two cohorts – Tanna and Eros – were played by Joanna Lee and Dudley Manlove in shiny space tunics. Best of all was Los Angeles TV horror hostess Vampira, as the resurrected 'Ghoul Woman', and her husband, also deceased, played by Bela Lugosi. Wood had a couple of minutes of footage of Lugosi, shot for a 1956 film entitled *Tomb of the Vampire*, with the actor wandering around in the guise of a vampire in his trademark Dracula cape. Lugosi then died and Wood made the most of his archived star turn. Wood deployed Tom Mason (his wife's chiropractor) who was taller than Lugosi, with a cape held over his face, to fill out Lugosi's posthumous role. This film and other 'bad films' of its ilk are often far more entertaining than their big-budget counterparts and continue to thrive via rabid cult followers.

Tim Burton's *Ed Wood* (1994), starring Johnny Depp as Wood and Oscar-winning Martin Landau as Lugosi, lovingly recreated the making of *Plan 9*. Burton's *Mars Attacks!* (1996) was a spoof of 1950s alien-invasion movies, based on the Topps trading-card series. Burton regular Danny Elfman provided the pastiche score, which includes the 1950s sci-fi staple, the theremin. The Martians swarm from their planet in a fleet of flying saucers and attack Earth. Jack Nicholson chewed the scenery in two roles: US President James Dale and crass Las Vegas Galaxy Hotel impresario Art Land. Glenn Close was the president's First Lady, Marsha (who is crushed to death by a Nancy Reagan chandelier), Rod Steiger was warmongering General Decker and Paul Winfield was peacemaking General Casey. Pierce Brosnan played Martian expert Professor Donald Kessler, Sarah Jessica Parker played dense *Today in Fashion* presenter Nathalie Lake, and Michael J. Fox was news anchor Jason Stone. Lisa Marie played a sexy, statuesque blonde Martian girl who infiltrates the White House. Pam Grier was bus driver Louise Williams and Jim Brown was her husband, washed-up ex-boxer Byron. Tom Jones appeared as himself – while performing 'It's Not Unusual' in Vegas he winds up with three Martian backing singers. The trailer-park Norris family (including Joe Don Baker, O-Lan Jones, Lukas

Haas, Christina Applegate and Jack Black) fight back, vowing, 'They ain't gittin' the TV.' Sylvia Sidney stole the film as dotty grandma Florence Norris, who inadvertently destroys the stern-faced Martians – their bulbous heads explode in splattering green slime inside their domed helmets when she plays Slim Whitman's yodelling 'Indian Love Call'. While its jumpy, cross-cutting plot is exactly what you'd expect from a screenplay adapted from a series of trading cards, a film where Sarah Jessica Parker's head is grafted onto a chihuahua's body can't be all bad.

Wells's *The War of the Worlds* also spawned some offbeat adjuncts, such as *Jeff Wayne's Musical Version of The War of the Worlds*, a bestselling 1978 concept album featuring Richard Burton as the narrator, with vocals from David Essex, Phil Lynott, Julie Covington and Justin Hayward. Timothy Hines directed the below-par *H.G. Wells' The War of the Worlds* (2005) which retained the Victorian setting, but collapsed under its 3-hour duration (a director's cut runs 135 minutes, and another, titled *Classic War of the Worlds*, runs 125 minutes). David Michael Latt's direct-to-DVD *H.G. Wells' War of the Worlds* (2005; *Invasion*) cast C. Thomas Howell, his son Dashiell, Rhett Giles, Andrew Lauer and Jake Busey. A modern retelling, it was followed by *War of the Worlds 2: The Next Wave*.

DreamWorks SKG and Paramount Pictures presented the most ambitious and successful adaptation of Wells's novel in Steven Spielberg's *War of the Worlds* (2005). Tom Cruise starred as crane-driving divorcee Ray Ferrier, a slob who lives on takeout food and works in the docks at Bayonne, New Jersey. While his children – Robbie (Justin Chatwin) and Rachel (Dakota Fanning) – are staying over, an ill-timed apocalypse strikes and ruins their weekend. A kinetic storm hits New Jersey and lightning bolts repeatedly strike the ground, but there's no thunder and the tornado's wind blows towards the storm clouds. From a lightning crater, a towering three-legged Tripod erupts. Ray and his children flee to the house of Ray's pregnant ex-wife Mary Ann (Miranda Otto) and her new partner Tim (David Alan Basche), but discover they have gone to Boston to visit her parents, so Ray and the kids embark on a mayhem-strewn cross-country dash.

The film was shot on a $132 million budget by Janusz Kamiński in New York, California, Virginia, New Jersey and Connecticut, and on sound stages at Twentieth Century-Fox and Universal Studios. A plane crash site, where a Boeing 747 ploughs into Mary Ann's house, still exists as a standing set on the backlot tour at Universal Studios.

Morgan Freeman adds gravitas, intoning the spoken prologue and epilogue. Cruise does his usual 'all-American hero' bit (he even sings a snippet of the national anthem), but with little time to establish character the film's main attractions are its many memorably apocalyptic set pieces staged by Industrial Light & Magic, as the Tripods wreak havoc. The Tripods are impressive creations – towering mechanical jellyfish with dangling tentacles and bloodsucking hoses to drain their human victims – crewed by slithery, gremlin-like alien beings. Their craft were buried on Earth many years before and the alien crewmen are catapulted into the craft via bolts of lightning. Fittingly, the booming, two-note warning sound the Tripods emit prior to attack is a root note followed by an echoing 'third'. They shatter buildings, topple church steeples, flip cars and zap fleeing people, reducing them to fluttering rags and dust. There's also an incredible massacre by the Tripods during an attack on refugees fleeing on the Hudson Ferry. In a heroic gesture, Robbie joins the army to face the Tripods, and Ray and Rachel shelter in the secluded farm basement of anchorite survivalist Harlan Ogilvy (Tim Robbins). The comic-strip finale, when Ray manages to trick a Tripod into ingesting two grenades, is risible. Eventually the Tripods' vampiric tendrils dry out like twigs, as Earth's bacteria destroy the aliens. For the Ferrier family reunion in Boston, Ann Robinson and Gene Barry from the 1953 version cameo as Mary Ann's parents. *War of the Worlds* was a considerable hit, grossing $234 million in the US alone, making it Cruise's most successful film. All versions of *The War of the Worlds* have their virtues and weaknesses, but perhaps the finest cinema version of Wells's model is discussed elsewhere in this book, in its unofficial retelling as *Independence Day* (1996).

Directed by Greg and Colin Strause, *Skyline* (2010) reworked *The Day of the Triffids*, *Fiend Without a Face* and *War of the Worlds* to depict a three-day alien attack on Los Angeles. Jarrod (Eric Balfour) and his expectant girlfriend, Elaine (Scottie Thompson), attend the party of their successful friend, Terry (Donald Faison), who is cheating on Candice (Brittany Daniel) with Denise (Crystal Reed). In the penthouse apartment the morning after the night before, blue lights rain down across the skyline and anyone who sees the blinding rays is drawn towards them. A vast alien craft unleashes harvesters which roam the city, capturing humans and eating their brains. The excellent visual effects, by hy*drau"lx, depict dozens of humans vacuumed up into the alien craft, which resemble metallic spiders, jellyfish or octopuses, with tentacled tendrils, suckers and claws. The quintet try to escape to Terry's boat, but he and Denise are flattened in their car as they attempt to speed from an underground car park. The B-grade acting is barely competent, but the alien attacks bring out the eye-popping harum-scarum in even the most wooden. Jarrod, Elaine and Candice hook up with the building's concierge, Oliver (David Zayas), hole up in Terry's penthouse and hope for the best. Unfortunately *Skyline* is hamstrung by its ruinous finale, which sees Jarrod and Elaine sucked up inside the alien craft amid a sea of corpses, where Jarrod, now reborn as an alien, protects Elaine from other crea-tures. Brainless fun, this is a future cult movie in the making which brings alien-invasion movies into the twenty-first century.

3

'GODZILLA IS JUST A LEGEND'

GOJIRA (1954)

Director: Ishirō Honda
Story: Shigeru Kayama
Screenplay: Ishirō Honda and Takeo Murata
Director of Photography: Masao Tamai
Music: Akira Ifukube
A Toho Film Production
Released by Toho Film
96 minutes

Akira Takarada (Hideo Ogata), Momoko Kōchi (Emiko Yamane), Takashi Shimura (Professor Kyōhei Yamane), Akihiko Hirata (Dr Daisuke Serizawa), Fuyuki Murakami (Professor Tanabe), Sachio Sakai (Hagiwara, a reporter), Toranosuke Ogawa (manager of the Nankai Shipping Co.), Keiji Sakakida (Mayor Inada), Ren Yamamoto (Masaji, a fisherman), Kan Hayashi (Chairman of Diet Committee), Takeo Oikawa (Chief of Emergency HQ), Toyoaki Suzuki (Shinkichi, Masaji's younger brother), Kuninori Kōdō (old fisherman), Kin Sugai (Ozawa-san), Katsumi Tezuka and Haruo Nakajima (Godzilla)

* * *

Although the greats of Japanese cinema – Kurosawa, Ozu, Mizoguchi – were responsible for some of the finest, most revered films in world cinema, there was another Japanese cinema, one that was much more lucrative internationally. Just as Italian cinema of the 1950s and 1960s produced both arthouse and popular cinema, so too did Japan. Their vivid sci-fi cinema deployed men in rubber monster suits wrestling amid dioramas of Tokyo or volcanic Mount Fuji, flying fire-breathing beasts suspended by wires, fantastic spacecraft, irritating children, caped superheroes and wackily dressed visitors from outer space. Toho was the studio that produced the best examples, often in glorious widescreen colour TohoScope, which opened with the company logo, a blue background with a radiant sun and rippling aura. Unlike in US sci-fi films, the

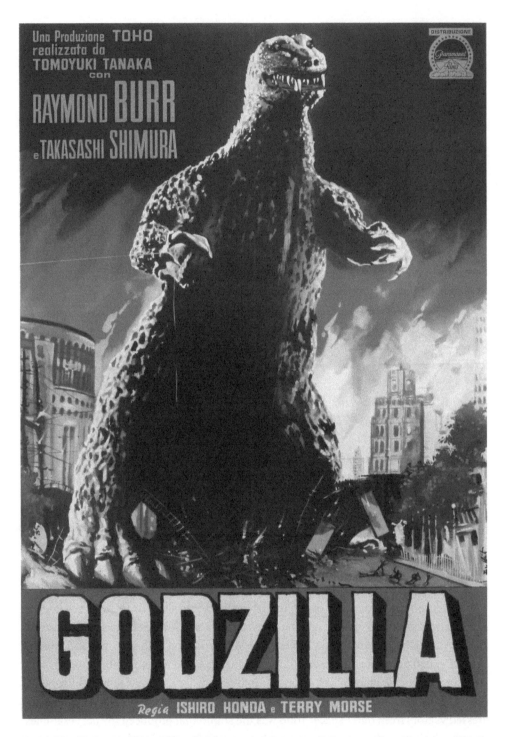

King of the Monsters: Italian poster for the re-edited version of *Gojira*, attributed to Ishirō Honda and Terry Morse, with new inserts featuring Raymond Burr.

deployment of atomic weapons is often considered or threatened but rarely used, with newly developed high-tech weapons of mass destruction favoured instead.

Gojira (1954), directed and co-written by Ishirō Honda, both initiated the Japanese *kaijū eiga*, or 'monster movie', genre and defined it. Ships vanish mysteriously in the sea near Japan and the authorities are at a loss as to the cause. The old fisher-folk of Odo Island know that it's not an underwater volcano, or a sea mine, but a monster from the ocean they call 'Gojira' – Godzilla. Following an attack on a fishing village, a research party led by Kyōhei Yamane (Takashi Shimura), a professor of palaeontology, is dispatched to Odo. They find a giant radioactive footprint, the village wells affected by radiation and a trilobite, a three-lobed creature that's been extinct for three million years. Then the monster, a giant lizard, appears. The scientists surmise that nuclear detonations in the vicinity have changed the beast's habitat and hydrogen-bomb tests may have dislodged it – humanity has created the radioactive monster. Frigates depth-charge the sea and a huge high-voltage electric fence is erected along the coast, but Godzilla walks through it and attacks mainland Japan, crushing houses, tearing up bridges, trains and power lines and leaving flaming ruins in its wake. It breathes a powerful heat ray that melts pylons and burns cars. A newly developed Oxygen Destroyer, which disintegrates the oxygen in water, is deployed and kills the monster in Tokyo Bay, though, as Professor Yamane observes, if the world continues nuclear testing, another Godzilla could appear at any time.

Gojira is a powerful human drama which delivers a potent anti-nuclear, anti-weapons message. Godzilla is a primal beast, a symbol of unleashed nuclear power born of the mushroom clouds of Nagasaki and Hiroshima. At the end of World War II, the USA dropped atomic bombs on these Japanese cities, thereby bringing the conflict to an emphatic conclusion. *Gojira* is an allegory of Japan's defeat, the power of scientific super-weapons and the ultimate futility of such destruction. Zoologist Yamane doesn't want the monster to die but wants to study it, and the beast's death is downbeat – a mixture of tears and jubilation, with the sense of loss aptly conveyed. After a final agonising roar as Godzilla breaks the water, the creature is reduced to a skeleton on the seabed. Dr Serizawa (Akihiko Hirata) is initially reluctant to allow the use of his invention, the Oxygen Destroyer, which is simply a weapon of destruction with no redeeming qualities. He worries that if it is used, then other world powers will see it and it will become a threat to mankind, so he burns all his research notes and, as the device activates, cuts the air line to his diving suit.

With the exception of colour and widescreen, all the Japanese monster-movie ingredients are present in *Gojira*, from the men of science who try to understand the beast and the military who attempt to obliterate it, to excited reporters, terrified crowds and a love story subplot between Professor Yamane's daughter Emiko (Momoko Kōchi) and salvager Ogata (Akira Takarada). Emiko is initially in love with researcher Serizawa, but means to break off her engagement to him. When she visits his laboratory, he demonstrates his invention – the Oxygen Destroyer – which reduces fish to skeletons in seconds: they are asphyxiated and liquefied. Serizawa himself is a reminder of the war – he wears an eyepatch and has a scarred face from the conflict. The aftermath of Godzilla's attacks, of smoking cities laid waste, are post-nuclear. Schoolchildren sing a lament, the masses pray for salvation and there are realistic scenes set in crowded hospitals, with vignettes of staff checking children for radiation and a child weeping for its dead mother.

Special-effects genius Eiji Tsuburaya worked on *Godzilla* and many of the finest Japanese sci-fi movies, while Teizo Toshimitsu was billed as 'Monster builder'. The mono-chrome cinematography was by Masao Tamai, and Akira Ifukube composed the effective score: the theme music features an insistent march, which is augmented by Godzilla's horrible roar. *Gojira* was a massive hit in Japan and was reworked for the US market by TransWorld Releasing as *Godzilla, King of the Monsters!* (1956), advertised on posters as 'Awesome! – And then some!' This version included newly filmed inserts directed by Terry Morse and featuring US star Raymond Burr as reporter Steve Martin, who 'witnesses' the events. The original Japanese version ran 96 minutes, but this reworking was 80 minutes and was X-rated in the UK. This version also omitted the anti-nuclear message, turning it into a monster-on-the-loose movie. In contrast to its American-dubbed edition (and an even worse colourised, re-scored version released by Luigi Cozzi in Italy in 1977, as *Godzilla*), *Gojira* is one of the great science-fiction monster movies and a masterpiece of 1950s Japanese cinema. Belying its 'creature feature' roots, it's pretty heavy drama: sombre, resonant and hard-hitting.

Hard-hitting turned out to be a keyword in the Godzilla oeuvre, as a host of imagina-tive monster movies jumped on the bandwagon. In Motoyoshi Oda's *Godzilla Raids Again* (1955; *Gigantis*), Godzilla (here looking rather toothy) is discovered living on one of the 'Southern Islands'. The original Godzilla was created by the effects of hydrogen-bomb tests. The tests have also awakened an ankylosaurus called Anguirus, which is somewhere between 70 million and 150 million years old. Godzilla and Anguirus invade Osaka and the pair fight, destroying Osaka Castle in the process, until Godzilla kills Anguirus. *Godzilla Raids Again* is similar in style to *Gojira*, with grainy monochrome cinematography, but is too plot-heavy truly to succeed as a monster movie, as the human characters and love stories clutter underfoot. Shimura reprises his role as Professor Yamane in a cameo and shows Osaka dignitaries Godzilla's attack on Tokyo (stock footage from *Gojira*). For the climax on ice-bound Shinko Island, jets attack and Godzilla is buried in an avalanche.

First out of the blocks in the imitation-Godzilla stakes was *Varan the Unbelievable* (1958), directed by Honda in monochrome TohoScope. Varan (called 'Baran' in Japanese) is a familiar lizardy creature with a lumpy complexion, powerful tail and spiked stickleback (actually made from sliced-up transparent plastic tubing), with the added gimmick that it has wings (flaps of skin between its limbs, rather like a flying squirrel) that enable it to fly. Varan is described as a Varanopode, which lived 185 million years ago. In the Tōhoku region, 'the Tibet of Japan', local natives worship their god, Baradagi, which is actually prehistoric Varan. It emerges from a lake, wreaks havoc and eventually attacks Tokyo in a final showdown at Haneda airport. The excellent atmosphere of the remote region – foggy jungles, cliffs, mountains, valleys and a lake – is dissipated by the generally poor special effects. Varan is eventually dispatched when it's conned into swallowing a new explosive, 20 times more powerful than dynamite. The re-cut, severely truncated (from 87 to 70 minutes) 1962 US release called *Varan the Unbelievable* had Varan disturbed from his lake by Myron Healy (as a US navy scientist trying to turn salt water into fresh water). *Varan* was also edited into a 54-minute, two-part miniseries for Japanese TV.

If *Gojira* is the archetypal 1950s Japanese monster movie, then Universal–International's *Creature from the Black Lagoon* (1954), directed by Jack Arnold, is the quintessential US equivalent of the same period. An expedition of ichthyologists and scientists in Brazil investigate a strange find, a Devonian-period webbed, clawed fossilised hand. In an Amazon tributary backwater known locally as the Black Lagoon, they find the scaly Gill-man. Arnold's tension-filled story is simple, but brilliantly executed. Beautiful Universal contract actress Julie Adams played Kay Lawrence, the story's bathing-beauty love interest, while the Gill-man was portrayed by Ricou Browning in the swimming scenes and by Ben Chapman on land. The party that embarks on the fateful trip on fishing barge *Rita* includes Dr David Reed (Richard Carlson), Mark Williams (Richard Denning), Carl Maia (Antonio Moreno), Dr Edwin Thomas (Whit Bissell) and ship's captain Lucas (Nestor Paiva). The scientists reason there are things unknown even on Earth, just like the vast unknown of space. The movie was shot on sets at Universal Studios, with Wakulla Springs, Florida as the Black Lagoon. A massive success on its release, *Black Lagoon* was originally exhibited in 3-D, and the rippling, bubbling underwater photography still looks magnificent today, as the monster stalks swimmer Kay, Mark tries to spear the beast with a harpoon or David squirts white clouds of native drug Rotenone at the monster. The score was written by three composers: Henry Mancini wrote the lighter incidental themes; Herman Stein the main and end title themes, as well as music for the underwater scenes without dialogue; and Hans Salter the horror sequences, plus cobbled-together source music from *The Wolf Man*, *The Ghost of Frankenstein* and *Bend of the River*. Two sequels followed: *Revenge of the Creature* (1955; in '3-D Horrorscope'), where the creature is brought back to Florida and runs amok at Marineland Studios, and *The Creature Walks Among Us* (1956), where the creature, badly burnt in the Everglades, is 'humanised' via surgery into a Frankenstein's monster which wears clothes. Thus the thing from the deep, from another age, evolves into something almost human throughout the trilogy.

In addition to their monsters, Japanese sci-fi cinema continued Hollywood's serial tradition from the 1930s and 1940s, with intergalactic Japanese hero Super Giant, a bulletproof 'man of steel' sporting cape and tights, who was re-dubbed for international audiences as Starman. The original Japanese nine-chapter *Super Giant* serial (1956–9) was co-directed by Teruo Ishii, Akira Mitsuwa and Koreyoshi Akasaka at the Shintoho Studio. Ken Utsui played the title role in all nine outings and the serial was syndicated by Walter Manley Enterprises on US TV in the mid-1960s, recut into a series of four feature films: *Atomic Rulers* (or *Atomic Rulers of the World*), *Invaders from Space*, *Attack from Space* and *Evil Brain from Outer Space*. Each entry begins with Starman and his watch-like gizmo, the Globe-Meter (which enables him to fly, detect radiation and speak and understand any Earth language), being dispatched from his home on the Emerald Planet by the strange-looking menagerie of the planet's high council (including some starfish-shaped oddballs), to save Earth from contaminating the universe with nuclear fallout.

Atomic Rulers is a spy thriller, as Starman tries to locate a powerful nuclear device that the Magolians threaten to blow up Japan with – their lair, labs and equipment anticipate the James Bond films. *Invaders* is livelier, as Starman takes on the Salamander Men of Kuleman, who unleash a deadly virus from space and high-decibel sound-wave attacks, and whose lungs expel a radioactive ray. This entry features eye-opening costumes, acrobatic fights, a menacing dance troupe, a scramble of action and chases, and some scary make-up: one villain's visage resembles the hideous grin of Batman's nemesis The Joker. The 'Starman' stories usually feature children in the plots, and there's a genuinely weird sequence not suitable for younger viewers where a creepy witch menaces some kids. *Attack from Space* is mostly a straightforward space opera with the Sapphirians threatening Earth with a deadly missile. The film rounds off with an epic and well-choreographed punch-up and shootout on the Sapphirians' space station, during which Starman fights his way through the entire bunch. It does, however, feature intriguing touches, such as a secret underground entrance through a grave and a scene on the fiery 'Death Star'.

The first three films were each culled from two *Super Giant* chapters, but the final instalment crammed three chapters into *Evil Brain from Outer Space*, making it the wackiest of the series. Starman is up against Zumarian invaders, who are a band of Batman-like villains with leotard-clad henchmen – fanged, clawed, acrobatic mutations that breathe radioactive vapour, germ warfare (deploying 'the original germ') and deadly throwing weapons that resemble cocktail sticks. There are gadgets, secret passages, elaborate weapons and a villainous rogues' gallery including evil Dr Kurokawa, a wheelchair user with a hawk perched on his shoulder, who is aided by his one-legged henchman on crutches. Another mad doctor, Kurokawa's brother Okawa, has a hideously scarred face and a henchman with a hook for a hand, who manifests the germ into a long-haired witch-like woman who battles Starman with jets of fire. The disparate plot threads include assassination plots on world leaders, a germ attack on Japan and supervillain Balcazar's still-living brain in a suitcase, which triggers some crazy dialogue ('I bring orders from Balcazar's Brain'). It's easy to see the joins in these US adaptations, but a prosaic narration was added to try to paper over the plot's gaping cracks. Starman was dubbed in English by Bernard Gordon and at the end of *Evil Brain* he returned to the Emerald Planet. The seeds of many cinema tropes, from J-horror and Japanese gangster movies to *Star Wars*, can be found in these refreshingly inventive yarns.

Back at Toho, *Rodan* (1956), directed by Honda, featured a beaky flying reptile, a pterodactyl–eagle hybrid, and was the first Japanese monster-movie to appear in colour.

Rodan hatches in a coal mine after eating giant dragonflies, creates a destructive shock-wave as it flies across the landscape and can whip up a whirlwind with its wings. Honda returned to Godzilla with *King Kong vs. Godzilla* (1963), which pitted two of the great movie monsters (a US one and a Japanese one) against each other in 'The Battle of the Century!' Godzilla is resurrected when US submarine *Seahawk* collides with an iceberg and the monster attacks Tokyo. Meanwhile, the Pacific Pharmaceutical Company, led by Mr Tako (Ichirō Arishima), plans to export sedative berries from the native island of Faroe, but King Kong intervenes. He saves the island from a giant octopus (a well-orchestrated sequence, featuring a live octopus) and drinks the red berry juice, which knocks him out. The company tow King Kong on a raft towards Japan to exploit him in their sponsorship campaign, but the monster breaks loose. King Kong is eventually sedated with rocket warheads tipped with the berry juice, and helium balloons towed by helicopters airlift him to Mount Fuji to face Godzilla. King Kong emerges victorious – he has elongated ape arms for extra reach in the combat scenes. In a sign of the era in which it was made, note the scene where the explorers arrive on the island and distribute cigarettes to the natives, including children. True to form, Kong wrecks a train and perches atop a building with a female hostage in his paw (Mie Hama, later Kissy Suzuki in *You Only Live Twice*). Jun Tazaki – a *Godzilla* series regular – played General Shinzō. This is 'gorilla filmmaking' at its best, a strange allegorical tale of US–Japanese post-World War II relations. Here the US monster saves Tokyo from the Japanese 'nuclear monster' and also gets top billing. It remains the most successful Godzilla film ever in Japan and was followed by a Kong-only sequel, Honda's *King Kong Escapes* in 1967, which pitted the ape against robotic Mechani-Kong.

In Honda's *Mothra* (1961), ruthless impresario Clark Nelson (Jerry Ito) kidnaps a tiny pair of telepathic 'little beauties' (played by twins Emi and Yumi Itō) from Infant Island and publicly exhibits them as 'The Secret Fairies Show'. Their protector Mothra, a 100-metre moth larva, swims to Japan to free them – sinking a luxury liner, busting a dam, attacking Yokota army base and demolishing Tokyo Tower. The heroes are Dr Chūjō (Hiroshi Koizumi), reporter Zen 'the Snapping Turtle' (Frankie Sakai), press photographer Michi Hanamura (Kyōko Kagawa) and their editor (Takashi Shimura). Mothra spins a cocoon, which the army attempts to incinerate with an Atomic Heat Cannon, and hatches as a giant moth. Nelson flees to his home country of Rolisica (a fictional Anglo-American country that is clearly the US) and Mothra attacks its capital, New Kirk City.

Honda's sequel is even better. In *Mothra vs. Godzilla* (1964), a hurricane washes a giant egg from its island home to the shores of Japan. Kumayama (Yoshifumi Tajima) of Happy Enterprises and rich businessman Torahata (Kenji Sahara) plan to exploit the egg and whatever hatches from it by building a theme park, the Shizunoura Happy Centre, around it. The egg's guardians, two tiny twins (in some prints called 'the Peanuts Twins', played by the Itōs), arrive from Infant Island (which has been laid waste by nuclear testing) to reclaim the egg with the help of its parent, Mothra, a giant female moth. When

Godzilla emerges from under Kurada Beach, a delegation pleads with the natives to convince Mothra to save Japan. *Mothra vs. Godzilla* deploys a threatening score from Akira Ifukube and is a great example of Japanese fantasy storytelling. Akira Takarada plays news reporter Ichirō Sakai, and Yuriko Hoshi was his photographer sidekick, Junko 'Yoka' Nakanishi. Maruda, their editor at the paper, was played by Jun Tazaki. The scenes of Godzilla's destructive rampage in Nagoya and at Osaka Castle are well done, as are the combat scenes with flapping Mothra (a string-operated puppet), and when the military drop metal nets on Godzilla and electrocute it. The moth agrees to save her egg – and Japan – even though she is dying. During a battle with Godzilla, Mothra deploys poisonous yellow pollen. She expires, her wing draped over her egg, which hatches twin larvae. The grubs then take on Godzilla on Iwa Island. The segmented avengers envelop Godzilla in a cocoon of silky thread and 'The Atomic Monster' plunges into the sea.

Again helmed by Honda, *Ghidorah, the Three-Headed Monster* (1965) marked the beginning of the second phase of the Godzilla series, with the lizard now a defender of Earth. Japan is suffering a heatwave in winter, which convinces scientists that the planet is going to explode, and there have been strange sightings of UFOs – the Saucer People – in the skies. A glowing, egg-like meteor lands in a mountain gorge and hatches Ghidorah (aka King Ghidorah), a ferocious three-headed winged dragon, with no arms and two tails, that fires yellow bolts of lightning. Godzilla, Rodan and larval Mothra team up to tackle Ghidorah with silken webs and rocks, with Mothra riding on Rodan's back as aerial artillery. The human-interest story is strong, with Yuriko Hoshi as news reporter Naoko and Yosuke Natsuki as Detective Shindō. He is assigned to protect visiting Himalayan princess, Salina, played by the remarkably beautiful Akiko Wakabayashi (later Aki in *You Only Live Twice*), who is the subject of an assassination plot. She is possessed by strange forces, claims to be a Martian and becomes a vagabond prophet of doom.

Honda's *Invasion of the Astro-Monsters* (1965; *Monster Zero*) shifted the emphasis of the series to science-fiction settings and monsters. Planet X is discovered in the Scorpion constellation beyond Jupiter, and World Space Authority astronauts Glenn (Nick Adams) and Fuji (Akira Takarada) investigate. On Planet X the Controller (Yoshio Tsuchiya) says that the planet is being terrorised by Monster Zero (actually King Ghidorah). In exchange for a tape containing the formula to a miracle drug that will cure all diseases, the Xians want to borrow Monsters 'Zero One' and 'Zero Two' – Godzilla and Rodan – to defeat Monster Zero. The two monsters are transported to Planet X, but when Earth's council play the tape containing the 'miracle cure', it is an ultimatum from the Xians. Earth will be governed as a colony of Planet X and the three monsters are unleashed on Earth. Planet X's ships are eventually derailed with 'A-cycle light rays' and piercing sonic weapons. The superb cinematography by Hajime Koizumi contrasts the autumnal atmosphere of the scenes on Earth with the psychedelic wonders of Planet X and the Xians, with their groovy space shades. The film displays great imagination, flamboyant sets and costuming, and laughable English dubbing. Jun Tazaki appeared as Dr Sakurai.

In a subplot, Tetsuo Torii (Akira Kubo), the inventor of a high-pitched sonic defence device – the 'ladyguard' – is approached by mysterious Miss Namikawa (Kumi Mizuno) from Planet X. There's a wonderful moment when Earth's council prepare to play the tape from Planet X and someone asks: 'Is their system the same?', a familiar worry for videotape and DVD film collectors worldwide. Godzilla does a victory dance when he defeats King Ghidorah – the man in the Godzilla suit is Haruo Nakajima, Rodan is Masaki Shinohara and King Ghidorah is Shōichi Hirose. Planet X. Monster Zero. Cloned spacewomen and a three-headed monster. Cult sci-fi doesn't get any better than this.

In Jun Fukuda's *Ebirah, Horror of the Deep* (1966; *Godzilla vs. the Sea Monster*), Godzilla (having been jump-started on Devil's Island by a primitive lightning conductor made of a scimitar and a length of wire) takes on Giant Eagle (which he grills with his heat ray), swats away military organisation Red Bamboo's jet air force and fights Ebirah, a giant lobster, in paw-to-claw action that begins with the pair 'playing ball' with a rock. With Devil's Island set to self-destruct in an atomic explosion, the stranded heroes are rescued by Mothra. The score, which includes surf guitars and brass, was by Masaru Satō. In Fukuda's *Son of Godzilla* (1967), on tropical Sollgel Island in the Pacific, scientists conducting weather experiments attempt to freeze the island and induce snowfall, but instead induce a radioactive storm and a heatwave that grows the already huge praying mantis on the island to gigantic proportions. Christened Gimantis by the scientists, the three beasts find an egg, which hatches Baby Godzilla (or Minilla). The baby's cries summon daddy Godzilla from across the Pacific, and the Big G defeats the flying mantis and tackles Spiga – a giant spider – which sprays Godzilla with web. Eventually the scientists instigate a big freeze, it starts to snow and father and son defeat Spiga and burn him. From the opening jaunty comedy music by Satō, this is obviously a kids' film. There's a scantily clad native girl, Riko Matsumiya (Bibari Maeda), the daughter of an archaeologist, and Gorō Maki (Akira Kubo), an amiable reporter, with whom she falls in love. Godzilla's opponents are formidable – the 'Kamacuras' giant mantis (string-operated puppets, accompanied by a screeching noise and a threatening, staccato, chugging theme from Satō) and Spiga (aka Kumonga). This film features father Godzilla teaching Godzilla Jr. how to roar and to use his flaming heat ray, but Baby Godzilla only manages to blow smoke rings.

Other Japanese studios got in on the act. Haruyasu Noguchi's *Gappa: The Triphibian Monster* (1967; *Gappa the Triphibian Terror*) was the only foray into the genre by Nikkatsu Studio, which was better known for the gangster movies *Tokyo Drifter* (1966) and *Branded to Kill* (1967). The Gappas are comical beasts, a kind of lizardy winged griffin, with beaks, powerful tails and the ability to emit a deadly blue 'heat ray'. They are 'triphibian', equally at home on land, at sea or flying through the air. The film is a send-up of the genre and is aimed at the children's market. Daiei Studios contributed *Gamera* (1965), starring a 200-foot-tall space turtle that has two tusk-like teeth, can breathe fire and flies with rocket propulsion like a revolving flying saucer. The original film was cannibalised for US release as *Gamera the Invincible* (1966), which featured an awful twisting 'Gamera

Theme Song' that sounds like *Batman*. Gamera is released from a glacier and the UN decides on 'Plan Z', to fire Gamera back to Mars. The finale is terrific – Gamera is lured to Ōshima Island by a trail of burning oil. It is then captured in a capsule that is attached to the nose of a rocket and fired into space. It was soon 'lights, Gamera, action!' again, as Daiei unleashed its sequels. In *Gamera vs. Barugon* or *War of the Monsters* (1966, 1967 in the US), the turtle does battle with Barugon 'the quick-freeze monster', a cross between a crocodile and a rhino, which fires a deep-freezing vapour from its stalk-like tongue. *Gamera vs. Gaos* or *The Return of the Giant Monsters* (1967, 1968 in the US) featured a winged, reptilian supersonic flying squirrel (or is it a foxbat?) with a flat, anvil-shaped head; it fires laser beams from its mouth and detests sunlight. In *Gamera vs. Viras* or *Destroy All Planets* (1968), the alien Virians travel in craft seemingly assembled from yellow-and-black striped beach balls and deploy their 'Super Catch Ray' to apprehend their turtle nemesis. The Virians' master, Viras, is a silvery, four-tentacled creature with glowing eyes and a beak that seems to be part octopus, part peeled banana. For *Attack of the Monsters* (1969; *Gamera vs. Guiron*), Gaos makes a reappearance, though painted silver for this outing, and manages to cut his own leg off with a deflected laser beam. Gamera's main adversary is the aliens' defender, Guiron, a dino-shark, with a knife blade for its head. *Gamera vs. Jiger* (1970; *Gamera vs. Monster X*) featured a spiky-faced dinosaur that walks on all fours. Daiei resurrected Gamera for Shūsuke Kaneko's *Gamera: Guardian of the Universe* (1995), which pitted the turtle (still a guy in a suit) against bat-like flat-headed Gaos and his brethren. The UK edition features a truly awful dubbing track and an irritating-as-noisy-neighbours-thudding intrusive techno soundtrack. Gamera protects Tokyo from Gaos, who nests in Tokyo Tower, and redeems the film in an incredible fireball finale.

To combat their competitors, Toho pulled out the stops for *Destroy All Monsters* (1968; *All Monsters Attack*), as Honda threw everything at the audience in this surreal celebration of 1960s cult Japanese cinema. Set in 1999, all the Toho monsters are now confined on the Pacific island of Ogasawara, known as Monsterland. Aliens the Kilaaks take over the island's control centre and release the monsters on the world's capitals – Rodan flattens Moscow, Mothra Beijing and giant, serpent-like dragon Manda (in some sources called Wenda) London. Godzilla takes a chunk out of the Big Apple and later sinks a passenger liner, while Mothra (in larva form) derails a train and Rodan downs a passenger jet. Gorosaurus (Baragon in the English dub) demolishes the Arc de Triomphe in Paris, then Godzilla, Rodan, Manda and Mothra launch a devastating all-out attack on Tokyo. This zesty monster mash is staged with élan by Honda, cinematographer Taiichi Kankura and special-effects man Tsuburaya. There are bits of James Bond espionage, yakuza gangster films, monster movies and sci-fi stirred into the brew. Akira Ifukube provided an urgent, heroic march theme. By 1999, the United Nations Scientific Committee (UNSC) has established a base on the Moon and spacecraft Moonlight SY-3, commanded by Captain Katsuo Yamabe (Akira Kubo), investigates the control base on Monsterland. The crew

Destroy All Monsters: The all-star cast for this 'monstrous' hit includes Godzilla, Anguirus, Baragon, Manda, Spiga, Baby Godzilla and King Ghidorah. It was unleashed in 1969 in the US by American International Pictures.

wear bright-yellow space suits and the sets are garishly pop art. The Kilaaks, led by their queen (Kyōko Ai), are beautiful women wearing glittery hoods and capes. Protected by a force field, they are living metal and can withstand high temperatures, so they hole up near volcanic Mount Fuji. When killed, the Kilaaks become molten 'worms' that hide in rocks. They demand to be allowed to stay on Earth and Earth must live by Kilaaks' laws.

Monster-movie regular Jun Tazaki played boffin Dr Yoshido. Earth's scientists – including Dr Ōtani (Yoshio Tsuchiya) and Kyōko Namabe (Yukiko Kobayashi) – are taken over by the Kilaaks during an attack on Monsterland (using billowing yellow gas) and have control transmitters implanted in their necks. There's a shoot-out on a beach, with Kilaak-controlled Kyōko and her black-suited gangster henchmen (armed with laser guns) versus secret service 'special police'. Action shifts energetically back and forth between Earth and the Moon space station. In one scene Katsuo destroys the Kilaaks' monster-controlling apparatus on the Moon with a laser gun, before the action returns to Earth for the grandstand finale. The all-star cast includes Godzilla, Baby Godzilla, Wenda, Baragon, Varan, Spiga, Anguirus, Manda, Gorosaurus, Mothra and Rodan. At Mount Fuji, the Kilaaks unleash King Ghidorah on the monsters, who are now fighting to protect Earth. Spiga and Mothra spray Ghidorah with web, others wrestle it to the ground and Ghidorah is vanquished as Godzilla viciously stamps on one of its necks to finish it off. The Kilaaks then deploy a flying ball of fire called the Great Fire Dragon, which nukes Monsterland. Godzilla smashes up the Kilaaks' underground base on Fuji, and Katsuo and the SY-3 take on the Fire Dragon. They zap it with a 'cooling missile', which reveals it's a Kilaak flying saucer. The film ends with peace on Earth and the monsters back on Monsterland Island. This comic-strip retro sci-fi movie, a favourite among sci-fi monster buffs, is the zenith of the series.

Godzilla's Revenge (1969; *All Monsters Attack*), directed by Honda, was an infantile adventure. Schoolboy Ichirō (Tomonori Yazaki) is bullied by Gavara, one of his schoolmates. Ichirō's parents are never home (his father is an engine driver and his mother 'works nights'), so when he visits a toy inventor (Hideyo Amamoto), Ichirō travels in his imagination to Monster Island, where he meets Baby Godzilla, known variously as Minya, Minara and Minilla (depending on the print), and his father. Ichirō witnesses Godzilla and son take on various opponents (battle footage from *Ebirah* and *Son of Godzilla*) cut to jaunty jazz-pop. Godzilla was played by Haruo Nakajima, Baby Godzilla was 'Little Man' Machan, and Gavara (in some sources Gabara) was Hiroshi Sekita (who had played Ebirah). Godzilla also takes on a projection of Ichirō's bullying tormentor, Gavara. This is a random creature, a green scaly dragon–cat with tufted ginger hair and the ability to electrocute its enemies. At one point Baby Godzilla grows and takes on Gavara himself. Just as Baby Godzilla learns life lessons from his father, so Ichirō learns from his monster heroes to stand up for himself against the bullies, which he eventually does.

Jun Fukuda's *Godzilla vs. Gigan* (1972; *War of the Monsters*) pitted Godzilla against giant cockroaches (aliens who have assumed human form) that are orchestrating an invasion of Earth using a giant computerised control room in a new construction development, 'Godzilla Tower', a replica of the monster that is part of a Tokyo leisure park, 'Children's Land'. The manic plot pits cartoonist Gengo (Hiroshi Ishikawa), his martial artist girlfriend and their hippyish allies against the aliens. The by-now-classic 'Godzilla March' is reprised on the soundtrack, and at one point cartoonist Gengo invents two new, rather boring cartoon monsters, 'Shukurah' and 'Mamagan': the 'Homework Monster' and a monster representing 'Strict Mothers'. The film is partly a remake of *Destroy All Monsters*, and the aliens' planet has been destroyed by pollution (stock footage from *Destroy All Monsters*, *Godzilla vs. Hedorah* and earlier entries is used). The aliens unleash King Ghidorah and Gigan (sometimes billed as Gaigan), a dragon–chicken with a beak, tail, stickleback wings, glowing red eyes, large metal hooks and a buzzsaw in its chest. Godzilla and Anguirus break out of Monster Island and come to Tokyo's rescue. This outing is particularly surreal, as Godzilla and Anguirus speak to each other in the English language dub. In Fukuda's *Godzilla vs. Megalon* (1973), underground nuclear tests in 1971 cause earthquakes in Japan and the subterranean Seatopians unleash Megalon, a bizarro pogo-jumping creature assembled from random bits of other Toho monsters. With scales, pointed metallic limbs and prawn features, it is topped off by a Christmas-tree star that fires a disintegrating heat ray. It is joined for the film's main bout by Gigan. Heroic remote-controlled robot Jet Jaguar (a silver-red-blue-and-yellow flying superhero with a Mephistophelian face) grows to great size to fight the villains. Godzilla is pretty much a guest star, with Jet Jaguar the main attraction. The obdurate villains are difficult to put away for good. Godzilla swings Megalon around by the tail, in a barn-dance showdown that's more 'swing your pants' than total war.

The Godzilla series continued in a similar vein with movies including *Godzilla vs. Mechagodzilla* (1974) and *Terror of Mechagodzilla* (1975). A third cycle of Japanese monster movies began with Yoshimitsu Banno's *Godzilla vs. Hedorah* (1971; *Godzilla vs. the Smog Monster* in the US), in which pollution was the threat. Godzilla saves Japan from Hedorah (from the Japanese word for 'sludge' or 'slime'), which is initially a small black tadpole, but soon grows to great size, resembling a heap of melted rubber tyres and seaweed, with red eyes that fire lasers. This toxic avenger can also transform into a flying manta ray and disperse clouds of sulphuric-acid vapour, wiping out the population like a deadly crop-duster and reducing humans to acid-burnt skeletons. The monster feeds on refuse drifting in the harbour, attacks tankers and drinks their oil, and puffs on factory chimneys bellowing black pollutant smoke. It has travelled from the Andromeda Nebula on a rock that has landed on Earth. The wrestling match between Godzilla and Hedorah on Mount Fuji is highly unconvincing, as Godzilla uses his heat ray as a jet pack, enabling him to fly, and Hedorah fires dollops of acidic, oily gunk. The film includes scenes in a groovy hippy nightclub (where one patron imagines the other clubbers to have turned into fish-headed mutants), psychedelic pop songs, an environmental movement sponsored by the 'All Japan Youth Foundation' and ecological-themed animations.

Hedorah's natural successor was the antagonist of highly successful South Korean monster movie *The Host* (2006), directed by Joon-ho Bong. When formaldehyde is dumped down the drain from a mortuary into the Han River in Seoul, it creates a massive aquatic horror, which resembles a tadpole. It emerges from the river to wreak hell along a waterfront, and the government later reveals it is hosting a deadly, unknown virus. Sleepy slacker Gang-doo Park (Kang-ho Song) runs a snack bar near the Han with his father Hee-bong (Hee-bong Byeon). When Gang-doo's daughter Hyun-seo (Ah-seong Ko) is captured by the beast and imprisoned with other humans in the sewer system, the family, including Gang-doo's sister, archery champion Nam-joo (Doo-na Bae) and brother, unemployed graduate Nam-il (Hae-il Park), stumble to the rescue. This winning entertainment blends tragedy and comedy to great effect, no better than in the film's most celebrated scene when the creature, huge and dark in the water, emerges from the river, attacks curious onlookers and ploughs through a waterfront park, with the giant scampering tadpole bounding along and causing havoc far more convincingly than Hedorah.

Over the decades, Godzilla has been reinvented for successive generations. A 1985 revamp, also called *Godzilla*, reworked the original film and even deployed 'flashback' footage from the 1954 version and cast Raymond Burr. There's been a Hollywood *Godzilla* remake, with a hefty $130 million budget. Roland Emmerich helmed this overblown tale of the Big G levelling New York. The film globetrots from French Polynesia to Chernobyl, Tahiti, Panama and Jamaica, before settling in a rain-sodden New York, where a selection of everyman heroes attempts to curtail the monster's rampage and scores of irritatingly kooky New Yorkers get deservedly flattened by the beast's enormous three-toed feet. Against the masonry-shattering backdrop of New York under attack, sappy worm expert Dr Niko Tatopoulos (Matthew Broderick) has a sloppy romance with cliché-ridden old flame Audrey Timmonds (Maria Pitillo), who has ambitions to become a news reporter and is in hot pursuit of that big scoop. There are some massive explosions, plenty of misplaced comedy (errant Sidewinder missiles destroy the Chrysler Building), a gloopy David Arnold score, a facile, route-one script, wooden acting and gung-ho militarism that makes James Cameron films look subtle. Hundreds of eggs are discovered incubating in Madison Square Garden, and the hordes hatch before the US Air Force nukes the nest. The leaden acid jazz of Jamiroquai's tie-in single 'Deeper Underground' is an apt complement to a film that won Razzies for Worst Supporting Actress (Pitillo) and Worst Remake or Sequel.

Toho countered this sacrilege with Takao Okawara's *Godzilla 2000* (1999) and, best of all the latter-day outings, *Godzilla, Mothra and King Ghidorah: Giant Monsters All-Out Attack* (2001; *GMK* for short). Writer–director Shūsuke Kaneko took the helm for this edition, as, 50 years after the original Godzilla stomped Tokyo, the military fear he's on the prowl again. This reboot ignores all the intervening 'Godzilla' films, as Godzilla is a white-eyed, savage atomic beast. Earth is defended by the 'Guardian Monsters', as foretold by an ancient legend – Baragon, Mothra (which emerges from a cocoon on Lake Ikeda) and King Ghidorah, the 1,000-year-old dragon. The monsters are still portrayed by men in suits, but they are incorporated into some wonderful widescreen action and special effects by Makoto Kimiya, rendered in Super-35. This is a proper monster movie, with wanton destruction, great effects, thumping action, shocks, an excellent score from Kō Ōtani (with a reprise of Ifukube's classic 'Godzilla Theme') and mild gore (it's a PG-13 in the US). There's a chilling scene where Godzilla causes a tidal wave that lifts a ship into the air on a harbour front, a picturesque pitched battle at a tourist spot between Baragon and Godzilla in Owaku Valley, and a night-time confrontation in Tokyo between Ghidorah, Mothra and Gozilla. Graceful, colourful Mothra's never looked better, and there's a brief appearance by the Peanuts Twins. Yuri Tachibana (Chiharu Niiyama) is a reporter for TV station 'BS Digital Q' ('the bargain basement of the airwaves') which specialises in sensationalist drama–documentaries with a fantastical edge. She is helped in her investigation by Teruaki Takeda (Masahiro Kobayashi) and hindered by her hippy boss Haruki Kadokura (Shirō Sano). Yuri becomes an on-the-spot eyewitness, filming the climactic battle as a live broadcast. The film also features texting and the internet and is a modern take on the formula, while being true to the spirit of the 1960s classic period. The film even references its horrible 1998 Hollywood cousin, with a mention that the only time Godzilla has been seen since the 1950s was in a recent attack on New York.

Kaneko spins a good yarn and this is one of the most intelligent, effective Japanese monster movies, which stirs in realistic human drama and elements of J-horror ghost stories, myths and legends. Wise old prophet Professor Hirotoshi Isayama (Hideyo Amamoto) is revealed to have died years before, and the energy that revives the 'Guardian Monsters' is the restless souls of the thousands of innocent Asians who died during the Pacific War. They are not protecting the people of Japan, but their own homeland: the mountains, the forests, the rivers. After Yuri's father, Admiral Taizō Tachibana (Ryūdō Uzaki), has confronted Godzilla in Tokyo Bay, in deep-sea salvage sub *Satsuma*, and killed the monster with a burrowing D-03 boring missile, the creature's beating heart continues to pump away on the bay floor, boding ill. You can't keep a good monster down and we'll never say 'Sayonara Godzilla' forever. It's just a question of how long before the one and only Toho monster rises again.

In Guillermo del Toro's gloriously epic *Pacific Rim* (2013), the menace to Earth – giant Kaiju beasts – emerge from a dimensional portal between tectonic plates beneath the Pacific Ocean. To fight the monsters, which resemble Godzilla's and Gamera's varied foes, Earth creates monsters of its own, the towering robot Jaegers (hunters). There are Jaegers representing Australia, China, Russia and America. This international mix is reflected in a cast that includes Charlie Hunnam, Idris Elba, Rinko Kikuchi, Charlie Day, Robert Kazinsky, Max Martini, Ron Perlman and Burn Gorman. The action sequences are hurricanes of furious combat, as man and war machine meld in harmony to slug it out with the behemoth Kaijus, to Ramin Djawadi's thumping score. *Pacific Rim* was a great success worldwide, taking over $400 million. Fittingly, the film is dedicated to two monster masters: Ray Harryhausen and Ishirō Honda.

4

'I NEVER SAW ANYTHING LIKE IT!'

TARANTULA (1955)

Director: Jack Arnold
Story: Jack Arnold and Robert M. Fresco
Screenplay: Robert M. Fresco and Martin Berkeley
Director of Photography: George Robinson
Music: Herman Stein
A Universal–International Pictures Production
Released by Universal–International
76 minutes

John Agar (Dr Matt Hastings), Mara Corday (Stephanie 'Steve' Clayton), Leo G. Carroll (Professor Gerald Deemer), Nestor Paiva (Desert Rock County Sheriff Jack Andrews), Ross Elliott (Joe Burch, reporter), Edwin Rand (Lieutenant John Nolan), Raymond Bailey (Townsend), Hank Patterson (Josh), Bert Holland (Barney Russell, mortician), Steve Darrell (Andy Anderson, rancher), Bing Russell (Deputy), Clint Eastwood (Sands Air Base squadron leader)

※ ※ ※

US science-fiction cinema was revitalised in the early 1950s, when filmmakers' imaginations ran riot in a series of 'creature features'. Earth was under attack from a new universal enemy – a monster that some commentators saw as representative of Communism, others as critical of the dangers of nuclear experimentation. The monsters in question were either terrestrial (of the Earth) or extraterrestrial (from outer space). Terrestrial beasts grew to gigantic proportions as the result of experiments by maverick, misunderstood, and often quite mad, scientists. Further threats emanated from the wide, unspecified 'outer space', while others were atomic mutations, the horrific by-products of radioactive fallout from atomic testing. Some were insects or dinosaur-like creatures, while others were inventive hybrids, such as the squawking, tufted chicken–vulture of *The Giant Claw* (1957) or the angry, clawed cucumber in *It Conquered the World* (1956).

It's Them!: Italian poster for Gordon Douglas's giant ant movie *Them!* (1954), the prototype for the 'giant-insect attack' subgenre.

The first 1950s 'creature feature' was Eugène Lourié's *The Beast from 20,000 Fathoms* (1953). Based on Ray Bradbury's *Saturday Evening Post* short story *The Fog Horn*, the film depicted a rampage by a giant reptilian dinosaur, a rhedosaurus (animated in stop-motion by Ray Harryhausen on his first movie assignment). The 100-million-year-old beast is awoken and thawed out at the North Pole by a US-government atomic test. It eventually makes its way to New York and is revealed to be carrying a plague. Professor Tom Nesbitt (Paul Christian) spends the movie attempting to convince his sceptical superiors that New York is being levelled by a real live dinosaur. Cecil Kellaway played jovial Professor Thurgood Elson, the dean of the Natural History Museum, and Paula Raymond was his palaeontologist assistant and Paul's love interest, Lee Hunter. Here all mention of the atomic age is indicative of a new and positive future, which is equated with writing 'the first chapter of a new Genesis', even if it is responsible for awakening primal, destructive forces. A state of emergency is declared in New York, the National Guard is called out and the beast is cornered at the roller coaster in the Manhattan Amusement Park. Sure-shot marksman Corporal Stone (Lee Van Cleef) shoots a radioactive isotope from a grenade rifle into its wound, killing the beast and neutralising the plague. Budgeted at $200,000, the film grossed over $5 million for Warner Bros and opened the floodgates for the assorted giant fiends that followed.

Them! (1954), directed by Gordon Douglas, is the prototype for the giant-insect sub-genre. South of Alamogordo, New Mexico, a dazed young girl clutching a doll is discovered wandering by two patrolmen – Sergeant Ben Peterson (James Whitmore) and Trooper Ed Blackburn (Chris Drake). The patrolmen soon encounter a wrecked car and caravan, sugar cubes, a strange footprint and an eerie, high-pitched noise on the desert wind. At Johnson's Store, a seemingly abandoned gas station, the corpse of Gramps Johnson is found. FBI agent Robert Graham (James Arness), Dr Harold Medford (Edmund Gwenn) of the Department of Agriculture and his daughter Pat (Joan Weldon) join Ben in trying to solve the case when Johnson's corpse is revealed to be pumped full of ants' formic acid. They locate the ants' nest in the desert and destroy it with phosphorous and cyanide, but two queens fly away. One hatches a nest on board the SS *Viking* and the crew are massacred before the ship is sunk, but the other queen takes refuge in storm drains in Los Angeles. The mutation has been caused by the first atomic test blasts at White Sands, New Mexico, in 1945. *Them!* is one of the most effective US sci-fi films of the 1950s. The desert scenes have a fine oppressive atmosphere, created by Bronislau Kaper's music, Sid Hickox's monochrome cinematography and the desolate New Mexico desert setting, with its whistling winds, shifting sands, ominously silhouetted Joshua trees (yuccas) and sparse, rustling undergrowth. It was shot in late 1953 in Palmdale, California, on the Blaney Ranch, and on location in Los Angeles. At a Los Angeles railroad yard, the police investigate the theft of 40 tons of sugar. Interiors were lensed at Warner Bros Burbank Studios. The open LA storm drain featured prominently at the climax, where the queen ant has made her nest. A military operation (using flame-throwers to incinerate the 12-foot-high ants) is launched to rescue two young boys – Jerry and Mike Lodge (Robert John Correll and Richard Bellis) – who are cornered in the half-constructed tunnel. Sandy Descher played the pigtailed 'Ellinson girl' found wandering in the desert in her dressing gown, who screams 'Them!' when she smells formic acid. Fess Parker has a cameo as pilot Alan Crotty, who is deemed crazy when he claims to have seen flying ants. *Them!* was supposed to be filmed in 3-D and colour, but it's more effective for its monochrome 'docu-realism'. It took $2.2 million in the US and was the highest-grossing Warner Bros movie of 1954.

The most famous 1950s US creature feature was Jack Arnold's seminal *Tarantula* (1955), which closely followed the blueprint of *Them!*. Biologist Eric Jacobs wanders dazedly through the Arizona badlands, his face and hands hideously disfigured. His condition is acromegaly, caused by an overactive pituitary gland. Local doctor Matt Hastings (John Agar) investigates and discovers that Jacobs has been injected with a super-nutrient, Nutrient Type 3Y, which he developed with Professor Gerald Deemer (Leo G. Carroll) in an isolated desert laboratory. Deemer is attempting to solve the world's food short-age, but the nutrient speeds body growth. His laboratory is filled with rapidly enlarging rabbits, white rats, guinea pigs and tarantulas. When Deemer's lab assistant Paul Lund is also affected by acromegaly, Paul goes berserk, injects Deemer with the serum, wrecks the laboratory and an outsized tarantula escapes to embark on a rampage through the desert towards Desert Rock. Matt, with help from lab assistant Stephanie 'Steve' Clayton, as well as the local police and air force, attempts to stop the creature.

Eight-Legged Freak: Jack Arnold's 1955 giant-spider thriller, starring John Agar, Mara Corday and Leo G. Carroll, was notable for its noirish atmosphere and eerie special effects.

Jack Arnold specialised in sci-fi/horror movies including *It Came from Outer Space* (1953), *Creature from the Black Lagoon* (1954) and *The Incredible Shrinking Man* (1957). *Creature* featured the amphibious, scaly Gill-man, one of the most famous sci-fi/horror creations that inspired many sequels and imitators, including *The Phantom from 10,000 Leagues* (1954), *Revenge of the Creature* (1955), *The Creature Walks Among Us* (1956) and *The Horror of Party Beach* (1964), the 'First Horror Monster Musical!' *Tarantula* was shot in black and white by George Robinson, on desert locations in the Lucerne Valley, California. Dead Man's Point – a jutting rock formation – appeared as Devil's Rock, where Matt and Steve narrowly avoid being crushed by a rock fall started by the spider. The town of Desert Rock was filmed at Courthouse Square, a backlot set at Universal Studios, California. Universal–International favourite John Agar played the lead. He also starred in B-pictures such as *The Mole People* (1956), *The Brain from Planet Arous* (1957) and *Zontar, the Thing from Venus* (1968). Leo G. Carroll was excellent as Deemer, whose acromegaly disfigurement results in his right eye sliding down his face. Steve Darrell was rancher Andy Andersen, who discovers his cattle reduced to a heap of bones and Eddie Parker (in acromegaly make-up) played both Eric Jacobs and Paul Lund. Deemer's replacement lab assistant, science student Steve Clayton, was played by 1950s cult movie star, model and pin-up Mara Corday in her most famous role. She and Agar tour the desert in a flashy Ford Skyliner convertible.

The spider's slow, deliberate walk as it makes its ominous progress through the empty, threatening desert was created with an actual spider spliced into matte shots of the desert, plus model work and a full-sized prop spider head and fangs. In the matte shots, the spider appears menacing the town of Desert Rock, or on the horizon above a ranch spooking the skittish horses in a corral. The arachnid leaves large white pools of spider venom near the victims' remains. Action highlights include the spider's attack on the ranch and a sequence when the local cops try to blow the spider to smithereens with dynamite. The spider devours two saddle tramps, destroys power pylons and flips trucks. It eventually levels Deemer's mansion as it kills the professor and menaces Steve: the spider's eyes and fangs appear at her window in an image that has come to epitomise this brand of sci-fi films. Finally an attack by four US Air Force jets from Sands Air Base incinerates the creature with rockets and napalm on the flats outside Desert Rock. The pilot in command of Sands Air Base in the film's finale, which incinerates the spider with rockets and napalm, was played by an unbilled Clint Eastwood.

Tarantula was released in the US in December 1955 to great success. Originally X-rated in the UK, it is now a PG for 'mild horror and threat'. *Variety* called it: 'quite credibly staged and played, bringing off the far-fetched premise with a maximum of believability'. The trailer noted, 'Even science was stunned!' *Tarantula* remains the quintessential 1950s creature feature and is high art compared to the drive-in schlock that flew, crawled, scuttled or crept in its wake.

Corday's breakthrough role in *Tarantula* led to her starring in several further 'creature features', including Edward Ludwig's *The Black Scorpion* (1959), which features atomically mutated scorpions, spiders and stop-motion worms with claws in caves beneath the Mexican desert. Corday also appeared in *The Giant Claw* (1957), directed by Fred F. Sears, as mathematician and systems analyst Sally Caldwell. Jeff Morrow played pilot and electronics engineer Mitch MacAfee. Earth is threatened by an extraterrestrial creature with an impenetrable force-field shield that flew in 'from some godforsaken antimatter galaxy'. The puppet creature, which was created on an insufficient budget by a Mexican special-effects crew, is part vulture, part chicken, mostly turkey. This squawking, flapping travesty, with talons, flared nostrils, tufted hair and staring eyes, aptly conveys what the script calls 'a feathered nightmare on wings'. The cast play the material straight, which makes the enterprise all the more entertaining. The beaky fiend attacks planes, trains and automobiles, and plucks parachuting survivors out of the sky. Having attacked New York and mangled the Empire State Building and the UN, its force field is disintegrated by a particle bombardment from a B-25 Mitchell, and rockets consign it to a watery grave. Shot in less than two weeks (and looking like it), *The Giant Claw* is not easily forgotten.

Mesa of Lost Women (1953) was filmed under the working title *Tarantula*. In the Mexican Muerto Desert, Dr Araña (Jackie Coogan) conducts experiments while hidden in a cave on Zarpa Mesa. As *araña* is Spanish for 'spider', it's no surprise that with help from his dwarf assistants, he creates a giant spider (an unconvincing, largely immobile prop) and spider women, such as talon-clawed Tarantella (Tandra Quinn), the film's best two features. A party, stranded following a plane crash, investigate the mysterious goings-on, but the plodding plot never takes flight. It also features probably the most irritating score of all time – an interminable, jagged Spanish flamenco cue. Quinn performs a spider-inspired dance routine to it in a Mexican cantina, the highlight of her all-too-brief five-film career.

Other filmmakers tried to cash in on money-spinners such as *Tarantula*, attempting to outdo them in size and threat, but often only succeeded in achieving incompetence and hilarity. Ray Kellogg's *The Giant Gila Monster* (1959) was shot on location in undergrowth in Cielo, Texas. Produced by cowboy star Ken Curtis for Hollywood Pictures Corporation (also responsible for the same year's *The Killer Shrews*), it pitted a roving giant Gila monster (enlarged due to pituitary-gland growth spurt) against assorted hot-rodding, drag-racing hipsters in jalopies. Fred Graham was flummoxed Sheriff Jeff, Don Sullivan played full-time mechanic, part-time rock-'n'-roll yodeller Chase Winstead, and Ken Knox was platter-spinning Texan disk jockey Steamroller Smith. The lizard wanders amiably through landscape dioramas and attacks the teens' barn-dance shindig, before being obliterated by Chase's nitroglycerine-laden jalopy.

The Monster That Challenged the World (1957), directed by Arnold Laven, created a nicely tense atmosphere in its story of giant molluscs (which resemble dribbling sea snails) threatening the inland Salton Sea in California, before slithering their way into the All-American Canal. Commander John 'Twill' Twillinger (Tim Holt), a naval intelligence officer based at El Centro Airbase, battles the radioactive monsters with help from research scientist Dr Jess Rogers (Hans Conried), in between romancing Gail MacKenzie (Audrey Dalton). The prehistoric snails' eggs have been dislodged from the lake floor by an earthquake and hatched by radiation. *Monster* features some atmospheric monochrome underwater photography of the seaweedy depths (shot mainly off Santa Catalina Island, California), and the snails, which the scientists claim resemble mythological Kraken, are impressive, full-scale monsters created by August Lohman and designed by Edward S. Haworth (later famed production designer Ted Haworth). Victims are discovered with dishevelled, petrified, googly-eyed faces, their bodies drained of blood and water.

Nathan Juran's *The Deadly Mantis* (1957), released by Universal–International, deployed a prehistoric praying mantis being thawed out at the North Pole. An expert is brought in (here palaeontologist Ned Jackson, played by William Hopper) as the creature flies south to menace the US. Eventually the wounded mantis is trapped in a tunnel and killed with chemical mines. *The Killer Shrews* (1959) featured shrews the size of Alsatians in this low-budget, effectively odd little shocker. Bernard L. Kowalski's *Attack of the Giant Leeches* (1959; *The Giant Leeches*), starring Ken Clark, was self-explanatory. Kenneth Crane's *Monster from Green Hell* (1957) saw Dr Quentin Brady (Jim Davis) battle giant wasps enlarged by cosmic radiation in the Green Hell jungle of Central Africa, until a volcanic eruption wipes them out. British entries include Quentin Lawrence's *The Crawling Eye* (1958; an adaptation of the TV series *The Trollenberg Terror*) and Eugène Lourié's *Gorgo* (1961), which deployed a sea monster in London. Lourié's *Behemoth, the Sea Monster* (1959; *The Giant Behemoth*) tried the same trick with a radiation-infused dinosaur threatening London. John Lemont's *Konga* (1961) ripped off *King Kong* with experimental scientist Dr Decker (Michael Gough) gigantically enlarging a chimpanzee.

In Angel County, California, a rocket crashes and an odd-looking monster emerges to terrorise the countryside in *The Creeping Terror* (1964). This creature, which resembles a giant slug that's been hit by a truck, was basically a large quilt. One person operated the front 'head' section (complete with wobbly tentacles) with several students from Glendale College following in its wake under the sheet and operating the 'body'. Victims of the shambling beast are hauled, awkwardly, into the creature's mouth. The monster attacks picnickers, a low-key teen hootenanny in a park, fishermen, a housewife, lovers smooching in lovers' lane and, most memorably, a community dance-hall shindig. Eventually it eats most of a squad of soldiers, before being dispatched with a grenade. There's also a second monster lurking inside the spaceship, which savages Dr Bradford (William Thourlby), until it's hit by a squad car. 'Vic Savage', who played the deputy Martin Gordon, also directed, produced and edited the film under his real name, Art J. Nelson. Virtually the entire film is narrated in monotonous deadpan fashion by Larry

Burrel, who describes dialogues that we see acted out, silent-movie-style, on-screen. The beasts are actually mobile laboratories and ingest the humans in order to analyse them chemically, to beam back their findings to their home planet. Nelson raised the budget for *The Creeping Terror* by getting the actors and crew to pay to work on the film. Many people wanted to appear in the movie, which is why the film is little more than the monster attacking people, with little semblance of a plot. Thourlby, a male model, paid $16,000 to play Dr Bradford, while Frederick Kopp paid $6,000 to write the score. Nelson's lover Shannon O'Neill played Martin's newlywed wife, Brett. Before the film was released, Nelson disappeared and was never seen again.

Bert I. Gordon (acronym B.I.G.) was renowned for outsized subject matter in films such as *The Amazing Colossal Man* (1957), *Earth vs. the Spider* (1958; *The Spider*) and *Village of the Giants* (1965). Gordon was producer–director–co-writer of *Empire of the Ants* (1977), a loose adaptation of H.G. Wells's 1905 story. The film is set on the Florida coast at 'Dreamland Shores', an exclusive, under-construction leisure resort. During a tour of the site hosted by bogus realtor Marilyn Fryser (Joan Collins) and her accomplice Charlie Pearson (Edward Power), the party of prospective buyers is attacked by giant ants. The creatures have been mutated by radioactive waste, which has been illegally dumped and washed up on the beach. The party struggle through the swamp and are whittled down by ant ambushes, as their ordeal becomes 'survival of the fastest'. When they reach civilisation the humans are suspicious of the vacant-eyed locals, and in a ridiculous twist (even by giant-ant movie standards) the creatures have brainwashed the locals with a pheromone. They work as their slaves in a sugar refinery, until heroic Joe Morrison (John David Carson) drives a gasoline tanker into their lair. Produced by Samuel Z. Arkoff for AIP, *Empire of the Ants* was shot on windy locations at Florida's Jensen Beach (as 'Dreamland Shores') and in Belle Glade (for the town scenes). The dozen-strong party includes a divorcee, a lecher, some pensionable timewasters, a pair of busybodies, a couple of lonelyhearts looking for love, and those there solely for the free food and boat trip. Albert Salmi was suitably shifty as County Sheriff Art Kincaid, who is in league with the ants, and Robert Lansing was heroic captain Dan Stokely. Dana Koproff provided the atmospheric, *Jaws*-like score, and Warren Estes was billed as 'Ant Coordinator'. For the most part *Empire of the Ants* is highly entertaining 1970s trash. Only in the rushed finale does the film disappoint, delivering such an anty-climax.

The year 1977 was a peak year for insect-rampage fans, with the release of John 'Bud' Cardos's *Kingdom of the Spiders*. Strange occurrences at the cattle ranch of Walt and Birch Colby (Woody Strode and Altouise Davis) near the sleepy Arizona town of Camp Verde are investigated by lothario cowboy vet Dr Rack Hansen (William Shatner) and sexy entomologist Diane Ashley (Tiffany Bolling). The Colbys' prized calf, their dog and bull are all killed by tarantula venom five times more powerful than normal. They discover a spider hill – a massive nest – on their property, which they torch, but Diane explains that it seems thousands of tarantulas are working together as an army, forging communities and migrating to this one place. They have been forced to find a new food source, as pesticides have wiped out their usual diet. Stubborn Mayor Connors (Ray Engel) refuses to cancel the upcoming county fair, a big tourist attraction. An attempt to obliterate dozens of further spider hills results in the crop-dusting biplane flown by the Baron (Whitey Hughes, also the film's stunt gaffer) crashing into a gas station. Rack, Diane and other fugitives shelter from the infestation in Washburn's Lodge, a guesthouse, which is soon completely surrounded. The town meanwhile is overrun and the panicky locals are slaughtered en masse. Rack is badly bitten when he attempts to change a fuse in the basement. As a new day dawns, Rack looks out to discover that their building (and the entire town) has been blanketed beneath an immense cocoon, the spiders' way of preserving their food.

Kingdom of the Spiders is undoubtedly a B-movie, but the performances are convincing and the tension and pace remain taut, making for a lively 91 minutes. In a humorous scene early on, entomologist Diane emerges from the shower to find a tarantula in her dresser drawer, but she simply picks it up and puts it outside, completely unfazed. The spiders were supplied by Lou Schumacher and the production's spider wrangler was Jim Brockett, who must have had his work cut out. The tarantulas are mostly normal sized, but there are hundreds of them – crawling over their spider hill, popping out of drawers, dropping down chimneys and through ventilation ducts and swarming across the landscape. And they're real. The actors battle them in close-up and their corpses are left cocooned for the beasts to feast on later. The film features some tremendous, skin-crawling set pieces, as when the crop-duster pilot discovers his cockpit is full of spiders while he's mid-air. In his terror he shrieks like a bird, as you would in such circumstances. During another attack, Birch shoots her own hand off with a pistol. Her husband Walt crashes his pickup down a ravine when arachnids accost him while he's driving. *Kingdom* was shot on location in dusty Arizona, including the distinctive sandstone rocks at Sedona. David McLean was Verde county sheriff Gene Smith, Lieux Dressler was lodge owner Emma Washburn, and Joe Ross and Adele Malis played Vern and Betty Johnson, two tourists from Colorado. Rack looks after Terry Hansen (Marcy Lafferty), the widow of his brother who has been killed in 'Nam, and her daughter Linda (Natasha Ryan). *Kingdom* is a very well-made little frightener that's edited for maximum shock value. It was scored by Jerry Goldsmith. Dorsey Burnette delivered the countryish, ironic title song, 'Peaceful Verde Valley' ('Down in peaceful Verde Valley, who knows what tomorrow may bring?'), in a resonant Elvis quiver and also provided a couple of tunes that are played on the radio during the movie.

Kingdom was part of another strain of 'what if?' sci-fi movies, where ecological destruction – pesticides, chemicals, unfettered land development and exploitation – led to nature fighting back in such movies as *Tentacles* and *Day of the Animals* (both 1977), *The Swarm* and *The Bees* (both 1978). Bert I. Gordon's *Food of the Gods* (1976) starring Marjoe Gortner, Pamela Franklin, Ida Lupino, Jon Cypher and Ralph Meeker was an adaptation of an H.G. Wells novel, which featured oversized rats and Gortner being viciously pecked by a giant chicken. It was followed by *Gnaw: Food of the Gods II* (1989). In Bill Rebane's *The Giant Spider Invasion* (1975), starring Steve Brodie, Barbara Hale, Leslie Parrish, Robert Easton and Alan Hale, spiders hatch from geodes following a gamma-ray shower, grow to enormous size and invade Hicksville, USA. Eventually the yokels go a-spider huntin' and crowds flee the beast en masse at a county fair. Microphones are visible at the bottom of the screen during dialogue scenes, and check out the wiggly-legged 'giant spider' effect rampaging through northern Wisconsin, which is just about passable at distance, but in close-up breaks the spell.

Although spiders, giant or otherwise, infest such mainstream movies as *Arachnophobia* (1990) and *Eight Legged Freaks* (2002), it's down to gross-out exploitation fare such as *Spiders* (2000) and *Spiders 2: Breeding Ground* (2001) to keep 1950s creature features truly alive. Gary Jones's *Spiders* starred Lana Parrilla as small-time college reporter and UFO-er Marci who finds herself trapped in a secret government facility. She discovers the MIL (Mother-in-Law) Project has injected a desert Funnel Web Spider with alien DNA aboard NASA's *Solaris* space shuttle in orbit. Something goes wrong, the spider gets loose and the shuttle crashes to Earth. There's an attempted cover-up as the spider lays its spawn in humans, which burst *Alien*-like from their hosts. Despite an awful script and patchy acting, this is proper, lively B-movie stuff, with some truly skin-crawling spiders. Sam Firstenberg's sequel set the claustrophobic creepy-crawly action on a ship, with Stephanie Niznik as heroine Alexandra.

Matt Reeves's *Cloverfield* (2008) was the most imaginative and innovative of a modern breed of creature feature. During a going-away party for Rob Hawkins (Michael Stahl-David), a monster attacks New York, leaving widespread destruction and hideous insect creatures it its wake. Rob and his friends – Marlena Diamond (Lizzy Caplan), Lily Ford (Jessica Lucas), Hud Platt (T.J. Miller) and Rob's brother Jason (Mike Vogel) – attempt to flee the island, but Jason is killed when the beast demolishes the Brooklyn Bridge. Rob tries to reach his ex-girlfriend, Beth McIntyre (Odette Yustman), who is trapped, badly injured, on the 39th floor of her teetering apartment block. *Cloverfield* cost approximately $25 million, but took over $80 million in the US. Memorable images include the Brooklyn Bridge's demise, the army and air force battling the beast through the streets, an oil tanker capsizing, a helicopter crash and the sight of the Statue of Liberty's severed head landing in a Manhattan street. The beast itself, designed by Neville Page, is a gangly-armed, screaming behemoth. 'Whatever it is,' notes a soldier, 'it's winning.'

If you've seen one monster stampeding through a city, you've seen 'em all, but *Cloverfield* offers an engaging gimmick. Hud has been instructed before the farewell party to record good luck messages for Rob from the guests with a video camera, and as the havoc unfolds, it is through his camera that we witness the events. The tape (and also *Cloverfield*) begins with the blurb stating that this is the property of the US Department of Defence and is filmed evidence of multiple sightings of a case designated 'Cloverfield'. The camera was

retrieved at Incident Site US-447, an area 'formerly known as Central Park'. The beginning of the tape has footage from 27 April, when Rob and Beth were in love and visited
a funfair on Coney Island. The tape then cuts to Rob's leaving party on 22 May, which
Beth attends with her new boyfriend, Travis (Ben Feldman). At various points in the
film, Reeves cuts back to the footage that has been wiped off – Beth and Rob's perfect
day. Caplan, Yustman and Stahl-David are excellent, and the finale is particularly effective. Rob and Beth, both trapped screaming under rubble, yell to each other, 'I love you.'
Cutting back to them on the sunny Coney Island Ferris wheel, Beth smiles and affirms,
'I had a good day', as the tape runs out.

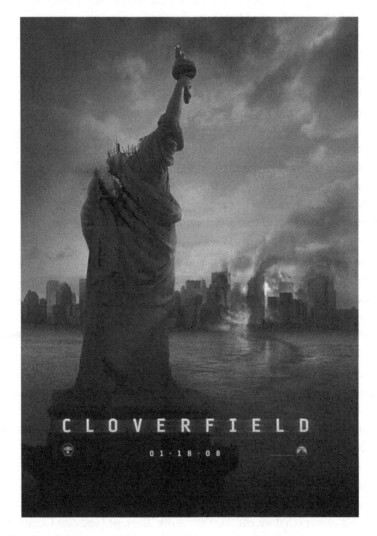

The End of Liberty: Matt Reeves's creature feature *Cloverfield* (2008) followed its protagonists
during an alien invasion of New York through the lens of a video camera.

5

'YOU'RE NEXT!'

INVASION OF THE BODY SNATCHERS (1956)

Director: Don Siegel
Story: Jack Finney
Screenplay: Daniel Mainwaring
Director of Photography: Ellsworth Fredericks
Music: Carmen Dragon
SuperScope
A Walter Wanger Production
Released by Allied Artists
77 minutes

Kevin McCarthy (Dr Miles Bennell), Dana Wynter (Becky Driscoll), Larry Gates (Dr Dan Kauffman), King Donovan (Jack Bellicec), Carolyn Jones (Theodora 'Teddy' Bellicec), Jean Willes (Nurse Sally Withers), Ralph Dumke (Chief of Police Nick Grivett), Virginia Christine (Wilma Lentz, Becky's cousin), Tom Fadden (Uncle Ira Lentz), Jean Andren (Eleda Lentz), Kenneth Patterson (Stanley Driscoll, Becky's father), Eileen Stevens (Anne Grimaldi), Beatrice Maude (Grandma Grimaldi), Bobby Clark (Jimmy Grimaldi, Anne's son), Sam Peckinpah (Charlie, gas-meter reader)

* * *

The 1950s unleashed a new modern brand of terror in 'science-fiction horror'. The old-fashioned horror of Dracula, Frankenstein, the Mummy and the Wolfman looked outmoded against such nuclear mutations as *Them!* and *Tarantula*. But amid the rampaging monsters, 50 feet high and spitting fire and venom, there was also a subtler strain of allegorical sci-fi horror. These films had paranoid resonance, contemporary relevance and social commentary, approached in lively, chilling fashion. Now 'them' could be one of us.

A classic example of this new breed was Don Siegel's *Invasion of the Body Snatchers* (1956). Dr Miles Bennell (Kevin McCarthy) is called back urgently from a medical

Don Siegel's groundbreaking *Invasion of the Body Snatchers* (1956) saw the Californian town of Santa Mira overrun by pod people.

convention to Santa Mira to tend his patients, only to find: 'Something evil had taken possession of the town.' Some of the local residents claim their loved ones have been replaced by impostors. They look and sound the same, but there is soullessness, a lack of humanity. Miles's former lover Becky Driscoll (Dana Wynter) tells Miles that her cousin Wilma Lentz claims her Uncle Ira is not her Uncle Ira. Miles's friend Jack Bellicec (King Donovan) finds a body on his billiard table, with no fingerprints or distinctive features, which begins to assume the physical characteristics of Jack. When the body disappears, psychiatrist Dr Dan Kauffman (Larry Gates) and chief of police Nick Grivett (Ralph Dumke) offer rational explanations. Miles, Becky, Jack and his wife Teddy (Carolyn

Jones) discover four seed 'pods' in Bellicec's greenhouse. The seeds hatch foetal human forms which quickly transform into likenesses of the quartet. They deduce that the pods assume the shape of their targets, becoming replicas. The 'switch' takes place while their victims sleep and Miles destroys them with a pitchfork. But almost the whole town has been overtaken by doppelgängers, including Jack. As Miles and Becky are hounded out of town and take refuge in canyon caves, Becky briefly succumbs to sleep and betrays her lover, giving away his position to their pursuers: 'He's in here – get him!'

Invasion of the Body Snatchers was based on the 1955 novel *The Body Snatchers* by Jack Finney, which had been serialised in *Collier's Magazine*.

The novel specifies that the story begins on Thursday 13 August 1953 and is narrated in the first person by Dr Miles Boise Bennell, a 28-year-old divorcee in Santa Mira (in some versions Mill Valley), California. The film adaptation stayed close to its source for the most part and some character names were altered. The character of Professor Budlong, who identifies the pods as 'space spores', parasitic fugitives from another planet, is not present in the film, nor is sinister librarian Mrs Wyandotte. In the novel, the pod people wear yellow and navy-blue button badges, and anyone on the streets not wearing one is waylaid by the pod police. In the finale, the pods admit defeat and fly off into space.

Don Siegel shot his film adaptation on a $300,000 budget during a 19-day shoot in March and April 1955. The story was set in a fictional Californian suburb of Los Angeles called Santa Mira, and many of the exterior Santa Mira locations were shot in Sierra Madre, California, including its open town square. Santa Mira railway station was Chatsworth Station, while other scenes were filmed in Chatsworth and Glendale. Further exterior locations included Bronson Cave (as the abandoned mine Miles and Becky shelter in) and Bronson Canyon in Griffith Park (for the pursuit scenes, including a chase up steep steps). Interiors and some exteriors were lensed at Monogram/Allied Artists Studio in Los Angeles. For the memorable climax, when Miles attempts to flag down cars on the jammed Hollywood Freeway, Siegel filmed on a seldom-used flyover. The pod people allow him to escape, reasoning, 'They'll never believe him.' Panic-stricken Miles tells motorists, 'They're here already! You're next! You're next!' The drama unfolds in a normal, everyday setting – the pod people, pottering about their daily business, are the enemy. A fine sense of paranoia is enhanced by Carmen Dragon's score and Ellsworth Fredericks's shadowy monochrome photography in widescreen SuperScope. Future film director Sam Peckinpah worked as 'dialogue director' on the film and also as a stuntman and actor. He can be seen as Charlie the gas-meter reader, who deposits pods in people's basements on his rounds. Peckinpah's wife Marie Selland also had a small role as Martha Lomax, the wife of a gas-station attendant who surreptitiously places pods in the boot of Miles's car. Art director Ted Howarth created the pod special effects for $30,000. They resemble outsized pea pods, which burst and emit frothing bubbles to reveal human-like life forms. The scientific explanation for their arrival is that seed spores drifted through outer space, germinating in farmers' fields. During filming Siegel completely freaked Wynter out when he left a pod in her house, under her bed.

Psychiatrist Dan explains to Miles and Becky the appeal of becoming a pod: 'Cell for cell, atom for atom […] reborn into an untroubled world.' In one of the film's most chilling moments, Nurse Sally Withers (Jean Willes) places a pod in her baby's room. The babe will soon be asleep, 'And there'll be no more tears.' Miles pitchforks his own replica and such simple imagery (the film has few 'special effects') is expertly utilised by Siegel for maximum shock. One such image is lorries loaded with pods, like farmers taking veg to market. Miles's surgery overlooks the town square, and Miles and Becky watch through the window as a typical lazy Saturday morning unfolds. But now those arriving by bus from out of town are quietly spirited away by the police before they can realise what's going on, and the zombified population gravitate to the square, where farmers' trucks distribute pods to the locals. Miles later discovers greenhouses cultivating pods in huge quantities, and in the finale he sees a freighter truck bound for San Francisco loaded with the strange cargo.

Invasion of the Body Snatchers, like Jack Arnold's *It Came from Outer Space* (1953), can also be interpreted as a suspicious allegory of 'Reds under the Bed' paranoia. In Cold War America, the House Un-American Activities Committee, headed by Republican Senator Joseph McCarthy, conducted witch-hunts to root-out perceived 'Commie' infiltrators during the Red Scare. In interviews Siegel has never discussed the film's politics, and it's apparently an amazing coincidence that the film has an actor named McCarthy in the lead. The pod people to Siegel 'possess no soul, emotion or culture' and are 'incapable of love'. Siegel 'knew many of our associates, acquaintances and family were already pods. How many of them woke up in the morning, ate breakfast (but never read the newspaper), went to work, returned home to eat again and went to sleep?'

At one point Dan tries to convince Miles to become 'one of us': 'Love, desire, ambition, faith – without them life's so simple.' The film could also be commenting on the loss of family values, or morality, or the essential soullessness of modern living, or critical of the herd mentality and the lack of individual thought. Presently it relates to the alienation of the individual via an increasingly solitary modern society. In *Invasion of the Body Snatchers*, bodily possession by alien life forms creates an 'alien nation'. When Miles and Becky walk among the glassy-eyed pods on the streets of Santa Mira, Miles tells Becky to 'Keep your eyes a little wide and blank. Show no interest or excitement.' It's surely not just coincidence that digital music players are called iPods.

Kevin McCarthy suggested *Sleep No More* as the title, but Allied Artists preferred something grabbier. They also intervened in the final cut. As Siegel remembered: 'Allied Artists, bursting at the seams with pods, took [producer Walter] Wanger's and my final cut and edited out all the humour.' Siegel's cut began with Miles's arrival at the railway station and ended with him babbling hysterically on the highway. Allied Artists made Siegel tack on two new scenes. The release version begins with Miles ranting at the City

Hospital and being questioned by Dr Harvey Bassett (Richard Deacon) and psychiatrist Dr Hill (Whit Bissell). The film's events then take place in flashback. At the end, the action cuts back to the hospital, where the doctors refuse to believe Miles's story. A truck driver injured in a road accident arrives at the hospital – to rescue him, the emergency crew had to retrieve him from under a cargo of strange seed pods. The docs immediately call the FBI to alert them to the emergency. So good is Siegel's film, these adjuncts don't diminish the film's power, as Miles sweats fearfully in the final shot. *Invasion of the Body Snatchers* was released in the US in February 1956 and was a success with public and critics alike. In the UK it was passed with minor cuts, rated X, in early 1956. It has since been re-rated PG. According to Siegel, in Europe and some 'underground' US venues, the original cut was screened, minus the studio tampering, which he termed 'The Siegel Version'.

Invaders from Mars (1953) was a combination of *Body Snatchers*-like human cloning and Martian-invasion movie. William Cameron Menzies designed and directed this colourful cult adventure, which depicted an alien invasion in rural America from the point of view of a sci-fi-mad little boy, stargazer David MacLean (Jimmy Hunt). One stormy night he witnesses a flying saucer land near his home and it buries itself in sandpits. Soon after, many of the local population, including David's own mother and father, are sucked into the pits and return as soulless human shells. They are being controlled by the invaders – tall, green bug-eyed alien 'mutants', synthetic humans who are led by a tentacled Martian head in a glass bubble, which is 'mankind developed to its ultimate intelligence'. Eventually the army attack the sandpits and destroy the Martians' subterranean caverns and saucer with demolition charges. Despite, or perhaps because of, its simple 'Gee whiz!' attitude to sci-fi – the result of the child's point of view of the invasion – the film avoids the sermonising of other 1950s sci-fi films, though we do learn from an astronomer that Earth has been on the Martians' radar for many years. Space itself is deemed 'a vast region of growing knowledge'. The bubbled walls of the Martians' caves, the towering mutants, their flying saucer and the glowing red ray guns are well presented, and the winding path leading to the sandpit is a suitably eerie setting. *Invaders from Mars* has been screened in two different versions – one ending with everything safely back to normal, with David fast asleep in bed ('Shhh, the little man has had a busy day') and another that reveals the events to have been simply the product of David's dreaming imagination.

In W. Lee Wilder's *Killers from Space* (1954), during an A-bomb test in Nevada, Dr Doug Martin (Peter Graves) goes missing in his jet as he flies over the Soledad Flats test zone. He later reappears with a strange scar near his heart and begins to act strangely, stealing information about the next A-bomb trials. While dosed with truth serum, Doug reveals that he was revived by aliens from the Astron Delta, who are operating from a cave near 'ground zero' (the bomb impact) in the desert. They are accumulating atomic energy on a grand scale. Out in space their comrades are waiting to invade, and they have used the energy to create a monstrous menagerie – giant tarantulas, lizards, cockroaches, grasshoppers and scorpions – which will be unleashed on Earth to kill the population and then destroyed to fertilise the ground for a new society. Doug's been hypnotised, his body snatched by the aliens, and he will tell the aliens when the next test will happen. No one, even his wife Ellen (Barbara Bestar), believes Doug. He figures out that the aliens are controlling the atomic energy by diverting an electricity supply and at the power station shuts off the region's supply. The atomic energy explodes and blows the Astron Deltans back into space. This is one problem that can be rectified by 'switching it off and on again'. The aliens wear hooded body suits, have googly ping-pong-ball eyes and perform open heart surgery on Doug with what appear to be welding torches.

Though Roger Corman's *It Conquered the World* (1956) is best remembered today for its Venusian monster, with fangs, arched eyebrows, snail antennae and wobbling crab claws, it also shares themes with *Invasion of the Body Snatchers*. The Venusian sets up camp in a cave at Elephant Hot Springs (actually Bronson Canyon), plotting world domination so that its eight fellow aliens, the last survivors of a dying race, can join it. Beginning with the town of Beachwood, California, it dispatches 'control devices', which resemble flying manta rays, to bite several leading dignitaries. The victims' minds are sapped, leaving robotic, inhuman zombies who are controlled telepathically by the Venusian. Dr Tom Anderson (Lee Van Cleef) is the Venusians' ally on Earth and Dr Paul Nelson (Peter Graves) compares the Venusian's theories to a polluting 'communist tract'. His wife Joan (Sally Fraser) falls victim to the monster. Corman favourites Jonathan Haze and Dick Miller appeared as two National Guardsmen. The monster itself was built and operated by Paul Blaisdell, who christened it Beulah. Beverly Garland was Anderson's wife Claire, who blindly loves her deluded husband. She is killed as she attempts to dispatch the beast in Bronson Caves and Anderson dies as he destroys the creature with a blowtorch. The scenes where the Venusian induces a power cut so that no telephones, vehicles or electrical devices function recalls *The Day the Earth Stood Still*. It certainly saved the budget production some money on vehicles and resulted in Graves's hurtling around to save humanity on a bicycle.

Another Corman cult classic, *Not of This Earth* (1956) starred Paul Birch as Paul Johnson, who with his black suit and hat, silver briefcase and shades resembles a gangster. Johnson is a vampiric alien from another world – when he removes his shades, his blank white eyes zap his victims. He drains their blood into bottles that he keeps in his briefcase, which he later refrigerates. Trailers dubbed him 'the screen's weirdest terror'. Johnson doesn't eat and lives on a 'superdrink' supplement in a luxury house with a servant (Jonathan Haze) and a nurse, Nadine Story (Beverly Garland), who gives him daily blood transfusions. Johnson is an emissary from Davanna, a world riven with war, whose blood is rapidly evaporating. Johnson sends back plasma samples and human 'specimens' to his home planet via a teleportation device, a Dimension Warp. Dick Miller has a walk-on as a door-to-door vacuum-cleaner salesman who winds up in Johnson's cellar incinerator. When another Davannan (Ann Carol) is accidentally given a transfusion of rabid canine blood, Johnson is exposed as the murderer behind a number of unexplained disappearances and the police investigate, whereupon Johnson releases a flying jellyfish-like creature that resembles an ornamental lampshade. Chased by the police, Johnson perishes in a car crash – his funeral epitaph reads: 'Here lies a man who was not of this Earth.' A good blend of horror and science fiction, this space vampire movie has been remade several times, including by Jim Wynorski in 1988, with Arthur Roberts as the alien and Traci Lords as his nurse.

Gene Fowler Jr.'s *I Married a Monster from Outer Space* (1958) yoked 'Reds under the Bed' scaremongering to alien invasion movies, in an imaginative sci-fi horror suspenser. On the eve of his wedding, Bill Farrell (Tom Tryon) brakes his car to avoid hitting a corpse, but when he investigates he is enveloped by a strange vapour. On their honeymoon, Bill's wife Marge (Gloria Talbot) becomes convinced that her husband has been replaced by an emotionless impersonator.

No one in Norrisville believes her, but her panic escalates when she realises that other male members of the community are not who they seem and that all lines of communication – telephone, telegram and roads – are controlled by telepathic alien beings inhabiting human hosts. Hulking, creepy Tryon is perfect as the man who is now a stranger to his own wife, and Talbot is in 1950s 'sweater girl' mode as his petrified spouse. The aliens are from the Andromeda Constellation, where their sun exploded and died, and so too their women. They have arrived on Earth hoping to breed with our women. In an interesting subtext, Marge is desperate to have children (tests ascertain that she is able to), but 'alien' Bill is understandably reluctant to visit the doctor. The aliens themselves are tall, glowing monsters, with tentacly faces. For the finale, menfolk who haven't been brain-napped (plus tracker dogs) attack the aliens' spacecraft, hidden in woodland, where they find the hostages of those now impersonated by aliens connected to a 'broadcasting circuit', which controls their avatars' actions. When they are disconnected, the avatars disintegrate into mushy sludge. Bill and Marge are reunited and the fleet of alien craft move on from Earth to pastures new. This is an excellent spine-chiller. Nothing in 1950s sci-fi horror equals the moment when cold killer Bill strangles 'Junior', the puppy Marge has bought him for their wedding anniversary. As the trailer screamed: 'Terrifyingly Different!'

An interesting European take on a race of aliens taking over earthlings was *No Survivors Please* (1964), a West German production co-directed by Hans Albin and Peter Berneis. In the superb opening scenes, a plane carrying US Senator John Farnsworth (Robert Cunningham) crashes into the Mexican jungle. The pilot has been instructed by his alien masters to kill everyone on Flight 112 except the ambassador: 'No survivors please.' Farnsworth, his body now a vessel for an alien being, returns to his job, as other aliens have possessed high-ranking politicians and scientists. These men in power plan to disrupt the UN and there'll be no survivors on Earth either if the aliens have their way and destroy the amity of mankind. Maria Perschy played Farnsworth's secretary Ginny Desmond, Gustavo Rojo played Armand, a heavy who carries out the aliens' bidding, and Uwe Friedrichsen was investigative reporter Howard Moore, who rumbles the alien takeover. He seeks to interview the alien cabal's key figures, who have all miraculously survived accidents – plane crashes, falls from bridges or from ocean liners. This jittery monochrome film played on the 'are they, aren't they' ambiguity of *Invasion of the Body Snatchers* as the action shifted between Rio, Paris and New York.

Freddie Francis's *They Came from Beyond Space* (1967), based on Joseph Millard's novel *The Gods Hate Kansas* and made by UK horror studio Amicus, melded *War of the Worlds*-style alien invaders with body snatching. With its gentleman hero driving a vintage Bentley and its genteel English village setting, it resembles a psychedelic episode of *The Avengers*, complete with hypno-swirls and light jazz score. A meteor shower lands in Cornwall, and when scientists attempt to break open the blue crystallised rocks they are possessed by alien beings. Soon the aliens have recruited labourers and scientists to construct a rocket to the Moon. The invaders have brought with them a contagion, the crimson plague, which results in a bloody, measly rash – the human corpses are then freighted to the Moon. Real-life TV newsman Kenneth Kendall reports on the plague. Dr Curtis Temple (Robert Hutton) has been involved in a car accident and has a metal plate in his head, immunising him against the aliens' brain takeovers. With help from Dr Farge (Zia Mohyeddin), he saves his lover Lee Mason (Jennifer Jayne) and kits Farge out with a silver-minted brainwave deflector that resembles a colander. Keep alert for the finale, where the heroes (wearing motorcycle crash helmets) face 'The Master of the Moon' from Zarn (Michael Gough), and there's no explanation why their Moon station is littered with metal milk churns.

Equal parts *Planet of the Vampires, Invasion of the Body Snatchers* and *Flight of the Phoenix*, Hajime Satō's *Goke, Body Snatcher from Hell* (1968) was high-calibre, wildly offbeat Japanese sci-fi horror. As an Air Japan airliner cruises through a blood-red sky where there have been reports of a UFO in the vicinity, birds commit suicide by flying into the plane's windows and a hijacker threatens to blow up the plane. There's a blinding yellow light and the jet crashes to earth. The survivors find themselves in a desert, but without food or water they have little chance of survival. The odds are further lowered when the hijacker flees with a hostage, stewardess Kazumi Asakura (Tomomi Satō), and finds a flying saucer. The hijacker's forehead splits open and a blob of blue pulsating space slime slithers into his open head wound, turning him into a bloodsucking vampire. This 'Flight of the Vampires' has vividly stylised colour photography, comic-strip graphics, gore and an ultra-weird oscillating, whining score by Shunsuke Kikuchi. The survivors include the plane's co-pilot Sugisaka (Teruo Yoshida), Senator Mano (Eizō Kitamura), Mrs Neal (Kathy Horan), an American war widow whose husband has died in Vietnam, Noriko Tokuyasu (Yūko Kusunoki), who is having an affair with the senator, psychiatrist Dr Momotake (Kazuo Katō) and scientist Sagai (Masaya Takahashi). There is also a political assassin on board, who is on the run, having murdered the British ambassador. The vampiric bloodsucking is coy, but the ashen, drained and crumbling cadavers are convincing, as is the wrecked aircraft's interior, with scavenging crows and corpses. The slithering alien amoeba is imaginatively done and the psychedelically coloured UFO's occupants are the Gokemidoro people, who speak through the possessed corpse of Noriko. They are preparing to invade Earth and wipe out mankind, a race already weakened by war. The film ends with Sugisaka and Kuzumi fleeing, as hundreds of alien saucers close in on Earth. Hideo Ko's hijacker – dapper in a pure white suit, matching white gloves and black shades – looks like the frontman of a 1960s beat combo and is the kind of flamboyant, unique villain that only exists in the world of cult movies.

Philip Kaufman's 1978 version of *Invasion of the Body Snatchers* relocated Finney's story to San Francisco. Matthew Bennell (Donald Sutherland), a deputy inspector at the Department of Public Health, becomes suspicious when his co-worker Elizabeth Driscoll (Brooke Adams) claims that her lover, dentist Geoffrey Howell (Art Hindle), has changed into an emotionless zombie. Matthew uncovers a citywide cover-up and goes into hiding with Elizabeth and Nancy and Jack Bellicec (Veronica Cartwright and Jeff Goldblum). The pods are 'space flowers' which germinate and propagate human forms. The city is taken over by pod people and only Nancy and Matthew escape, but they are separated. Months later, Matthew has managed to assimilate into pod society by showing no emotion. But when he is approached by Nancy, who has avoided becoming a pod, Matthew points at Nancy and emits a piercing, agonisingly shrill scream (a sound effect achieved by recording a pig squeal), singling Nancy out as human. Kaufman's *Body Snatchers* is more concerned, post-Watergate era, with political conspiracies and paranoia than the Red threat. Matthew offers reasons to Elizabeth as to why Geoffrey might have changed: he could be having an affair, have become gay, have caught a social disease or become a Republican. The mayor, the police and other prominent public figures are orchestrating the pods' dissemination throughout San Francisco, to the accompaniment of a spooky score by Danny Zeitlin. The grisly hatching pods, their foetal emissions and creeping tendrils are graphic and convincing. Leonard Nimoy is subtly menacing as celebrity psychiatrist Dr David Kibner. Robert Duvall played an intimidating priest on a swing, watching children pick the blooming 'space flowers'. Don Siegel played a cabby and Kevin McCarthy reprised his role as Miles, who runs in panic through the streets of San Francisco, ranting, 'They're coming!', and is knocked down and killed by a car on the corner of Leavenworth and Turk Streets. The film's finale, when Matthew becomes James Bond and destroys a warehouse where the pods are grown, seems tacked on, but Kaufman's film is a worthy treatment and superior 1970s sci-fi.

Abel Ferrara's chillingly nervy *Body Snatchers* (1993) set the story in Fort Daly army camp (shot at Craig Air Force Base, Alabama) and told the pod takeover via familial strife from the perspective of teenager Marti Malone (Gabrielle Anwar). Her father Steve (Terry Kinney) is an Environmental Protection Agency officer who is posted to inspect the base, accompanied by her stepmother Carole Malone (Meg Tilly) and stepbrother Andy (Reilly Murphy). To Marti, Carole is already the 'woman who replaced' her mother. The pods, which are harvested by the soldiers in a misty swamp, are taking over the garrison.

Forest Whitaker played Dr Collins, who suspects what's occurring and blows his own brains out rather than joining the pods. Christine Elise played Marti's friend Jenn Platt, the tearaway daughter of the camp's commander and a bad influence on Marti. The shrill primal scream, when the pod people point out 'normals', is heightened here to become truly horrific, while the creeping tendrils of the pods and their pseudo-human clone forms are gruesomely depicted. The genius of setting the story in an army camp results in the presence of rigid military discipline, a certain coldness of emotion, before the clones take hold. Carole becomes a pod; so too do Steve and, finally, little Andy. Marti manages to escape with chopper pilot Tim Young (Billy Wirth), and they launch a missile attack on a convoy of army trucks freighting pods across the US. But as they land at Atlanta Air Base in the ambiguous finale, it is implied that the menace has spread and they can't stay awake forever.

Veronica Cartwright, from Kaufman's adaptation, went on to appear as Wendy Lenk, who tells psychiatrist Carol Bennell (Nicole Kidman), 'My husband is not my husband' in another adaptation of Finney's novel, *The Invasion* (2007). Oliver Hirschbiegel's thriller has the spores brought back to Earth on the space shuttle *Patriot*, which crash-lands and disperses a flu contagion, causing seizures and vomiting. Those who sleep succumb and the integration of alien DNA results in a complete lack of emotion. Some, like Carol's son Oliver (Jackson Bond), are immune to the bacteria. Daniel Craig is good as Carol's love interest, Dr Ben Driscoll, who attempts to find a cure for the pandemic. This so-so Finney reimagining is itself strangely emotionless and was a missed opportunity in an era when the fear of mass contagion and pandemics continue to occupy people's minds.

Roger Spottiswoode's *The 6th Day* (2000) looked at a world where cloning is outlawed, though the duplication of pets (RePet) is commonplace. In the near future, family man and chartered helicopter pilot Adam Gibson (Arnold Schwarzenegger) returns home to find he has been replaced by a double. The mastermind behind the illegal cloning racket, Michael Drucker (Tony Goldwyn), is revealed to be a clone himself. This is an Arnie movie, so there are also grandiose laser-pistol shoot-outs, swooping jet-helicopter stunts, cliff jumps and a house-smashing, fence-flattening, tyre-screeching car chase; although Arnie's character is strong, he's no superman and consequently more believable than other Schwarzenegger sci-fi protagonists. In the world of the near future, where your fridge tells you when you're low on milk, Gibson's chief nemeses are Drucker's heavies, who upon their deaths are simply re-cloned. Gibson and his clone team up to rescue their wife Natalie (Wendy Crewson) and daughter Clara (Taylor Anne Reid) from Drucker's headquarters. The ending is ambiguously played: does the clone Adam return to Gibson's quiet life as a family man, while the real one heads off to a life of adventure in Patagonia, carrying out charter flights, or vice versa? The themes of Finney's *The Body Snatchers* and its film adaptations and derivatives are still relevant today. If we've learnt nothing else from this story about losing your identity as an individual to 'body snatchers' in modern society, then at least you're never alone with a clone.

6

'WE ARE, AFTER ALL, NOT GOD'

FORBIDDEN PLANET (1956)

Director: Fred McLeod Wilcox
Story: Irving Block and Allen Adler
Screenplay: Cyril Hume
Director of Photography: George J. Folsey
Music: Louis and Bebe Barron
CinemaScope/Eastmancolor
An MGM Production
Released by MGM
94 minutes

Walter Pidgeon (Dr Edward Morbius), Anne Francis (Altaira 'Alta' Morbius), Leslie Nielsen (Commander John 'J.J.' Adams), Warren Stevens (Lieutenant 'Doc' Ostrow), Jack Kelly (Lieutenant Jerry Farman), Richard Anderson (Chief Quinn), Earl Holliman (Cook), George Wallace (Bosun), Bob Dix (Grey), Jimmie Thompson (Youngerford), Harry Harvey Jr. (Randall), Roger McGee (Lindstrom), Peter Miller (Moran), Morgan Jones (Nichols), Richard Grant (Silvers), James Best and William Boyett (crewmen), Robby the Robot (himself), Les Tremayne (Narrator)

✻ ✻ ✻

During the 1950s, as man began to address the exploration of space, cinema reflected these developments, as intrepid screen space travellers flew to other worlds populated by all manner of beasts and alien planets in the deep unknown of space. A key factor in the most successful 1950s sci-fi films was the introduction of colour and widescreen, which the genre was relatively slow in deploying. Most US 1950s sci-fi films are in monochrome, but with the addition of colour, imaginations ran riot in filmmakers' depictions of faraway planets and warring worlds.

An early example of far-off worlds rendered in glorious Technicolor was Joseph Newman's *This Island Earth* (1955). Nuclear researcher Dr Cal Meacham (Rex Reason)

This Island Earth: Joseph Newman's 1955 sci-fi film had Earth's scientists kidnapped to save the planet Metaluna. Poster artwork depicts Faith Domergue being menaced by a Metalunan mutant.

is contacted by Electronic Service Unit No. 16 to build an Interocitor, a machine through which he is then contacted by Exeter (Jeff Morrow). Meacham is invited to join a team of nuclear experts working for Exeter at a luxurious research facility, 'The Club', in Georgia. Exeter is an alien from the planet Metaluna, which is under attack. Time is running out for the Metalunans, and Meacham and another scientist, Dr Ruth Adams (Faith Domergue), are kidnapped and taken by flying saucer to the green planet of Metaluna, a rocky, smoking-cratered landscape under constant meteor bombardment from the Zaghon. *This Island Earth* is one of the top US sci-fi films of the 1950s. When the Metalunans take the scientists to their planet, the visuals include floods of Technicolor and sweeping planetary spacescapes, as in the film's nebular title sequence, the hazy ionised layer of colourful space mist that protects Metaluna from aerial attack and the Metalunans' futuristic subterranean world. It was one of the last films to be shot in the sumptuous three-strip Technicolor process, with cinematography by Clifford Stine, and the special effects by Stine and Stanley Horsley are the film's main assets. The scientists have been enlisted to turn lead into uranium, as the Metalunans need it to reinforce their protective ionised layer. The Zaghons guide meteors with their spaceships. Outside the world of Saturday-morning serials, this was one of the first examples of interplanetary warfare involving planets other than Earth. The destruction of Metaluna, as the planet is transformed into a burning, radioactive sun, was directed by Jack Arnold. The 'Earth being' scientists are attacked by a Metalunan mutant, which has been bred by the Metalunans to carry out menial work. This creature (played in a suit by stuntman Regis Parton) has a bulbous, brain-like cranium and elongated arms with pincers. The Metalunans themselves, such as Exeter, have an orange suntan, high, prominent foreheads and white hair. Orangey, credited in some films as Rhubarb, played Neutron the cat. *This Island Earth*'s vigorous use of colour, trendsetting special effects and literate script proved influential on the best 1950s US sci-fi.

One of the most thought-provoking sci-fi movies of the era, *Forbidden Planet*, was an uncredited reworking of Shakespeare's 1613 play *The Tempest*, relocated to the distant Earth-like planet of Altair-IV. At the end of the twenty-first century, man has landed on the moon. By AD 2200 Earth has begun the conquest and colonisation of deep space. In AD 2257 United Planets Cruiser C57-D, commanded by John Adams (Leslie Nielsen), travels to Altair-IV to investigate what became of a prospecting party of scientists that travelled there from Earth 20 years previously. The astronauts are warned not to land by Dr Edward Morbius (Walter Pidgeon), but they do and discover that the doctor lives there with his 19-year-old daughter Alta (Anne Francis) and Robby the Robot. All the other colonists are long dead, including Morbius's wife, who died from natural causes. The other survivors succumbed to the planet's dark forces and were torn limb from limb by a savage beast, while their ship, the *Bellerophon* (named after a monster-slaying hero from Greek myth) was vaporised. Morbius reveals that thousands of years ago the planet was occupied by the Krell, whose civilisation was a million years ahead of Earth's.

Krell even visited Earth before man inhabited it and brought back specimens, hence the presence of wild animals such as tigers and deer on Altair-IV. But 2,000 centuries ago catastrophe struck and the Krell were wiped out. Nothing of Krell society exists above ground, but their vast subterranean world is still intact. Morbius, a philologist (an expert in the science of languages), deciphered the Krell history books. In the Krell laboratory he took the 'Krell Test' (via an apparatus called the Plastic Educator), which expanded his intellect and enabled him to materialise his own thoughts. When Adams romances Alta against her father's wishes, a ferocious invisible beast attacks the C57-D, killing several of the crew. Eventually the beast is revealed to be a 'monster from the id', unleashed by Morbius's subconscious. In psychoanalytic theory the id is the deepest level of primitive personality, and only Morbius's own death can destroy the beast.

Forbidden Planet was the first sci-fi film to cost over $1 million and was shot entirely on sound stages at MGM Studios, Culver City. The trailer stated: 'MGM's great technical staff brings you a magnificent picture of that distant tomorrow – Far and away the most provocative and unusual adventure film you've ever seen [...] two years in the making.' Morbius constructed Robby the Robot according to Krell plans, but in reality Robert Kinoshita built Robby at a cost of $125,000. Frankie Darro was inside the suit, which rather resembled a lumbering, metallic Michelin Man and incorporated pincer-like 'hands', a domed glass head, revolving gyroscopic devices, antennae, a flashing neon 'mouth' and flickering lights. Robby featured prominently in advertising material and proved especially popular with juvenile audiences. He has been programmed not to harm humans and it is his refusal to attack the monster that clues in Adams that the id is of human origin. Robby traverses the planet's desert in a moon buggy and the astronaut's cook (Earl Holliman) coaxes Robby into manufacturing 60 gallons of genuine Kansas City bourbon, so the robot delivers a vast stack of whisky bottles. Robby is Morbius and Alta's rather housewifey home help, able to rustle up a meal or make Alta an evening gown. 'I beamed and beamed,' moans Alta to Robby, when she has been 'ringing' for her servant, who replies, 'Sorry miss, I was giving myself an oil job.' He is also fluent in 187 languages. Marvin Miller provided Robby's matter-of-fact voice, which was post-synched, as was the dialogue by other actors in scenes involving Robby, due to the machine's chattering workings making such a rattling din on set.

One of the relief party mentions as they approach Altair-IV, 'The Lord sure makes some beautiful worlds', but appearances can be deceptive. The alien world of Altair-IV was created at MGM Studios using a combination of matte paintings, model work, photo trickery and sets. The flat desert plain, where the C57-D flying saucer lands, stretches away to distant jagged mountains. The saucer is an unusual choice of craft for earthling heroes, who usually travelled in rockets, while villainous alien invaders use saucers. The astronauts also deploy a 'space tractor' with a magnetic hoist and four-barrelled artillery pieces. The planet, with its strangely hued sky and two moons, also features a graveyard and the landscape around Morbius's residence is exotically wooded. The residence itself

Forbidden Planet: Robby the Robot carries off Alta (Anne Francis) in Fred McLeod Wilcox's 1956 uncredited take on Shakespeare's *The Tempest*.

features airy, open rooms, automatic triangular-shaped sliding doors (the Krell architectural style) and labs with futuristic contraptions (the mind-blowing IQ-boosting Plastic Educator, a disintegrating waste-disposal unit, banks of dials indicating the Krell power levels), flashing lights and glowing beams. Only the massive protective steel shutters hint at outside dangers. In the depths of the planet we see the 'Krell wonders' – 400 vast ventilator shafts that stretch 20 miles on 7,800 levels, creating a single machine 20 miles by 20 miles in dimension. *Forbidden Planet* is the best-looking US sci-fi film of the 1950s and was only surpassed by the wonder and invention of Japanese cinema.

In this planetary utopia, Altaira, called 'Alta', has a coy naivety that the visiting astronauts find shocking – she skinny dips in a pool and recognises no danger from wild animals. She has never known humans apart from her father – she terms Morbius and herself as 'exceptions', who haven't succumbed to the 'planetary force'. With her blonde hair and minidresses, Alta is desirable, inadvertently provocative, and it is her father's protection of his daughter that triggers the id, the 'elementary basis of the subconscious mind [...] the beast, the mindless primitive'. When the monster attacks the residence, melting its way through the metal doors, Morbius pleads with Alta: 'Tell it you don't love this man.'

As in so much 1950s sci-fi, the monster is unseen for much of the film. Something invisible but heavy-breathing steals onto the C57-D and sabotages their Klystron Monitor. The monster leaves footprints that, when the astronauts make a 37 inch by 19 inch plaster cast, reveal a large clawed toe (an arboreal hook resembling that of a tree sloth) implying considerable size. A laser-gun battle between the astronauts and the monster takes place when it attempts to break the crew's electrified perimeter fence. Now the behemoth's massive, hunched outline and gaping jaws are revealed by the neutron-beam blasts. The animated effects here were produced by Joseph Meador from Walt Disney Studios, in collaboration with the MGM special effects crew. *Forbidden Planet*'s score is billed as 'Electronic Tonalities' by Louis and Bebe Barron, an apt description for the futuristic montage of hums, stutters, squalls, pops, throbs, beeps, squeals, blips and descending whirs. In the film Morbius explains to the astronauts that these 'tonalities' were created by Krell musicians half a million years ago – thus it is their music, the first such entirely electronic score in cinema, which accompanies the film.

At face value, *Forbidden Planet* is a monster movie, a kids' sci-fi flick with a cute robot, but it is also intelligently plotted sci-fi, with subtle plot nuances, hints of theology and Freudian references. It demonstrates very 1950s values, with nuclear power still the overriding energy source, weapon and threat. Walter Pidgeon played Dr Morbius as black-clad, bearded and satanic. He creates the monster from his own subconscious (it could have been called *Id Came from Another World*). The manifest, unleashed id – the unconscious conflicts and desires that can surface in dreams or madness, according to psychoanalyst Sigmund Freud – is a hideous monster that won't harm Alta. As the murders begin, the literate script conveys subtle menace, as Morbius notes, 'The *Bellerophon* pattern is being woven again.' Later he realises, 'My evil self is at that door and I have no power to stop it', and when Morbius is mortally wounded, his 'other self' perishes too. Morbius has engineered the destruction of the planet on a 24-hour timer, enabling Adams, Alta, Robby and the surviving crew to make their escape before Altair-IV and the Krell legacy detonate. As they flee, Adams tells Alta: 'It will remind us that we are, after all, not God.'

The film's classic poster depicted Robby holding an unconscious Anne Francis in its arms, as though he is an aggressor carrying her away (echoing the poster for *This Island Earth*), but a promotional featurette had Pidgeon presenting Robby as a benevolent character. The trailer blurb stated: 'Today, man prepares to take his first step outward into space – tomorrow he will explore the stars.' The trailer's voice-over narration was provided by Robby's dubber Marvin Miller – in the trailer Robby is billed only as 'the Robot'. The film was a great success, but it eventually cost so much (an estimated $1.9 million) that its profits were small. At the 1957 Academy Awards, A. Arnold Gillespie, Warren Newcombe and Irving G. Reis were nominated for Best Special Effects, but lost out to the parting of the Red Sea in *The Ten Commandments*, as staged by Moses and John Fulton.

Forbidden Planet's enduring legacy can be seen in such disparate areas as the chain of comic and cult merchandise stores named 'Forbidden Planet' and *Return to the Forbidden Planet*, a late-1980s stage musical featuring rock-and-roll hits and B-movie atmosphere. MGM producer Nicholas Nayfack and director Fred McLeod Wilcox planned a sequel to *Forbidden Planet*, entitled *Robot Planet*, but Nayfack died of a heart attack in 1958 before the project began. Robby the Robot went on to appear opposite Richard Eyer in *The Invisible Boy* (1957), an unofficial sequel to *Forbidden Planet*, again written by Cyril Hume and produced by Nayfack for MGM, which for its child's point of view was a key influence on *E.T. the Extra-Terrestrial* (1982).

Forbidden Planet's grey space uniforms cropped up in Edward Bernds's cult classic *Queen of Outer Space* (1958). Captain Neal Patterson (Eric Fleming), Lieutenant Mike Cruze (David Willock, the comedy relief) and Lieutenant Larry Turner (Patrick Waltz, the romantic relief) escort Professor Conrad (Paul Birch) to Space Station 8. A mysterious beam destroys the station and their ship travels 26 million miles from Earth. They land on Venus, a planet populated by women ruled by masked queen Yllana (Laurie Mitchell), who has been hideously scarred by radiation burns (a result of men and their wars). She plans to destroy Earth with a disintegrator ray, but the astronauts find allies in scientist Talleah ('Miss Hungary 1936' Zsa Zsa Gabor) and other Venusians, who help them overthrow Yllana. *Queen of Outer Space* was shot at Allied Artists' studios and reused *Forbidden Planet*'s blasters (which resemble hairdryers) and parts of the exotic forest set. The miniatures and special effects were from Allied Artists' own *World without End* (1956) and the spacecraft is from Monogram's *Flight to Mars* (1951). The film looks fantastic in CinemaScope and garish DeLuxe Color, despite the spangly backdrops, sparse sets and a pathetic rubber giant spider. The first 14 minutes of this 75-minute film (until the spacecraft crashes on the snowy planet) is a lengthy pre-title sequence, which is unusual for the era. The astronauts are called 'space jockeys' and the scene when they travel at super speed, their faces contorted by g-force, is not to be missed. Fleming, shortly before he hit the big time in *Rawhide*, is a wooden hero. The astronauts romance the local beauties, demonstrating the old adage 'a man chases a woman until she catches him'. The Venusian 'space babes', shapely beauty contestants wearing minidresses or flowing evening gowns, resemble 1950s pin-ups. They pack lethal ray guns and walkie-talkies that look like perfume atomisers. Gabor's accent mangles such dialogue as 'vimmin can't be happy viz-out men' and love is 'zat varm feelink zat makes my heart zing'. Most of the humour in this sexy, camp classic is intentional. It's a B-movie spoof of sci-fi movies, and in that respect it was years ahead of its time.

In Arthur Hilton's *Cat-Women of the Moon* (1953; *Rocket to the Moon*), Moon Rocket 4: Code 63 lands on the dark side of the moon, thanks to its possessed navigator, Helen Salinger (Marie Windsor). She communicates telepathically with the Moon-dwelling cat-women, led by Alpha (Carol Brewster), who live in an ancient city with eclectic interior design. The Moon's oxygen supply is depleting, due to the vanishing atmosphere, and the cat-women plan to invade Earth, where they will embark on world domination, presumably between naps. This epic of space travel has a score by Elmer Bernstein and a rocket ship equipped with lilos and hammocks. The astronauts included Kip (Victor Jory), Walt (Douglas Fowley, also the film's dialogue coach), youngster Doug (William Phipps) and Grainger (Sonny Tufts), all of whom the cat-women attempt to seduce, with wines, treats, dances and tales of golden caves. But these superintelligent women only want to learn how to fly the rocket. As Walt observes of cat-woman Beta (Suzanne Alexander): 'You're too smart for me, baby, I like 'em stupid.' This is a real B-movie, with stagy interior sets, tarted up with 3-D (the film's lone in-your-face special effect is a meteorite) and the essential giant puppet spider. The moonscapes were painted by Chesley Bonestell. The cat-women, who slink around in black all-in-one body suits, heavy make-up, jewellery and ornate collars, were played by 'The Hollywood Cover Girls'. The film was remade in colour in 1958 as *Missile to the Moon*, and the pair makes a masochistic double bill.

Such films as *Cat-Women* and *Queen of Outer Space* were spoofed in *Amazon Women on the Moon* (1986), which included a 1954 space opera from Universal–International starring 'Lyle Talbot and Greta Van Zandt'. In 1980, Moon Rocket One lands on the Moon (shot at Vasquez Rocks Natural Park, California), where a trio of astronauts (Steve Forrest, Robert Colbert and Joey Travolta) and Loony the space monkey encounter a giant lizard, an (off-screen) giant spider and a race of busty space 'dames'. The US president was played by *Famous Monsters of Filmland* author Forrest J. Ackerman and the music is from *This Island Earth*. Sybil Danning played the Amazon's cleavaged queen, Lara, and Lana Clarkson was Alpha Beta. The costuming and sets are dead-on, with the crew's grey uniforms resembling those from *Forbidden Planet*, while the spear-chucking Amazon women wear colourful minidresses almost identical to *Queen of Outer Space*.

But even when budgets were vast, the results were often mixed. David Lynch's *Dune* (1984) offered a glimpse into far-off worlds on a grand scale, for an adaptation of Frank Herbert's landmark 1965 sci-fi novel. It was a tale of spice mining on the barren, stormy desert planet Arrakis (Dune). The invaluable spice, melange, is vital to interstellar travel – it folds space, enabling travel to anywhere in the universe without moving. In 10191, two clans vie for control of the planet: the House of Atreides on Planet Caladan and the House of Harkonnen on Planet Giedi Prime. An expedition from Atreides begins mining on Arrakis, but the Harkonnen invade and overrun them. Paul Atreides (Kyle MacLachlan), the son of the dynasty's rulers, joins the subterranean, blue-eyed Fremen, led by Stilgar (Everett McGill). He falls in love with Fremen Chani (Sean Young) and through his demonstration of bravery, including riding a vast sandworm, he becomes leader Muad'Dib to the Fremen, while his mother, Lady Jessica (Francesca Annis), becomes a matriarchal reverend mother when Reverend Mother Ramallo (Silvana Mangano) dies. Padishah Emperor Shaddam IV (José Ferrer), the ruler of the universe, orders genocide on Arraki, and Paul leads the Fremen against the Harkonnen and their allies, until finally the rains come to arid Dune.

A long-delayed project, *Dune* finally got off the ground in the early 1980s as a $40 million Dino De Laurentiis production, filmed at Estudios Churubusco, Mexico City, and the Samalayuca Dunes at Ciudad Juárez, Chihuahua. The creatures (including a massive talking slug) were created by Carlo Rambaldi, foreground miniatures were by Emilio Ruiz Del Rio and creative make-up was by Giannetto De Rossi. Toto provided the score and the 'Prophesy Theme' was by Brian Eno. *Dune* was photographed in widescreen Todd-AO and Technicolor by Freddie Francis and is a visual spectacular. Particularly memorable are the giant sandworms, which whip up tornado sandstorms as they move through the landscape. On Dune, people wear suits that store and recycle the wearers' bodily fluids. Paul teaches the Fremen how to use sonic weapons, and, with help from the sandworms, they defeat the Harkonnen. Chief villain, Baron Vladimir Harkonnen (Kenneth McMillan), hovers around the room like a balloon, his face disfigured with pus-filled boils. There are some startling moments of violence, one great threat ('Or you'll live your life in a pain amplifier') and some genuinely weird imagery, but there are too many explanatory voice-overs and expository dialogue, as in the intro by Princess Irulan (Virginia Madsen). Paul's allies include Duncan Idaho (Richard Jordan), Gurney Halleck (Patrick Stewart), Fremen Dr Kynes (Max von Sydow) and Alicia Roanne Witt, who played Paul's sister Alia. In the House of Atreides, Freddie Jones was Thufir Hawat and Dean Stockwell was Dr Wellington Yueh, who betrays and murders Duke Leto (Jürgen Prochnow). Reverend Mother Gaius Helen Mohiam (Siân Phillips) was Shaddam IV's 'truthsayer' clairvoyant. Among the Harkonnen are Piter De Vries (Brad Dourif), the 'Beast' Rabban (Paul Smith) and Feyd Rautha (a manic Sting). The film's collision of ancient and ultramodern, mystical and technological, is certainly unique, but it was almost universally panned and lost $10 million on its release. Lynch blamed post-production tampering and disowned the project. Most prints run 131 minutes (140 in the US in NTSC), but there's a 177-minute cut available too. The novel was remade as a 3-part TV miniseries, *Frank Herbert's Dune*, in 2000 (photographed by Vittorio Storaro), which was in turn followed in 2003 by *Frank Herbert's Children of Dune*.

Space travellers adrift in the cosmos were central to Stephen Hopkins's *Lost in Space* (1998), an update of Irwin Allen's popular US TV series (1965–8). Essentially *Swiss Family Robinson* in orbit, the premise has a family of colonists setting off on *Jupiter 2* to Alpha Centauri, but they become stranded on a mysterious planet. The Robinson family were Professor John Robinson (Guy Williams), wife Maureen (June Lockhart) and their children Will (Bill Mumy), Judy (Marta Kristen) and Penny (Angela Cartwright). Also aboard were pilot Don West (Mark Goddard), mischievous Dr Zachary Smith (Jonathan Harris) and a robot (voiced by Dick Tufeld, designed by Robert Kinoshita) that resembles Robby from *Forbidden Planet*. The 1998 retread featured the family (William Hurt, Mimi Rogers, Heather Graham, Lacey Chabert and Jack Johnson), Gary Oldman as Dr Smith (who plans sabotage) and Matt LeBlanc as pilot Major West. The original series was set in 1997, while this redo takes place in 2058. They leave Earth on a ten-year mission to Alpha Prime, to bring civilisation to the stars and to construct a hypergate to facilitate space travel, but Smith reprograms the ship's robot to wipe the family out. They travel through a time portal and encounter the *Proteus*, a ghost ship that is overrun with six-legged biomechanoid spiders, and land on an icy planet that seems to be from their future, where they find gravestones inscribed Maureen, Judy and Penny. When the robot is rebuilt by Will, it resembles the one from the 1960s TV series and is voiced by Tufeld – plus there are cameos from Lockhart, Goddard, Cartwright and Kristen. Even John Williams's lively, popular horn-led theme tune from the TV series is reworked by Apollo 440. But the cutesy chameleon space monkey is wholly irritating and, lumbered with a clichéd script enacted by walking cliché characters, *Lost in Space* soon becomes the worst kind of tedious shoot-'em-up before imploding under its own ridiculousness, as the heroes battle shrouded spidery mutant Smith. The optimistic finale sets up a prospective sequel, and an insightful review in *Mizz* pointed out that the film had 'More special effects than *Star Wars*'. Not better, or more entertaining, or intricate and convincing, but more.

Intrepid earthlings battling alien menaces on faraway worlds was the backbone of Paul Verhoeven's 1997 adaptation of Robert A. Heinlein's *Starship Troopers*, the exploitation-movie antithesis of *Forbidden Planet* that both satirises and exalts militarist warmongering in the outer reaches of space. There have been few films that have glamorised violence and military hardware as this one does in its depiction of a campaign against giant bugs from the planet Klendathu. On graduating from Buenos Aires High School, students Johnny Rico (Casper Van Dien), his girlfriend Carmen Ibanez (Denise Richards), Carl Jenkins (Neil Patrick Harris) and Dizzy Flores (Dina Meyer) all join the armed forces and become space cadets at Fleet Academy. Rico and Dizzy join the Mobile Infantry, Carmen the Fleet air force and Carl military intelligence. When the bugs launch a meteor that destroys Buenos Aires and millions of people, war is declared. Rico has since been dumped by Carmen, who has fallen for flying instructor Zander Barcalow (Patrick Muldoon), and Dizzy's right there for Rico on the rebound. The Federation Forces attack Klendathu, but the Mobile Infantry are slaughtered by the spiky, deadly bugs, with thousands dead in an hour. The Federation changes its tactics and tackles Klendathu's outlying planets in an effort to capture a 'brain bug', brain-sucking slugs that direct the arachnid hordes.

Starship Troopers is essentially a World War II combat movie – a beleaguered outpost in a valley swarming with insects recalls frontier forts in old 'Cavalry and Indians' pictures and the desert campaign scenes (filmed in Hell's Half Acre, Wyoming) resemble Gulf War footage. The battle scenes are unrelentingly savage, with the darting, rushing insects charging en masse, with devastating effects. We have already witnessed veterans of the campaign with limbs missing, and new recruits are referred to as 'fresh meat for the grinder'. During the graphic battle scenes, we discover how such amputations (and worse) occur. There are massive beetle-type bugs that jet corrosive acid and launch blue fireballs into space, smaller louse-like creatures, huge blubbery, disgusting 'brain bug' slugs and the huge, scuttling mantis-like soldiers that impale and tear the infantry to pieces.

The aftermath of their grisly handiwork is hideous and, when machine-gunned, the beasts splatter green and orange gunk (the film is rated 18 in the UK and R in the US). The convincing creature effects were created by the Tippet Studio, and the spaceship visual effects (such as Fleet Battleship *Ticonderoga*) were by Sony Pictures Imageworks. Industrial Light & Magic and other effects teams were also involved. The comic-book visuals are courtesy of cinematographer Jost Vacano. The toothsome cast features the unfeasibly beautiful leads – square-jawed Aryan Van Dien, tough-girl Meyer, and Richards, all mile-wide smile and glittery eyes. Zander and Dizzy are killed, leaving Rico and Carmen together for the fadeout. Jake Busey portrayed violin-playing infantryman Ace Levy, Clancy Brown was drill sergeant Zim, Seth Gilliam was Sugar Watkins and Michael Ironside played Jean Rasczak, the mechanical-armed commander of the 'Roughnecks' infantry unit. There's not much subtlety here, from the rousing, militarist score by Basil Poledouris and crunching battle scenes to the 'Federal Network' TV announcements, recruitment drives and news items ('Would you like to know more?'), but it's a glorious success. Sequels *Starship Troopers 2* (2004) and *Starship Troopers 3: Marauder* (2008) followed, but the original is a fine example of sci-fi 'pulped fiction', a guilty pleasure that good taste should decree forbidden.

The Time Machine: This Italian poster for George Pal's 1960 adaptation of H.G. Wells's 1895 novel retitles the film *The Man Who Lived in the Future.*

7

'HE HAS ALL THE TIME IN THE WORLD'

THE TIME MACHINE (1960)

Director: George Pal
Story: H.G. Wells
Screenplay: David Duncan
Director of Photography: Paul C. Vogel
Music: Russell Garcia
Metrocolor
A Galaxy Films Production
Released by MGM
103 minutes

Rod Taylor (H. George Wells), Alan Young (David and James Filby), Yvette Mimieux (Weena), Sebastian Cabot (Dr Philip Hillyer), Tom Helmore (Anthony Bridewell), Whit Bissell (Walter Kemp), Doris Lloyd (Mrs Watchett), Bob Barran and James Skelly (Eloi men), Josephine Powell (Eloi woman), Paul Frees (voice of the rings)

* * *

H.G. Wells wrote his first successful book, *The Time Machine*, in 1895. In Victorian England, inventor the 'Time Traveller' regales his contemporaries with fantastical tales. He arrives dishevelled from the future, where he has been adventuring in the fourth dimension (as opposed to the dimensions of length, breadth and depth). As time rapidly passes, his time-travelling machine occupies the same area, but travels through time itself. The inventor visits AD 802701, where the landscape is unrecognisable. The world is now Utopia, inhabited by four-foot-tall vegetarians, the Eloi. They are passive, friendly and completely without thought or purpose. The inventor's time machine is stolen and hidden in a white sphinx statue's pedestal by the aggressive Morlocks – subterranean, nocturnal troglodyte beasts who fatten the Eloi up before eating them in their cavern lair. The inventor befriends Eloi Weena and discovers a museum ('some latter-day South Kensington') full of artefacts, dinosaur bones, machinery, books, weapons and other ephemera of the past, plus two sticks of dynamite. The inventor tackles the Morlocks, but in the fracas Weena is killed. He escapes and accidentally travels forward in time, to a landscape of red beaches populated by giant crabs and butterflies. Thirty million years into the future, the burning sun ensures hardly anything lives, and there is a great darkness and terrible cold as the inventor witnesses the end of the world. He puts the machine in reverse and hurries back to his own time. In the book's epilogue, we are told the time traveller vanished three years ago and is yet to return.

Allied Artists' cheapie *World without End* (1955), directed and scripted by Edward Bernds, resembled parts of Wells's story. Four astronauts (Christopher Dark, Nelson Leigh, Rod Taylor and Hugh Marlowe) piloting the rocket XRM vanish in March 1957 during a recon mission to Mars and travel through time to Earth in A D 2508. Shot in Technicolor and CinemaScope, this B-movie reused rocket footage from *Flight to Mars* (1951). Earth has been destroyed by nuclear Armageddon. The XRM lands in a snowscape and the astronauts wander into a barren land (resembling California), where they are ambushed by primitive, mutated cyclops cavemen. Exploring caves, the quartet is jumped by giant rubber spiders and encounters a wimpy subterranean civilisation whose population is depleting. The astronauts help them rise up against the mutants with the aid of an improvised bazooka. Unusually, the film ends with the astronauts remaining in 2508 to aid in the repopulation of the planet. Among the subterranean folk Nancy Gates played Garnet, Lisa Montell played Deena, Shawn Smith was Elaine, Everett Glass played Timmek, the president of the council, and Booth Coleman (who resembles Kelsey Grammer) was the conniving villain, Mories. In this future civilisation, men wear tunics, tights and domed helmets, while the 1950s space belles wear minidresses designed by *Esquire* magazine illustrator and pin-up painter Alberto Vargas. He also drew a poster design featuring the scantily clad, elfin 'Varga Girls', with the strapline: 'Vargas interprets the women of the future for the screen's science fiction sensation.' The plot, involving 'exponential time displacement' was so close to Wells's story that the film was the subject of a lawsuit.

In 1959 Wells's book was brought to the screen by producer–director George Pal, who had worked splendidly on *The War of the Worlds* (1953). Wells's estate was so pleased with *War* that they allowed Pal the pick of Wells's library. The film was budgeted at $750,000 and shot at MGM's Culver City Studios, California. The trailer pointed out that 'It took the creative magic of George Pal and the fabulous production know-how of Metro-Goldwyn-Mayer to catapult you through time into a world that is yet to be.' Adapted for the screen by David Duncan, the film adds more specific historical references to the future (events that had occurred since the book's publication) that would resonate with contemporary audiences. On New Year's Eve 1899, inventor George (*World without End*'s Rod Taylor) demonstrated his time machine to four of his friends – David Filby, Dr Philip Hillyer, Anthony Bridewell and Walter Kemp. Five days later, the quartet convenes at George's for dinner, where the time traveller returns dramatically, having travelled far into the future, and tells his disbelieving friends of his exploits, before setting off again at the film's denouement back to the future. Though he's addressed as George by his friends and his housekeeper Mrs Watchett (Doris Lloyd), a plaque on the time machine indicates that it was 'Manufactured by H. George Wells'. Thus Wells became his own protagonist.

When George speeds into the future, the sun sears across the sky, days pass in an instant and the landscape around the time machine evolves as society changes. As George gently accelerates time, flowers bloom and close, a candle burns down and a snail speeds across the floor. George pauses in 1917 and finds his lab derelict and boarded up, the garden overgrown and the world at war. By June 1940, George finds himself in the midst of another war – George suspects the same war from 1917 – and his house under fire during the Blitz. Hurtling forward to August 1966, an atomic satellite zeroes in to attack and George realises he has witnessed the eve of the Earth's destruction by nuclear war, as volcanic eruptions and lava destroy the street he once knew. Encased in cooled volcanic rock, George speeds far into the future, until the rock has naturally eroded. He eventually stops on 12 October 802701, where the once-lunar post-nuclear landscape is overgrown with thriving tropical greenery. The film then follows the book closely, with George adrift, a stranger in paradise. Only in the finale does it diverge once more. George makes his escape and hurtles back to 1900, without first travelling millions of years into the future. George returns to his own time with a pink flower in his pocket that botanist Filby agrees couldn't possibly bloom in wintertime.

For the film's bookend scenes, Pal created an idealised Hollywood evocation of picturesque Victoriana, as George and his guests discuss travel through time as though chatting about the weather or cricket scores. Taylor is well cast as the urbane inventor and it remains probably his best-known role. Alan Young played both David Filby and, in the time-travelling scenes, his son James. Sebastian Cabot played doubting Dr Philip Hillyer and Tom Helmore was tipsy Anthony Bridewell. Whit Bissell, who played Walter Kemp, later appeared as a regular cast member in the US TV series *The Time Tunnel* (1966–7), created by Irwin Allen, which featured scientists who are trapped in time and become witnesses and participants in important historical events of the future and the past, including Pearl Harbor, the Trojan War, the Battles of Gettysburg, Little Bighorn and the Alamo, and the D-Day landings.

George's ever-changing street was recreated with matte shots, model work and miniatures, as a clothes shop grows into a department store and cars are replaced with a mid-air monorail. Changing women's fashion on a dress shop store mannequin indicates the passing of time. George's time-travelling exploits utilised impressive back-projected landscapes and stop-motion and speeded-up photography. The Time Machine itself is an eccentric Heath Robinson contraption, primarily consisting of a sledge fitted with a velvet-upholstered chair and a large revolving dish, presumably for propulsion. On the machine's dashboard, dates whizz by like revolving icons on a fruit machine.

The Time Machine was shot in vivid Metrocolor entirely on studio interiors, from the utopian, post-nuclear Garden of Eden (ruined buildings, a sphinx statue, a roofless domed dining hall, amid a choking, viny jungle) to the Morlocks' cavernous underground lairs. The mutant Morlocks are convincingly troll-like, with ugly grimaces, mops of white hair, blue skin and loincloths, while the Eloi are easier on the eye (and not four feet tall), as played by blond men and women draped in pastel robes. No one grows old – the Morlocks see to that – so everyone is young and beautiful. Weena was played by elfin starlet Yvette Mimieux. Her love affair with George is more conventionally romantic than in Wells's novel, and at 'The End' George goes forward in time to be reunited with Weena, who survives the film but is unable to flee with George. This provides romantic closure for a Hollywood audience.

The Eloi are clothed and fattened up by the Morlocks, want for nothing, never working nor wondering about their plight. The Morlocks fear fire, though they are masters of primitive science and lure the Eloi below ground with a siren to be slaughtered. The Eloi wander into the Morlocks' trap, a conditioned reaction from years of air raids, their only sense of 'history'. An addition to the film was the 'rings that talk' (voiced by Paul Frees), which recount the postwar history of the world. Earth was dying, no one could breathe and oxygen was produced in factories. The Morlocks became the masters and the Eloi their sustenance. Humans enslaved by a superior race reappeared in *Planet of the Apes*.

The film depicts travel not through space (the machine remains in the same place) but through time. When asked where he's from, George answers, 'I'm from right here', and his obsession is reflected in the many timepieces that litter his parlour. George expresses his dissatisfaction with his present time and longs to see the future. He wonders, 'Can man control his destiny? Can he change the shape of things to come?' The impact Wells's story had on Victorian literature is difficult to comprehend today, as George travels into a future so distant it will have no impact on the lives of his companions and sees only war and destruction. The wider implications of being able to travel in time – to reroute and remould future events – are not explored. George sees into the future without ever being able to change its predestined outcome.

The Time Machine was released to great success in the US in August 1960 by MGM, with the tagline 'Whirls you to a world of Amazing Adventure in the year 800,000!', rendered 'In Futuristic Metrocolor!' The trailer's narrator marvelled at shapely Mimieux wearing a pink dress: 'Ah, the shape of things to come.' The film was an extravaganza of its era and won an Oscar for Best Special Effects in 1961. Taylor, Bissell and Young reprised their roles in Clyde Lucas's semi-documentary *Time Machine: The Journey Back* (1993), which looked at the film's making and the Time Machine prop's restoration and also nostalgically reunited George Wells and David Filby for old times' sake.

Ib Melchior helmed a *Time Machine* sequel, *The Time Travellers* (1964), which was remade in 1967 as *Journey to the Center of Time*. Terry Marcel's *Prisoner of the Lost Universe* (1983) plays like a dire parody of *The Time Machine*. When Carrie Madison (Kay Lenz), the presenter of a sensationalising TV show, *The Weird and the Wacky*, visits 'dimensional physicist' (read 'mad professor') Dr Hartmann (Kenneth Hendel), she, he and electrician-cum-martial artist Dan Roebuck (Richard Hatch) are whisked via the professor's matter transmitter to another dimension (filmed in South Africa), where they encounter primitive fly-headed beings with red glowing eyes, goggles and loincloths, a giant caveman, green-skinned hunters, fishy aqua men and John Saxon as Kleel, a sadistic warlord.

Wells's story has continued to fascinate audiences and filmmakers with its possibilities. For the wonderfully 1970s TV adaptation of *The Time Machine* (1978) by Henning Schellerup, in addition to romancing Weena (Priscilla Barnes) and battling the Morlocks, inventor Neil Perry (John Beck) ends up in jail in the Wild West, and the skull-faced Morlocks wear boiler suits and are armed with electrocuting laser batons. *The Time Machine* (2002), directed by Simon Wells (H.G.'s great-grandson), was a radical reworking of the story. In 1899 New York, Dr Alexander Hartdegen (Guy Pearce) witnesses the death of his fiancée Emma (Sienna Guillory), who is shot during a bungled mugging. Four years later he has created a time machine, which he uses to travel back to save her, but this time she is trampled by runaway horses. In an effort to discover the secret to changing past events Alex travels to AD 802701, where he encounters the Eloi (a primitive, jungly, cliff-dwelling tribe) and the Morlocks (who eat and breed with the Eloi). The Morlock leader (Jeremy Irons) tells Alex that as long as the time machine exists, Emma will die. During a battle with the leader on the time machine, Alex zooms into the future, to AD 635427810, which is a volcanic, fiery wasteland. Back in 802701, Alex destroys the Morlocks' underground caverns by blowing up the time machine, but is stranded forever with Eloi Mara (Samantha Mumba). The film's impressive time machine is a glittering contraption, with two rotating propellers and blinding laser beams, which travels through time in its own protective bubble. In the finale we see two parallel worlds – then and now – in a split-screen effect, as Alex remains with the Eloi and Filby and Watchett walk through Alex's house in 1899. Alan Young has a blink-and-you'll-miss-him cameo as a flower-shop owner, while Orlando Jones's holographic 'library information unit' Vox was the film's equivalent of the rings that talk. At only 96 minutes, this *Time Machine* seems rushed and its depiction of snowy Victoriana is straight out of *The Muppet Christmas Carol*. If only H.G. really had invented time travel, he could have restrained his great-grandson from directing this film. The poster tagline was 'Where Would You Go?' Judging by the film's disappointing grosses, not to the cinema.

The UK TV series *Doctor Who* has since 1963 sent a succession of time-travelling Time Lords from the planet Gallifrey on adventures through time and space in a police box TARDIS (Time and Relative Dimension in Space). He is often pitted against now-classic villains such as the Cybermen or the Daleks, and the series has sometimes played out in Wellsian Victorian settings. Peter Cushing played the Doctor as an absent-minded professor in two movie spin-offs directed by Gordon Flemyng, in Techniscope and Technicolor: *Dr Who and the Daleks* (1965) and *Daleks – Invasion of Earth: 2150 A.D.* (1966). Set on the planet Skaro, *Dr Who and the Daleks* was essentially a reworking of *The Time Machine* (1960), with the Daleks (familiar from Terry Nation's TV series) subbing for the oppressive Morlocks and the peaceful Thals as the Eloi. In its sequel, the Doctor and his companions, including police constable Tom Campbell (Bernard Cribbins), arrive in the ruins of London in the title year, where the Daleks have enslaved the population, turning them into black-PVC-outfitted Robomen or making them work in a massive excavation in Bedfordshire. Andrew Kier and Ray Brooks are particularly good as members of the human resistance. The Daleks plan to dig to the Earth's core, explode a bomb and pilot Earth back to their home planet. With its 1960s scenes of the destruction of London and evocative special effects, this is the version of Wells's *The War of the Worlds* that never was.

While time travel remains a futuristic concept, the plethora of films has lessened its novelty value as subject matter. Its concept has opened up limitless plot possibilities – week after week on TV for the series *Quantum Leap* (1989–93) – plus the chance to use up all those old period costumes. Time travellers were whisked back into history, or forward from the past, in such oddities as *Les Visiteurs* (1993), *Time Bandits* (1981), *Bill & Ted's Excellent Adventure* (1988), *Bill & Ted's Bogus Journey* (1991), *Hot Tub Time Machine* (2010) and *A Connecticut Yankee in King Arthur's Court* (1949). The last, a Mark Twain story, was updated by Disney as *The Spaceman and King Arthur* (1979; *Unidentified Flying Oddball* in the US), starring Dennis Duggan as hapless NASA astronaut Tom Trimble and his robot assistant Hermes, Jim Dale as land-grabbing villain Sir Mordred, Ron Moody as Merlin, Kenneth More as King Arthur, Rodney Bewes as the page Clarence and John Le Mesurier as Sir Gawain. It was set in Ye Olde England, a verdant Arthurian Cornwall, in the year of Our Lord 508. In the film's classic scene, Mordred's sword is magnetised and attracts all manner of heavy objects: 'My trusty sword and I seem to be at odds.' A similar idea was played straight in Fernando Colomo's Spanish *Star Knight* (1985), with Klaus Kinski as alchemist Boetius, Harvey Keitel as knight Sir Clever and Manuel Bose as alien visitor IX.

Edgar G. Ulmer's *Beyond the Time Barrier* (1960) had pilot Robert Clarke shot into a bleak post-nuclear future while testing a new superfast jet. Don Taylor's *The Final Countdown* (1980) offered an interesting selection of hypothetical 'What ifs?', as nuclear-powered aircraft carrier USS *Nimitz* is snarled up in a violent Pacific storm that transports the carrier through a swirling time tunnel to the eve of the attack on Pearl Harbor on 6 December 1941. Time travel was key to action-movie blasts from the past such as *The Terminator* (1984) and *Highlander* (1986) and their spin-offs. The subgenre had a teen makeover in the 1980s with *Back to the Future*, which itself spawned many imitators. In Nicholas Meyer's gleefully contrived *Time after Time* (1979), Wells himself (Malcolm McDowell) chased Jack the Ripper (David Warner) through time, from Victorian London to 1979 San Francisco. Time and distance may provide perspective, but when time travel is done well, the possibilities remain endless.

8

'DAMN YOU ALL TO HELL'

PLANET OF THE APES (1968)

Director: Franklin J. Schaffner
Story: Pierre Boulle
Screenplay: Michael Wilson and Rod Serling
Director of Photography: Leon Shamroy
Music: Jerry Goldsmith
Panavision/DeLuxe Color
An APJAC Production
Released by Twentieth Century-Fox
107 minutes

Charlton Heston (Colonel George Taylor), Roddy McDowall (Cornelius), Kim Hunter (Dr Zira), Maurice Evans (Dr Zaius), James Whitmore (President of the Academy), James Daly (Honorious, deputy minister of justice), Linda Harrison (Nova), Robert Gunner (Landon), Lou Wagner (Lucius), Woodrow Parfrey (Dr Maximus, commissioner for animal affairs), Jeff Burton (Dodge), Buck Kartalian (Julius, prison guard), Norman Burton (leader of the hunters), Wright King (Dr Galen), Paul Lambert (minister), Robert Lombardo (gorilla photographer), Dianne Stanley (Stewart)

* * *

For most of the 1960s, sci-fi films were out of favour, as other genres – musicals, epics, Westerns and Gothic horror – dominated the box office. But 1968 was a key year for science fiction, a year defined by two very different films. *Planet of the Apes* premiered in February 1968 and *2001: A Space Odyssey* followed in April. Both films set out to delineate the dawn of time and the end of the world, and both featured actors dressed in monkey suits.

In *Planet of the Apes*, following a six-month mission from Earth into deep space – during which the astronauts estimate 700 Earth years have passed – a US rocket crashes into a vast lake in a desert on an unnamed planet, in the constellation of Orion. According to the craft's calendar, it's 25 November 3978 and 2,000 years have passed, though the three male astronauts in their hibernation pods have barely aged. Their female companion, Stewart (Dianne Stanley), had an air leak and is long dead. Landon (Robert Gunner), Dodge (Jeff Burton) and their skipper, Colonel George Taylor (Charlton Heston), explore the arid planet. They eventually reach a lush landscape, with waterfalls and crops, but the primitive human population are Neanderthal in progress. They are oppressed by the planet's dominant race – apes – who walk, talk, dress in clothes, have organised government and society, and hunt the humans to use in experiments in the Academy of Science. Dodge is killed, Landon disappears and Taylor is shot in the throat, rendering him mute. Dr Zira (Kim Hunter), an animal psychologist, becomes interested in Taylor, who exhibits great intelligence. Zira and her archaeologist lover Cornelius (Roddy McDowall) try to convince Dr Zaius (Maurice Evans), the minister of science, that Taylor is an important 'missing link' between un-evolved primates and apes. This heresy (that men can speak, can think) contradicts the old teachings of the Sacred Scrolls. When Taylor's voice returns and he states his own case, the ape elders plan to dispose of him, as they have done with Landon. When Taylor is reunited with his comrade, he discovers Landon has been lobotomised by the apes' brain experiments. Condemned by Zaius to the 'final disposition' – to be emasculated and have his brain experimented on, resulting in 'a kind of living death' – Taylor resolves to escape into the eastern desert 'Forbidden Zone'.

Planet of the Apes offered the idea that distant planets would not be inhabited by aliens or unrecognisable beings with tentacles and one glowing eye, but a species that is generally considered to be our inferior. It was based on the 1963 novel *La Planète des singes* by Pierre Boulle, which was published in the UK in 1964 as *Monkey Planet*. The book has the framing device featuring two space tourists – Phyllis and Jinn – who are floating through the cosmos and find a message in a bottle which recounts the adventures of three French astronauts – physician Arthur Levain, Professor Antelle and the story's narrator, Ulysse Mérou. They set off in 2500 and two years later are exploring the Betelgeuse system when they discover Earth's twin, which they christen Soror. The planet is inhabited by naked, grunting humans, who live in primitive Stone Age fashion and are oppressed by the planet's ape rulers. Ulysse learns the apes' language and delivers a speech to the Congress. The apes are excavating an archaeological site of a 10,000-year-old ruined city. There they find human skeletons, evidence of cars and aeroplanes, and a child's doll that says 'Papa' – a human doll, not an ape one, signifying that it was once humans who ruled Soror. In the book, Ulysse and his cellmate Nova sire a child in captivity, but the orangutans seek to eradicate any form of human evolution or threat to 'Monkey Science'. Zira and Cornelius arrange for Ulysse, Nova and their son Sirius to escape in a manned artificial satellite and board Ulysse's spacecraft, which is still orbiting Soror. They leave Soror far behind and land at Orly airport – in Earth terms 700 years later – to discover that apes rule this planet too. *La Planète des singes* loses something in translation, but the story is a sound one. To check they can breathe outside the spaceship, the astronauts send out their monkey

Monkey Planet: UK poster for Franklin J. Schaffner's *Planet of the Apes* (1968), which highlights the contribution of Pierre Boulle. Boulle wrote the 1963 source novel, originally published as *La Planète des singes*, and also authored the inspiration for *The Bridge on the River Kwai* (1957).

companion, Hector, 'to make doubly sure, we tried it out first on our chimpanzee'. When they first encounter Nova at a waterfall, without hesitation Nova throttles their harmless chimpanzee, a moment more shocking than anything that appears in the film version. But the book's ending is quite different, with Phyllis and Jinn mocking the implausibility of the document, as they themselves are chimpanzees.

The film's screenplay by Michael Wilson and Rod Serling (the creator of the seminal sci-fi TV series *The Twilight Zone* [1959–64]) is a massive improvement on the novel. Plot and characterisation are strong and throughout the story familiar human phrases are adapted for the apes, such as 'I never met an ape I didn't like' or 'You know what they say – human see, human do'. The film was shot from May to August 1967 for $5.8 million, in DeLuxe Panavision by Leon Shamroy. The rocket crashes in Lake Powell, a vast man-made reservoir with bleak desert mesas rising around it, part of the Glen Canyon National Park in Utah. For the desert landscape of the radiation-ridden, infertile 'Forbidden Zone', scenes were also shot on the Colorado River at Page, Arizona, and in the surrounding desert landscape. The atmospheric sun-baked desert scenes highlight Jerry Goldsmith's Oscar-nominated score, the first mainstream Hollywood score to use atonal, avant-garde musical stylings. Goldsmith deployed chiming echoes, dissonant whines, flute hoots, flurries of percussion and jagged, tumbling piano riffs. As the astro-nauts near 'civilisation', they encounter roughly constructed scarecrows, which resemble crucified bears: each scarecrow is a towering, crude X of animal hide and sticks. The lush green landscape beyond this boundary was filmed at the Fox Ranch, Malibu, California, where the forest, waterfall and hunt scenes were shot. Also built there was the Ape City, a strange mixture of stretched, Daliesque futuristic shapes and primitive construction methods (including a stepped amphitheatre and irregular arches), which resembles a Mexican pueblo designed by Gaudí. Interiors – including the tribunal set, the jail cells, the rocket interior, the church-like 'place of worship' and the museum – were constructed on Stages 20, 21 and 22 at Twentieth Century-Fox Studios, Los Angeles. The film's final scenes, as Taylor and Nova ride along the coast, were shot at Westward Beach, Malibu, between Zuma Beach and Point Dume.

Charlton Heston was a big star in the late 1960s; sci-fi was small fry. A hokey movie about an ape world may not have been the obvious choice for the actor, but it turned out to be one of the most intelligent decisions of his career. Colonel Taylor is a pompous cock-sure bully, chomping on a cigar and mocking Landon when he plants a small American flag in the dust, a futile gesture in this arid alien world. Taylor muses that there has to be something 'better than man' in outer space. Fox-contracted actress Linda Harrison played mute Nova. The actors cast as apes wore John Chambers's flexible, highly convincing latex ape make-up, which cost over $300,000 and was painstakingly applied by 80 make-up artists. Chambers received an Honorary Award at the 1968 Oscars for his outstanding make-up achievement on this film. There are three strata of ape society – orangutans, chimpanzees and gorillas. The most violent level are the gorillas: guards, hunters, jailers, soldiers, who wear black and dark-purple uniforms. The chimpanzees, society's artisans and intellectuals, wear green clothes, and the elder orangutans wear sandy orange and khaki. Kim Hunter played chimpanzee Dr Zira, Roddy McDowall was Cornelius and Lou Wagner played Zira's teenage nephew Lucius, the voice of discontented youth, who Taylor memorably tells: 'Remember, never trust anybody over thirty.' Maurice Evans was Zaius, the disingenuous orangutan doctor, and James Whitmore, James Daly and Woodrow Parfrey played the other orangutan elders who presided over ape society. Zaius is 'defender of the faith', who is also the guardian of a terrible secret that the presence of Taylor threatens to reveal.

One of the film's key themes is Taylor's unravelling of this reverse evolution – or rather 'retro-lution' – that has occurred on this planet. As Taylor notes when he first encounters the primitive human inhabitants, scavenging fruit and corn, 'If this is the best they've got around here, in six months we'll be running this planet.'

But Taylor is the specimen under their microscope, while other humans are experi-mented upon, become waxworks in the Zaius Museum, have their brains wiped or their souls crushed. There's an interesting moment when Nova is placed in Taylor's cell, presumably so their behaviour and mating can be observed first-hand. Whether Taylor finds Nova attractive is not an option, in the same way that animals are thrust together in zoos, an interesting take on 'they all look the same to me'. The infertile Forbidden Zone is a metaphor for Stewart, the rocket's precious cargo, a new Eve on whom civilisation hinged. For Taylor, Nova is 'the only girl in town'.

The apes are governed by orangutan elders, who adhere to the Sacred Scrolls – old testaments that the lawgivers decreed are society's moral glue. Zira and Dr Galen (Wright King) are accused of being 'perverted scientists' for apparently creating Taylor, a 'speaking monster', and Zira and Cornelius are charged with 'contempt of the tribunal, malicious mischief and scientific heresy'. In the Forbidden Zone, in a coastal cave, Cornelius has unearthed artefacts that predate the Sacred Scrolls. When Taylor visits the excavation, he sees false teeth, spectacles, an artificial heart valve and a human doll that cries and squawks 'Mama!' This evidence of man's presence predates the entire ape civilisation by 700 years and explains the paradox of the ancient race being more advanced.

Planet of the Apes includes two of the great revelatory moments in science fiction. The first is the hunt though the crop fields, as it dawns on Taylor that he is being chased by gorillas riding horses. This frantic sequence, expertly orchestrated by Schaffner and scored by Goldsmith, has the apes deploying beaters, nets, hunting horns and guns. This scene demonstrated that not only were the apes capable of working together and thinking for themselves, they were superior beings to the human 'savages'. Some humans are driven off a riverbank into the water, while others are shot into pits or scooped up in nets. Later Taylor snarls at his tormentors: 'Take your stinking paws off me, you damn dirty ape', when he has been treated 'like an animal' by these superiors. At the film's conclusion, Taylor and Nova ride along the coast, further into the Forbidden Zone, though Zaius warns him, 'You might not like what you find.' Taylor finally finds out why this planet's ancient human race was so advanced. At the end of a cove, Taylor finds the towering remains of a ruined statue, half buried in the sand but rising defiantly from the rocky beach. The torch, forlornly held aloft, and the jagged spiked headdress is unmistakable as the Statue of Liberty, signifying both the last bastion of civilisation and the definitive confirmation of its end. Its doomy endgame message is one of the most resonant in post-apocalyptic cinema, while the ruined statue is the most chilling image in all science fiction. 'Oh my God, I'm back,' realises Taylor, as the grim truth dawns on him. 'I'm home [...] they finally really did it, you maniacs, you blew it up! Damn you, God damn you all to Hell.'

The film's trailer voice-over warned, '*Planet of the Apes* – Beyond your wildest dreams', and featured Heston on set describing how the production assembled the largest ever number of make-up artists. To remind audiences who's behind the make-up, there are images of the ape characters and the actors who play them. *Planet of the Apes* was initially rated M (mature audiences) then re-rated G (suitable for general audiences). In the UK it was classified as an A in 1968 and remains a PG on video. It was a massive success, taking $32 million in the US, making it the most successful science-fiction film released up to that point, though it was quickly surpassed by *2001* later that year.

Ted Post's *Beneath the Planet of the Apes* (1969) started where the original film left off. Taylor and Nova continue to ride into the Forbidden Zone, where they witness unexplained phenomena (walls of flame, lightning storms and earthquakes) and Taylor dematerialises into a sheer rock face. Meanwhile another US rocket crashes in the desert zone in AD 3955, searching for Taylor's party. Astronaut Brent (James Franciscus) encounters Nova and travels to the 'City of the Apes' to contact Zira and Cornelius, who are now married. Heston returned as Taylor, but Franciscus took centre stage as Nova's new companion. Harrison, looking more beautiful here than she did in the original, reprised Nova. Evans returned as Zaius, Cornelius was now played by David Watson, and Hunter reappeared as Zira. Brent and Nova flee into the Forbidden Zone, where they find a cavernous underground city, which is the rock-encrusted ruins of New York, including the crumbled facades of the Public Library, the Stock Exchange, Radio City Music Hall and 5th Avenue. When Brent realises he is standing in the ruins of Queensboro Plaza subway station, it's his 'Statue of Liberty' moment.

Some of this wreckage was originally part of the $2 million set created at Fox for *Hello Dolly!* (1969). There were many gorilla extras needed for the impressive scenes of the ape army on the march. Exteriors were filmed at Red Rock Canyon State Park and on the standing 'ape village' set at the Fox Ranch, with interiors on Stage 16 of Fox Studios.

Ape society is clearly divided into peaceful elements (such as Zira and Cornelius), the followers of the Lawgiver – an ape Moses edified in stone – (such as Zaius and the science council) and the ape army and its commander, the warmongering General Ursus (James Gregory). In old New York resides a subterranean secret society of telepathists, who wear masks to conceal their hideous disfigurements. Paul Richards played their leader Mendez, with the senior council portrayed by Jeff Corey, Victor Buono, Don Pedro Colley and Natalie Trundy. In a ruined cathedral, these survivors worship a cobalt-encased atomic bomb, the Doomsday Bomb, which bears the Greek letters alpha and omega, and their creed includes, 'Glory be to the Bomb and to the Holy Fallout [...]world without end, Amen.' Brent finds Taylor imprisoned, and the two are forced to fight. The apes storm the underground city and during their attempted escape, Nova, Brent and Taylor are machine-gunned down. Proving the apes' belief that man is evil, capable only of destruction, mortally wounded Taylor detonates the missile, destroying the Earth. A voice-over recounts the planet's demise: 'In one of the countless billions of galaxies in the universe lies a medium-sized star, and one of its satellites, a green and insignificant planet, is now dead.' Made for a modest $3 million, *Beneath* took over $17 million in the US.

In Don Taylor's *Escape from the Planet of the Apes* (1971), Colonel Taylor's rocket ship lands in the Pacific off the coast of southern California in 1973, about 2,000 years before its destruction in 3955, with apes Zira (Hunter), Cornelius (McDowall) and Dr Milo (Sal Mineo) on board. These three 'apeonauts' are taken into captivity in Los Angeles Zoo, where they complete intelligence tests and reveal they can speak. Milo is throttled by a depressed gorilla, and Zira and Cornelius become celebrities until it's discovered that

Zira is expecting. Initially they become kooky celebrity darlings to a curious public, as Zira addresses the 'Bay Area Women's Club', the pair enjoy wine (or 'grape juice-plus') and host parties in their luxury suite at their Beverly Hills hotel. But with Zira's pregnancy come moral questions and problems. Under interrogation by the CIA at Camp 11, the apes recount how a plague wiped out cats and dogs, and apes became humanity's favoured pets. Over the centuries they evolved and became able to carry out menial tasks, in a state of servitude, until one of them, named Aldo, was able to utter 'No' and the apes overthrew their masters. Zira reveals that apes carried out atrocious experiments on humans, living and dead (depicted in yellow-tinted flashbacks from *Planet of the Apes*). The government commission decide to terminate her pregnancy, but the apes escape and hide at Armando's Circus (run by Ricardo Montalbán), where Zira gives birth to a male ape, which she christens Milo. Eventually they are forced to flee again, through oilfields to Los Angeles Harbor, where they are cornered on a rusting oil tanker and all three are fatally shot. In the film's opening scene, the three astronauts are greeted by troops on the beach and remove their helmets to reveal they're monkeys, while in the great twist ending Zira and Cornelius have switched their son with a normal baby chimp in the circus, and baby Milo utters 'Mama, mama', just like the toy doll in *Planet*. Bradford Dillman and Natalie Trundy played animal psychologists Dr Lewis Dixon and Dr Stephanie Branton, and Eric Braeden was the villain of the piece, Dr Otto Hasslein, who wants to terminate the advanced ape line. Shot for $2.5 million, the series was still popular enough to take over $12 million.

J. Lee Thompson took the helm for the final two *Apes* films. *Conquest of the Planet of the Apes* (1972) recounted how the apes came to power. A mysterious plague from outer space, brought by returning astronauts, wiped out cats and dogs. Humans took simian pets, which became their servants and slaves. Set in 1991 in California, almost 20 years after the events of *Escape*, Armando (Montalbán) has raised Zira and Cornelius's son, now named Caesar (McDowall), in secrecy. As apes are ever more mistreated, superintelligent Caesar leads a rebellion against the city's cruel Governor Breck (Don Murray). Caesar is captured and tortured with electroconvulsive therapy in a facility known as 'Ape Management', where beasts are domesticated. He is freed by the governor's aide, MacDonald (Hari Rhodes), who is sympathetic to the apes' cause. Natalie Trudy played Caesar's mate Lisa and Lou Wagner played a busboy. The city exteriors were shot at the University of California, Irving, and at Century City Shopping Center and Avenue of the Stars, Los Angeles. Filmed for $1.7 million, it took $9 million. Now the chimpanzees are dressed in green boiler suits, the gorillas in red ones, and the intricate face make-up of the early films has been replaced with masks. As the apes overthrow their masters – the black-clad, fascist riot police – and overrun Breck's command post, Caesar proclaims, 'Tonight we have seen the birth of the planet of the apes.'

Battle for the Planet of the Apes (1973) begins in North America in A D 2670, where orangutan The Lawgiver (John Huston), who is immortalised in stone in the early 'Apes' films, tells the story of how the ape God sent the world a saviour, the son of two speaking apes, and how both parents were brutally murdered. Caesar led the enslaved apes out of bondage and took them out of the city to found their own settlement. This 'story so far', rendered with footage from *Escape* and *Conquest*, is narrated in Huston's familiar 'biblical' tones. The ape revolt was followed by 'the vilest war in human history', where nuclear weapons were used and cities were destroyed. Now apes live alongside humans, such as MacDonald's brother (Austin Stoker), but the warlike gorillas, led by General Aldo (Claude Akins), creates tension. McDowall and Trundy again played Caesar and Lisa, who have a son, Cornelius (Bobby Porter). Aldo murders Cornelius, breaking the commandment 'Ape shall never kill ape', and seizes power, as mutant atomic survivors from the Forbidden City attack the ape settlement. This last chapter attempts to tie up the series' loose ends. Caesar, MacDonald and wise orangutan Virgil (Paul Williams) travel to the Forbidden City to locate archived tape recordings of 'Alien Visitors in 1973' which show Caesar's parents warning of doomed Earth's fate in 3950. Lew Ayres played orangutan armourer Mandemus, 'the keeper of Caesar's conscience'. The post-nuclear survivors in the city are in the early stages of mutation, while their radioactive 'Forbidden City' looms out of the desert. Severn Darden played Kolp, Breck's chief inspector in *Conquest*, who is now Governor Kolp. Exteriors were shot at Fox's Ranch and at Fox Studios. The trailer states that it's 12 years since the nuclear war, and the survivors' prize is 'the right to inherit what's left of the Earth'. Though it is hamstrung by a limiting budget (especially in the half-baked battle between the apes and the mutants), the $1.8 million investment yielded $8.8 million. The film ends 600 years after Caesar's death, with the Lawgiver schooling ape and human children about their history. Apes and humans continue to enjoy a harmonious existence, but a little girl asks, 'Lawgiver, who knows about the future?' 'Perhaps only the dead,' he answers, as the camera pans to a statue of Caesar, which appears to shed a tear. In scenes cut from most versions of the film, mutants discuss launching the Alpha–Omega bomb. Even in this alternative future, perhaps Earth is doomed after all.

There also followed a TV series of 14 hour-long episodes in 1974, with McDowall playing ape Galen in events before the original film, where two astronauts, Alan Virdon (Ron Harper) and Pete Burke (James Naughton), are time-warped 1,000 years into the future, to the ape-ruled world. It was shot at the 'ape city' set at the Fox Ranch, Malibu, and boasted a great title sequence. In 1981, some of the episodes were edited together to create new *Planet of the Apes* TV features: *Back to...*, *Forgotten City of...*, *Treachery and Greed on...*, *Life, Liberty and Pursuit on...* and *Farewell to the Planet of the Apes*. Fox also distributed a 13-episode cartoon TV series, *Return to the Planet of the Apes* (1975), shown on NBC in the US.

The year 2001 saw the release of a reimagining of the original film and Boulle's novel in Tim Burton's *Planet of the Apes*. Captain Leo Davidson (Mark Wahlberg) sets off from space research station USAF *Oberon* in 2029 in pursuit of a pod manned by chimpanzee

Pericles. Davidson passes through an electromagnetic storm, a time portal that hurtles him thousands of years into the future. He crashes on a planet where humans are hunted by apes, and familiar events ensue. In this version, the primitive human inhabitants of the planet – such as Karubi (Kris Kristofferson) and his beautiful daughter Daena (Estella Warren) – are able to speak. Davidson leads a small group of apes and humans from the Ape City into the 'Forbidden Area', where he discovers that the sacred ruins of Calima – 'where creation began' – are in fact the wreckage of his space station, *Oberon*. The apes in the space station rose up and overran the staff, founding the ape dynasty. Calima is a partially obscured sign: 'Caution Live Animals'. Meanwhile, the ape army led by General Thade (Tim Roth) arrives in the desert for a final showdown between the apes and the humans, who see Davidson as their saviour.

This $100 million venture has fine production values and visuals. The detailed ape make-up was designed and created by Rick Baker. Among the ape characters are chimpanzee Ari (Helena Bonham Carter), the daughter of Senator Sandar (David Warner), and chatty slave trader Limbo (Paul Giamatti). Charlton Heston had a cameo, in full ape regalia, as Thade's father, Zaius, whose dying words are: 'Damn them all to hell', while an ape tells Davidson, 'Take your stinking hands off me, you damn dirty human.' Linda Harrison made a brief cameo when the human prisoners are brought in the cage cart; Davidson asks, 'What is this place?' She shakes her head. Danny Elfman composed the percussive industrial score. During the final confrontation between the apes and humans, a spaceship lands, piloted by Pericles, in one of the hokiest moments in sci-fi, and he's exalted as an ape god. Davidson uses Pericles's ship to return to Earth, skims across the Reflecting Pool and lands near the Lincoln Memorial in Washington, DC. It isn't a statue of the sixteenth US president in the chair, but one of General Thade. Though Burton's dark visual artistry is present, this murky reimagining lacks the original film's élan, and a middling script pays lip service to the big themes (ethics, allegory, humanity and religion) without developing them. But it was a financial success, taking over $180 million in the US. In the 'history of the world' montage, look fast for clips from *Triumph of the Will* and *The Day the Earth Stood Still*, two very different moments in world 'history'.

It was followed by Rupert Wyatt's *Rise of the Planet of the Apes* (2011). In present-day San Francisco, human experiments into a cure for Alzheimer's disease, a formula ALZ-112, result in the breeding of a superintelligent chimp, named Caesar (Andy Serkis). Caesar develops at an alarming rate and is finally able to speak, in a reversal of the 'damn dirty ape' scene from *Planet of the Apes*. Will Rodman (James Franco) and Caroline Aranha (Freida Pinto) are the scientist and vet who raise Caesar as their own, before the authorities place him in captivity, where Caesar foments a revolt in the manner of *Conquest of the Planet of the Apes*. The franchise has come full circle and rather like the apes themselves, continues to evolve. John Lithgow played Will's father Charles, who has Alzheimer's, and Brian Cox was the animal pound's uncaring owner. Amid the tumbling monkey stunts, clichéd human baddies and great locations (shot in Hawaii and Canada) there's a good story. The ape army rampages across the Golden Gate Bridge to Redwood Park, where they make their home, while a rapidly disseminating virus that the apes are immune to begins to wipe out mankind. The biggest problem with staging talking-monkey movies is that they are awfully difficult to take seriously, ever since the famous *Not the Nine O'Clock News* (1979–82) TV sketch, where Professor Timothy Fielding (Mel Smith) demonstrates the huge leaps forward in human communication with animals, with help from Gerald the gorilla (Rowan Atkinson). During an interview with Pamela Stephenson, Fielding notes, 'When I caught Gerald in '68, he was completely wild', only for Gerald to pipe up: 'Wild? I was absolutely livid!'

9

'MY GOD, IT'S FULL OF STARS'

2001: A SPACE ODYSSEY (1968)

Director: Stanley Kubrick
Producer: Stanley Kubrick
Story: Arthur C. Clarke
Screenplay: Arthur C. Clarke and Stanley Kubrick
Directors of Photography: Geoffrey Unsworth and John Alcott
Music: Johann Strauss, Richard Strauss, Aram Khachaturian and György Ligeti
Metrocolor, Technicolor/Super Panavision and Cinerama
A Metro-Goldwyn-Mayer/Polaris/Stanley Kubrick Production
Released by MGM
143 minutes (including Overture, Intermission and Exit Music)

Keir Dullea (Dr David Bowman), Gary Lockwood (Dr Frank Poole), William Sylvester (Dr Heywood R. Floyd), Daniel Richter (Moon-Watcher), Leonard Rossiter (Dr Andrei Smyslov), Margaret Tyzack (Elena), Robert Beatty (Dr Ralph Halvorsen), Sean Sullivan (Dr Bill Michaels), Frank Miller (voice of mission control), Edward Bishop (Aries-1B lunar shuttle captain), Kevin Scott (Miller, on Aries-1B), Alan Gifford and Ann Gillis (Frank Poole's parents), Edwina Carroll (Aries-1B stewardess), Vivian Kubrick ('Squirt', Floyd's daughter), Kenneth Kendall (BBC-12 announcer), Douglas Rain (voice of HAL 9000)

* * *

In the 1950s and early 1960s, space exploration on film was epitomised by such fare as *Conquest of Space* and *First Spaceship on Venus*, as astronauts ventured beyond the Moon and stars, and into the black yonder of deep space. Byron Haskins's *Conquest of Space* (1955) depicted a Mars mission launched from a rotating space station, 'the Wheel', 1,000 miles from Earth. Paramount's limited budget forced producer George Pal, who saw this as a sequel to *Destination Moon*, to cut planned diversions to Jupiter and Venus. This is a striking-looking film and the Wheel and the astronauts working on the exterior of the craft were key influences on Antonio Margheriti's Italian sci-fi movies, such as *The*

2001: A Space Odyssey: Stanley Kubrick's 1968 sci-fi spectacular raised the bar for special effects and was grandly presented in widescreen-process Cinerama.

Wild, Wild Planet and *War of the Planets*. In *Conquest*, the mission is commanded by the 'inventor of the Wheel', Samuel Merritt (Walter Brooke), a religious man, and his son Barney (Eric Fleming). Others in the international crew include Sergeant Mahoney (Mickey Shaughnessy), New Yorker Siegle (Phil Foster), Austrian Fodor (Ross Martin) and Japanese Imoto (Benson Fong). The film, which blatantly plugs international (and in particular US–Japanese) amity, was based on the book *The Mars Project* by Chesley Bonestell and Willy Ley. It features some great 'space faces', the facial distortion that occurs due to the superspeed forces during take-off, an essential ingredient of sci-fi cinema. Samuel, who is struggling with the theological ethics of their journey and his own mental instability, tries to sabotage their landing on Mars, believing it to be a blasphemous act against God, and Barney accidentally shoots and kills his own father. The crew collect soil and mineral samples and set off home to assure Earth that Mars's arable red dust can sustain life. The Martian landscapes are impressively staged, and this is a realistic depiction of a mission through deep space, even down to the crew's condensed-food pellets. It's probably best to ignore the risible scene when it snows during Martian Christmas and dialogue such as, 'We'll have no unnecessary floating on this ship.'

Following *Conquest of Space*'s failure at the box office, there were few 'realistic' space exploration movies, as US sci-fi concentrated on creature features, UFOs and alien-invasion flicks. The East German/Polish co-production *First Spaceship on Venus* (1960) was originally released as *Der schweigende Stern* ('The Silent Star'). The film follows an international space mission in 1985 to Venus aboard the spacecraft *Cosmostrator One*. On Venus they discover a long-dead ancient civilisation that had developed nuclear power and planned to attack Earth, but an atomic accident destroyed the Venusian population. The film has rich visuals, in Technicolor and Totalvision. Venus is a tempestuous planet, a wild, swirling world wracked by storms and wreathed in clouds, populated by bounding metallic insects. Other Venusian space oddities include an immense white sphere (a transformer and force-field generator) that resembles a giant golf ball, a vitrified forest, wilted icy forms, shadows of the Venusian victims projected forever on rock walls by the atomic blast and other misty oddness. The planet pours forth bubbling black lava and boiling tar, and *Cosmostrator One* is forced to take off and return to Earth, having abandoned three astronauts on the planet. *Cosmostrator One*'s voyage is covered by a TV company on Earth called Intervision. The expedition includes cute robot Omega, which is unbeatable at chess and bears a rather strained expression. The film's most interesting aspect is the international crew. The nominal star is Japanese actress Yōko Tani, but the crew includes black and Asian astronauts, who were noticeable by their absence from most 1950s US sci-fi movies. Is this multicultural crew inclusive or simply decorously exotic? Unfortunately the English dub is awful and the astronauts' hooded spacesuits, with protruding earmuffs, resemble oversized teddy bears.

William Marshall's *The Phantom Planet* (1961) was *Gulliver's Travels*. The film boasts 'Interplanetary Sound' by Hayes Pagel and Walter Dick and 'Electronic Space Equipment' by Space Age Rentals. Captain Frank Chapman (Dean Fredericks, a bargain-basement Lex Barker) drifts in the powerless *Pegasus IV* rocket and is stranded on Rayton, a mysterious world populated by tiny people. The air makes Chapman shrink to their size and he becomes involved in their primitive society. He is tried by great sage Sessom (silent great Francis X. Bushman, here unfortunately speaking), is torn between Liara (Coleen Gray) and Zetha (Dolores Faith), and clashes with Herron (Tony Dexter). Eventually the Solarites, fire people from a Sun satellite, attack the planet in craft that resemble flaming meteors. The Raytons have a captured Solarite monster restrained in a cave. During the attack, which the Raytons repulse with a 'Gravity Curtain', their prisoner breaks free and lumbers amok. This bulky, bug-eyed alien – with arching shoulders and three weird tubular fingers – was played by towering Richard Kiel.

Voyage to the Prehistoric Planet (1965) was written and directed by 'John Sebastian' (Curtis Harrington). Set in 2020, it follows the first landing on Venus by astronauts and automaton John (a 'Robby the Robot' clone), who explore the wacky planet, which features tentacled, bulbous plants, lizard men, dinosaurs, moaning winds, mist, volcanic eruptions and lava, and a vast ocean. Eventually they find evidence of civilisation on the planet – a pterodactyl statue, a face carved in a rock – but have to flee when rainstorms flood the planet. After they have left, a mysterious horned Venusian is seen reflected in a pool of water. This US production was largely created from footage lifted from the excellent Russian sci-fi film, Pavel Klushantsev's *Planeta bur* (1962; *Planet of Storms*), which had great special effects, including a hovering moon car. Producer Roger Corman bought the Russian film, chopped it to pieces, redubbed the Russian cosmonauts in English and then inserted new scenes (directed by Harrington) into the Russian plot. In *Prehistoric Planet*, Marsha (Faith Domergue) helps the stranded astronauts from an orbiting spacecraft, while Professor Hartman (Basil Rathbone) oversees the operation from Lunar Station 7. Ironically this cut-price mutation of Klushantsev's work is seen more widely than the original *Planeta bur*.

Corman also used the Russian footage in *Voyage to the Planet of Prehistoric Women* (1968; *Gill Women of Venus* or *Gill Woman*). The story, recounted in flashback by a narrator in 1998, follows *Prehistoric World*'s Venus mission, but removes Rathbone and Domergue. A subplot introduces Moana (Mamie Van Doren) and her blank-faced, haunting 'sisters'. These wailing sea sirens are a selection of shapely blondes and redheads who bask on a misty, rocky Venusian beach. They wear silvery slacks, scallop-shell brassieres, false eyelashes and seashell necklaces. The sirens communicate telepathically, feast on raw fish, collect shells and worship a statue of a pterodactyl called Ptera. Later they devote a new idol, the astronaut's lava-encrusted robot. Though the film's credited director is 'Derek Thomas', the siren scenes are the directorial debut of Peter Bogdanovich, who was also the narrator. Bombshell Van Doren looks beautiful here, even when she bizarrely dons a chef's hat. The titles inform us: 'Costumes executed by Maureen of Hollywood'. Let's hope they didn't suffer.

Corman tried a similar trick with *Battle beyond the Sun* (1963), which is credited to 'Thomas Colchart' (actually Francis Ford Coppola) and is the 1959 Russian film *Nebo Zovet* redubbed and with added footage of a duel, for no apparent reason, between two grisly space monsters: an eyeball on a tentacle and a Venus-flytrap-toothed chomping mouth. The main plot recounts the space race to Mars (Project Red Planet) in November 1997 (after a nuclear war) between two rockets, *Typhoon* and *Mercury*, of the North and South Hemis. These rival space agencies are obviously representative of the Eastern and Western Cold War superpowers. The impressive Russian footage, of cosmonauts dwarfed by massive spacecraft and space stations, influenced later sci-fi movies, as did its realistic depiction of space travel.

Director Stanley Kubrick wrote to sci-fi author Arthur C. Clarke in the spring of 1964, with a view to their creating the 'proverbial good science-fiction movie'. Clarke had just edited Time Life's *Man and Space*, which was published in 1965. Kubrick had secured the rights to a story, 'Shadow of the Sun', but Clarke preferred to concoct something completely original, or at least from his own pen. Clarke provided Kubrick with a list of his short stories and the director liked 'The Sentinel' and 'Encounter in the Dawn' (aka 'Expedition to Earth'). 'The Sentinel' was written over Christmas 1948 as an entry to a BBC writing competition (it didn't win) and was eventually published in 1951, while 'Encounter' dated from 1953.

'The Sentinel' recounted a moon expedition in late summer 1996 to Mare Crisium – the Sea of Crises – where a glistening, mirrored, pyramidal structure has been discovered standing on a levelled plateau: 'Was it a building, a shrine – or something for which my language had no name?' It has a force field surrounding it and is a machine, a sentinel, one of millions scattered throughout the universe 'watching over all worlds with the promise of life'. Once activated, it sends a signal to whoever erected it, signifying that it is only a matter of time before its creators' arrival. 'Encounter in the Dawn' recounted a three-man space mission to search out new planets. Captain Altman, Bertrond and Clinder alight on an Earth-like planet and explore it by robot, where they see giant beasts and primitive savage tribes. They befriend one of the natives, whom they name Yaan. When they depart they leave various artefacts as gifts and 'Yaan's descendants would build the great city they were to call Babylon', signifying that the astral visitors predate the history of the Earth. These stories were augmented with material from four short stories, plus original input from both Clarke and Kubrick, to create *2001: A Space Odyssey*. By July 1964 Clarke noted in his journal that he had everything 'except the plot', and the story was completed by Christmas 1964. Clarke wrote the story as a novel and turned it into a script later. The film had now begun production, so visual ideas Kubrick used in the film were worked into Clarke's novel, in a two-way creative process. The published book states: 'Based on the screenplay by Stanley Kubrick and Arthur C. Clarke'.

Clarke's book is divided into six parts: 'Primeval Night', 'TMA-1', 'Between Planets', 'Abyss', 'The Moons of Saturn' and 'Through the Star Gate'. 'Primeval Night' describes ape-men living on Earth in the harsh desert lands of the African veldt, where 'the reign of the Terrible Lizards was over long ago'. The ape-men live in harmony with warthogs and are menaced by a leopard. The fifth chapter of this first section, 'Encounter in the Dawn', echoes Clarke's 'The Sentinel' and 'Encounter in the Dawn', with the sudden appearance of a transparent monolith, 'the new rock'. After its arrival, the ape-men begin their evolutionary path to becoming men. They develop human-like responses, self-awareness and consciousness and learn how to use tools, to become hunters to feed themselves, and to make weapons to kill the leopard. The narrative concentrates on one of the ape-men, Moon-Watcher (Daniel Richter), who kills the leader of a neighbour-ing ape clan. By the end of the primeval night, they have developed speech and become 'early man'. 'TMA-1' jumps forward into the era of space travel and describes a trip by

Dr Heywood Floyd from Earth to the Moon to examine a new excavation that has been unearthed in a crater: a monolith similar to the one encountered by the ape-men, which has been designated Tycho Magnetic Anomaly One (TMA-1 for short) and is believed to be over three million years old. 'Between the Planets' and the remainder of the book detail a mission to Jupiter and finally Saturn by the spacecraft *Discovery*.

The film closely resembles Clarke's book, with the exception that the *Discovery*'s mission is to Jupiter – Kubrick wasn't convinced his special effects could recreate Saturn's rings. The film begins with 'The Dawn of Man'. The desert-dwelling ape-men encounter the black slab monolith and evolution begins. The story then catapults forward to 1999, an era where space travel is commonplace, and follows Dr Heywood R. Floyd (William Sylvester) on his Moon visit. He docks in an Aries-1B lunar shuttle on a revolving space station en route, where he's questioned by Russian scientist Dr Andrei Smyslov (Leonard Rossiter). There are mysterious rumours that there is an epidemic at the Clavius moon base: radio contact with the station has been suspended and a Russian spacecraft has been refused permission to emergency-land. Floyd is from the National Council of Astronautics and is there to examine a scientific discovery in the Sea of Tranquillity. With other members of the Clavius team, including Dr Ralph Halvorsen (Robert Beatty), Floyd travels to the excavation in a crater. The discovery, a black monolith, was deliberately buried four million years ago and was located by its magnetic field. As the sun rises on the monolith for the first time in eons, the object emits a deafening high-pitched signal to beings unknown.

For 'Jupiter Mission 18 Months Later', the story jumps forward to 2001, with the spacecraft *Discovery I* on a mission to Jupiter. On board are Dr David Bowman (Keir Dullea) and Dr Frank Poole (Gary Lockwood). Three further surveyors – Whitehead, Kamiński and Hunter – are in sarcophagi-like hibernation pods (hibernacula) in a deep sleep, while the craft's brain and central nervous system is onboard computer HAL 9000: a Heuristically programmed Algorithmic Computer known as HAL. The HAL 9000 series has never been known to make errors. HAL reports that *Discovery*'s AE-35 unit will fail within the next 72 hours. When Bowman disconnects the AE-35 it is found to be fault-free. HAL seems to be in error and the astronauts plot to disconnect the computer. As Poole is replacing the unit, he is killed by the space pod. Bowman retrieves Poole's body, but HAL refuses to allow Bowman to re-enter the ship and also kills the three 'hibernauts' in their sleep by cutting their life support systems. Bowman manages to gain entry to the ship through an airlock and removes HAL's Logic Memory Centre, disabling the machine. Bowman views a pre-recorded briefing from Dr Floyd and learns that the monolith on the Moon signified that there is intelligent life on planets other than Earth. The monolith's emission was directed at Jupiter. Bowman continues into deep space and pilots the pod into 'Jupiter and Beyond the Infinite', as the craft is sucked into a mind-bending 'star gate', where all, or nothing, will be revealed.

2001 was financed by MGM and shot in the Cinerama process. The working title was *Journey beyond the Stars (aka How the Solar System Was Won)* in joking reference to the

Cinerama hit *How the West Was Won*. Clarke noted that NASA was spending the film's $10 million budget every day on space exploration projects, a comment that had particular resonance as *2001*'s budget eventually reached $10.5 million. Kubrick began shooting in December 1965 and the considerable post-production work lasted until March 1968. Interiors, some lunar exteriors and the special effects were shot at MGM British Studios, Borehamwood, and at Shepperton Studios. The visual authenticity was scrupulous – this was a new type of science fiction, where the spacecraft and planetary scapes looked wholly convincing. Kubrick's future vision includes voice-print identification, phone credit cards, a zero-gravity toilet, 3-D computer graphic mapping, and processed food that is sucked through straws. Kubrick himself took credit for designing and directing the film's 'special photographic effects', which were supervised by Wally Veevers, Douglas Trumbull, Con Peterson and Tom Howard. The scenes of space travel, shot in 2.21:1 widescreen by Geoffrey Unsworth and John Alcott, are magnificent, with the bulbous nose and elongated superstructure of *Discovery 1* sweeping majestically through starfields, while eclipses burst from behind orbiting planets and red-bathed spacecraft cockpits are awash with flickering lights. The 'Dawn of Man' scenes highlight some magnificent desert landscapes bathed in sunlight, and the costumed actors portraying the apes are totally convincing, more so than the Oscar-winning primates of *Planet of the Apes*. Life on the Moon is also rendered in considerable detail, the year before man set foot on it.

The film's pace is slow and languorous, and the rhythm stately, even for moments of jeopardy, drama and tension – for example, when Bowman attempts to reboard the *Discovery* ('Open the pod-bay doors, HAL'), and the ensuing frozen stand-off. In Bowman's 'murder' of HAL, he accesses the computer's Logic Memory Centre. 'Just what do you think you're doing?' asks HAL, as his memory banks are removed. 'Stop, I'm afraid [...] my memory is going.' Is HAL actually capable of emotion, or merely programmed that way? He methodically beats Poole at chess but gives his opinion of Bowman's improving sketching skills. With HAL's only presence a threatening, all-seeing red eye with a yellow iris, Kubrick manages to imbue cold, computerised hardware with personality, through the hushed, matter-of-fact tones of Douglas Rain's voice.

Kubrick and his team's cinematic ingenuity creates startling imagery, such as stewardesses on a lunar shuttle who, in their 'grip shoes', can walk upside down, or astronaut Poole jogging around the 'hamster wheel' of his rotating spacecraft. The effects won an Academy Award for Kubrick, who was also nominated as Best Director, Best Original Story and Screenplay (with Clarke), and the film for Best Art Direction/Set Decoration. It was under-appreciated at the Oscars, in a year where safe-bet musical *Oliver!* triumphed. *2001*'s pacing and visual beauty are arthouse, even if the settings are otherworldly and futuristic. This is further stressed in the juxtaposition of futuristic technology and classical music. Kubrick used the waltzing 'The Blue Danube' by Johann Strauss (conducted by Herbert von Karajan and performed by the Berlin Philharmonic Orchestra), *Atmosphères*, *Lux Aeterna* and *Requiem* by György Ligeti, and music from Armenian composer Aram

Khachaturian's ballet suite *Gayaneh* (performed by the Leningrad Philharmonic Orchestra). Most memorable is Kubrick's deployment of *Thus Spake Zarathustra* by Richard Strauss, the build-up of brass and timpani reaching a triumphant euphoria in a musical 'eureka moment'. This piece accompanies the celebrated shot when an ape, having discovered the use of primitive tools, throws a bone into the air. Kubrick cuts from prehistory to future history in an instant, as the bone becomes a spacecraft. The brilliant planetary spacescapes and rotating space stations are choreographed by Kubrick to the melodious music, or else the distressed, sorrowful chorus of Ligeti's shrill *Lux Aeterna* and *Requiem*, the ominous leitmotif to the black slab monolith.

The film is open to many interpretations and there have been many theories and explanations. The monolith at the 'Dawn of Man' could be the equivalent of the Tree of Knowledge in the Garden of Eden, which leads Eve and Adam to self-awareness, knowledge and evolution. The film's third and final act, 'Jupiter and beyond the Infinite', is the narrative's most discussed and confounding. As Bowman approaches Jupiter in a pod, he sees a larger, free-drifting monolith. The pod is sucked into a 'star gate', a vertical then horizontal corridor of speeding coloured lights, a vortex of fantastical visual experiences that are the antithesis of the science-based images that have preceded it. In the novel (but not in the film), Bowman observes, 'My God, it's full of stars.' Bowman witnesses milky plasma, starbursts, swirling fractals, whizzing, rippling colour fields, and he speeds over multi-hued, hallucinogenic landscapes – location shots for this were lensed on the Isle of Harris (South Harris), Outer Hebrides, Scotland, and Monument Valley (including the Totem Pole aiguilles) in Utah. This head rush is accompanied by Ligeti's dissonant chorus and feedback. For the film's mind-blowing finale, Bowman finds himself in a hotel room with the monolith, sees himself accelerated into old age and then finally returns to youth (the 'Dawn of Man' again) as a baby, the 'star child', in an aura bubble, looking down in awe on the Moon and Earth. *Zarathustra* swells once more, the musical 'answer' to what remains a cinematic enigma. Is the star child a new phase of human evolution? Or are we seeing the interior of a lab – the equivalent of a guinea pig in a cage – with the monolith collecting specimens so extraterrestrials can study us?

2001 was released in April 1968 in the US, and in May 1968 in the UK, rated U. It was a tremendous success both with audiences and most critics. The dazzling widescreen images heralded a new kind of screen sci-fi epic. It took $24 million on its initial US release and became a popular 'midnight movie' with the druggy counterculture, with the star-gate sequence (also dubbed the 'cosmic ride') a popular visual experience for those with expanded minds. Kubrick cut *2001* by 17 minutes after the premiere, from 160 minutes to the 143-minute version now widely available. This running time includes a dissonant, humming Overture introduction, set against the dark abyss of space, an Intermission (featuring a distant engine roar and feedback) and the full play-out Exit Music. Never has the Overture and Intermission score been so effective and essential to a 'film experience'. Clarke's novelisation was published in July 1968. It literalises and clarifies many of the more obscure, ambiguous plot points. He published three further books, *2010: Odyssey Two* (in 1982), *2061: Odyssey Three* (1987) and *3001: The Final Odyssey* (1997).

In 1984, Peter Hyams directed, produced and adapted *2010*, which was subtitled *The Year We Make Contact*. Heywood Floyd (Roy Scheider) has been disgraced following the failure of the *Discovery I* mission and nine years later works as a teacher. He joins a joint Russian–American mission on the Russian craft *Leonov*, to find out what happened to *Discovery*. The US part of the team is Floyd, Walter Curnow (John Lithgow), who designed *Discovery I* and Dr R. Chandra (Bob Balaban), HAL's designer. The Russian contingent includes Captain Tanya Kirbuk (Helen Mirren), Dimitri Moisevitch (Dana Elcar) and Maxim Brajlovsky (Elya Baskin). Investigating Jupiter's moons, Europa and Io, the *Leonov* finds the *Discovery* drifting in a decaying orbit. Chandra reboots HAL, but they receive a message from Bowman, warning them to leave the area as 'something wonderful is going to happen'. There are also unexplained occurrences back on Earth – Bowman appears on his wife's TV screen, and his mother, who is in a coma, sits up in bed. The mission is put under strain by diplomatic unrest on Earth, where Russo-US tensions in Central America lead to war. Eventually *Discovery* is used as a booster rocket to launch *Leonov* towards Earth, but HAL realises it is to be sacrificed and Chandra must lie to him to save the mission. Meanwhile, millions of rapidly multiplying monoliths consume Jupiter, and a massive explosion creates a 'wonderful happening', a new star that becomes a powerful second sun for Earth. Dullea reprised his role as Dave Bowman. The film replays when Bowman ages drastically and also recreates some of the *Discovery*'s key sets, including HAL's red-bathed Logic Memory Centre. HAL was again voiced by Douglas Rain, and his reboot resurrection is an edgy scene. The scientists worry if the murderous computer is 'homicidal, suicidal, neurotic, psychotic, or just plain broken'. A *Time* magazine cover depicts Clarke and Kubrick as the US and Russian presidents. *2010* literalised Kubrick and Clarke's cerebral sci-fi, and its message of peace between squabbling nations is driven home in the 'we must all get along together' finale. Floyd's introductory scene was filmed at the Very Large Array (VLA), the distinctive astronomy observatory made up of rows of dished radio telescopes on the Plains of San Agustin, near Socorro, New Mexico, which also appears in *Contact*, *Independence Day* and *Terminator: Salvation*. Though David Shire composed the score, *Lux Aeterna* and *Thus Spake Zarathustra* (as *Also Sprach Zarathustra*, the original German title) also reappear. *2010* is a much more conventional sci-fi movie, which in trying to explain what happened to Bowman dispels his disappearance's mystique.

Special-effects expert Douglas Trumbull made his directorial debut with *Silent Running* (1972). On the American Airlines space freighter *Valley Forge*, Freeman Lowell (Bruce Dern) lovingly tends the natural environment of trees, grass, pools and vegetation that's home to woodland animals and birds, flourishing in an artificial dome that drifts through deep space. Earth has been laid waste and Lowell hopes that one day his plants will refoliate the planet and that he will be selected to oversee the operation. When his superiors decide to terminate the cultivation programme, distraught Lowell protects 'his forest'. As other domes on other freighters are destroyed with nuclear detonators, Lowell kills his three co-workers, Marty Barker (Ron Rifkin), Andy Wolf (Jesse Vint) and John Keenan (Cliff Potts). Claiming it has been damaged by an explosion, he hijacks the craft and sets a course for Saturn. Lowell reprograms the ship's three maintenance drone robots to be his helpers – he teaches them to be mechanical park keepers, tending his 'Garden of Eden' paradise, the last remaining such oasis in space. Drone number 3 is lost as *Valley Forge* makes a turbulent passage through Saturn's rings, and Lowell christens the two remaining robots Huey and Dewey. He teaches them how to play poker, and they become his companions, but on the dark side of Saturn, the forest begins to die for lack of sunlight, and contact is unexpectedly re-established between *Valley Forge* and its command craft, *Berkshire*, which has launched a rescue mission. Trumbull's looming spacecraft exteriors are equal to his work on *2001*, and one of the college students he hired was John Dykstra. Spacecraft interiors were filmed inside the aircraft carrier USS *Valley Forge*. Peter Schickele provided the imaginative, understated score, which included two folk songs, 'Silent Running' and 'Rejoice in the Sun', performed by Joan Baez. Without sunlight, Lowell rigs up artificial lighting which ensures the plants will begin to grow. But with the relief party en route, Lowell reasons: 'Things just haven't worked out for me', the self-apologetic excuse for so many suicides. He sets the nuclear detonators and blows up himself, Huey and *Valley Forge*, but not before he has launched Dewey and the dome into space: 'Take good care of the forest, Dewey.' The poignant final image is of a little bubble of life, with Dewey and his watering can drifting into space.

The protagonists of *The Doomsday Machine* (1972; *Armageddon 1975* or *Escape from Planet Earth*) flee Earth for deep space in search of another planet to colonise. The machine of the title is a deadly device that resembles a fishbowl in a red cage, to which 'only Chairman Mao has the key'. It's going to destroy the world in less than 72 hours, so project Astra, a mission to Venus, sets off with a mixed-sex crew played by Ruta Lee, Lorri Scott, Mala Powers, Scott 'Denny' Miller, Bobby Van and Grant Williams, who will create a new nation in 'a rerun of Adam and Eve'. 'Those chopstick jockeys couldn't come up with a planet buster, could they?' one of the astronauts subtly wonders, but Earth is indeed destroyed by the nuclear chain reaction (which resembles a Christmas light shorting out). Backed by a mellow jazz score, the romancin' commences and the spacecraft soon resembles *The Love Boat*. The interiors are bathed in a colourful rainbow lighting scheme and the seating is of the comfy, reclining Parker Knoll variety. This resembles an outmoded 1950s sci-fi film, with 1960s trappings, made in the 1970s. It was shot mostly in 1967, but the makers ran out of money and it was finally completed in 1972, with space special-effects shots lifted from *Gorath* (1962).

Killing machine HAL had equally inhuman, conscienceless cousins, as in Stanley Donen's UK sci-fi movie *Saturn 3* (1980), set in an experimental synthetic food-research station on Titan, Saturn's third moon. Major Adam (Kirk Douglas) and his beautiful assistant-cum-playmate Alex (Farrah Fawcett) enjoy a paradisiacal idyll of research and recreation. But during an eclipse, their 'Garden of Eden' is invaded by an interloper from Earth, Captain Benson (Harvey Keitel), who has been sent to speed up their research, as Earth is starving. Benson has designs on Alex ('You have a great body, may I use it?') and assembles an eight-foot-tall headless robot, Hector, 'the first of the demigod series', to help him get rid of the only obstacle to his 'Eve': Adam. Unstable Benson is a psycho killer and when he inputs his cerebral contents into Hector's huge brain (which is part of its torso) the robot becomes psychotic and runs amok. This results in a familiar 'when technology goes bad' scenario, as Adam and Alex flee Hector through the endless corridors of Saturn 3. *Saturn 3* features mediocre acting and heavy-handed attempts at religious and mythological allegory. Keitel is dubbed by someone else in the English-language print. The film does boast impressive production designs at Shepperton Studio Centre in Middlesex, and the exterior moon shots, starfields, planets and spacecraft are well done. Other bad computers include the rapacious machine in Donald Cammell's *Demon Seed* (1973) and the destructive supercomputer in charge of defence systems in Joseph Sargent's *Colossus: The Forbin Project* (1969).

A would-be sci-fi epic, Gary Nelson's *The Black Hole* (1979) was Disney's first PG-rated movie. The spaceship *Palomino* is searching for life in outer space. In the vicinity of a giant black hole, the most destructive force in the universe, it encounters the long-lost spacecraft *Cygnus*. On board is scientist Dr Hans Reinhardt (Maximilian Schell), a wild, bearded genius teetering on the edge of sanity, who has almost attained 'ultimate knowledge'. In his 20 years alone in space he has created a part-human, part-robot humanoid staff using the crew of the *Cygnus*. He has also created a monstrous robot named Maximilian (which appears to be half robot, half Swiss Army knife) and an army of Stormtroopers, led by Darth Vader-like Captain S.T.A.R. (Tommy McLoughlin). Reinhardt plans to travel beyond the 'event horizon' and explore the black hole. The *Palomino* is destroyed and its crew manage to flee the *Cygnus* in a probe as Reinhardt and his crazy dreams are dragged into the black hole and destruction. The talky plot is as plodding as John Barry's score, which features rolling orchestral themes more appropriate for *Spartacus* or long biblical desert treks. The crew of the *Palomino* includes Robert Forster, Anthony Perkins, Ernest Borgnine, Joseph Bottoms and Yvette Mimieux. The film also features two cute, resourceful robots of the Dusty Bin variety: VINCENT LF396 (voiced by Roddy McDowall) and a battered earlier version of the same model, a Mk 28 (voiced by Slim Pickens). The black hole itself, a swirling celestial whirlpool, is the film's best aspect, and there's an exciting scene where huge, rolling meteorites destroy the *Cygnus*. When the probe is sucked into the black hole, the trippy special effects reveal that the experience is akin to being trapped in the title sequence of a 1960s sci-fi TV series. The ending, clutching in vain for *2001* profundity, has the probe emerge safely from the other side and travel towards a new planet.

Other science fiction missions launched their intrepid heroes towards the Sun. The US–Japanese co-production *Solar Crisis* (1990) blended Earthbound plots (in Skytown and the desert) and outer space, as the *Helios* seeks to deliver its payload of five tons of antimatter to destroy a solar flare on the Sun that will cremate the Earth. Three generations of the Kelso family contribute to the drama. Charlton Heston played Admiral Skeet Kelso, who oversees the operation (called the Ra Mission), Tim Matheson was his son Steve, aboard the *Helios*, and Corin Nemec was Steve's son Mike, a pilot who crash-lands in the desert, where he encounters Jack Palance, who acts everyone off the screen as crazy desert hermit Colonel Travis. The desert scenes resemble *Mad Max 2*, while aboard the *Helios* scientist Alex (Annabel Schofield) attempts to sabotage the mission at the bidding of industrialist Teague (Peter Boyle), the head of IXL Corps. Teague has invested in seeds, water and other vital commodities, and is 'stockpiled up to his ass' in preparation for Earth's demise. Alex pilots the probe payload into the sun, which triggers a psychedelic star-gate sequence. The special effects are good, the story pacy and the staging never less than interesting. Reshoots after the film fared badly in Japan meant that director Richard C. Sarafian signed himself with that common indicator of artistic dissatisfaction, 'Alan Smithee'.

A reversal of this premise appeared in *Sunshine* (2008), from the director–writer team of Danny Boyle and Alex Garland. A mission through the Dead Zone by *Icarus II* will deliver an explosive payload to reignite the dying sun, to save Earth from a solar winter. The original mission, *Icarus I*, was lost seven years previously. *Sunshine* turns into one of those 'everything goes wrong' movies, where a slight detour off-mission has serious repercussions. The crew investigate a distress beacon from *Icarus I*. When the life-giving plants in the second ship's oxygen garden are destroyed, it becomes touch and go whether they will be able to carry out their mission, as their air supply dwindles and so do the crew, due to accidents and unexplained phenomena. The crew includes Cillian Murphy, Chris Evans, Rose Byrne, Michelle Yeoh, Hiroyuki Sanada, Cliff Curtis, Troy Garity and Benedict Wong, with Mark Strong as Pinbacker, the badly burnt captain of *Icarus I*. Murphy's good as physicist Robert Capa, but the film, in striving for artiness, is caught between two styles, as the narrative develops the less interesting 'monster on the loose' subplot, with Pinbacker bloodily attempting to sabotage their mission. The spacey score by John Murphy and Underworld is ideal, and Boyle makes great use of the smoky ballad 'Avenue of Hope' by I Am Kloot under the end titles.

At the opposite end of the intellectual spectrum to *2001* is Brian De Palma's prosaic *Mission to Mars* (2000), which details a rescue mission dispatched from the World Space Station to a NASA space station at Cydonia on Mars. The Mars recovery-mission crew includes Gary Sinise, Tim Robbins, Connie Nielsen and Jerry O'Connell. On the red-desert planet, they find half-mad Luke Graham (Don Cheadle), a sort of celestial Ben Gunn, the lone survivor of the Mars team. His fellow astronauts were killed during a ferocious dust storm. The exploratory party has discovered water and have cultivated plants. In the desert the rescuers find a huge monolith of an ancient face which transmits 3-D sound waves that are revealed to be DNA patterns. De Palma's film is visually beautiful and has some lovely musical themes from Ennio Morricone. The rescue ship's slow, revolving orbit, like a hamster wheel, recalls *2001* and there's a marvellous moment when Woody and Terri cut some non-gravitational rug to Van Halen's 'Dance the Night Away'. The film's realistic depiction of space travel is offset by the extraordinary events on Mars. The finale implodes under its own pretension, as it is revealed that life on Earth is derived from Mars. Morricone's scores have often lifted or even saved mediocre outings, but even Ennio can't work his magic here.

Anthony Hoffman's *Red Planet* (2000), a US–Australian co-production, was another doomed mission to Mars, with Val Kilmer, Terence Stamp and Tom Sizemore among a team undertaking the first manned mission to the planet. By 2057, our Earth is dying and Mars is an option for colonisation. The expedition becomes stranded on Mars, with only Commander Kate Bowman (Carrie-Anne Moss) remaining on the orbiting *Mars-1* craft. The planet's HAB artificial habitat is wrecked and the astronauts have to engineer their escape in Russian probe *Cosmos*. The astronauts discover algae growing on the planet, which enables the air to contain breathable oxygen, and tiny predator bugs feast on the algae and devour interlopers. The astronauts are also stalked across the wastes by their own surface navigator robot, AMEE, which resembles a canine Terminator. This standard space opera is essentially an update of 1950s deep-space explorations such as *Conquest of Space*, with souped-up special effects.

But what about when science fiction becomes fact? There have been many films detailing exploratory missions to the Red Planet, but on 4 November 2011, a 520-day simulated Mars mission – Mars-500 – was completed in a mocked-up spacecraft in a Moscow warehouse. The six-man crew of three Russians, a Frenchman, a Chinese and an Italian–Columbian, set off on their 'journey' on 3 June 2010. The project even included simulated space walks and Mars landings. It was intended to discover the psychological effects of extended seclusion on the human mind and body. There was no resupply of the crew, who carried everything they needed for the trip, and they were in complete isolation from physical contact with the outside world. There was even a 20-minute delay in communications, to recreate the sense of distance properly. The project was filmed by 30 cameras. On their return, the smiling dazed 'astronauts' were quarantined, as they were susceptible to germs and infection. Each volunteer received $100,000 for taking part in the 17-month experiment. With the technology in place, all findings from the experiment will count towards launching an actual mission to Mars, perhaps as early as 2025.

10

'I LOVE ALL THE LOVE IN YOU'

BARBARELLA (1968)

Director: Roger Vadim
Story: Jean-Claude Forest
Screenplay: Terry Southern, Roger Vadim, Claude Brulé, Vittorio Bonicelli, Clement Biddle Wood, Brian Degas, Tudor Gates and Jean-Claude Forest
Director of Photography: Claude Renoir
Music: Bob Crewe, Charles Fox and The Glitterhouse
Panavision/Technicolor
A Marianne (France)/Dino De Laurentiis Cinematografica (Italy) Production
Released by Paramount Pictures
94 minutes

Jane Fonda (Barbarella), John Phillip Law (Pygar), David Hemmings (Dildano), Anita Pallenberg (The Black Queen, aka The Great Tyrant), Milo O'Shea (Concierge, alias Dr Durand-Durand), Marcel Marceau (Professor Ping), Ugo Tognazzi (Mark Hand, 'the Catchman'), Claude Dauphin (President of the Republic of Earth), Véronique Vendell (Captain Moon), Serge Marquand (Captain Sun), Catherine and Maria Therese Chevallier (Stomoxys and Glossina), Giancarlo Cobelli (Jean-Paul), Talitha Pol (bong-smoking girl), Fabienne Fabre (the woman tree), Fred Robsahm (Dildano's assistant), Nino Musco (Black Guard general), Umberto Di Grazia and Angelo Susani (brigands who kidnap Barbarella)

❊ ❊ ❊

While US, UK and Japanese production dominated 1950s sci-fi, by the 1960s Continental filmmakers – particularly in Italy and France – made their mark on the genre with imaginative, transgressive sci-fi fantasises and pastiches, wreathed in colour, shadow and space fog. An early Italian–French sci-fi movie was Paolo Heusch's *The Day the Sky Exploded* (1958), which fired intrepid astronaut John McLaren (Paul Hubschmid) into space in an atomic-powered rocket. When he is forced to bail out, McLaren is unable to disconnect its atomic motor. The atomic missile detonates in

The Wild, Wild Planet:
Lisa Gastoni takes
centre stage in MGM's
1967 US poster for
Antonio Margheriti's *I
criminali della galassia*.

the Delta Zone, releasing a shower of asteroids, which bond together into a single mass towards Earth. Animals evacuate the coastal regions, tidal waves sweep in and storms rage, while the Earth heats up, causing fires and panic. The UN fires dozens of atomic missiles to destroy the threat. Most of the story's action takes place at the Cape Shark space base in Australia, and despite its interesting monochrome effects photography by Mario Bava and Carlo Rustichelli's score it plainly imitates low-grade US sci-fi.

Italian Antonio Margheriti worked in many genres, but it is his bold science-fiction features for which he is best remembered. The title of Margheriti's *Assignment: Outer Space* (1960; *Space Men*) clued audiences in that the story followed Ray Peterson (Rik Van Nutter), news reporter for the *New York Interplanetary News*, on a ten-day mission on spacecraft Bravo Zulu 88 to check infra-radiation flux on Galaxy M-12. The mission is diverted when drifting spacecraft Alpha Two doesn't respond to radio contact and BZ 88 encounters a stricken spaceship, which collides with Phobos, one of Mars's satellites. On Alpha Two, the photonic generators have created a high-temperature force field equal to the Sun, which will transform Earth into 'a mass of boiling mud'. BZ 88 lands at a space base on Venus, but atomic missiles launched at Alpha Two disintegrate harmlessly. The astronauts' only chance is a narrow channel in Alpha Two's force field. Al (Archie Savage) flies an atomic rocket at Alpha Two, but perishes, and finally Peterson, piloting a tiny space taxi, manages to navigate the channel, board the errant ship, disconnect the electronic brain and turn off the photonic generator. Margheriti's film is the first of several Technicolor Italian space movies that have since developed a cult following. The special effects are patchy, but the filmmaker's enthusiasm comes over loud and clear.

Margheriti followed this with *Battle of the Worlds* (1961) and the *Gamma I* series, a quartet of films featuring the space station of the title. *War of the Planets* (1965; *The Deadly Diaphanoids*) was an *Invasion of the Body Snatchers*-style scenario, with groovy New Year's Eve celebrations being interrupted by a spate of possessions. The effective, eerie opening features Captain Dubois (Michel Lemoine) being overtaken by the Diaphanoids, green glowing-light creatures and swirling space mists, and the ending has the heroes escaping from the body snatchers' clutches on Mars. Tony Russel played Commander Mike Halstead, Lisa Gastoni was Lieutenant Connie Gomez, Franco Nero was Jake Jackovich and Umberto Raho was General Paul Maitland. In a stroke of genius, the clouds of mist that are so prevalent in Italian sci-fi are deployed as the aliens themselves.

The sequel, *The Wild, Wild Planet* (1965), was even better, with Mike (Russel) and Connie (Gastoni) mixed up with Professor Nurmi (Massimo Serato), who carries out experiments on kidnapped humans on planet Delphos. Nurmi aims to create a race of perfect beings and to fuse his body with Connie's. The film was originally titled *I criminali della galassia* (*The Galaxy Criminals*) in Italy, and the supporting cast, carried over from *War of the Planets*, includes Nero, Raho, Enzo Fiermonte, Carlo Giustini, Franco Ressel and Goffredo Unger. Angelo Lavagnino composed the lush space symphonies, supplemented by ominous horror stylings. This spaced-out movie – showcasing four-armed space mutants with long macs and shades, inflatable zombie women, grooving space discos, domed space cars and flame-thrower laser guns – ends with Nurmi's space station being flooded with a destructive tidal wave of blood plasma. This is the best Italian sci-fi movie and a gloriously entertaining cult movie in its own right, as Margheriti's imagination-on-a-budget runs riot. Nurmi's oddball jobbery on Delphos considerably jiffs up proceedings. The kidnap victims on Earth are miniaturised and shipped off in packing cases – and don't forget, forewarned is four-armed. The *Gamma I* movies were completed by *War between the Planets* (1966; *Planet on the Prowl*), with Commander Rod Jackson (Giacomo Rossi-Stuart) tackling a rogue planet on a collision course with Earth (a replay of Margheriti's own *Battle of the Worlds*), while *The Snow Devils* (1967;

Space Devils) pitted Jackson against seven-foot-tall space yetis (resembling hairy blue Vikings) that have ensconced themselves in the Himalayas and plan to take over Earth by flooding the world and then freezing it, creating another Ice Age.

In Mario Bava's body-snatching *Planet of the Vampires* (1965; *The Demon Planet*), the *Argos* and the *Galliot* approach planet Aura, a world wreathed in fog, in answer to a strange signal. Dragged down by the gravitational pull, the *Argos*'s crew fight among themselves and only Captain Mark Markary (Barry Sullivan) prevents them killing each other. The crew discover the *Galliot* nearby, its astronauts dead. They bury the corpses, but later the zombie crew rise again and steal the *Argos*'s meteor rejecter, without which the *Argos* cannot leave Aura. The Aureans – possessive parasitic spirits – have occupied the dead crewmen's bodies and plan to hitch a lift on the *Argos* to another planet and safety: their sun is dying and soon their planet will too. For his only foray into astral sci-fi, Bava, a director of the macabre, is at home in this tale of space horror. *Planet* was an Italian–Spanish–US co-production, partly financed by AIP. Bava shot on sets at Cinecittà Studios, Rome. With its jagged rock formations, rocky pinnacles and outcrops, lava beds in the bubbling space marsh, whooshing, darting coloured lights, bubbling fog, moaning voices and howling winds, *Planet of the Vampires* is highly atmospheric. Carlo Rambaldi worked uncredited as the model maker, and the effects are good, from the horseshoe-shaped spacecraft *Argos* and *Galliot* to the hulking, rusting spacecraft crewed by the skeletal remains of giant creatures that had been lured to Aura years before (a setting that was recreated in *Alien*). Gino Marinuzzi's atmospheric score was replaced in some English-language prints by abrasive electronics from Kendall Schmidt. Having retrieved the rejecter and blown up the *Galliot* and its zombie crew with plutonium, Wes (Angel Aranda), Sanya (Norma Bengell) and Mark take flight on the *Argos*. But Wes's cohorts are zombies, so he destroys the rejecter, forcing them to divert to 'a puny civilisation', Earth. Sanya worries how they will be accepted. 'I hope well,' says Mark, 'for them.'

Pietro Francisci tried his hand at sci-fi with *2+5: Missione Hydra* (1965; *Star Pilot*). An alien rocket crash-lands in Sardinia and research scientists Professor Solmi (Roland Lesaffre), Dr Paolo Bardi (Anthony Freeman) and the professor's daughter Luisa (Leontine May) investigate. In an underground cavern, they find the craft crewed by aliens who want to return to their home in the constellation Hydra. They kidnap the scientists, plus two nosy Chinese agents, and head for Hydra. Leonora Ruffo played flame-haired, sexily attired Hydran Kaena, while Alfio Caltabiano and Kirk Morris played her beefy, black-clad henchmen Arti and Belsi. Gordon Mitchell made a very brief cameo as Murdu, the commanding officer at Hydra Central. May wore some skimpy outfits (including a fluffy bikini and body-stocking combo), Nico Fidenco provided the score and the film was largely shot at Cinecittà. The space adventurers land on a planet and are attacked by apes, and in the downbeat ending Earth is destroyed by nuclear war. The ship eventually lands on Hydra, after Kaena has drugged everyone with gas (to the strains of Bach's *Toccata and Fugue in D Minor*). On an exotic coastline, with brightly coloured plants, palm trees

Barbarella: Jane Fonda stars as the five-star double-rated Astronominatrix, who travels on a secret mission into the Tau Ceti galaxy to locate renegade scientist Dr Durand-Durand and his Positronic Ray.

and a ruined overgrown city, a monolith message informs the travellers that following the threat of nuclear pollution and mutation from Earth, the Hydrans have departed to found a new, perfect civilisation elsewhere. The Italian version of the film closes with the travellers making contact with a group of survivors, a primitive race whose leader resembles a caveman, on the shoreline.

Mission Hydra was an odd mix of sci-fi and espionage, a formula that was repeated in Primo Zeglio's *Mission Stardust* (1968), which began as an outer-space mission to the Moon and was commanded by Major Perry Rhodan (Lang Jeffries) and Captain Bull (Luis Davila). The team encounter a spacecraft with aliens Thora (Essy Persson) and Kress (John Karlsen) on board. Kress is dying of leukaemia, so Rhodan agrees to take the alien to Mombasa, Kenya, to be treated by blood specialist Dr Haggard. Much of the action takes place in the East African desert and the aliens and astronauts are the targets of criminals (including Pinkas Braun and Gianni Rizzo) and the African Federation Army (commanded by John Bartha). Danish bombshell Persson makes an alluring alien and the story was based on the 'Perry Rhodan' novels. Though the score was by Antón García Abril, the film's best feature is its groovy title song, 'Seli', composed by Marcello Giombini, and sung by Edda Dell'Orso and the Cantori Moderni. In additional to conventional Italian sci-fi, Italian masked superhero or supervillain movies, some of which were based on *fumetti* comic strips (including *Superargo Against Diabolicus*, *The Fantastic Argoman*, *Satanik* and *Diabolik*), occasionally incorporated sci-fi trappings such as robot henchmen, futuristic gadgets, implausible weaponry and otherworldly settings and costumes.

Colourful, visually eye-popping Euro sci-fi reached its zenith in 1968 with Roger Vadim's *Barbarella* (1968), the ultimate 1960s space opera of pop-art psychedelics, free-love promiscuity and free-for-all politics – a film adaptation of a comic strip, with the accent on 'strip'. In the forty-first century Barbarella (a five-star, double-rated Astronominatrix) is sent by the president of Earth (Claude Dauphin) on a secret mission. She must travel to the Tau Ceti galaxy to locate 25-year-old scientist Dr Durand-Durand (pronounced in the English dubbing Duran Duran, and played by Milo O'Shea), who has disappeared while on a trip to the North Star. The doctor has invented the Positronic Ray, a deadly device which transports its victims to 'a fourth dimension, irretrievably'. During a magnetic hurricane, Barbarella's spaceship *Alpha 7* crash-lands on Lythion, planet 16 of the Tau Ceti system. In the iniquitous metropolis Sogo, the City of Night ruled by Black Queen known as the Great Tyrant, Barbarella discovers that Durand-Durand is the queen's concierge. A megalomaniac, he plots to usurp the throne, foment rebellion and become 'Master of the Universe'. During Durand-Durand's coronation, Sogo's rebels rise up, but the doctor uses the Positronic Ray to quell the insurrection. With help from Pygar (John Phillip Law) – a blind angel – and the Black Queen herself, Barbarella escapes the cataclysm.

Barbarella was shot on a $9 million budget at Rome's Dino De Laurentiis Studios. De Laurentiis co-produced the film with France's Marianne Productions. Jean-Claude Forest's erotic comic-book *Barbarella*, published in France in the early 1960s by Éditions

Le Terrain Vague, depicted the space-age sexual adventures of the heroine, whose physique was based on Brigitte Bardot. Vadim called the film 'a sexual *Alice in the Wonderland* of the future'. Actresses considered for the role included Virna Lisi and Raquel Welch, but Vadim cast his wife from 1965 to 1973, Jane Fonda, who via her films with Vadim became a sex symbol dubbed 'the American Bardot'. When Barbarella, with her mane of golden hair, is asked if she is representative of earthly womanhood, she answers with understatement, 'I'm about average.'

Vadim fielded a stellar international supporting cast for his interstellar protagonists. Angelic John Phillip Law modelled wings and a feathered loincloth as Pygar, the last of the winged 'ornithanthropes' (birdmen). Anita Pallenberg, playing the dagger-spinning sadist Black Queen, was dubbed in the English print by Joan Greenwood, who added purring menace to such lines as, 'Hello, my pretty-pretty.' Barbarella's allies include mad scientist Professor Ping (French mime Marcel Marceau) and hairy 'Catchman' Mark Hand (Ugo Tognazzi), who rounds up feral children in the icy Forests of Weir. David Hemmings played incompetent freedom fighter Dildano, who refers to Earth as 'Planet of the Revolutions', which in 1968 chimed with cinema audiences. His organisation's use of Anglesey village Llanfairpwllgwyngyllgogerychwyrndrobwyllllantysiliogogogoch as their secret password is surely the oddest in-joke in international sci-fi cinema. Nino Musco was the commander of the Black Queen's Black Guard, her 'Leather Men'. O'Shea's Durand-Durand has been aged 30 years by the Mathmos, a bubbling magma lake of liquid energy that thrives on evil (named after the British company that sold the lava lamp, which was invented in 1963).

The innuendo-laden script functions as the flimsiest narrative pretext to strip Fonda. During the title sequence, Barbarella performs a zero-gravity striptease – the 'weightless' effect was achieved by shooting Fonda writhing on a sheet of transparent Plexiglas above a picture of the spacecraft's interior. The titles were designed by Maurice Binder and strategically placed lettering spells out the film's personnel and unsuccessfully attempts to preserve Fonda's modesty. On her travels Barbarella encounters and survives all manner of futuristic mayhem, including feral children in the wreck of *Alpha 1* (Durand-Durand's spacecraft). As blue-hued rabbits hop about, twins Stomoxys and Glossina and their little friends tie up Barbarella and unleash their clockwork dolls with chomping metal teeth. Barbarella permissively sleeps with everyone who saves her from jeopardy, including Pygar ('It was just heavenly') and Mark Hand. The film's most memorable love scene involves the 'exultation transference pellet'. In this futuristic sex act, participants sit opposite one other and place the palms of their hands together for a minute 'or until full rapport is achieved'. Later Durand-Durand restrains Barbarella in a pipe-organ-like execution device, the Excess Machine, in which she is to die of pleasure, but she burns the machine out ('It couldn't keep up with you'). 'This is really much too poetic a way to die,' deadpans Fonda in another scene, when she's locked in a giant birdcage and assaulted by dozens of pecking budgies.

Barbarella really scores in its production design and costumes. This was something of a departure for Fonda, as she threw caution, and her modesty, to the wind for the sexy title role. Fonda has a costume change every ten minutes, due to her outfits being shredded or removed in the previous scene. Her skimpy, revealing outfits incorporate leotards, bodices, tights, thongs, knee-high boots and armoured brassieres. Fonda's delivery of the trashy script and her formidable beauty holds the film together. Claude Renoir's 2.35:1 Panavision cinematography looks better than ever on DVD. The film's lava-lamp visuals create bubbling, throbbing explosions of colour, accentuating the film's sensual mood and comic-strip origins. Production designer Mario Garbuglia created the labyrinth of the City of Night, where all that is not evil has been exiled. It is populated by ghostly lost souls, who live on orchids and are imprisoned in the cobwebby, misty, Bavaesque stone maze. Other vivid settings include the ice lake in the Forest of Weir, the suicide Chamber of Ultimate Solution, the queen's Chamber of Dreams and the furry interior of Barbarella's spaceship, which features the 1884 Impressionist painting *A Sunday Afternoon on the Island of La Grande Jatte* by Georges Seurat. The city of Sogo (a contraction of Sodom and Gomorrah) is a phantasmagorical nightmare of glass, girders and tubes populated by the wasted and the wicked – a trashy collision of high fashion and low art, fuelled by sex and drugs. In such a den of iniquity, pure angel Pygar is crucified by the Black Queen, giving Fonda (armed with a space Derringer) the excuse to threaten Pallenberg with the classic line: 'De-crucify the angel… or I'll melt your face.'

Barbarella's score features lively compositions combining a brassy big-band sound with twee pop, spacey atmospherics and spaced-out psychedelia. The score was performed by The Bob Crew Generation and conducted by Charles Fox. The soundtrack also features four songs written by Crewe and Fox, performed by psychedelic outfit The Glitterhouse. 'Barbarella' is an upbeat big band lounge number, with 'ba-ba-ba' backing singers, mambo percussion and brass: 'Barbarella, psychadella, there's a kind of cockleshell about you. Dazzle me with rainbow colour, fade away the duller shade of living.' 'Love, Love, Love Drags Me Down' is a bluesy fairground stomp, 'I Love All the Love in You' (also called 'Love Theme from *Barbarella*') is a breathy number, and 'An Angel Is Love' plays over the end credits as Pygar flaps to safety, carrying Barbarella and the Black Queen.

Charles Bluhdorn of Paramount's parent company Gulf and Western didn't want the studio to release *Barbarella*, but was pleasantly surprised by the film's success in October 1968, where it took $5.5 million. Paramount's suggestive trailer announced: 'Meet the most beautiful creature of the future' and 'We wish to thank the following planets making this picture possible: Lythion, Jupiter, Venus, Saturn, Earth and many special guest stars!' The film was later re-released as *Barbarella: Queen of the Galaxy*. It was X-rated on its release in the UK in 1968 and has since been re-rated 15. Some UK prints are abridged and blur the lettering in the title sequence, to obscure Fonda's nudity. There are also two different end-title sequences: in one version the end credits recede into the distance, in another the multicoloured titles glide towards the foreground. The film has since spawned a *Barbarella* musical written by Dave Stewart, and one line from the film gave New Romantic band Duran Duran their name and the title of their first single. Barbarella asks Ping if he has heard of the doctor: 'Durand-Durand?' answers Ping. 'From the planet Earth?' Duran Duran also released the single 'Electric Barbarella' in 1997, in homage to the film's influence on their career. Like other European space oddities of the 1960s, *Barbarella* has gathered a considerable retro cult following. It's a surreal extravagance in a galaxy far, far away, where all you really need is love.

Like *Barbarella*, Mario Bava's *Diabolik* (1968; *Danger: Diabolik*) was bankrolled by Marianne Production and De Laurentiis, shot at Dinocittà and based on comic strips. With John Phillip Law cast as the futuristic superthief, and with Bava's magnificent visuals, it has worn much better than *Barbarella*. Luigi Cozzi shot *Starcrash* (1978; *Female Space Invaders*) at Cinecittà, which he envisioned as 'Sinbad Goes to Space'. He cast beautiful British 'Hammer glamour girl' Caroline Munro as Stella Star, a sexy intergalactic heroine in the Barbarella mould. The scantily clad smuggler is sent by the Star Emperor (Christopher Plummer) to locate three missing imperial launches, one of which contains his only son, Simon (David Hasselhoff). Stella must also find the Doom Machine, a weapon of mass destruction created by Count Zartharn (Joe Spinell). *Starcrash* is essentially *Barbarella and the Argonauts*, with Stella and her cohorts – Akton (Marjoe Gortner) and automaton Elle (Judd Hamilton) – facing assorted robots, cavemen, Amazons and traitorous baddies, before launching Starcrash ('fourth-dimensional attack'), where Stella and Elle pilot the Emperor's Floating City into Zartharn's spaceship. Elle's drawling American accent (voiced by Hamilton Camp) wears on the nerves, and in a replay of *Barbarella* Elle frees Stella by threatening the Amazonian Queen Corelia (Nadia Cassini): 'Release her, or I'll blast your queen!' Robert Tessier played green-faced imperial policeman Thor, and John Barry's lush score anticipates *Moonraker*. *Starcrash* was a lost opportunity that can't decide if it's serious science fiction or a spoofy send-up. It certainly doesn't measure up to its promotional photographs, nor does it deliver on the promise of its posters. Less *Starcrash*, more car crash.

Due to the film's success in the US, distributors AIP wanted Cozzi to direct Munro in a sequel, *Star Riders*, with Klaus Kinski as the villain Baron Waalk, but the deal fell through. A gaudily awful sequel did surface in Bitto Albertini's *Escape from Galaxy 3* (1981; *Starcrash II*), with Cheryl Buchanan as Belle Starr. Don Powell played villain Oraclon and also composed the disco soundtrack. Special-effects shots from *Starcrash* reappear as Belle lands on planet Earth, where following a nuclear war the population has reverted to life which looks suspiciously like an early 1960s Lazio-shot Italian 'sword and sandal' epic. Dancers prance about like Pan's People and Stella wears revealingly slashed outfits and strategically positioned stars. Oraclon instructs his henchman to deploy the 'megametric teleprobe' to scan the eastern galaxy 'including the equidistant conic tangents'. The script is attributed to the untraceably pseudonymous 'John Thomas'.

Like *Barbarella*, David Hogan's pulpy *Barb Wire* (1995) opens with its heroine performing a striptease under the credits. Here Barb (former *Baywatch* star Pamela Anderson Lee) struts her stuff to 'Word Up' by Gun. With buxom bounty hunter Barb packed into revealing leather fetish gear, it is easy to deduce the film's cult popularity as a guilty pleasure, as *Barb Wire* exists solely to display its star's figure. She tracks down bail jumpers and hisses, 'Don't call me babe.' Based on the Dark Horse comic of the same name, *Barb Wire* depicted a stark, Gothic future world of 2017 during the Second American Civil War. The Congressional Directorate have overthrown democracy and freedom fighters are society's last hope. In this lawless city seemingly inhabited exclusively by cops, hookers and bikers, multitasking Barb also moonlights as hooker 'Olivia Lewis', is a gun for hire who's sympathetic to the resistance, and is the owner of rock nightclub 'Hammerhead', where she lives with her guard dog Camille and her bald manservant Curly (Udo Kier). The plot details the search, by both the resistance and the authorities, for a set of contact lenses that can fool the city's retinal scanners. The ending – as Barb helps her one-time lover Axel (Temuera Morrison) and his wife Cora D. (Victoria Rowell) escape to Canada on a UN plane – is a bizarre replay of *Casablanca*.

A strong, sexy female lead was the selling point of Karyn Kusama's *Æon Flux* (2005), with Charlize Theron as the eponymous heroine. In 2011 a virus has killed 99 per cent of the world's population. Scientist Trevor Goodchild invents a cure and the Goodchild dynasty rules the 5 million survivors in the walled city of Bregna. In 2415, rebels strive to overthrow the regime in this seemingly utopian city, which is actually oppressed by the government. Rebel Æon Flux is assigned to sabotage the central surveillance facility and to assassinate Chairman Goodchild (Marton Csokas). The cast included Jonny Lee Miller, Frances McDormand, Pete Postlethwaite (wearing a costume that resembles a cardboard toilet roll tube) and Sophie Okonedo as Æon's accomplice Sithandra, who through 'modification' has had her feet replaced with hands, which aids her acrobatics. Dressed in figure-hugging outfits, lithe, elastic assassin Æon was played by Theron, amid bold, futuristic designs, as equal parts *La Femme Nikita* and *Diabolik*.

In the wake of *Star Wars*' success in the late 1970s, Italo-sci-fi was resurrected when Alfonso Brescia directed a series of hilariously low-budget movies under the pseudonym 'Al Bradly'. Throughout the series, the acting was variable, but the inept special effects always took centre stage. *Cosmos: War of the Planets* (1977) was a remake of *Planet of the Vampires*, with spacecraft MK-31 lured to a planet populated by green goblin creatures ruled by supercomputer The Immortal Monster. John Richardson and Yanti Somer starred as the heroic astronauts and Aldo Canti played lead goblin, Etor, while the rest of the cast cower behind aliases including West Buchanan, Percy Hogan, Romeo Constantin and Max Bonus. Look out for the spaceship's console panel, which includes such controls as 'Time', 'Alarm', 'Stop Watch' and 'Lap'. In *The War of the Robots* (1978), scientist Professor Carr (Jacques Herlin) and his assistant Lois (Malisa Longo) are kidnapped by golden androids, the 'Men of the World of Anthor', who look like ABBA. Captain John Boyd

(Antonio Sabàto) and the crew set out to rescue him, while on Earth an atomic reactor is about to blow. In *Star Odyssey* (1979; *Captive Planet*, *Metallica* and *Seven Golden Men in Space*) alien invaders round up earthlings to be shipped off as slaves. The aliens are protected by inderium and master scientist-cum-hypnotist Professor Mori (Ennio Balbo) and his niece Irene (Yanti Somer) are asked to discover a way of defeating them. Mori regroups his old team, including swashbuckling gambler Dirk Laramie (Gianni Garko) and heroic astronaut Lieutenant Oliver 'Hollywood' Carrera (Nino Castelnuovo). They are aided by two irritating male and female robots, Tilt and Tilly, with babyish voices and resembling silver Donald Ducks with fairies' wands attached to their heads. Claudio Undari played an auctioneer who sells off Earth and other planets to the highest bidder. Marcello Giombini, a regular on Brescia's sci-fi movies, provided a noodling synth score that is less fanfare, more funfair. Brescia also reused footage from his space operas in the sci-fi sex movie, *The Beast in Space* (1980).

Like *Barbarella* and *Starcrash*, *Galaxina* (1980) is best remembered for its sexy leading lady. *Playboy* 'Playmate of the Year 1980' Dorothy Stratten played the title role in this would-be spoof from writer–director William Sachs. Galaxina is an android on the *Infinity* police cruiser, skippered by Captain Cornelius Butt (Avery Schreiber), which patrols space in the year 3008, until they are diverted to planet Altair One to pick up the precious 'Blue Star'. The colour-tinted scenes on Altair One are vividly photographed in eye-popping red and yellow Panavision, as Galaxina arrives in a Wild West town (filmed at the Paramount Ranch) and takes on villain Ordric from Mordrik (Ronald Knight) in a laser gunfight at high noon. Galaxina teaches herself how to speak, transforms from a robotic 'doll' into a 'real woman' and falls in love with Sergeant Thor (Stephen Macht). The film features widescreen clips of *First Spaceship on Venus*, the best reasons for watching *Galaxina*. It was Stratten's last role, as she was shot dead by her husband and manager Paul Snider shortly after its release.

For a garish but entertaining redo of an old favourite, producer De Laurentiis talked Mike Hodges into helming a $35 million extravaganza adaptation of Alex Raymond's comic strip *Flash Gordon* (1980). Flash (Sam J. Jones), the star quarterback for the New York Jets, and Dale Arden (Melody Anderson) are shanghaied into helping eccentric scientist Dr Hans Zarkov (Topol) topple Ming the Merciless (Max von Sydow), emperor of the planet Mongo, who plans to obliterate Earth. Hodges shot on location on the Isle of Skye and at Shepperton, EMI and Brooklands Industrial Park, Weybridge. The enterprise is saved by lively plotting, Hodges's improvisational genius with the hokey material, fantastic costumes and sets (from Fellini associate Danilo Donati), and the cast. Ornella Muti played Ming's sultry, treacherous daughter Princess Aura, and Mariangela Melato was Ming's ruthless General Kala. Peter Wyngarde appeared as Ming's councillor Klytus, and Flash's allies included Timothy Dalton's Robin Hood-inspired Prince Barin, from the forested planet of Arboria, and Prince Vultan of the winged Hawkmen, played with inimitable bluster and volume by Brian Blessed. Hodges even managed to convince playwright John Osborne to appear as an Arborian priest, and familiar British faces include Richard O'Brien, Robbie Coltrane, Suzanne Danielle and *Blue Peter* presenter Peter Duncan.

Flash Gordon features swirling multicoloured skies, gleaming spaceships, opulent, exotic costumery and vast sets. Ming's guard includes squealing, red-robed pig-men in gas masks (they couldn't see out of their costumes, so Hodges made them blind). Flash speeds through space on a rocket cycle that resembles an exercise bike and Aura leads around a goblin jester called Fellini on a leash. The tongue-in-cheek action is constantly undercut with humour, as in Ming's wedding day felicitations to his subjects: 'All creatures will make merry... under pain of death.' The blisteringly colourful cinematography prompted Pauline Kael to call it 'disco in the sky'. The score consisted of traditional orchestrations by Howard Blake and bombastic rock-opera songs from British band Queen. Hodges's film was preceded by the surprisingly successful, though strangely unsexy sexploitation parody *Flesh Gordon* (1972), which itself inspired a crass sequel, *Flesh Gordon and the Cosmic Cheerleaders* (1989). But it took Sybil Danning's statuesque Valkyrie Saint-Exmin in *Battle beyond the Stars* (1980) and Fonda's Barbarella to demonstrate how to get 'sexy in space' exactly right.

11

'THE MYSTERIES REMAIN'

THE MAN WHO FELL TO EARTH (1976)

Director: Nicolas Roeg
Producers: Michael Deeley and Barry Spikings
Story: Walter Tevis
Screenplay: Paul Mayersberg
Director of Photography: Anthony B. Richmond
Original Music: John Phillips and Stomu Yamashta
Panavision/Technicolor
A British Lion Film Production
Released by Cinema 5 Distributing (US) and Lion International (UK)
133 minutes

David Bowie (Thomas Jerome Newton, alias 'Mr Sussex'), Rip Torn (Professor Nathan Bryce), Candy Clark (Mary-Lou), Buck Henry (Oliver Farnsworth), Bernie Casey (Peters), Jackson D. Kane (Professor Canutti, Bryce's boss), Rick Riccardo (Trevor), Tony Mascia (Arthur, chauffeur), Linda Hutton (Elaine), Hilary Holland (Jill), Adrienne Larussa (Helen), Lilybelle Crawford (jewellery-store owner), Richard Breeding (hotel receptionist), Terry Southern (reporter at space launch), Jim Lovell (himself), the preacher and congregation of Presbyterian Church, Artesia (themselves)

✻ ✻ ✻

Britain has always produced interesting, idiosyncratic and original sci-fi. From the many TV series, such as *Doctor Who* and *Blake's Seven*, to *Quatermass* and other space oddities, we now turn our attention to filmmakers' distinctively British contributions to science fiction.

The first truly successful UK sci-fi was Hammer's *Quatermass* trilogy, which were adaptations of Nigel Kneale's popular UK TV serial. Val Guest's *The Quatermass Xperiment* (1955; *The Creeping Unknown* in the US) was an adaptation of Kneale's six-part 1953 TV serial *The Quatermass Experiment*. The 'X' in the film title reflected the 'X' rating

The Quatermass Xperiment: Returning astronaut Victor Carroon (Richard Wordsworth) and his mutating cactus arm feature prominently in this UK poster for Val Guest's seminal X-rated 1955 sci-fi horror.

it garnered from censors. Britain's first space rocket *Q-1*, masterminded by Professor Bernard Quatermass (Brian Donlevy), crashes near Bray, Berkshire, but only one of the three astronauts has returned alive. The others have vanished, leaving only their space-suits. Inspector Lomax (Jack Warner) ponders whether the explanation is scientific or criminal. Catatonic astronaut Victor Carroon (Richard Wordsworth), in deep shock, is treated by Dr Briscoe (David King-Wood), but with help from his wife Judith (Margia Dean) Victor escapes, triggering a manhunt that mobilises police, troops and civil defence. On his hand, Victor's cells have become fused with a cactus and he becomes a hybrid of man and plant. In a lab, a small sample regenerates itself and grows into a tentacled blob, a fate that also befalls Victor. The tentacled 20-foot-wide mass is spotted atop a scaffolding platform inside Westminster Abbey during a BBC outside broadcast. London's electricity supply is diverted through a cable that is attached to the scaffolding pole, and with a mighty scream the mass burns. *The Quatermass Xperiment* builds a fine, unnerving tension. Wordsworth was ideally cast as monstrous Victor, with his sunken eyes and sallow, cadaverous visage, his face and body wracked with torment and torture. Victor, his hideously deformed, enlarged hand wrapped in his coat, murders a pharmacist

(Toke Townley) and leaves other withered corpses – man and beast – in his wake. The film was shot at Bray Studios, Berkshire, and at Chessington Zoo, Surrey (where Victor feeds on leopards, antelopes and lions), and at Deptford, where Victor hides out in a derelict boat and encounters a little girl (Jane Asher). Inspector Lomax is a Bible-reading man of religion, while Quatermass is an ever-delving man of science. The film ends with Quatermass resolutely launching another space rocket.

Guest's *Quatermass 2* (1957; *Enemy from Space* in the US) was the first film to use '2' as a sequel suffix. In the north of England, a meteor shower leads Quatermass (Donlevy) to investigate a suspicious industrial plant en route to Carlisle, Cumbria. It's a 'Top Secret' installation that purports to be a synthetic food project. The area is patrolled with armed guards and the nearby village of Wynnerton Flats has been destroyed. Quatermass discovers a cover-up that reaches the government and police. The plant is breeding huge, destructive alien beings in vast domes, fed by corrosive, highly poisonous concentrated ammonia which is deadly to living things. In the finale, the locals who work at the plant rebel, while Quatermass tries to destroy the silo monsters, blubbery colossi of oily tar. *Quatermass 2* is fast paced and eerily threatening in the best traditions of UK sci-fi/horror. There aren't gallons of gratuitous gore on display, but the movie remains disturbing – for example, when Quatermass pumps oxygen into the alien silos and the aliens block the pipes with 'human pulp' of other workers and blood begins to drip from the pipes. The atmosphere is greatly enhanced by Gerald Gibbs's monochrome cinematography and James Bernard's unusual score.

Quatermass 2 was shot at New Elstree Studios and on location in the UK, including Westminster and Trafalgar Square in London. The production thanked Hemel Hempstead New Town Development Corporation for its assistance, and the industrial domes and pipes of the vast alien food factory were filmed at the Shell Haven Refinery, Essex. The cast includes Bryan Forbes and William Franklyn as Quatermass's fellow scientists, Marsh and Brand, Vera Day as barmaid Sheila and John Longden as Scotland Yard's Inspector Lomax. Sid James, as drunken reporter Jimmy Hall, meets a memorable demise when he's machine-gunned to death behind a bar by the plant's security guards as he attempts to phone-in his big scoop. *Quatermass 2* is filled with memorable images, such as the death of MP Vincent Broadhead (Tom Chatto), who falls into one of the domes and emerges staggering, coated in burning, corrosive ammonia slime. There are eerie, gas-masked decontamination crews and meteors that emit a gas, scarring their victims with a 'V' and turning them into mindless zombies. Quatermass destroys an alien asteroid, the source of the menace, with a prototype atomic missile, and the mighty blobs burn. At the conclusion, Lomax ponders: 'You know what worries me? How am I going to make a final report about all this?' Quatermass is more pessimistic: 'What worries me is how final can it be?'

Hammer cashed in on *Quatermass* with *X the Unknown* (1956), scripted by Jimmy Sangster and directed by Leslie Norman. During an army 'radiation location' exercise in a Scottish quarry (Beaconsfield Gravel Pits, Buckinghamshire) an explosion causes a fissure to open up in the ground, leaving one soldier badly burnt and another killed. Dr Adam Royston (Dean Jagger) discovers that their enemy is a bubbling mass of ever-growing radioactive mud that emerges from the bowels of the earth through the fissure and seeks radiation. As it grows larger and more unstable, it heads for the Atomic Energy Establishment at Lochmouth, Scotland, but Royston and his team neutralise it with radar wave emissions. Royston is helped by scientists, the army and McGill (Leo McKern), an agent from the UK Atomic Energy Commission. Interiors were shot at Bray Studios, with some village exteriors in the Buckinghamshire village of Gerrards Cross. The supporting cast included Edward Chapman, William Lucas, Michael Ripper, Kenneth Cope and Anthony Newley. Much of the shocking effects of radiation are described in dialogue rather than depicted, but the primitive special effects (melting faces, hideous scars and the creeping blob) are helped by the monochrome cinematography. Nowadays it's quaint to see police in an emergency noting that they're half a mile from the nearest telephone.

In Robert Day's *First Man into Space* (1958), a test pilot returns as a hideous blood-drinking space mutation and AIP's effective, creepy *Night of the Blood Beast* (1958), directed by Bernard L. Kowalski, was an American take on the *Quatermass* scenario, with manned satellite X-100 crash landing with its pilot, John Corcoran (Michael Emmet), dead. As the recovery team investigate, Corcoran revives, while a crusty monster, with beak and claws, emerges from the craft and rips Dr Wyman's head off. Corcoran is the host for the monster's spawn ('Something foreign is inside me, alive'), but during the finale at Bronson Canyon and Caves, Corcoran stabs himself rather than hatch the aliens, while the monster is dispatched with Molotov cocktails and a Very pistol.

The third instalment of the *Quatermass* TV saga, *Quatermass and the Pit*, was originally broadcast in six parts during 1958–9. In 1967, the big-screen version from Hammer and Seven Arts was directed by Roy Ward Baker. It was released as *Quatermass and the Pit* in the UK and *Five Million Miles to Earth* in the US, and was shot at MGM British Studios, Borehamwood, in DeLuxe Color. During the redevelopment of Hobbs End underground tube station in London, an archaeological dig uncovers the skeletal fossils of several apemen, which date from five million years ago. They also uncover an unexploded German bomb. Bomb disposal experts are called in, but when the object is fully unearthed, it is revealed to be a missile-like craft. The terraced houses above the site are empty, as the area is riven with weird happenings and mystery, tales of ghostly apparitions, goblins and hideous dwarves. The plaster on the walls is strangely scratched, and feudal superstitions stem from the area's old name (Hob's Lane) and its associations with the Devil. The craft emits a high-pitched sonic defence and disorientating vibrations when the investigators try to drill into it; the exterior shatters into shards and reveals the craft's alien occupants – strange, three-legged, green-oozing arthropods that resemble outsized locusts. Scientists theorise that the apes discovered in the tunnel arrived with the aliens, millions of years ago, when the Thames Valley was a swamp. They are in fact our ancestors.

Quatermass and the Pit is superior British sci-fi, with a good score by Tristram Cary and a superior, intelligent script from Nigel Kneale. Andrew Kier made a fine Quatermass, James Donald played archaeologist Dr Matthew Roney, and Barbara Shelley was Roney's fellow researcher Barbara Judd. Julian Glover played sceptical Colonel Breen and Sheila Staefel was an inquisitive journalist. Drill operator Sladden (Duncan Lamont) is pursued, petrified, through the streets by a swirling mini tornado of alien energy. The insecty demons, resembling gargoyles or horned devils, reappear when the alien entity manifests itself in a mass of white energy over the city. Rocks, flagstones and rubble fly through the air, burying unfortunate bystanders, a howling wind surges from the excavation, the heaving ground smokes hellishly, buildings collapse and water mains burst, in a brilliantly staged whirlwind apocalypse during a live TV broadcast. 'The thing in the pit' unleashes an ancient and diabolical evil, as humans turn on their own in a manner that recalls strange alien footage of ritual slaughter on their planet. In order to dispel the alien energy mass, Roney climbs out on the jib of a McAlpine crane, which he uses as a huge lightning conductor to earth the energy mass and destroy it.

Joseph Losey's *These Are the Damned* (aka *The Damned*), made in 1961 but released in 1963, was set in mysterious Dorset. In Weymouth, holidaying American yachtsman Simon Wells (Macdonald Carey) is mugged by a thuggish biker gang led by King (Oliver Reed). King's sister Joan (Shirley Anne Field) befriends the tourist, and when they explore the coastline they are chased by the bikers towards a wired military compound, the Edgecliff Establishment. In a cave Joan, Simon and King encounter nine children, who are ice cold to the touch. The Edgecliff Establishment, run by Dr Bernard (Alexander Knox), is keeping the radioactive children segregated from society. In the event of nuclear war they will be the only survivors capable of living in the postwar fallout conditions. These children will inherit the Earth. As Joan, Simon and particularly King begin to feel the ill effects of radiation, they decide to help the children escape. But helicopters and guards pursue them, and the children are rounded up and returned to the compound. King is killed when he drives his Jaguar off a bridge (near the Royal Victoria Hotel, now the Ferry Bridge Inn, Wyke Regis). As the captive children cry for help, contaminated Simon and Joan flee in a boat that is shadowed out to sea by a helicopter.

These Are the Damned was based on H.L. Lawrence's novel *The Children of Light* and was shot in monochromed Hammerscope. Interiors were lensed at Bray Studios, with location work in Dorset on the coast above Chesil Beach, at Portland Harbour and in Weymouth itself. The film begins as a seaside drama of violent Teddy Boys but soon shifts gear into something altogether more sinister, as the eerie coastline and nefarious activities at Edgecliff take centre stage. Bernard's lover, artist Freya Neilson (Viveca Lindfors), lives in Bernard's clifftop property, 'The Birdhouse', where she creates weird animal and human statuary that resembles charred, crumpled A-bomb corpses (actually works by Elizabeth Frink). Bernard communicates with the children, seated at desks in their 'classroom', via TV monitors, and when the guards come into contact with the kids they wear anti-radiation suits. Members of this post-nuclear dynasty fittingly bear the names of kings and queens of England: Victoria, Elizabeth, Mary, Anne, Richard, Henry, William, Charles and George. *These Are the Damned* is the best UK sci-fi film of the 1960s.

British sci-fi has taken many forms. Throughout his acting career, Sean Connery attempted to outrun his association with James Bond by taking on all sorts of odd roles. Never was this more apparent than his part as Zed in John Boorman's trippy, cerebral, New Age, medieval sci-fi epic *Zardoz* (1973). Set in 2293, this bizarre vision of the future depicts two zones – the frontier-like Outlands and the picturesque Vortex – shot on location in the Wicklow Mountains (with interiors at Ardmore Studios) in Ireland. The Outlands are policed by armed brigands, the exterminators who kill the lawless brutals in the name of the god Zardoz. Zed travels from the Outlands to the Vortex in the giant flying stone head of the fierce-looking Zardoz. He is enslaved and studied by the Vortex's curious intellectual folk, including Consuella (Charlotte Rampling), May (Sara Kestleman) and Friend (John Alderton), who live a seemingly utopian existence. When they commit crimes, their sentences – for example six months, or five years – are the period of time the wrongdoers are aged, but the people of the Vortex are immortal, so they just get older and older. The film's key theme of 'look behind the mask for the truth' is a veiled reference to L. Frank Baum's book *The Wonderful Wizard of Oz*, of which 'Zardoz' is a contraction (<u>Wiz</u>ard of <u>Oz</u>). Connery's costume is a sight to behold. His long hair plaited down his back, and with a fiery Mexican bandido moustache, Zed wears nothing more than red bullet bandoliers, a red nappy and knee-high boots. Striving for arthouse significance, *Zardoz* only achieves campy magnificence.

From the ridiculous to the sublime. Along with *Solaris* (1972), *The Man Who Fell to Earth* is perhaps the most enigmatic science-fiction film ever made. British director Nicolas Roeg began his career as a cinematographer on such films as *The Masque of the Red Death* (1964) and François Truffaut's dystopian sci-fi *Fahrenheit 451* (1966). An adaptation of Ray Bradbury's first novel, *Fahrenheit 451* starred Oskar Werner, Julie Christie and Cyril Cusack, and envisioned a book-free future. Roeg's *The Man Who Fell to Earth* (1976), an elliptical sci-fi parable, was adapted from the 1963 novel by Walter Tevis. Thomas Jerome Newton (David Bowie) emerges from the New Mexican desert. Apparently from England, he approaches a lawyer, Oliver Farnsworth (Buck Henry), with a series of nine basic patents, which Farnsworth estimates to be worth $300 million. Soon Newton and his business partner make a fortune, building a New York empire, World Enterprises, which becomes one of the largest corporations in America. Newton and Mary-Lou (Candy Clark), a hotel maid he hooks up with, return to New Mexico and use his formidable business acumen to create a space programme, with a view to building a rocket that will take extraterrestrial Newton to his home planet. He employs Nathan Bryce (Rip Torn), a college professor expert in fuels, who becomes suspicious of his strange employer. Newton is an alien in human disguise and his planet (in the novel called Anthea) is suffering a draught. Newton left his alien wife and two children to travel to Earth in search of water. But Newton becomes sidetracked by Earthly vices. He's corrupted by alcohol (preferring gin to water), sex (with Mary-Lou) and TV. Eventually his business empire is overthrown, Farnsworth is murdered and Newton is betrayed by Bryce. Newton is imprisoned in a hotel suite, experimented upon and almost blinded. He escapes this hell and years later an aged Bryce catches up with him. Newton, who hasn't aged at all, has recorded an LP, 'The Visitor', which he hopes his wife will hear one day broadcast on the radio. Asked by Bryce if he's bitter, ruined Newton replies: 'Bitter? No. We'd have probably treated you the same if you'd come over to our place.'

This linear summary of the film's plot is a simple 'alien visiting Earth from a dying planet' story. But Roeg's idiosyncratic editing style and elastic sense of time and space result in a completely original work. Roeg's technique involves avant-garde editing, with scenes intercut with seemingly unrelated events, or sudden jump cuts between people and places, tangling story threads in ways only multiple viewings can unravel. To complement Roeg's mosaic filmmaking style, there is an array of sonic juxtapositions on the soundtrack (though no Bowie songs). The original music was by John Phillips and Stomu Yamashta, and the soundtrack also featured tracks by Roy Orbison, Jim Reeves, Bing Crosby and Grace Kelly, Louis Armstrong, Joni Mitchell, The Kingston Trio, Steely Dan, as well as excerpts from *The Planets Suite* by Gustav Holst, the carol 'Silent Night' and 'Songs of the Humpbacked Whale'. The jazz tune over the end titles is 'Star Dust' by Artie Shaw.

It was a stroke of genius to cast David Bowie in his film debut as Newton. Bowie rose to prominence with the 1969 space-themed 'Space Oddity' single, which detailed a space mission, and its timely release coincided with the Apollo 11 Moon landing. It included the famous line: 'Ground Control to Major Tom'. In 1972 Bowie launched his 'Ziggy Stardust' alien alter ego, a spacey, alien glam-rock star for *The Rise and Fall of Ziggy Stardust and the Spiders from Mars*. Bowie's androgynous appearance, stylised futuristic costuming and bisexuality enhanced his mystique. Ziggy is a 'space oddity', impossible to categorise, like Roeg's cinema. Alien Newton has taken on humanoid form so that he can infiltrate Earth society, to implement his business plan and space programme. In reality, Newton is an alien, with pallid skin and no defining features such as nipples, genitals or eyebrows. Newton's adopted persona is a comment on the artificiality of fame, of a performer's 'act'. Newton's disguise – the red hair, the contact lenses concealing his yellow, cat-like eyes – is a mask, like Bowie's Ziggy enigma. Roeg is warning of the perils of adopting such artifice in the 'real world', of being found out and revealed as a phoney. As Newton notes, people on Earth think he's 'a freak or a fake'.

Though it was a British production, *The Man Who Fell to Earth* was largely shot in the US, on location in New Mexico, including Albuquerque, Alamogordo, White Sands, Artesia and wooded Fenton Lake (where Newton's space pod splashes down and he later constructs a Japanese-style lakeside chalet). Interiors were shot at Shepperton Studios in England. Jim Lovell, the commander of the ill-fated Apollo 13 moon mission, appears in a scene when Newton attempts to leave in his spaceship. *The Man Who Fell to Earth* was photographed in Panavision and Technicolor by Anthony B. Richmond, though

Roeg's flair for beautiful, often disturbing, imagery is in evidence. The New Mexican landscapes are artfully photographed – as Mary-Lou tells Newton, 'Lord, I never knew America was so beautiful.' The New Mexican desert resembles Newton's home planet, a drought-plagued land of barren, featureless dunes, where his wife and children slowly die of thirst. The desert flashback scenes to Anthea are eerily beautiful, with the spindly aliens in their silver suits and backpacks, fragile in the inhospitable landscape. At one point Bryce, suspicious of his employer, conceals an X-ray camera and takes a picture of Newton, which when developed reveals that he has no skeleton. One of Newton's inventions is film that develops pictures instantly inside the camera, but most of the science-fiction elements of Roeg's film are low-key, a spacey mood often created through suggestion rather than vision.

Newton becomes addicted to TV – first one, then four, then seven, then a bank of 12 – simultaneously showing different programmes, which reflects Roeg's narrative style, a collision of images, as the film itself resembles someone channel-hopping with a TV remote control. Water is important to the story: Newton's craft lands in a lake, he meets Mary-Lou in the hotel in Artesia (an Artesian well is a deeply bored hole that supplies water naturally) and aliens know Earth as the 'Planet of Water'. There are many images of mirrors and reflections, which address our perceptions of ourselves and how others see us. Newton's mirror-gazing could imply the narcissism of a rock star, though 'Moon rock' has a totally different meaning here. There are juxtapositions of time (Earth/Anthea), place (city/country) and love/lust, the last of which via near-pornographic sex scenes, a Roeg motif. Roeg depicts Bryce's romps with his teenage students and three love scenes between Newton and Mary-Lou, which progress from tenderness, to alien–human love, to wanton lust. Their final sexual encounter is strobe-lit, savage and often cut from prints of the film. Newton fires blanks from a pistol at drunken Mary-Lou, as 'Hello Mary-Lou' (covered by John Phillips and Mick Taylor) plays on the soundtrack, in this debauched mix of lust, sex, booze and guns, from which 'love' is entirely absent. As announced by the film's title, the key theme is falling. Newton's arrival is a fall from space, and the alien is called Newton, after the English scientist Sir Isaac Newton, who identified gravity. Roeg depicts alien beings gymnastically falling through space, amid slow-motion splashes of a milky substance. This echoes Newton's downward spiral into moral bankruptcy, his fall from grace.

This British Lion production crash-landed in UK cinemas in March 1976 (rated X) and in the US in May (rated R). Publicity predictably highlighted Bowie, and the trailer noted: 'Another dimension of David Bowie, one of the few true originals of our time.' The film enhanced Roeg's stature as one of the most interesting, visually compelling artists of the 1970s. *The Man Who Fell to Earth* was remade for US TV in 1986 by Robert J. Roth as the pilot for a never-commissioned TV series. Lewis Smith played alien visitor John Dory and Beverly D'Angelo was Eva Milton. It was rated PG for video in the UK in 1987 but, despite derivative video-box artwork, will never be mistaken for Roeg and Bowie's artful masterpiece.

With UK studios often the production base for hit sci-fi films, such as *Star Wars* and *Alien*, British science fiction continued to thrive throughout the 1980s. Shot at Pinewood Studios, London, Peter Hyams's *Outland* (1981) featured federal district marshal Bill O'Niel (Sean Connery), who polices the Con-Am 27 titanium-mining operation on Io (the third moon of Jupiter). People are inexplicably running amok on violent sprees and, with the help of Dr Lazarus (Frances Sternhagen), O'Niel deduces the cause to be a synthetic narcotic, PDE, an amphetamine developed to increase labourers' work rates, but that fries users' brains. It's being shipped in with the backing of mining general manager Sheppard (Peter Boyle). As O'Niel digs deeper, identifying the culprits and threatening to spoil the traffickers' operation, Sheppard decides to have O'Niel erased, resulting in a *High Noon* replay, with marshal O'Niel waiting for the arrival of the shuttle with Sheppard's two hired assassins onboard. O'Niel asks various people for help, but only Lazarus stands by him in the final showdown. The sentimental backstory has O'Niel abandoned even by his wife and son (Kika Markham and Nicholas Barnes), who return to Earth. There's even a digital clock countdown in the terminal for O'Niel's waiting game, but the shuttle docks early.

Terry Gilliam's *Brazil* (1985) depicted a drab Orwellian future British society that's controlled by fascist secret police and oppressed by a 13-year-long terrorist bombing campaign. Sam Lowry (Jonathan Pryce) works in the Ministry of Information, in the Department of Records. Like Roeg's editorial juxtapositions, Gilliam's hero escapes from his mundane job into wild flights of fantasy, where he imagines himself as a winged knight in shining armour who battles a giant samurai warrior, or a monster made of bricks, to save his idealised dream girl (Kim Greist). When there's a glitch in the system (a swatted fly drops into a computer), innocent Archibald Buttle is arrested instead of Archibald Tuttle (Robert De Niro), a terrorist heating engineer who abseils between jobs. Sam is also suspected of being a terrorist and his life begins to enact his fantasies. This is triggered when he sees his 'dream girl' in real life – Jill Layton (Greist), a truck-driving neighbour of Buttle's. This is a wild fantasia from Gilliam, the animator of the cartoon links for *Monty Python's Flying Circus*. Gilliam combines the Big Brother society of *1984* with eye-opening fantasy visuals, à la Fellini. There are satirical digs at petty government officials and labyrinthine bureaucracy, and everything is noted, classified, filed, stamped and receipted. You 'can't make a move without a form', 'the rules are the rules' and Churchillian bureaucrats and yes-men talk in public-school cricketing and horse-racing metaphors. This city resembles the London of the Blitz and is lodged in retro-futurism; everywhere there are ducts and swarms of wires creating Heath Robinson computers and other archaic hardware. The Ministry of Information is a rushing, frantic hive of activity, while street-urchin Blitz kids in woollen tank tops roam the streets. It's a noirish netherworld, a city in fear of doing or even thinking the wrong thing. Genial Michael Palin is cast against type as Jack Lint, who is revealed to be a sadistic, baby-masked torturer. Sam's interfering mother Ida (Katherine Helmond) is obsessed with facial plastic surgery, as performed by oily Dr Jaffe (Jim Broadbent), which eventually transforms her into Jill, while Ida's friend Alma Terrain (Barbara Hicks) becomes more disfigured, with 'complications on the complications'. The lovers appear to escape the choking city in her Scammell truck into country greenery, but actually Sam has finally lost his sanity under torture. *Brazil's* totalitarian sci-fi vision is original and, at times, brilliant.

Tobe Hooper's *Lifeforce* (1985) references and remixes Britain's rich horror and sci-fi heritage to great effect. HMS *Churchill*, a UK–US space mission, investigates Halley's Comet, which appears to Earth once every 76 years and is a harbinger of doom. The *Churchill* returns to Earth with its crew dead – there was a fire on board and only Colonel Tom Carlsen (Steve Railsback) escaped in a pod. The *Churchill* has picked up some alien beings from a craft near the comet, which revive and suck the life from their victims, leaving only wizened corpses. The script was concocted by Dan O'Bannon and Don Jakoby from the novel *The Space Vampires* by Colin Wilson. The aliens are space vampires and their 150-mile-long needle-like mother ship, the Collector, arrives and hovers over London in a geostatic orbit, drawing up swathes of blue light that are the ripped-out souls of victims (this imagery reappeared in *Skyline*). This transforms the population of London into plague-wracked, rampaging zombies, prompting the authorities to declare martial law and ready a thermonuclear device. The eclectic cast includes Peter Firth as SAS colonel Caine, Frank Finlay as Dr Hans Fallada (a role originally slated for Klaus Kinski), Patrick Stewart as Dr Armstrong (the head of Thurlstone asylum for the criminally insane), Nancy Paul as nurse Ellen Donaldson, Aubrey Morris as Home Secretary Sir Percy, and Michael Gothard as Dr Bukovsky. It was shot on location in London and in Thorn EMI Studios, Borehamwood. Henry Mancini wrote the score and John Dykstra created the excellent effects. Amid the grand-scale B-movie mayhem there are nods to *The Exorcist*, *Alien*, *Quatermass and the Pit*, *The Sweeney*, *Night of the Living Dead*, Kate Bush's pop videos, a prehistoric bat from *One Million Years B.C.*, chunks of *The War of the Worlds*, and the final confrontation is a Hammer horror-inspired extraterrestrial vampire staking, which takes place in the crypt of St Paul's Cathedral. The film has attracted a cult following over the years for the presence of Mathilda May. Billed as 'Space Girl', she is nude as she wanders around London, sucking the essence or 'life force' from humans via her kiss of death. A costly failure for Cannon Films, this British hokum is unmissable.

From the man who fell to Earth to the man on the Moon, as David Bowie's son Duncan Jones made his directorial debut with the idiosyncratic *Moon* (2009). At Mining Base Sarang – a Moon-based outpost of Lunar Industries Ltd, a clean energy provider – Helium-3 is harvested and shipped back to Earth for use in nuclear fusion. The base is operated by Sam Bell (Sam Rockwell) and the GERTY 3000 Robotic Assistant (voiced by Kevin Spacey). Sam is nearing the end of his three-year tenure and is looking forward to seeing his wife Tess (Dominique McElligott) and infant daughter Eve (Rosie Shaw). Sam begins to see hallucinations of other people on the base and GERTY seems to be concealing something from him. When one of the vast harvesters collides with Sam's Lunar Rover, he is injured and wakes up inside the base. At the collision site, Sam finds his own corpse in the Rover, but which Sam is real? With the relief ship *Eliza* due, the Sams resolve to discover Lunar Industries' secret on the dark side of the Moon.

Moon was shot in Shepperton Studios, England, for $5 million, on sets which resemble the retro white interiors of *2001*. This retro feel is reinforced by the presence of 1980s pop hits 'Walking on Sunshine' (Katrina and the Waves) and 'The One and Only' (Chesney Hawkes). The lunar exteriors, the base and its machinery were created with models. The cratered lunar landscapes are striped with furrowed harvested tracts, as man exploits the Moon. The story has a thriller's pace and an unsettling score by Clint Mansell. Though the story includes such clichés as the apparently benevolent robot and the desolate, secluded space station, it foxes audience expectations, as we discover Sam has been manning Mining Base Sarang for considerably longer than three years. GERTY indicates its mood with 'smiley' or 'unsmiley' face icons and its passionless voice recalls HAL. The Sams explore beyond the base's lunar perimeter into the outland, and Sam Mk 1 communicates with Earth, discovering his wife is dead and his daughter is now 15. He also finds a secret store chamber containing many more Sam clones. Each replacement Sam is implanted with memories. As the rescue ship *Eliza* arrives, one of the Sams escapes in a pod back to Earth. Fragmented news reports inform us: 'Lunar Industries stocks have slipped a further 32 per cent after accusations [...] Clone 6, the clone of Sam Bell, has been giving evidence at CEA's Board of Directors meeting in Seattle.' The film itself is designated '© Lunar Industries Ltd 2009'. *Moon* was warmly received by critics and is a fine example of how to make gripping, effective sci-fi with a modest budget. Versatile Rockwell is more than up to the challenge of the roles in this complex, rewarding film.

Perhaps the most famous and certainly one of the most eccentric British sci-fi creations was Douglas Adams's radio series *The Hitchhiker's Guide to the Galaxy*. This satire, variously a cult 1978 BBC Radio 4 show, several books and a six-part 1981 TV series in the UK, finally reached the big screen in 2005, directed by Garth Jennings. Arthur Dent (Martin Freeman) has his house demolished to make way for a bypass, but moments later he is saved by alien Ford Prefect (Mos Def), just before Earth is demolished to make way for a Hyperspace Expressway to be built by the Vogons. The film then follows Arthur's tour of the galaxy, which includes the restaurant at the end of the universe and an exact replica of Earth Mk II, with the revelation that mice are experimenting on us (not the reverse). Adams's inventions, including Babelfish translators, the Improbability Drive and the Point-of-View gun, have since passed into sci-fi folklore, as have his galaxy of oddballs, such as Trillian (Zooey Deschanel), Galaxy president Zaphod Beeblebrox (two-headed Sam Rockwell), Questular Rontok (Anna Chancellor), Slartibartfast (Bill Nighy), Humma Kavula (John Malkovich) and Marvin the Paranoid Android (played by Warwick Davis and voiced by Alan Rickman). The voice of the guide itself was provided by the reassuring tones of Stephen Fry, and, of course, as we all suspected, 'The answer to life, the universe and everything' is 42.

12

'THE FORCE WILL BE WITH YOU, ALWAYS'

STAR WARS (1977)

Director: George Lucas
Story and Screenplay: George Lucas
Director of Photography: Gilbert Taylor
Music: John Williams
Panavision/Technicolor
A Lucasfilm Ltd Production
Released by Twentieth Century-Fox
121 minutes

Mark Hamill (Luke Skywalker), Harrison Ford (Captain Han Solo), Carrie Fisher (Princess Leia Organa), Peter Cushing (Grand Moff Tarkin), Alec Guinness (Obi-Wan 'Ben' Kenobi), Anthony Daniels (C-3PO), Kenny Baker (R2-D2), Peter Mayhew (Chewbacca), David Prowse (Lord Darth Vader, voiced by James Earl Jones), Phil Brown and Shelagh Fraser (Owen and Beru Lars), Paul Blake (Greedo), Eddie Byrne (General Willard)

* * *

A long time ago in a galaxy far, far away an Imperial starship attacks a Rebel blockade runner carrying Princess Leia Organa (Carrie Fisher). She is a senator for the Rebel forces, which are fighting the Empire in a civil war. She has encoded important technical data about the Empire's planet-busting battle station called the Death Star into droid R2-D2 (Kenny Baker). Lord Darth Vader (David Prowse) of the Empire captures Leia, but R2 and his companion C-3PO (Anthony Daniels) escape to the desert planet of Tatooine. The droids are captured by Jawas and are sold to moisture farmers Owen and Beru Lars and their nephew Luke Skywalker (Mark Hamill). The message is meant for Ben Kenobi (Alec Guinness), an old hermit who now lives in Tatooine's Jundland Wastes, who was once a Jedi Knight known as Obi-Wan, so Luke and the droids contact him. When the Lars farmstead is sacked by Imperial Stormtroopers and Luke's aunt and uncle are killed, Luke's fate is sealed. Luke's father was a powerful Jedi, until he was killed

The special effects developed for *Star Wars*, which was written and directed by George Lucas, changed the science-fiction landscape. Mark Hamill's Luke Skywalker took centre stage on this US one-sheet poster, style 'C', from 1977.

by Vader, and Luke decides to follow Ben. Luke is given his father's weapon, a lightsabre: 'an elegant weapon for a more civilised age'. At the Mos Eisley spaceport ('a hive of scum and villainy') they hire a smuggler, Captain Han Solo (Harrison Ford), and his freighter, the *Millennium Falcon*, to take them to Leia's home planet of Alderaan, but before they reach it, it's destroyed by the Death Star and they are pulled in by the space station's tractor beam. They manage to rescue Leia and escape, but Ben is killed in a lightsabre duel with Vader and the Empire tracks them with a homing beacon. From their secret stronghold, the Massassi Outpost base on the fourth moon of Yavin, the rebels launch an attack in X-wing fighters as the Death Star approaches to destroy the planet with its ray. Sweeping down a trench on the base, the pilots (including Luke) aim for the Death Star's weak point – a thermal exhaust port only two metres wide – the shaft of which leads directly to the reactor system. A precise hit from a proton torpedo causes a chain reaction and obliterates the battle station, but Vader escapes to fight another day.

Star Wars, the brainchild of producer–director–writer George Lucas, was made for $10 million, a modest budget for a Hollywood sci-fi movie. His script was rather long, so he decided only to shoot the first third. It was shot on location in the Tunisian desert and at Death Valley National Monument (the Dune Sea and badlands of Tatooine), in the Takal National Park in Guatemala (the forested Rebel base on Yavin IV) and at EMI Studios, Borehamwood. The cast included star-making performances from Mark Hamill, Carrie Fisher and Harrison Ford (who was working as a carpenter at the time), and old hands such as Alec Guinness and Hammer-horror favourite Peter Cushing as the evil Galactic Empire's Grand Moff Tarkin. Their performances craft what could have been a collection of clichéd characters – the farm boy, bored of his chores, who seeks adventure, the spunky tomboy princess, the mercenary pirate, the wise old sage, the blacker-than-black baddie – into iconic, timeless screen heroes and villains.

A fifth of the budget was spent on special effects, which were created by, among others, John Dykstra, Richard Edlund and Les Bowie. *Star Wars* married the episodic serial escapades of Lucas's beloved *Flash Gordon Conquers the Universe* (all the *Star Wars* films open with a scrolling 'story so far' blurb) to grandiose *2001* special effects. Lucas effectively built his own special-effects team to create the wizard visuals. The film opens with the famous shot of the giant Imperial Star Destroyer cruising overhead, seemingly forever, as its vastness crawls across the screen in a nod to *2001*. The convincing milieu of glittering starfields and bright planets and moons is a fitting backdrop to the kinetic aerial combat sequences, as Imperial TIE fighters attack Solo's *Millennium Falcon* or the Rebels career in to attack the Death Star. On the ground too there is derring-do, with laser-gun battles, lightsabre duels and cliffhanging heroics.

Perhaps even more memorable than the human cast was Lucas's gallery of creature creations for the film, from the warlike Sand People (also referred to as Tusken Raiders, desert-dwellers on Tatooine who ride mammoth horned steeds, the banthas) to the chattering, pint-sized, monk-robed Jawas and their immense tracked sandcrawler. In Lucas's take on a Wild West saloon, the array of good, bad and ugly beasties in the Mos Eisley cantina contains a gallery of oddball furry, lizardy freaks. It is here that Han shoots first and guns down green bounty hunter Greedo, who plans to turn Solo in for the reward posted by Jabba the Hutt, whom Solo has crossed. Peter Mayhew played Chewbacca, the hairy Wookiee (reputedly based on Lucas's dog) and Solo's first mate, whom Leia refers to as 'a walking carpet' – though he doesn't resemble *The Creeping Terror*. Vader's Stormtroopers, with their white plate armour and helmets, became instantly recognisable in pop culture, as did Vader himself, with his demonic presence and booming, asthmatic voice provided by James Earl Jones. There is also an impressive array of robots and droids, including the film's two most memorable creations. R2-D2, the cute, resourceful domed tripod robot, which communicates by emitting squeaking blips, and C-3PO, the golden ditherer, as though Machine Man from *Metropolis* had been played by Charles Hawtrey.

The film's key theme is the mystical 'Force', which 'binds the galaxy together'. Those who have it are endowed with powers beyond natural talent, and there's also a religious element – 'May the Force be with you' – recalling 'And also with you', the blessing at the conclusion of Christian worship. In *Star Wars* the Force is described alternatively as an 'ancient religion' or 'simple tricks and nonsense', but later films attempted to explain the Force scientifically as midi-clorians, which are part of Jedi's biological make-up, dispelling the mystique of the Force's elemental, spiritual power. Darth Vader's story echoes that of God's fallen angel Satan, who turned to the Dark Side and became the Devil. Lucas incorporated elements of fairy tales, myths, legends, sword-and-sandal epics, drag-racing movies (Luke's landspeeder is essentially a hovering 1950s convertible), chunks of John Ford (including the farmstead attack from *The Searchers*) and Akira Kurosawa's epic samurai cinema, including the two bickering farmers and the basic plot outline of a fugitive princess from *The Hidden Fortress* and the sword fight and severed arm from *Yojimbo*, as well as Kurosawa's trademark screen-wipe transitions. The gauntlet-running rebel attack down the Death Star trench is said to have been inspired by the World War II movie *The Dam Busters*, but more closely resembles the fjord attack at the climax of *633 Squadron* (1964), as Mosquito fighter-bombers swoop in and try for a direct hit on the rocky overhang above a German rocket-fuel factory, while avoiding ack-ack anti-aircraft guns. In *Star Wars*, these disparate elements and many more, plus Lucas's incredible vision and imagination, came together to create a near-perfect work of action-packed science fiction, which was given extra oomph by John Williams's triumphant, sweeping score – one of cinema's most popular – played with exultant élan by the London Symphony Orchestra. Lucas wanted a full-blooded orchestral score, from the 'golden era' of film scoring, in the manner of Viennese composer Erich Wolfgang Korngold.

The film was released in the US in May 1977 and was an instantaneous smash hit, proving so popular that it played in some theatres for a year. It took $260 million on its first run in the US, making it the most successful film in history up to that point. There were also massive residual profits from a range of merchandise tie-ins, including toys, stickers, comics and books. The toys recreated the film's characters, their props, weapons, costumes and craft, in admirably meticulous detail, even down to Chewie's crossbow and retractable lightsabres for the heroes and villains. *Star Wars* was released in the UK in 1977. At the Oscars, Williams won Best Score, and the film also won Oscars for Art Direction, Costume Design, Editing, Sound and, of course, Visual Effects. Early versions of the film were simply titled *Star Wars*, but since 1981's re-release it's become known as *Star Wars Episode IV: A New Hope*, with reference to the beginning of Luke's education as a Jedi and his destruction of the Death Star. It was a colossal hit that became a cultural phenomenon that continues to spawn a labyrinthine, ever-expanding 'Star Wars Universe'.

The original *Star Wars* encouraged film- and TV-makers to head spaceward, as sci-fi became the golden ticket – but success was by no means guaranteed. The short-lived *Battlestar Galactica* teleseries ran for 24 hour-long episodes in 1978–9, and was later revived with a pilot in 2003 and a series from 2004 to 2009. Created by Glen A. Larson, the original was the subject of an unsuccessful plagiarism lawsuit from Lucas. Two theatrically released feature films were assembled from the series: *Battlestar Galactica* (1978) and *Mission Galactica: The Cylon Attack* (1979). Larson followed *Galactica* with another series, *Buck Rogers in the 25th Century* (1979–81), starring Gil Gerard as the hero and featuring cute robot Twiki (voiced by Mel Blanc) and Erin Gray as Colonel Wilma Deering. The 1978 *Galactica* movie epitomises Larson's approach. The plot was part biblical epic, part wagon-train trek. In the seventh millennium Commander Adama (Lorne Greene) leads his convoy of 220 assorted ships containing the only survivors of the 12 planet colonies on an exodus through space to the Promised Land – their thirteenth colony, Earth. The villains are the armoured Cylon warriors. The action is mainly set on the colonists' last remaining battlestar, the *Galactica*, and foregrounds hotshot pilots – Adama's son Apollo (Richard Hatch) and cigar-smoking lothario Starbuck (Dirk Benedict). Maren Jensen played Adama's daughter Athena, Laurette Spang was 'socialator' (prostitute) Cassiopeia, and Herbert Jefferson Jr. was Lieutenant Boomer, while the guest stars were Ray Milland, Jane Seymour, Lew Ayres and Wilfred Hyde-White. There's even a cute robot dog called Muffit 2, which resembles a baby bear wearing a gas mask. The wanderers visit Carillon, a corrupting palace of gambling and entertainment pleasure, run by the bug-like Ovion people, who are in league with the Cylons. There's a *Star Wars*-like score from Stu Phillips and *Galactica*'s producer was special-effects maestro John Dykstra. Little wonder then that the colonists' fighter craft, laser blasts and some of the costumery closely resemble *Star Wars*, but it remains entertaining on its own terms. It was given added zap in theatres with the addition of ear-jangling, sub-woofing Sensurround.

In Roger Corman's *Seven Samurai*/*Magnificent Seven* remake *Battle beyond the Stars* (1980), Shad (Richard Thomas), an Akirian, rounds up a motley space crew of space cadets to save the planet Akir from villainous Sador (John Saxon), who plans to destroy the planet with his 'Stellar Converter'. Shad's gang are a 'magnificent seven' because they travel in seven ships, but there are actually more of them: intergalactic hitman Gelt (Robert Vaughn), whisky-swigging Space Cowboy (George Peppard), Shad's love inter- est Nanelia (Darlanne Fluegel), who is the daughter of weapons expert Dr Hephaestus (Sam Jaffe), scantily-clad Valkyrie warrior Saint-Exmin (Sybil Danning), green, lizardy Cayman (Morgan Woodward) of the Lambda Zone, two twin, bald 'thermal creatures', the Kelvins (Larry Meyers and Lara Kody), and five white, telepathic clones, the Nestor, who think and act as one. Sador has a selection of ugly-faced, mutated, scarred minions, the Malmore, and the film is filled with candy-coloured disco-light special effects and hokey dialogue. James Horner provided the score and James Cameron worked on the film as art director, miniatures designer and construction. His future wife, Gale Anne Hurd, was assistant production manager. *Battle beyond the Stars*, a co-production between Corman's New World and Orion Pictures, cost $5 million, but grossed $11 million. When John Dykstra asked for $2 million to do the special effects, Corman bought the Hammond Lumber Company's lot in Venice, California, and built his own studio. It became known as the 'The Lumberyard' and its sets and effects were subsequently used by many other productions, notably *Android* (1982, starring Klaus Kinski as a mad doctor in space and Don Opper as his creation, Max 404), while Corman reused his own special-effects foot- age in the *Star Wars* rip-off *Space Raiders* (1983).

In the wake of *Star Wars*' mega-success, every kid wanted to be a star pilot and take on the Empire. Nick Castle's *The Last Starfighter* (1984) was a tale of such wish fulfilment, offering hope to those who spent their entire lives playing video games. Alex Rogan (Lance Guest) lives in a Californian trailer park with his mother (Barbara Bosson) and little brother Lewis (Chris Hebert), but dreams of escape. When he trashes the record score on the 'Starfighter' arcade game, he is recruited by Centauri (Robert Preston) of the Star League to pilot one of its craft, *Gunstar One*, against the Xurians, who are about to invade across the Frontier with the Kodan armada. The Xurians destroy the Starfighters' base on Rylos, leaving Alex as the universe's last hope. This B-movie has an appealing cast and plenty of aerial combat (in then-pioneering CGI), as Alex and his alien co-pilot Grig, a 'gung-ho iguana' (Dan O'Herlihy in scaly face make-up) wipe out the evil Xur's armada of deckfighters with untried rapid-firing weapon 'Death Blossom' and destroy the mother ship, though villain Xur (Norman Snow) escapes. The story cross-cuts between Alex in space and his robotic alien 'simuloid' twin Beta (also Guest), who stands in for Alex on Earth. Beta awkwardly romances Alex's girlfriend Maggie Gordon (Catherine Mary Stewart), while avoiding interstellar 'hit-beasts' that have been dispatched to kill him. Eventually Alex returns to Earth victorious, having proved to his mother that he's not a waster, by saving the universe. The other Starfighter pilots look like locals from the Mos Eisley cantina, while Centauri's car-cum-spaceship resembles Marty McFly's DeLorean. The 'Starfighter' video game is actually a recruitment device, which assesses potential pilots' combat skills – the controls to the *Gunstar One* are identical to the video game's joystick and buttons.

Star Wars revolutionised moviemaking, and the integral role of spin-off merchandising, including tie-in computer games, was never the same again. Lucas's saga continued with the Irvin Kershner-directed *The Empire Strikes Back* (1980; *Star Wars Episode V: The Empire Strikes Back*), with most of the actors reprising their roles, including, in ghostly form, Guinness as Obi-Wan. *Star Wars* had ended with a medal ceremony, with Luke and Han decorated by Leia in the Massassi Outpost's main throne room. The final shot resembles a big family photograph, a portrait of the film's heroes, with Luke and Han centre stage. *Empire* is darker – in theme, content and look. Having escaped the destruction of the Death Star, Darth Vader had some major news for Luke in this sequel, which led to the now iconic exchange of dialogue: 'I am your father' [...] 'Noooooooooo!'

Following an Imperial attack on the secret Rebel base on the ice planet of Hoth, Luke and R2-D2 travel to the Dagobah system for Luke to learn the ways of the Force and receive Jedi Knight training from master Yoda. This green, pointy-eared goblin philosopher, who talks in a distinctive gravelly voice with an unusual reverse syntax ('Help you, I can') is a fine puppet creation. He was performed and voiced by Frank Oz, who created such memorable puppet characters as Miss Piggy, Fozzie Bear, Cookie Monster, Bert and Grover. Han, Chewie, Leia and C-3PO evade the Imperial forces in the *Millennium Falcon* ('the fastest piece of junk in the galaxy') by hiding out in an asteroid field. They later travel to the Cloud City above rosy-tinted gaseous planet Bespin, where Han teams up with Lando Calrissian (Billy Dee Williams), the original owner of the *Millennium Falcon* and the administrator of the gas mining facility. Lando betrays them to the Imperial forces, but when he sees Han tortured, he sides with the Rebels. The downbeat ending sees Han frozen in Carbonite to be taken away by bounty hunter Boba Fett (Jeremy Bulloch) to Jabba the Hutt. Having detected that 'The Force is strong in this one', Vader and his master, the Emperor (Ian McDiarmid), try to tempt Luke to the Dark Side, to rule the Galaxy as father and son. During a lightsabre duel between Luke and Vader – where Luke discovers his parentage – Luke loses his right hand and is later fitted with a mechanical replacement.

Photographed in Panavision and DeLuxe Color by Peter Suschitzky and again scored by Williams, *Empire* cost $32 million. For all the first film's technological advances (particularly in the depiction of space flight), this sequel often relies on good old-fashioned stop-motion trick photography, as with Hoth steeds, the horned Tauntaun, or with the huge, rumbling mechanical Imperial AT-AT walkers during Vader's attack on Hoth (exteriors were shot on a glacier at Finse, Norway). This sequel had a screenplay by Leigh Brackett and Lawrence Kasdan and was based on a story by Lucas. *Empire* careers episodically, briskly rushing along the action. The obvious parallels with Nazism continue, with the Imperial commanders petrified of Vader and death their reward for failure, while the Stormtroopers enforce Vader's and the Emperor's will through terror, intimidation and persecution. The acting in this sequel is often sloppy, and despite the story's big reveal this is primarily a minor, middle-act transitional work to the third film in the series. The film's darker tone deploys horror-movie aesthetics, with the harsh snow of Hoth, the snow cave and its yeti-like Wampa snow creature (Des Webb), or Yoda's murky, dry-iced tangled swamp bog. *Empire* strives for maturity, like a child dressed as an adult, but it fails to convince. It was nevertheless a smash hit with cinema audiences and took over $222 million in the US by December 1982.

Despite the presence of the Ewoks of Endor in *Return of the Jedi* (1983; *Star Wars Episode VI: Return of the Jedi*), it is a vast improvement on its predecessor. Directed by Richard Marquand and written by Lucas and Kasdan (from a story by Lucas), it is the best-executed of the trilogy. Han is now hanging, encased in Carbonite, as a wall decoration in Jabba's desert palace on Tatooine. Soon Luke and the gang spring him, and the heroes are reunited. Vader and the Emperor are overseeing the reconstruction of the Death Star, which is using a generator in a bunker on the planet of Endor as its power-shield defence source. The story resolves its various loose ends via an intercut three-way slice finale. Solo and Leia try to knock out the shield's power generator, Luke faces Vader on the Death Star, while Calrissian leads the Rebel fleet against the Imperial forces.

Filmed with the working title *Blue Harvest* on a $32 million budget, *Jedi* begins with the best scenes of the series. In gangster Jabba's palace stronghold – which despite its cabaret singer, dancers and funky disco music is the debauched rat's-nest antithesis of the Mos Eisley cantina – blubbery slug Jabba holds court and speaks in subtitled Huttese. Luke and Leia's escape plan fails and they all end up being taken to the Dune Sea in Jabba's hovering craft to be cast into the Pit of Carkoon, which is home to the massive, many-toothed creature, the Sarlacc. As Luke is made to walk the plank to certain death, R2-D2 fires him a lightsabre and a splendidly staged shoot-out ensues, during which Boba Fett ends up in the pit and Leia (now Jabba's slave and garbed in a minuscule golden bikini) throttles Jabba with a chain. Tatooine's desert scenes were shot in Buttercup Valley and Death Valley.

Jedi does what *Star Wars* did so well – ranks of cannon-fodder Stormtroopers, the Death Star and great creatures and monsters, including Jabba's gremlin-like minion Salacious Crumb, Jabba's ogre-like Gamorrean guards and the grisly Rancor in Jabba's pit. Yoda reappears, but only to confirm that Vader is Luke's father and that Leia is Luke's sister, before dying. Much of the film takes place on the lushly forested planet of Endor (shot in Redwood National Park and Smith River, California), populated by the cutesy Ewoks – small, hairy bear creatures that look like a walking merchandise campaign. In Lucas's original concept, they were Wookiees. The cutest, Wicket, who Cheetah-style befriends Leia in the forest, was played by Warwick Davis. They live in a primitive Stone Age village of huts and treetop walkways, and Leia goes native when she lives with them, her flaxen hair and costuming resembling Maid Marian. The Ewoks gamely battle the Empire's mighty AT-AT walkers with makeshift primitive weapons such as hand gliders, spears, catapults, clubs, bolas and bows and arrows, and the more cynical in the audience will cheer when some of the furry little critters get killed. There's also the film's special-effects highlight, the exhilarating speeder bike chase (inspired by a horseback chase in

The Hidden Fortress) through thickly wooded Endor, as Luke and Leia pursue Imperial guards to prevent them from raising the alarm, on jetting speeders. Like *Empire*, *Jedi* walked away with the Best Visual Effects Oscar for its year.

In the final act of Luke and Vader's story, Luke cannot escape his destiny. They duel and Vader, who is more machine than man, has his mechanical right hand cut off by Luke's newly minted, green-hued sabre. The Emperor (Ian McDiarmid) attacks Luke with lightning bolts, and when it's obvious Luke will die in the face of the Emperor's superior power Vader throws his master down a chasm to his death. Mortally wounded, Vader – now simply Luke's father Anakin Skywalker (Sebastian Shaw) – has his helmet removed, to look upon his son with his own eyes, and Luke sees his scarred, pale face. Following a funeral pyre send-off for Vader, the film ends with the Ewoks' percussive celebrations to please the kiddies, but Luke is watched over by the spirits of Yoda, Anakin and Ben. *Jedi* was another huge success on its release, taking $252 million in the US alone.

After the original *Star Wars* trilogy, Lucas embarked on the *Clone Wars* trilogy – the fall of the Old Republic and the rise of the Evil Empire. Some fans think these prequels tarnish the original trilogy's gilt-edged reputation, while others admire Lucas's telling of the wider backstory. As posters put it, 'Every Saga has a Beginning.' *Star Wars Episode I: The Phantom Menace* (1999) is set 30 years before the original *Star Wars*. It details an attempt to broker peace in the galaxy, when due to trade embargoes and blockades the Planet Naboo is invaded by the Trade Federation's droid army. The heroes are two Jedi Knight ambassadors: Qui-Gon Jinn (Liam Neeson) and his Padawan apprentice Obi-Wan Kenobi (Ewan McGregor). They steal a Naboo cruiser and break out through the blockade, saving Queen Amidala of Naboo and her entourage, but their ship is damaged and they take refuge on the planet Tatooine. Looking for parts in a nearby spaceport, Qui-Gon meets nine-year-old mechanic Anakin Skywalker (Jake Lloyd), a slave to hovering, bulbous-nosed parts dealer Watto, and recognises in him the powerful force, concluding: 'He will bring balance.'

The title sounds like an old *Flash Gordon* episode, but *The Phantom Menace* was greeted by fans with a heady mixture of euphoria and outrage in May 1999. Visually the movie is tremendous, with knockout spectacular imagery – the huge advances in technology readily apparent and adding much to Lucas's cinematic arsenal. But the script is flat and most of the performances (Neeson, Portman and Yoda excepted) are unbelievably two-dimensional. Portman played Queen Amidala (in a variety of outlandish Oriental-style outfits) and also appeared in disguise as her handmaiden Padmé, with Keira Knightley as her decoy double Sabé. Ian McDiarmid played Palpatine, the benevolent Naboo Galactic Republic senator, who later becomes Darth Sidious, the Emperor. The chief baddie is Sith apprentice Darth Maul (Ray Park, voiced by Peter Serafinowicz), a red-and-black-faced horned devil, with a black hooded cape and a double-bladed lightsabre, who is cut in two by Kenobi in a duel, after Jinn has been killed. Anakin's mother (Pernilla August) describes Anakin's birth as a Christ-like virgin birth. Terence Stamp played Chancellor

Valorum and Brian Blessed was Boss Nass, the wobbly-jowled, froggy-faced leader of the Gungan. Greg Proops and Scott Capurro voiced two-headed pod-race commentator Fode and Beed. Samuel L. Jackson was Jedi Knight Mace Windu and series regulars Frank Oz played Yoda, Anthony Daniels, C-3PO (who we see being built by Anakin as a protocol droid), and R2-D2 also crops up. The improvement in visual effects creates some fantastic landscapes, particularly the paradisiacal Naboo, the golden orbs of the underwater Gungan city and the deserts of Tatooine. In the finale, Anakin destroys the droids' control ship, which orbits Naboo (echoing the Death Star's destruction of the original film), while the Gungan army take on the droids in a massive land battle and Darth Maul duels with Jinn and Kenobi. The innumerable droids have been lumbered with voices that sound like 'Speak & Spell'. *Phantom Menace* features one major miscalculation: the tiresome high jinks of Naboo-native Jar Jar Binks the Gungan, an awkward, animated, flappy-eared jackass creation more appropriate for Sesame Street, with a voice like Donald Duck on helium, who blithers across the screen.

Phantom Menace also features the show-stopping Boonta Eve Podrace, an adrenaline-charged futuristic Grand National gambling event that's one part *Ben-Hur* chariot race, one part *Jedi* speeder bike chase. This superb set piece, a circuit race though the Arizona-like red desert of Tatooine on rocket-propelled contraptions, pits young Anakin against a variety of opponents, chiefly the hideous Sebula, who before the race assures Anakin: 'You're bantha fodder'. When Jabba the Hutt starts the race and Tuscan raiders take potshots at the competitors, while Jawas watch the pod units speed by, this is the magic of *Star Wars*. Made for $115 million, *The Phantom Menace* took $431 million in the US on its release. The Advance Style A posters featured young Anakin beside an adobe igloo, with his shadow casting the outline of his older self, Lord Vader.

The title of *Star Wars Episode II: Attack of the Clones* (2002) turned out to be prophetic, as this is more of the same from Lucas. Ten years later, Anakin is Obi-Wan Kenobi's Padawan apprentice, while Padmé is a senator amid further political turmoil, talk of a separatist movement and the creation of an Army of the Republic to help the Jedi keep order. Kenobi investigates an assassination attempt on Padmé when she arrives on Coruscant, which brings him into contact with bounty hunter Jango Fett (Temuera Morrison), who has a young son, Boba (Daniel Logan), and unveils the secret clone army (patterned after Jango) on the stormy ocean planet Kamino. We also see the droid foundry on Geonosis. Anakin is assigned as Padmé's bodyguard, and while in hiding in the Lake Country of Naboo they fall in love.

All the major players are back, with the addition of Christopher Lee as villain Count Dooku. McGregor, now promoted to the lead, is much better in this instalment, with his beard and longer hair, and again he wields a mean lightsabre. But the story's weak link is again Anakin (Hayden Christensen). Emotions are skin-deep and characterisation two-dimensional, with love scenes in a fairy-tale lakeside palace that are pure Disney. There's even a 'meet the parents' segment filmed for Anakin and Padmé, which was wisely left on the cutting-room floor. Padmé begins to resemble Princess Leia and in the end they marry. In other developments, Windu beheads Jango in combat, the Republic is falling under the control of Darth Sidious and the senators are in his thrall.

The film is at its best when it is alluding to *Star Wars* mythology – the teasing glimpse of Dooku's Death Star designs, ninja Yoda in an acrobatic lightsabre duel with the count, or the first sight of a certain moisture farmstead igloo on Tatooine (complete with Owen Lars and his wife Beru). Such moments create a fan tingle that the rest of the film sorely lacks. Anakin loses his right arm during a duel with Dooku, and Anakin's mother dies in his arms when she's been taken hostage by Tusken Raiders, which begins to tilt the young Jedi towards the Dark Side. Meanwhile Palpatine becomes Supreme Chancellor, while masking his alter ego, Darth Sidious. There's a fine sense of technological development (in one scene baddie Dooku escapes on a futuristic broomstick), but it's undermined by another flat script (with facile pronouncements such as 'Good call, my young Padawan' and 'Attack those Federation starships quickly') and too-flashy precipice-dangling adventures, verging on superheroism. There's an excellent aerial battle between Kenobi and Jango in an asteroid field and a scene in a magnificent, maleficent sandstone arena with Padmé, Anakin and Kenobi versus an odd squad of creatures, which is old-school gladiatorial combat, Ray Harryhausen style. Yoda wonders if all this fighting has resulted in a victory ('The shroud of the dark side has fallen. Begun the Clone War has') as armies amass for a confrontation. The film was another massive success for Twentieth Century-Fox and Lucasfilm, taking over $300 million in the US. The climactic battle is the first engagement of the Clone Wars.

Dave Filoni's *The Clone Wars* (2008) depicted the conflict in a computer-animated film. It features the vocal talents of Daniels, Jackson and Lee and is a fast-moving, imaginative adventure. At the height of the Clone Wars between the separatist droid army and the Republic's clones, Jedi are dispatched to rescue Jabba the Hutt's son. Anakin and his feisty new Padawan, Ahsoka Tano, manage to rescue the bawling baby Huttlet, who falls ill ('He's turning every shade of green except the one he's supposed to be'), but find themselves blamed by Dooku for the kidnapping. The actual culprit is Jabba's uncle, Ziro the Hutt, in league with Count Dooku, and the climax features a lightsabre duel between Dooku and Anakin in the Dune Sea on Tatooine. Eventually Jabba Jr. is reunited with his father, and the Hutt clan agree to join the Jedi and allow the clone armies to travel through their territories in the Outer Rim. This animated feature is visually tremendous, with some of the characters more three-dimensional than their live-action counterparts. The combat scenes of legions of droids attacking the clones are impressive, and the whole enterprise is backed by an excellent score from Kevin Kiner, with a couple of Williams's themes carried over from the movies.

Return of the Jedi was originally to have been called *Revenge of the Jedi*, but this was deemed inappropriate for a family movie, and it's arguable whether a Jedi would be a revenge-seeker. For *Star Wars Episode III: Revenge of the Sith* (2005), the title worked fine, as a Sith Lord was perfectly capable of vengeance. Set three years after *Attack of the Clones*, this is the best of the prequels. As the separatists fight the Jedi, Anakin beheads Dooku at Palpatine's orders and then becomes Palpatine's pupil. Palpatine is revealed to be Darth Sidious, and Anakin, through costuming and demeanour, becomes Darth Vader. Already adopting a black glove on his mechanical right hand, Anakin now wears black clothes and a cloak, as he becomes 'twisted by the Dark Side'. Convinced Padmé will perish during childbirth, he allies with Palpatine, who promises Anakin he will save her. Though much of the *Star Wars* political jargon alludes to Roman history – the senate, Imperial and Republic – Palpatine's rise to chancellor is Hitlerian, right down to a scene where many of the key Jedi Council are ruthlessly murdered in 'Order 66', an echo of the Night of the Long Knives, where Hitler consolidated his position via politically motivated murder. Darth Sidious's hood partially conceals his pale-skinned, wrinkled, evilly deformed countenance. Kenobi manages to convince Padmé that Anakin is no longer the man she loved, when he sees security hologram images of his one-time pupil slaughtering 'younglings' (young Jedi) as part of the chancellor's purge. The special effects are often overdone and the acrobatic Bruce Lee somersaults during lightsabre duels continue to look ridiculous. There's a big battle, with Wookiee and clone armies versus the droids (which features a cameo from Chewbacca), and numerous duels in vibrant settings. Having failed to defeat the chancellor in combat, Yoda heads into obscurity and exile. The leader of the droid army, General Grievous, is a cloaked skeletal Terminator. While attempting to do Grievous bodily harm, Kenobi chases the villain. Grievous flees in what appears to be a mechanical hamster wheel, pursued by Kenobi on a stampeding giant iguana.

But there's drama, urgency, heart-stopping emotion and excellence in *Revenge*, and McGregor, Portman, McDiarmid and Christensen give great performances. General Kenobi is seen wearing a brown monkish robe, while Padmé adopts a Leia-like duo-bun hairstyle. In the volcanic red hell of Planet Mustafar, Kenobi defeats Vader and leaves his corpse on lava shores as smouldering, limb-severed human wreckage. Sidious saves Vader's still-living remains and rebuilds him, with Anakin's body ensconced in the iconic black costume (a mechanical life-support system) in a bravura moment of drama. Vader's minions of the First Galactic Empire are now garbed in familiar grey uniforms and caps (as modelled in *Star Wars*), the clone troopers begin to resemble Imperial Stormtroopers and the ominous shot of the Death Star under construction bodes badly for the universe. Padmé gives birth to twins, during which she dies. The girl, Leia, is fostered by Senator Bail Organa (Jimmy Smits) and his wife on Alderaan, while the boy, Luke, is taken by Kenobi to Tatooine to the Lars farmstead. It's a fantastic, emotional ending to the story, which is successful on its own terms, but masterfully sets the scene for the original trilogy. In line with its dark subject matter, the film is rated PG-13 in the US and 12A in the UK. It was another success, taking almost $400 million in the US and $848 million worldwide.

Lucas has since gone back and enhanced the original trilogy, so the special effects more closely resemble the three films that were made in its wake. For example, *Star Wars* was reissued as a 'special edition' in 1997, with jazzed-up visuals and tweaks to dialogue and sound, including major changes to a now-expansive Mos Eisley sequence (with all manner of beasts in the crowded streets of this busy spaceport, which now resembles a city) and spectacular laser blasts and explosions (particularly the destruction of Leia's Alderaan and the Death Star's demise). Although there is only a two-minute difference in running time between the original print and the special edition, they are very different films. Added scenes have Han chatting to Jabba the Hutt in Docking Bay 94 (with Boba Fett present) and a conversation between Luke and Biggs (his friend from Tatooine who featured more prominently in the original shooting script) before the climactic attack on the Imperial star base. Fans were angered when Lucas altered the scene where Han shoots Greedo without warning in the cantina, so that Greedo now fires first and hits the wall before Han shoots him. This was to make Han more of a good guy, but fans responded with outrage and the cult favourite 'Han Shot First' T-shirts. Subsequent video, DVD and Blu-Ray releases continue to be tweaked by Lucas, to the joy or consternation of fans. Additions to the *Return of the Jedi* special edition include an animated musical number in Jabba's lair and the Sarlacc's pit now resembles something from *The Little Shop of Horrors*. *Star Wars* and its progeny have entrenched themselves forever in popular culture and have been parodied by everyone from Mel Brooks to *Family Guy*. 'Star Wars' was even the name assigned by the Reagan administration to the US ground- and space-based nuclear defence system, the Strategic Defence Initiative, a case of life and fact imitating art and fiction.

13

'WHEN YOU WISH UPON A STAR'

CLOSE ENCOUNTERS OF THE THIRD KIND (1977)

Director: Steven Spielberg
Screenplay: Steven Spielberg
Director of Photography: Vilmos Zsigmond
Music: John Williams
Panavision/Metrocolor
A Phillips/Columbia/EMI Production
Released by Columbia
126 minutes

Richard Dreyfuss (Roy Neary), François Truffaut (Claude Lacombe), Teri Garr (Ronnie Neary), Melinda Dillon (Jillian Guiler), Bob Balaban (David Laughlin), J. Patrick McNamara (project leader), Warren Kemmerling (Wild Bill), Roberts Blossom (farmer), Philip Dodds (Jean Claude), Cary Guffey (Barry Guiler), Shawn Bishop (Brad Neary), Adrienne Campbell (Silvia Neary), Justin Dreyfuss (Toby Neary), Lance Henriksen (Robert), George DiCenzo (Major Benchley), Gene Dynarski (Ike), Mary Gafrey (Mrs Harris), Josef Sommer (Larry Butler), Revd Michael J. Dyer (himself)

* * *

In contrast to such alien invasions as *The War of the Worlds* and *Earth vs. the Flying Saucers*, Earth has experienced cinematic extraterrestrial visitations of another kind, ones where they came in peace, even if they left in pieces. For his study *The UFO Experiment* (1972), astronomer, professor and ufologist Dr Josef Allen Hynek devised the Hynek Close Encounter Classification System. In a CE-I case, a UFO comes into close proximity (within about 500 feet) of the witness. CE-II is a UFO sighting that leaves markings on the ground, causes burns or paralysis, interferes with car engines, or TV and radio reception, while CE-III is a CE-I or CE-II that has visible occupants.

Robert Wise's *The Day the Earth Stood Still* (1951) was adapted for the screen by Edmund H. North from Harry Bates's short story *Farewell to the Master*. A flying saucer from another world lands in Washington, DC, with emissaries – human-like Klaatu (Michael Rennie) and his tall robot Gort (Lock Martin in a robot suit). Having been wounded, Klaatu hides out in a boarding house as 'Mr Carpenter' and befriends widow Helen Benson (Patricia Neal) and her son Bobby (Billy Gray), who is particularly taken with the stranger. Helen and her lover Tom Stevens (Hugh Marlowe) realise that Klaatu is the wanted alien, but Klaatu claims he is there for the world's good. The alien visitors here adopt a softly-softly approach, gently (though threateningly) prodding earthlings towards a better future. The aliens' worldwide show of strength is conveyed by stopping everything powered by electricity – with certain exceptions such as hospitals and planes in flight – from noon until half past, which paralyses the modern world.

Klaatu is a tall, urbane, benevolent alien (not a little green man), who is intelligent and literate. Having travelled 250 million miles to Earth proffering peace and goodwill, he is met with hostility. Gort is more what we expect from the genre: a silver-suited robot that fires a disintegrating laser beam from a slit in its visored head. For the finale, Helen activates Gort with the words 'Klaatu barada nikto', the robot breaks Klaatu out of jail and revives him in the flying saucer. At a summit with the world's scientists, Klaatu addresses

The Day the Earth Stood Still: Emissaries Gort and Klaatu arrive on Earth to warn us that our actions will have consequences if we continue our nuclear research, in Robert Wise's 1951 sci-fi parable.

them on behalf of the 'other planets'. In the light of Earth's experimentation and nuclear advancement, Klaatu calls for tolerance, peace and responsible actions. In space, the planets have their own police – indestructible robots like Gort – who patrol in saucers. The robots have absolute power, which cannot be resisted or revoked. The inhabitants of outer space behave themselves, as the consequences are too great to risk. If Earth's nuclear violence extends beyond Earth itself, action will be taken. The options are simple. Join the other planets in peace, or risk obliteration by Gort and his robotic brethren. Before Klaatu takes off into space, he leaves Earth with a stark warning: 'The decision rests with you.'

The Day the Earth Stood Still was shot at Twentieth Century-Fox Studios and in Washington, DC, at the George Washington Monument, the White House, the Lincoln Memorial, the Arlington War Cemetery, and the flying saucer lands on the grassy Ellipse. Bernard Herrmann composed the ebbing, atmospheric score, which includes the trend-setting use of the eerie, oscillating theremin. For its underplayed action, compelling story and timeless message, *The Day the Earth Stood Still* remains one of the most highly regarded sci-fi films of the 1950s.

The Day the Earth Stood Still suffered an ill-advised remake in 2008, directed by Scott Derrickson. In this modern retelling, Dr Helen Benson (Jennifer Connelly) – a widowed astrobiologist – and other scientists and engineers are called to Fort Linwood Military Academy, New Jersey, to form a crisis team, as a meteor is about to flatten Manhattan. The foreign object slows down and the saucer (now a swirling, planet-like sphere) lands in Central Park, New York. Klaatu the alien is shot, but recovers in hospital and sheds its blubbery outer layer to reveal Keanu Reeves. Klaatu wants to meet with the UN and becomes a fugitive, aided and abetted by Helen and her son Jacob (Jaden Smith, Will's son). Other orbs have landed around the world and they are there to save our planet's animals, a fleet of Noah's Arks. Earth is enduring a slow, painful environmental disaster, and Klaatu Reeves is here to save the planet. For some reason, Reeves decided to play Klaatu as a bad impersonation of Clint Eastwood. The actual moment when he makes the Earth 'stand still' is wastefully shifted to the climax, reducing one of the great moments of science fiction to an afterthought.

In the 1970s, UFOs and UFO sightings were everywhere, from books and newspapers to hokey documentaries. Eyewitness accounts had slack-jawed lollygaggers claiming, 'I seen it. I don't know what it was, but I seen it.' *UFO: Target Earth* (1974), directed by Michael A. DeGaetano and released by Jed Productions, opens with several such 'eyewitness interviews' recounting incredible UFO sightings and abductions. Shot in Atlanta, Georgia, this incredible sci-fi 'film' features a plot that makes no sense whatsoever. Scientist Alan Grimes (Nick Plakias) and UFO abductee Vivian (Cynthia Cline) trace the alien signals to an eerie lake, but the movie is so cheap as to be oddly unsettling, in the way only very low-budget cinema sometimes can be.

Following his blockbuster *Jaws* (1975), Steven Spielberg began work on his first foray into science fiction: *Close Encounters of the Third Kind* (1977), which he wrote and directed.

The film depicts the arrival of alien visitors, via various stages. A close encounter of the first kind is a sighting of a UFO, the second kind is physical evidence and the third kind is contact (these three stages were also used on posters advertising the film). Brightly lit alien craft are spotted reconnoitring over the US, and locals gather at night to watch them. Electrical engineer Roy Neary (Richard Dreyfuss) witnesses these lights while investigating a massive power outage in Indiana, while Jillian Guiler (Melinda Dillon) finds her 3-year-old son Barry (Cary Guffey) abducted by the aliens, after his toys have magically but inexplicably sprung to life. Those who have had some form of contact with the crafts' lights (which cause sunburn-like scorches to the skin) become obsessed with a mysterious mountain: Jillian sketches it, while Roy recreates a large-scale model of it in his lounge. This icon is revealed to be Devil's Tower in Wyoming, which will be the point at which the aliens will make contact. The authorities evacuate the surrounding area by claiming that a train carrying nerve gas has crashed in the vicinity, and set up a phoney decontamination unit, which is in fact a scientific base in the shadow of the mountain, with an illuminated runway. Roy and Jillian manage to negotiate the cordon and watch as the reconnaissance spacecraft return, this time accompanied by an immense, glittering, tiered mother ship, which communicates to the scientists with music – first a distinctive undulating five-note phrase and later with a full-scale celestial recital. Barry and other abductees (including US pilots who have not been seen since 1945) are released from the alien ship, and Roy has a close encounter with the aliens as he boards their craft.

Close Encounters is the classic UFO movie and Spielberg's most cinematic, visually beautiful sci-fi film. In this, he is abetted by master director of photography Vilmos Zsigmond, whose artistry, particularly with blindingly bright lights and expansive Panavision vistas, won him an Academy Award for Best Cinematography. Additional photography was done by John Alonzo and László Kovács. Locals in Muncie, Indiana, camp out at night and watch the UFO's vivid light show for entertainment, and the scene of Gary's abduction, through the cat flap – which mixes paranormal horror with science-fiction wonderment, as mysterious lights descend outside the Guiler residence and appliances suddenly activate – is one of the great sci-fi set pieces.

Close Encounters was filmed for $19 million, on location in Alabama, Wyoming, California and India, near Mumbai, and in two massive aircraft hangars in Brookley Field Industrial Complex, Mobile, Alabama. Devil's Tower is in the Black Hills National Forest, Wyoming. The supervisor for special photographic effects was Douglas Trumbull, while Carlo Rambaldi designed the child-like bug-eyed, bulbous-headed extraterrestrials that emerge from the mother ship. The supporting cast includes French New Wave director François Truffaut as scientist Claude Lacombe, who pieces together the clues on the trail of strange phenomena, from discovering the US Air Force planes from 1945's missing Flight 19 in the Sonora Desert, Mexico, to investigating religious chanting of the five-note musical 'codex' in India. In later cuts of the film prepared by Spielberg, this

Sighting, Evidence, Contact: Steven Spielberg's 1977 alien-visitation movie *Close Encounters of the Third Kind* both capitalised on and fuelled the public's interest in UFOs.

oddness includes the ship SS *Cotopaxi* being discovered dumped in the middle of the Gobi Desert in Mongolia.

Spielberg's imaginative story throws out the idea of aliens making war on Earth and instead proffers a peaceful message, with friendly aliens who communicate with us through musical phrases. John Williams's score is key to the film and the success of this theme, with music central to the aliens' making contact with us and the euphoria of playing music translated here into the pleasure of making 'first contact'. The five-tone 'communication' the aliens use has passed into sci-fi mythology, while the 'concert' by the mother ship, all flashing lightshow and musical arabesques, resembles a contemporary pop concert in its showmanship and immediacy. There are even snatches of 'When You Wish upon a Star', which, since its use in *Pinocchio* (1940), has become the Walt Disney Company's leitmotif. This communal musical experience brings people together, like those present at the Devil's Tower concert or the UFO 'nuts' who have converged on the site from all over the US (like Roy and Jillian on their odyssey from Indiana to Wyoming) and are rounded up by the authorities. But Roy's obsessive behaviour, which in some scenes resembles mental illness, drives his wife Ronnie (Teri Garr) to leave with the children. Dreyfus (recast by Spielberg after *Jaws*) is excellent as the visionary who doesn't know what he's looking at. But eventually those who seek 'an answer' are rewarded with contact with the visitors. This 'shared vision' aspect of the story gives the finale religious significance. The authorities crop-dust the area with sleeping gas, to knock out any stray members of the public, so there are no unauthorised witnesses to this scientific 'miracle'. Roy and Jillian are clear examples of one of the key themes of Spielberg's cinema: ordinary people in extraordinary circumstances, witnessing extraordinary events.

Columbia rushed Spielberg into releasing the film in November 1977 and it was very successful (taking almost $300 million worldwide), but Spielberg was dissatisfied with some aspects of it and re-edited a 'special edition' in 1980. Among several changes to this version (including the SS *Cotopaxi* scene), we see inside the alien mother ship with its windows of light at the climax. Spielberg also prepared a third version in 1998, the 'collector's edition' or 'director's cut', which further re-edited material, reverted to the original ending and doesn't show the craft's interior. With *Star Wars* and *Alien*, *Close Encounters* is among the most influential science-fiction films of the 1970s, and it can be seen in everything from *Signs* and *The X-Files* to Spielberg's own 2002 TV miniseries *Taken*, which dramatised alien abduction and the Roswell Incident in 1947. A flying saucer allegedly crash-landed in the New Mexico desert, and its existence was supposedly covered up by the US government in Area 51 in Nevada, a military base that it didn't even admit existed until 1995.

Spielberg revisited the theme of friendly alien visitors from space in *E.T. the Extra-Terrestrial* (1982), which was originally to be called *Night Skies*. During an alien sortie to Earth to collect botanic samples in a Californian forest, one alien is left behind. As the trailer stated: 'He's lost, he's alone and he's three million light years from home.' The creature hides in a Los Angeles garage and becomes adopted by little Elliott (Henry Thomas), who lives with his mother Mary (Dee Wallace), brother Mike (Robert MacNaughton) and sister Gertie (Drew Barrymore). The children discover E.T. has special powers (including healing) and Elliott telepathically empathises with the alien. E.T. constructs a device from various bits and pieces, including a buzzsaw and the children's electronic 'Speak & Spell' teaching aid, to send a transmission home, and the mantra 'E.T. phone home' quickly passed into cinema history. Meanwhile, government agents become interested in the extraterrestrial visitor and keep Elliott's household under surveillance.

Spielberg shot the movie on location in California in late 1981 for $10.5 million. The film's fairy-tale atmosphere was enhanced by murky, ethereal cinematography by Allen Daviau and John Williams's soaring score. Some commentators have interpreted the film as a story of a Messianic arrival, while others see E.T. as a surrogate father figure to Elliott. Erika Eleniak (later of *Baywatch* fame) played a cute schoolgirl with whom Elliott recreates a kiss between John Wayne and Maureen O'Hara in *The Quiet Man*, when, intoxicated, he disrupts a dissection class and frees all the frogs. There are also sci-fi and fantasy pop-culture references littered throughout the film, including *Earth vs. the Flying Saucers* on TV, Elliott playing with *Star Wars* figures and Mike mimicking Yoda's voice. When they go trick-or-treating, with E.T. dressed as a ghost, they pass a child dressed as Yoda and E.T. waddles towards him, saying, 'Home.' In the film's iconic moment, Elliott (dressed as a hunchback) and E.T. pedal across the starry night sky by bike, passing a fir treetop silhouetted against a bright October moon, which became the logo for Spielberg's production company, Amblin Entertainment.

E.T. is a sentimental, magical children's film which features Carlo Rambaldi's incredible puppet creation. The child-sized, shuffling, wrinkled E.T. has long arms, spindly digits, an extendible, stretchy neck and a triangular face that resembles a tortoise's. Spielberg reputedly created the face by superimposing Albert Einstein's eyes and forehead on a photo of a baby. E.T. was voiced by rasping heavy smoker Pat Welsh and actress Deborah Winger. In the film's famous conclusion, Elliott, Mike and three of their schoolmates – Greg, Steve and Tyler (K.C. Martel, Sean Frye and C. Thomas Howell) – speed on their choppers, with the government agents in hot pursuit and E.T. in a carrier basket on the front of Elliott's bike, to keep their rendezvous with the rescue ship in the woods. On its release in 1982, *E.T.* was a smash, outgrossing even *Star Wars*, and remained the biggest hit in film history until *Jurassic Park* (1993). On its first run *E.T.* took almost $350 million in the US and Canada. It was re-released in 1985 and an extended, slightly tweaked version appeared on the film's twentieth anniversary in March 2002. This version famously altered the government agents' pump-action shotguns to walkie-talkies, in a perceived 'softening' of the film's content. The film's current worldwide gross is approaching $800 million.

In the wake of *E.T.*'s success Spielberg formed Amblin in 1984, an independent with a lot at Universal Pictures. Under its aegis, Spielberg presented movies with broad family appeal, such as the *Back to the Future* and *Men in Black* films and Matthew Robbins's *batteries not included* (1987). A New York apartment block is slated for demolition, as all about it has been levelled in preparation for a new development, Lacey Plaza. The plucky residents (an elderly couple, an artist, a pregnant Hispanic woman, a washed-up ex-boxer) are aided in their fight with the big corporation and its muscle by cute alien spaceships that are nesting on their roof – two cute flying saucers and three smaller, cuter little robots. The film is really about human relationships, especially Frank Riley (Hume Cronyn) and his eccentric wife Faye (Jessica Tandy), and artist Mason (Dennis Boutsikaris) and expectant Marisa (Elizabeth Peña). The film's most interesting reading is as a depiction of mental illness and senility, with Faye's ramblings and UFO sightings of 'the little guys' initially written off as figments of her aged imagination.

Simon Wincer's *D.A.R.Y.L.* (1985) combined juvenile sci-fi and technology with a surprisingly effective weepy tale of adoption and fostering. Daryl (Barret Oliver), a lost boy suffering from amnesia, is taken into care. He is temporarily placed with foster parents, Andy and Joyce Richardson (Michael McKean and Mary Beth Hurt). Daryl befriends Turtle Fox (Danny Corkill), a boy his age who lives nearby, and everyone soon realises that Daryl is a very gifted child with a natural talent for everything from piano and computer games to baseball. His foster parents dote on him and are distraught when his real parents show up. Daryl is taken away to a research facility. He is a secret government project, D.A.R.Y.L. (Data Analysing Robot Youth Lifeform), an experiment in artificial intelligence. A pre-programmed computerised brain has been installed in a boy who has been genetically created in a test tube. He is a walking memory bank, designed for sensory data analysis via the five human senses. When Daryl begins to experience sensitive human emotions, such as anxiety and fear, the Pentagon decides the project has run its course. They want a ruthless, superintelligent soldier, not a talented kid, and Daryl is to be terminated. The project's head, Dr Jeffrey Stewart (Josef Sommer), helps Daryl escape. The Marvin Hamlisch score and ballad 'Somewhere I Belong', belted out by Teddy Pendergrass, may telegraph kiddie schmaltz, but this simple, low-key drama is much more about genuine human emotions than special effects.

Joe Dante's *Explorers* (1985) explored the relationship between three school friends – sci-fi geek Ben (Ethan Hawke), boffin Wolfgang (River Phoenix) and cool dude Darren (Jason Presson). They convert a fairground waltzer into a spacecraft pod, which they christen 'Thunder Road' after a Springsteen song, and travel into space, whereupon the film careers off the rails when the kids encounter blubbery, jabbering aliens which have absorbed terrestrial TV shows and adverts, and whose irritating antics sink the film. *Explorers* features Tron-like circuitry in Ben's dream and spectacular aerial travel graphics, with alien make-up from Rob Bottin. Dante includes plenty of sci-fi clips (including *The Thing from Another World*, *The Day the Earth Stood Still*, *The War of the Worlds*, *This Island Earth* and *IT! The Terror from Beyond Space*) and references, such as the newspaper, the *Davanna Gazette* (the planet Davanna featured in *Not of This Earth*). Roger Corman regular Dick Miller had a cameo as a sky marshal, and *Starkiller*, Dante's spoof sci-fi B-movie at the drive-in, is named after Anakin Starkiller (Luke Skywalker's original name).

Randal Kleiser's *Flight of the Navigator* (1986) was a US–Norwegian production in which 12-year-old David Freeman (Joey Cramer) goes walking in a wood in 1978, stumbles down a ravine and on his return home discovers eight years have elapsed. His family have moved house and aged, while he is still a 12-year-old boy. David is taken to a NASA facility to be studied, but escapes hidden in robot R.A.L.F. (Robotic Assistant Labour Facilitator, which resembles a boxy, wheeled photocopier). He boards a clamshell-shaped spacecraft that NASA has impounded and the onboard computer MAX recognises him as its pilot, the Navigator. Under David's orders the ship takes off to David's family's home in Fort Lauderdale, Florida. It is explained that the alien ship had taken David as a specimen to study and travelled 560 light years to the planet Phaelon, which took 2.2 solar hours at light speed, or the equivalent of eight Earth years. MAX, the metallic armature and 'head', which communicates with David, was voiced by Paul Reubens (billed as Pall Mall, before he became known as Pee-Wee Herman). Veronica Cartwright and Cliff De Young played David's parents, Howard Hesseman played NASA researcher Dr Faraday and Sarah Jessica Parker played NASA intern Carolyn McAdams. The clamshell spacecraft is beautifully designed and its dripping, liquid metal steps are the film's best feature. The speeding aerial travelogue sequences are also well photographed. The Beach Boys' 'I Get Around' is particularly fitting on the soundtrack. On the spacecraft there are other specimens that have been collected throughout the galaxy (including a giant screaming eyeball) of the cutesy alien muppet variey. In the film's best scene, the spacecraft pulls into 'Al's Gator City' gas station for David to use a telephone to ring his parents. Tourists photograph the craft as though it's an attraction, until it takes off and they are left dumbstruck, while hick Al intones, 'Just said he wanted to phone home.'

Close Encounters and *E.T.* sired the expected Continental derivatives. Cary Guffey went on to appear as alien visitor H7-25 opposite Italian comedy superstar Bud Spencer (as Sheriff Hall) in Michele Lupo's two Italian–US sci-fi comedies aimed at the matinée market – *The Sheriff and the Satellite Kid* (1979) and its sequel *Why Did you Pick on Me?* (1980). Juan Piquer Simón's *Extraterrestrial Visitors* (1983; *The Pod People*) was a low-budget Franco-Spanish sci-fi travesty. In a perpetually misty wood (Sierra De Guadarrama, near Madrid), a meteor crash-lands. Various characters – a bunch of illegal poachers (including Frank Braña and Guillermo Antón) and pop singer Rick (Ian Sera) and his entourage – are menaced or killed by a hairy, bear-like predator that strikes from the mist. Young Tommy (Óscar Martín) finds an egg in a cave. At home, it hatches out an alien which resembles a bear with an elephant's head that can hoover up peanuts with its trunk. Tommy christens it Trumpy and the trundling minibeast has special powers, rendered via the wonders of primitive stop-motion animation. Meanwhile, outside, the evil alien, Trumpy's twin, ambles amok on a low-key yet murderous shuffling rampage, as the continuity editor takes a holiday and the action switches freely from day to night. If Trumpy ever got around to phoning home, it would surely have been a trunk call.

Mario Gariazzo's *The Eyes behind the Stars* (1978) was an Italian *Close Encounters* without the special effects. When a photographer takes pictures of a model in an eerie wood, he notices two alien figures in the image. Inspector Jim Grant (Martin Balsam) investigates when the photographer is abducted. Reporter Tony Harris (Robert Hoffman) suspects a government cover-up, while a secret society of agents, The Silencers (led by George Ardisson), seek to destroy any photographic evidence and 'prove the inexistence of UFOs'. The film seems to be set in England (though looking at the architecture, it was probably shot in Italy) and offers the opportunity to hear Balsam dubbed with a Lancashire accent. This plodding story makes alien abduction as dull as car theft and ends with the astonishingly random disclaimer: 'Portions of the events depicted in this film actually happened, although at different times and in other places.'

More convincing was Robert Zemeckis's *Contact* (1997), which was carried by the central performance by Jodie Foster as lifelong star-watcher Dr Eleanor 'Ellie' Arroway. Since she was a little girl, experimenting with radio transmitters and telescopes with her father Ted (David Morse), Ellie has been forever seeking extraterrestrial life. Ellie picks up a throbbing transmission from the Vega star in deep space. Interlaced in a visual broadcast of Hitler's speech at the 1936 Berlin Olympic Games (the first Earth broadcast to reach outer space) are instructions to build a spacecraft and its gyroscopic launcher. The contraption is built by a worldwide consortium at a cost of trillions of dollars. Ellie pilots the shuttle to Vega, where she converses with alien intelligence, which manifests itself in the form of her father. On her return she claims to have been away for 18 hours, but witnesses simply saw Ellie's shuttle drop straight through the machine. Ellie is cross-examined by sceptical national-security advisor Michael Kitz (James Woods) until it is revealed that official recording equipment present filmed 18 hours of static. *Contact* was adapted from Carl Sagan's bestselling novel of the same name. When Ellie is seeking financial backers, she suggests they visit Hollywood: 'They've been making money off aliens for years, right?' Ellie's loneliness is key to her quest for 'contact'. She never knew her mother and she lost her father when she was nine years old. The contact she seeks in this mystical, spiritual fable is contact with people. Uniting the scientific and the spiritual is Palmer Joss (Matthew McConaughey), a self-styled author and religious humanitarian ('a man of the cloth without the cloth'). Palmer is anti-technology and anti-science, but the two come to love, respect and believe in one another. Tom Skerritt played Ellie's long-time nemesis Dr David Drumlin, who scoffs, 'Still waiting for E.T. to call?' And John Hurt played Ellie's shadowy, space-mad backer S.R. Hadden. The film opens with a fantastical journey through the solar system, whizzing past planets and constellations, which is space as imagined in Ellie's mind's eye. Later, Ellie's trip through tunnel-like wormholes to Vega and back, past celestial wonders, is a zooming swirl of light, as she's sucked through a vortex of energy that resembles the 'star gate' in *2001*.

Andy Fickman's *Race to Witch Mountain* (2009) told of a close encounter between teen aliens Seth and Sara (Alexander Ludwig and AnnaSophia Robb) and Vegas cab driver Jack Bruno (Dwayne Johnson), as the fugitives are whizzed across country to their ship, which has been impounded in a top-secret US government facility inside Witch Mountain. Johnson displays a fine line in self-deprecating humour, allowing himself to be upstaged by, among others, a dog who tags along on their adventure. There are jokes at the expense of a UFO space expo (deemed by Bruno a 'nut-job convention') at Planet Hollywood, and Carla Gugino played UFO 'science fact' expert Dr Alex Friedman. Garry Marshall portrayed conspiracy theorist and UFO 'crank' Dr Donald Harlan, while stoner icon Cheech Marin breezed in as the helpful mechanic, Eddie Cortez. Breakneck pacing papers over the film's plot holes and it plays like a kids' *Terminator* with a deadly armoured alien in relentless pursuit.

Race to Witch Mountain was a high-tech reworking of John Hough's *Escape to Witch Mountain* (1975), which was partly filmed on the spectacular Californian coast and was a massive hit for Disney. Orphans Tia and Tony Malone (Kim Richards and Ike Eisenmann) are kidnapped by Lucas Deranian (Donald Pleasence), who takes them to live with wealthy but scheming Aristotle Bolt (Ray Milland). They plan to put the children's powers (telepathic communication with animals, object moving, sixth-sense precognition and levitation) to good use. The duo go on the run and with help from Winky the black cat, a bear, a horse and grumpy widower Jason O'Day (Eddie Albert), they are reunited with Uncle Bene (Denver Pyle). The children are actually extraterrestrial 'castaways' from another planet. The special effects look patchy now, but don't miss when bad guy Sheriff Purdy (Walter Barnes) is attacked by a raincoat, a broom and a hat. *Return from Witch Mountain* (1978) had the children returning to Earth and Tony being kidnapped by Letha Wedge (Bette Davis), mad scientist Dr Victor Gannon (Christopher Lee) and Letha's nephew Sickle (Anthony James). What could have been just another Disney matinée is considerably enlivened by Lalo Schifrin's 'Dirty Harry' out-takes score and a comedy goat.

Alien Nation (1988) looked at aliens' integration into Earth society via a buddy–cop movie and a snapshot of murky drug subculture. By 1991 aliens have landed in the Mojave Desert and live among us, but they are referred to as Newcomers, suffer prejudicial treatment from humans, and their community is referred to as Slagtown or Slagville. In Los Angeles, Detective Sergeant Matthew Sykes (James Caan) investigates his partner's murder with a new sidekick, Sam Francisco (Mandy Patinkin), the first Newcomer to be promoted to detective. It's a typical chalk-and-cheese partnering of Sam, the happy family man, with Matthew, who lives alone in a house so untidy that George thinks its been 'burglarised'. Their teaming highlights racial tensions, with the duo christened 'ETPD'. The homicide procedural leads them to rich businessman William Harcourt (Terence Stamp in alien make-up) and his henchman Rudyard Kipling (Kevyn Major Howard), both Newcomers, who are making and distributing a powerful narcotic. This tough thriller is leavened with humour. Newcomers' pithy insults include, 'Your mother mates out of season', and they get wasted on sour milk and instead of hamburgers enjoy portions of raw beaver. Stan Winston Studios convincingly created the dappled, dome-headed alien make-up and Leslie Bevis was unexpectedly attractive as Newcomer exotic dancer Cassandra, who performs to a cover of 'Sympathy for the Devil' by Jane's Addiction. Directed by Graham Baker, this quirky film later spawned a sanitised TV series, also called *Alien Nation* (1989–90), plus several TV-movie spin-offs.

Hangar 18 (1980), starring Darren McGavin and Robert Vaughn, had two astronauts (Gary Collins and James Hampton) colliding with a UFO, but no one believes them, so they must expose the government cover-up of the extraterrestrial craft, which is hidden in the building of the title in Texas. The award for 'Vaguest Alien Close-Encounter Movie' is easily won by M. Night Shyamalan's *Signs* (2002). In Bucks County, Pennsylvania, former reverend Graham Hess (Mel Gibson) has suffered a loss of faith since the death of his wife. Graham lives with his brother, former baseball player Merrill (Joaquin Phoenix) and Graham's children, Morgan (Rory Culkin) and Bo (Abigail Breslin). They discover crop circles in their cornfield and call in local sheriff Carline Paski (Cherry Jones) to investigate, but it soon becomes apparent that the strange manifestations are a worldwide phenomenon, when alien craft arrive using the crop-circle 'signs' to navigate. The film proffers two reasons why aliens come to Earth: peaceful contact or hostile attrition. But the aliens here carry out human harvesting using a poisonous gas, and an illustration in UFO-enthusiast Morgan's book features a flying saucer attacking a house that looks remarkably like theirs.

Graham and his family barricade themselves inside their home and end up trapped in their dimly lit basement. As Merrill notes, 'It's like *War of the Worlds*.' Fittingly, baseball hero Merrill beats the alien up with a baseball bat and they can also be dispatched by being splashed with water. The film has a good, creepy small-town atmosphere and at least one excellent shiver, during a video clip taken at a children's party in Mexico, where a stalking green alien makes a brief appearance. *Signs* is an eccentric film, which often digresses, with offbeat performances (especially from Gibson and Phoenix) in which familial guilt and blame are as much in evidence as sci-fi action, though it is the aliens' eventual defeat that restores lapsed Graham's faith. As in *Contact* and other alien visitations, these close encounters bring people closer together.

14

'IN SPACE NO ONE CAN HEAR YOU SCREAM'

ALIEN (1979)

Director: Ridley Scott
Story: Dan O'Bannon and Ronald Shusett
Screenplay: Dan O'Bannon
Director of Photography: Derek Vanlint
Music: Jerry Goldsmith
Panavision/DeLuxe Color
A Brandywine/Shusett/Twentieth Century-Fox Production
Released by Twentieth Century-Fox
117 minutes

Tom Skerritt (Captain Dallas), Sigourney Weaver (Ripley, third officer), Veronica Cartwright (Lambert, navigator), Harry Dean Stanton (Brett, engineer), John Hurt (Kane, executive officer), Ian Holm (Ash, science officer), Yaphet Kotto (Parker, chief engineer), Helen Horton (voice of Mother), Bolaji Badejo (The Alien)

* * *

With *The Terminator*, *Mad Max* and *Star Wars*, *Alien* is one of the most imitated sci-fi films in cinema history. The film's premise – an alien monster at large on a spaceship – made it easy to restage, with minimal sets and cast. But what marked this space shocker out from earlier such offerings was the stomach-churning special effects. As sailors fear fire at sea, astronauts fear aliens hitching a ride across the universe, where, according to *Alien*'s tagline, 'In space no one can hear you scream.'

Though 1950s sci-fi movies were reasonably restrained in their deployment of gore, with most atrocities occurring off-screen, Arthur Crabtree's sci-fi shocker *Fiend without a Face* (1957) was the *Alien* of its day. At US Air Force Experimental Station No. 6, near Winthrop, Manitoba, locals' suspicions are aroused following a series of mysterious deaths in which victims have been throttled, had the nape of their necks punctured, their brains sucked out 'like an egg' and their spinal cords extracted. The army are conducting powerful radar experiments using atomic energy to spy on the Russians across the Bering Strait. Investigating the deaths, Major Jeff Cummings (Marshall Thompson) meets Barbara Griselle (Kim Parker), the assistant to Professor Walgate, an authority on psychic phenomena and the 'materialisation of thought'. The professor diverts nuclear energy from the base – his research into brain power and thought control has created an invisible entity. When the nuclear-reactor levels rise, the flying faceless fiends become visible and lay siege to the professor's house. *Fiend* was shot in the UK, at Walton Studios, Walton-on-Thames, and is based on Amelia Reynolds Long's short story 'The Thought Monster'. Plodding for the most part, as did many creature features, the film's finale really delivers,

The flying brains of Arthur Crabtree's *Fiend without a Face* (1957) heralded a new brand of grisly sci-fi horror.

as several characters (including Walgate, Jeff and Barbara) barricade themselves inside Walgate's house. The brain-sucking creatures, described as 'mental vampires', drain their victims' intelligence. They resemble human brains with the addition of antennae, feelers and a whip-like propellant spinal-cord tail. The tail coils around victims' necks, while the victim's brains are extracted. For their attack on the house, there's a fair amount of bubbling gore on display. The defenders shoot and axe the brains, which in this monochrome film ooze black blood. Jeff escapes and blows up the nuclear reactor with dynamite and the brains disintegrate into mush. A cut version of *Fiend without a Face* was passed in 1958 in the UK as an X certificate, and it remains a pleasantly beastly B-movie *tour de gore*.

The key influence on *Alien* was Edward L. Cahn's *IT! The Terror from beyond Space* (1958; *IT! The Vampire from beyond Space*). In 1973, US space rocket *Challenge 142*, the second mission to Mars, lands on the planet to find out what became of the first expedition, which vanished six months earlier. Of the 10 crewmen, they find only Colonel Edward Carruthers (Marshall Thompson again), who is charged with the murder of his fellow astronauts. Carruthers says that they were marooned on the planet and during a sandstorm they were wiped out by a mysterious monster. *Challenge 142* takes off, but something large and unpleasant has climbed aboard through an open emergency hatch. Soon crewmen are attacked, their desiccated corpses left with pasty skin and black-ringed eyes. The monster absorbs by osmosis its victims' edible fluid: water, oxygen, blood, glandular secretion, bone marrow and moisture in the tissues, leaving withered remains which die of 'cellular collapse and dehydration'. The crew try to destroy the monster with grenades, bullets, gas bombs,

IT! The Terror from Beyond Space: The principal inspiration for *Alien*, Edward L. Cahn's creature feature had its planetary explorers pick up an unwelcome stowaway on Mars.

electrocution and radiation, which just make IT angry. Paul Sawtell and Bert Shefter provided the tension-filled score and Kenneth Peach photographed the action in moody, noirish monochrome, which creates dark spaces as the monster stalks the ship. The monster – a tall, vicious, clawed beast that roars like a lion and resembles a cross between a scaly gorilla and the Creature from the Black Lagoon – was created by Paul Blaisdell and played by Ray 'Crash' Corrigan. With the dwindling survivors trapped on the control deck, Carruthers realises that their oxygen consumption is 40 per cent up since the arrival of their passenger. Its enormous Martian lungs consume vast quantities of oxygen, due to the thin air on Mars. The crew don their space suits, open the airlock into space and drain the oxygen, and the monster runs out of puff and dies. Of the 19 astronauts who set out to explore Mars, only six return. The film's tagline was: '$50,000 guaranteed! By a world renowned insurance company to the first person who can prove IT is not on Mars now!' (the small print specified 'Offer expires on Jan 1st, 1960'), while the trailer wisely advised: 'Don't miss IT!'

IT! was remade in a week for $65,000 by Curtis Harrington for AIP as *Queen of Blood* (1966; *Planet of Blood*), which owed its space visuals to archive footage lifted from the Russian sci-fi film *Mechte navstrechu* (1963; *A Dream Come True*). In 1990, Professor Farraday (Basil Rathbone) oversees a mission by two spacecraft, *Oceano* and *Meteor*, from moon base Lunar 7, while a team of astronauts (including John Saxon, Judi Meredith and Dennis Hopper) carry out the rescue of aliens who have crash-landed on Mars and Phobos. They take in a mute alien survivor (Florence Marly), who's a sucker for blood. They feed her plasma, but when it runs out, the crew become her victims. Marly's space vampire is a fine, creepy creation. With her blonde beehive hair, bright hypnotic eyes, green skin and leotard, she resembles a menacing, though strangely seductive, spring onion. The queen bee is defeated (she is a haemophiliac and bleeds to death), but she has laid pulsating tomato-like eggs all over the ship, which Faraday plans to examine back on Earth.

Alien was also partly influenced by Italian sci-fi. The astronauts awaken from hibernation pods at the beginning of *Assignment: Outer Space* (1960), and amid swirling space mists on planet Aura another group of astronauts explores a rusting spacecraft crewed by the skeletal remains of giant primeval creatures in *Planet of the Vampires* (1965). When the Japanese and US teamed up to make a rampaging alien movie, the results were Kinji Fukasaku's *The Green Slime* (1966), shot at Toei Studios, Tokyo. Rogue asteroid Flora is on a collision course with Earth. Commander Jack Rankin is sent to space station Gamma 3 to lead the operation to land on the asteroid and blow it up. Gamma 3's commander is Vince Elliot (Richard Jaeckel), Jack's one-time friend, now his love rival, as Vince is engaged to Jack's old flame, Dr Lisa Benson (Luciana Paluzzi). While planting the explosives on Flora, Dr Halvorsen (Ted Gunther) discovers pulsating blobs of green slime, a small blob of which ends up back on Gamma 3, where it generates into first one, then many, green, bubbly, walking creatures with one red eye, clomping feet and lobster-clawed tentacles. These shambling cyclops creatures (played by Japanese children in foam suits) emit a noise akin to gulls screeching, and they thrive and grow on the absorption of energy. They transfer this into a weapon and electrocute and fry their victims. With its dinky spaceship special effects and groovy theme song ('Green Slime', sung by Richard Delvy) this is retro classic stuff. The publicity department couldn't decide if 'slime' was singular or plural, veering between 'The Green Slime are Coming!' and 'The Green Slime is Here!' Judging by the film, they're definitely plural.

Ridley Scott's *Alien* (1979) was set aboard the *Nostromo*, a commercial starship towing a refinery processing 20 million tons of mineral ore. The seven crew members emerge from hibernation only to find they have been roused too soon and are off course. The onboard computer, Mother, has woken them due to a distress signal from a nearby planet. Kane (John Hurt), Lambert (Veronica Cartwright) and Captain Dallas (Tom Skerritt) investigate, and they find the wreck of a giant spacecraft with the skeleton of a monstrous alien at the controls. Kane delves into the bowels of the ship and finds a nest of alien eggs, while on the *Nostromo* the crew discover too late that the beacon transmission wasn't an SOS but a warning. One of the eggs hatches and a strange, octopus-like creature attaches itself to Kane's face. As the *Nostromo* heads home, the alien lays eggs inside Kane and the baby alien bursts from still-living Kane's chest. As they search *Nostromo*'s dark corridors and air ducts for the roving alien, Brett (Harry Dean Stanton) and Dallas are killed by the beast, which has rapidly grown to giant proportions and is navigating the ship's air ducts. Third Officer Ripley (Sigourney Weaver) decides to corner it, 'And then we'll blow it the fuck out into space.' Ripley accesses Mother and discovers 'Special Order 937': the *Nostromo* has been rerouted to investigate a life form and gather a specimen: 'Priority one. Insure return of organism for analysis. All other considerations secondary. Crew expendable.' This order is for the ship's science officer, Ash (Ian Holm), who has been protecting the alien and is revealed to be a robot. Ash tries to kill Ripley, but Lambert and Parker (Yaphet Kotto) manage to behead him. Lambert and Parker are killed and before Ripley and Jones, the ship's cat, escape, she sets the *Nostromo* to self-destruct. Drifting through space, Ripley realises the alien has stowed aboard the shuttle.

Dan O'Bannon and Ronald Shusett wrote the story, which was adapted into a screenplay by O'Bannon. The property was then bought and reworked by producers Walter Hill and David Giler. *Alien* created a powerful new style in cinema sci-fi horror, where realistic drama, violent set pieces and special effects were used intelligently, making it much more than its initial pitch of '*Jaws* in space'. Ridley Scott had previously directed TV commercials and had one feature, the Napoleonic drama *The Duellists* (1977), to his credit. *Alien* was shot in England on a budget of $11 million from July to December 1978 at Shepperton Studio Centre and at Bray Studios in Windsor. Post-production was done at EMI Elstree Studios. Bray was a particularly appropriate shooting location for this 'killer on the loose' movie, as it had been the production base for Hammer horror films. The UK–US ensemble – of established, but not yet massively famous, actors – proves how a good cast can add a realistic edge to flimsy material. The crew's conversations, featuring overlapping dialogue, mumbling and banter in the manner of a Robert Altman film, adds to their interactions' spontaneity and veracity. It also assured each of them a place in sci-fi mythology.

The *Nostromo*'s 'eighth passenger' (an alternative title for the film in foreign territories) was played by seven-foot-two-inches tall Nigerian design student Bolaji Badejo. The alien is perhaps the most terrifying of all science fiction monsters, a 'biomechanoid' beast of metal and flesh fused into a killing machine. The creature features extending rows of teeth upon teeth, claws, a tail and a chromed, phallic head. As it skulks in the shadowed corners of the ship, it's difficult to tell where the *Nostromo* ends and where the beast begins. The alien was designed by Swiss surrealist illustrator H.R. Giger, whose work Scott had seen in the 1977 collection *Necronomicon*. The Alien head effects were created by Carlo Rambaldi, with the 'small alien forms' co-designed and made by Roger Dicken. These included leathery eggs and an octopus-like creature that catapults itself onto Kane's space helmet, burning through the visor and clinging, still breathing, to his face. This 'face hugger' wraps its skeletal tendrils around the back of Kane's head, coils a tail around his neck and won't be detached, bleeding yellow acid which fizzles through the ship's decks. This creature's body and tail recall *Fiend without a Face*. The face hugger's progeny bursts from thrashing Kane's chest – it is this blood-splattering 'chest buster' that is the film's most shocking moment.

In *IT!* there's a fine sense of the *Challenge 142*'s geography and shape. The rocket is tall and thin, and the action is up and down, as the monster climbs the ladders and attacks the hatches between the craft's six levels. To reach the lower decks – and to surprise IT – the two astronauts walk down the rocket's exterior in spacesuits. *Nostromo*'s claustrophobic interior has more depth, the interiors wider, longer and more spacious, accentuated by the Panavision frame. Instead of the candlelit corridors of a haunted country house, the monster stalks the strobe-lit passages and decks of a space cruiser, a vast maze of corridors and storage areas that provides the alien with plenty of hiding places. Parker even utters the classic horror line: 'This place gives me the creeps.'

Alien's score was composed by Jerry Goldsmith, who was best known for his pastiche genre scoring of *Chinatown* (1974) and *The Omen* (1976), and his avant-garde themes for *Planet of the Apes*. He also worked extensively in the sci-fi genre, on *Logan's Run*, *Innerspace*, *Outland*, *Capricorn One*, *Total Recall* and *Star Trek: The Motion Picture* among many others. *Alien* has the sense of a 'classic' mainstream sci-fi film, while simultaneously being quite abstract and arty. Dallas listens to Mozart's *Eine kleine Nachtmusik*, and classical orchestrations score the *Nostromo*'s approach to the planet, a reference to *2001*. Goldsmith's main title theme is haunting, abstract and fragmentally threatening, setting the film's edgy tone from the outset.

The *Nostromo*, with its vast, towering ore refinery in tow, glides through spacescapes with all the elegance of *2001*. *Nostromo* detaches itself from the refinery platform to investigate the distress beacon, and the spacecraft and the planet effects were achieved with models and matte shots. The rocky planet is not wreathed in space mist, nor is it a Monument Valley expanse, but an inhospitable wasteland in the eye of a howling dust storm. Inside the ancient, wrecked, horseshoe-shaped spacecraft, the visitors find a long-dead, fossilised alien life form at the helm. The *Nostromo* is a utilitarian ship and the crew are dressed in customised fatigues, not smart uniforms. The crew are workers, not fighters, and their improvised arsenal includes electric prods, flame-thrower 'incinerator units' and nets. They attempt to locate the alien in the air ducts using a primitive tracking device that resembles a dustbuster. Having destroyed *Nostromo*, the refinery and its ore, Ripley realises that the alien has joined her and Jones on board the shuttle. When she silently climbs into a spacesuit and dons a helmet, this revealing 'striptease' ensured that Weaver became the pin-up girl for male sci-fi fans of the era. Ripley opens the airlock doors and the alien is sucked through them. It clings onto the frame, so Ripley shoots the monster with a grappling hook, but the thing still manages to climb back into the thrusters, until it is jettisoned, blasting into outer space, when Ripley fires the engine.

The film's subtext is the recurrent visual cycle of birth and rebirth. At the beginning of the film, Mother reboots and the ship springs to life. The crew, awoken by Mother from their sleep, rise from slumber. The ovary of the wrecked spaceship, where Kane discovers the alien eggs, is wreathed in a mist and his touch activates the egg to hatch. The alien uses Kane's human body as an incubating 'host' to hatch its young, and Kane's bloody chest burst – an 'unnatural' Caesarean birth – occurs in the bright 'hospital delivery room' interior of the ship's galley. The alien beast is referred to at one point as Kane's son, which could also be a biblical reference to Abel's murderer. To communicate with Mother, the crew sit inside a warmly glowing room with banks of lights, a safe haven from the ship.

There's circularity to the 'life cycle' of the film's plot, which suggests it could have been Ripley's nightmare. Having dispatched the alien, she returns to the hibernation chamber. Scott fades Ripley's serene sleeping face into a star field, as Howard Hanson's Symphony No. 2 ('Romantic'), a lush orchestral 'love theme', the calm after the storm, washes over the end titles.

Alien's 'advance' US poster, designed by Steve Frankfurt, featured the tagline 'A word of warning', but it was the subsequent release poster, designed by Frankfurt and featuring art by Philip Gips, that has become a classic: the planet-like egg hatching a glowing green light, with the tagline 'In space no one can hear you scream'. This is true, as sound waves can't travel through a vacuum, so there is no sound in outer space. Real space apparently smells of steak, though if you're being chased around a spaceship by an eight-foot shape-shifting alien, it probably smells of something else too. *Alien* was rated R in the US and X in the UK, which later became an 18 on video (it's now re-rated 15). It won Oscars at the 1980 Academy Awards for Visual Effects, shared by Giger, Rambaldi, Brian Johnson, Nick Allder and Denys Ayling. The film is available in various versions including a 'director's cut' or '25th Anniversary Edition' in 2003, which substituted and excised material and runs a minute shorter than the theatrical release. There is also a 'Definitive Edition', but there are many more versions of the film, with cuts made for foreign distribution, TV broadcasts and censorship. It grossed almost $80 million on its original release in May 1979. Scott returned to the story in 2012 with an *Alien*-related film called *Prometheus*, starring Noomi Rapace, Michael Fassbender, Guy Pearce, Idris Elba and Charlize Theron, which followed the spacecraft *Prometheus* as it explored the outer reaches of space for alien life.

Alien's huge popularity immediately unleashed a slew of slithering, gut-busting progeny, with the Italians predictably leading the field in gross-out special effects with Luigi Cozzi's *Alien Contamination* (1980; *Contamination*). John Carpenter's Earth-bound *The Thing* referenced Scott's film, with its poster tagline, 'The Ultimate in Alien Terror', and *Alien* was even spoofed in *The Creature Wasn't Nice* (1981), with Cindy Williams, Leslie Nielsen and Patrick Macnee. Roger Corman produced two unsavoury *Alien* knock-offs for New World Pictures. B.D. Clark's *Galaxy of Terror* (1981; *Galaxy of Horrors*, or *Mindwarp: An Infinity of Terror*) recounted a rescue mission to Morganthus, a mysterious, foggy planet where the spacecraft *Remus* has been lost, which results in the expected spooky tension and extreme gore. The eclectic cast in the search party included Ray Walston, Edward Albert, Grace Zabriskie, Bernard Behrens, Zalman King, Sid Haig, Erin Moran (Joanie Cunningham in *Happy Days*) and Robert Englund (Freddy Krueger in *A Nightmare on Elm Street*). The special effects, sets and decor are way above average for a junky B-movie. James Cameron worked as production designer, and the production manager was *Android*'s Aaron Lipstadt. *Galaxy of Terror* took $4 million in North America and has gained notoriety for its nonsense plotting: the tasteless scene where crew member Damaia (Taaffe O'Connell) is assaulted by a giant slithery maggot, and several bone-crunching, disremembering death scenes perpetrated by tentacled, clawed, insecty aliens. Corman's equally bloody follow-up, *Forbidden World* (1982; *Mutant*) reused sets from *Galaxy of Terror* and footage from *Battle beyond the Stars*.

The grisly UK sci-fi *Inseminoid* (1981; *Horror Planet*), directed by Norman J. Warren, had its imperilled astronauts attacked while on the Xeno archaeological expedition, an investigative dig of a tomb-like cave complex (shot in Chislehurst Caves, Kent) which is based at an on-site space station (shot at Lee International Film Studios, London). Sandy (Judy Geeson) is impregnated by a monstrous alien, and following a hideous, prolonged labour, during which she embarks on a murderous killing spree to protect her offspring, she gives birth to twins, both of which resemble Stewie from *Family Guy*. When Sandy is killed by Mark (Robin Clarke), he finds the alien twins devouring their new surrogate mother, Sharon (Heather Wright). The Anglo-US crew included Jennifer Ashley, Steven Grives, Barrie Houghton, Rosalind Lloyd, Victoria Tennant and Stephanie Beacham, all of whom play it completely straight and collectively approach their roles with all the dynamism of estate agents. John Scott provided the necessary spooky synth score. *Inseminoid* features particularly unpleasant, gross-out action – in one scene a trapped

victim attempts to cut off her own foot with a chainsaw. The film ends with an exploration party discovering the corpse-littered station devastated, and the twins hitch a ride
off the planet in their craft.

Lively little shocker *The Titan Find* (1984; *Creature*) was directed, co-scripted and
co-produced by sci-fi buff William Malone. Competition between two multinational
corporations for new materials and manufacturing techniques pushes their exploration
further into deep space. On Titan, Saturn's largest moon, a US research team crash-lands
its craft *Shenandoah*. They find a shipwreck of their West German rival, Richter Dynamics.
Its sole survivor, Hans Rudy Hofner (Klaus Kinski), explains that a 250,000-year-old
anthropological discovery has reawakened and broken out of its storage capsule. Of the
22 crewmen, only Hofner has survived. As the trailer put it, they 'Find the one thing
they never expected… was expecting them.' The film follows Mario Bava's maxim of
more mist than plot, while the Find itself, a large lizard-like creature resembling Scott's
alien, was created by Michael McCracken and played by Jeff Solomon. The astronauts
attempt to kill it by electrocuting it, as one of them recalls seeing a movie where this
method was used by people trapped in an ice station on a 'carrot from another planet'.
The creature deploys brain-sucking parasites, which are described as biological control devices (as in *Fiend without a Face* and *It Conquered the World*), which turn their
victims into flesh-eating zombies. The special effects are closer to Italian zombie flicks,
with blood, torn flesh and a memorable exploding head. The blue-tinted, misty, eerie,
lightning-strobed planet owes much to *Alien*, and the trailer concluded: 'Suddenly those
who had travelled across the galaxy had run out of space. *Creature*… it kills to live and
it lives to kill.'

Following his success with *Alien*, H.R. Giger designed Sil, the alien beast seeking a
mate in Los Angeles, in Roger Donaldson's *Species* (1995). A team of scientists at US
government labs in Dugway, Utah, led by Fitch (Ben Kingsley), create Sil (Michelle
Williams), a genetically modified little girl, using an alien DNA formula. The scientists
put the alien DNA in a female because she'll be 'more docile and controllable'. When
they try to gas her with cyanide, Sil escapes and heads for Los Angeles, growing into
beautiful blonde Canadian model Natasha Henstridge en route. Sil enters the next stage
of her life cycle – to find a man and procreate as soon as possible. Finch follows her with
his crack science team, including hunter Preston Lennox (Michael Madsen), British
cross-cultural behavioural expert Stephen Arden (Alfred Molina), empath Dan Smithson
(Forest Whitaker) and biologist Dr Laura Baker (Marg Helgenberger). The plot follows
sexy Sil picking up men and trying to mate with them, while the team attempt coitus
interruptus, with the emphasis on interruptus. This trash eventually runs out of steam,
with Giger's alien rampaging through sewers and underground caves, but a tentacled
beast and *Alien*-like female are nightmarish creations. Any science team that fields Mr
Blonde, Bird and Gandhi is bound to be interesting. Sequels, beginning with *Species II*
(1998; also with Henstridge, Madsen and Helgenberger) followed.

Tours de force: For *Alien* sequel *Aliens* (1986), Sigourney Weaver returned as Ripley, this time packing some extra-heavy firepower. The US one-sheet poster depicted the genre's first sci-fi action heroine protecting Newt (Carrie Henn) deep within the alien queen's nest.

In *Event Horizon* (1997), United States Aerospace Command (USAC) vessel *Lewis and Clark* goes into deep space to salvage research vessel *Event Horizon*, which has disappeared beyond Neptune. The salvage crew includes Laurence Fishburne, Sam Neill (as the *Event Horizon*'s designer), Kathleen Quinlan, Joely Richardson, Richard T. Jones, Jason Isaacs and Sean Pertwee. The *Event Horizon* is eerily deserted and video data reveals the crew were brutally massacred by a malevolent force. The ship is actually an experimental vessel that can fold space to travel from one place to another by creating an artificial black hole with its onboard gyroscopic gravity drive. The ship's impressive interiors were based on Notre Dame Cathedral. A US–UK co-production directed by Paul Anderson, this would-be *Alien* is simply a 'ghost galleon' in space, and there's a gory redo of the flood of blood from *The Wild, Wild Planet*. It features strong, disturbing footage, as the crew are whittled down by the oppressive, possessive force. They witness gory manifestations – hallucinations of 'the dark inside', their deepest fears – before expiring bloodily. When the salvagers wonder where the ship has been for the last seven years, the implication is to hell and back.

Renny Harlin's *Deep Blue Sea* (1999) was a *Jaws*-meets-*Alien* combo set in Aquatica, an oceanographic research facility, where during a storm the genetically modified sharks go on the rampage and terrorise a cast that includes Samuel L. Jackson, Saffron Burrows, Thomas Jane and LL Cool J. Andrzej Bartkowiak's *Doom* (2005), a co-production involving Czech, German, UK and US companies, was a screen adaptation of the computer game of the same name. In 2046 in the Union Aerospace Corporation Olduvai Research Facility on Mars, something is running amok. The Marine Corps Special Ops HQ dispatch an eight-man Rapid Response Tactical Squad (including Karl Urban and Dwayne 'The Rock' Johnson) on a search-and-destroy mission. This violent, unrelentingly ferocious exercise, which pits the marines against ghoulish mutants, is augmented by a thumping score and incessant gunfire. In one scene, traumatised Dr Carmack (Robert Russell) rips off his own ear – deafened viewers will sympathise with him. Rosamund Pike played Urban's sister, Dr Samantha Grimm. The heavy artillery on display includes the ever-popular six-barrelled Minigun (an alien-combating essential), and the action strongly resembles the first-person shooter action of the *Doom* video game, as heavy steel doors slide open and victims disintegrate in splattered plumes of flesh and blood.

In addition to the many rip-offs and imitators of Scott's original *Alien*, the film also inspired an official series. *Aliens* (1986), directed by James Cameron, was quite different in tone to Scott's film, as a squad of Colonial Marines packing state-of-the-art weapons headed back to the planet (now designated LV-426) where *Nostromo* discovered the alien eggs. As posters stated: 'There are some places in the universe you don't go alone.' The story begins with Ellen Ripley (Weaver) and Jones in hypersleep. They are revived in the Gateway space station, where Ripley discovers that she has been drifting for 57 years. Her daughter, Amanda, who was ten when Ripley departed, died two years ago, aged 66. At an inquiry into the loss of *Nostromo*, the refinery and its cargo, Ripley's licence is revoked and she finds employment in the docks, operating a hydraulic 'loader', a human-operated, walking robot. When Gateway loses contact with LV-426 (in some sources referred to as Acheron), the marines are dispatched, with Ripley as their adviser.

Expending an estimated $18.5 million budget, *Aliens* was shot at Pinewood Studios and Acton Lane Power Station. The screenplay was written by Cameron, based on a story by Cameron, Walter Hill and David Giler. Cameron's directorial debut, Italian B-movie *Piranha 2: Flying Killers* (1981), featured a 'chest buster' shock similar to *Alien*, as a piranha fish flies out of a corpse's chest and savages a nurse's throat. *Aliens* features Michael Biehn (from *Terminator*) as marine Corporal Dwayne Hicks, and Lance Henriksen (from *Terminator* and *Piranha 2*) as matter-of-fact robot Bishop, a synthetic or 'artificial person'. Other marines include Private Hudson (Bill Paxton), Sergeant Apone (Al Matthews), Private Drake (Mark Rolston), muscly Latina 'Ramba' Vasquez (Jenette Goldstein) and their indecisive lieutenant, Gorman (William Hope). The planet is undergoing 'terraforming' by the Weyland-Yutani Corporation, whose adverts state they are 'building better worlds'. Paul Reiser appeared as corporate representative Carter Burke, who is more concerned with his company's holdings on the planet than saving the colonists of the community of Hadley's Hope.

Aliens follows *Alien*'s structure, beginning and ending with Ripley in hypersleep, and as the earlier film featured the theme of birth and rebirth, *Aliens* is concerned with motherhood. Having learnt that she has lost her daughter, Ripley becomes the adoptive 'mother' of the colony's lone survivor, Rebecca Jordan, known as Newt (Carrie Henn). With explosives set to obliterate the planet, Ripley and Newt find themselves trapped in the alien queen's nest, where the giant insectoid is laying hundreds of eggs. The final confrontation is fought between two female antagonists. The colonists have been cocooned by the creatures as incubating hosts – an alien breeding factory. There's a chest burst, face huggers menace Ripley and Newt, and the marauding large alien creatures resemble Giger's creations in the first film. Instead of a single fully grown alien, the marines encounter hundreds of the creatures, which attack en masse, and the film resembles a war movie (the tagline warned 'This Time It's War'). The marines wear helmets, body armour, lights, cameras and camo gear. Other hardware on display includes the formidable six-wheeled armoured personnel carrier (APC) and automatic sentries, which are sensor-activated machine guns. For the finale Ripley tapes two guns together, creating a death-dealing machine gun/grenade-launcher/flame-thrower combo. Weaver's strong female action persona inspired a new generation of kick-ass heroines, including Michelle Rodriguez, Angelina Jolie and Carrie-Anne Moss. With his marines trapped on the planet, Cameron piles on the jeopardy, as survivors Ripley, Newt, Hicks and a torn-in-half Bishop try to escape. As the queen alien menaces Newt, Ripley operates a hydraulic loader and grapples with the beast, which is sucked into space through an airlock. 'Not bad, for a human,' notes Bishop. *Aliens* grossed over $85 million in the US on its release in 1986. The original cut runs 137 minutes, but a later director's cut adds 17 minutes of new footage. The theatrical cut was rated R in the US and 18 in the UK (now re-rated 15, though the longer cut is still 18). For this *tour de force*, Weaver was nominated for Best Actress at the Academy Awards.

David Fincher took the helm for *Alien³* (1992). Spacecraft *Sulaco* lands on Fiorina 'Fury' 161, which houses the Outer-Veil Mineral Ore Refinery and is also a prison. It once contained 5,000 inmates, but now houses only a skeleton crew of 25, who operate the lead work's foundry and furnaces. Aboard the *Sulaco*, Hicks and Newt are dead, synthetic humanoid Bishop 341-B (Henriksen) is out of commission and only Ripley (Weaver) is alive. There is also an alien aboard, which incubates in a dog and runs amok through the prison. The inmates and staff have no weapons, but with Ripley they manage to destroy it in the foundry. Realising that she has an alien growing inside her, Ripley commits suicide by throwing herself into the molten lead as the alien bursts from her chest. Henriksen also played Bishop's creator, who works for the corporation Weyland-Yutani, which owns the prison, and arrives with the intention of taking the alien for experimentation. The supporting cast included Charles S. Dutton, Charles Dance, Paul

McGann, Brian Glover, Ralph Brown, Danny Webb and Pete Postlethwaite. The film was shot at Pinewood and at Blyth Power Station, Northumberland. Originally released at 115 minutes, a longer cut of 144 minutes is available. If Scott had encouraged his audience to confront its fears in darkened theatres, and Cameron his to blast its fears through the head, this third instalment was content to allude to and lazily reproduce noteworthy moments from its predecessors.

Jean-Pierre Jeunet's *Alien: Resurrection* (1997) continues the theme of birth, rebirth and motherhood, and also accentuates the dual meanings of such sci-fi-associated words as 'hatch' and 'breach', though the ship's onboard computer is now called 'Father'. Two hundred years after her death, Ripley is reborn aboard the United Systems Military craft *Auriga*, a medical research vessel, where scientists are illegally breeding aliens, which they plan to tame. Ripley is resurrected because she has an alien queen inside her, which is surgically removed and grows to full size (she introduces herself, saying, 'I'm the monster's mother'). The freighter *Betty* arrives with its cargo of alien eggs and hosts. Ripley is now a part-alien hybrid herself, while Call (Winona Ryder), one of the *Betty*'s crew, is a second-generation robot (an android built by robots) who is out to destroy the alien strain for good. A considerable improvement on its predecessor, *Alien: Resurrection* has pace, imagination, a rough sense of humour and finely drawn characters (a mark of scripter Joss Whedon). Originally released at 108 minutes, a special edition runs to 116. The *Betty*'s crew include Dominique Pinon, Ron Perlman, Gary Dourdan, Kim Flowers and Michael Wincott, and Brad Dourif played one of the experimenting scientists. The *Auriga* boasts nifty breath-activated security doors, vast, rusty interiors and miles of corridors. There's an excellent underwater scene when the fugitives try to outswim the aliens and an incredible overhead basketball shot from Ripley. As the *Betty* heads for Earth, an alien–human hybrid stowaway, with a skull-like face, is sucked into space through a small hole, in a cascading flume of blood and guts.

Twentieth Century Fox united the *Alien* franchise with the *Predator* movies for *Alien vs. Predator* (2004) and *Alien vs. Predator: Requiem* (2007). Rather like the *Godzilla* films, these modern monsters – pitched against each other in random bouts – have become empty vessels for the lumbering advancement of plot and action. Scott's original *Alien* was one of the goriest films of its era, and while its bloody story isn't to everyone's taste, it's difficult to see how this sci-fi horror movie could have been improved. But Scott wasn't done with sci-fi just yet either – his next film was *Blade Runner*.

15

'NOBODY GETS OUT OF HERE ALIVE'

MAD MAX 2 (1981)

Director: George Miller
Producer: Byron Kennedy
Screenplay: Terry Hayes, George Miller and Brian Hannant
Director of Photography: Dean Semler
Music: Brian May
Panavision/Technicolor
A Kennedy Miller Production
Released by Warner Bros
96 minutes

Mel Gibson ('Mad' Max Rockatansky), Bruce Spence (Gyro Captain), Mike Preston (Pappagallo), Max Phipps (the Toadie), Vernon Wells (Wez), Kjell Nilsson (the Humungus), Emil Minty (feral kid), Virginia Hey (warrior woman), William Zappa (Zetta), Arkie Whiteley (Gyro Captain's girl), Steve J. Spears (mechanic), Moira Claux (Big Rebecca), David Downer (Nathan), Jimmy Brown (Wez's golden youth), Harold Baigent (narrator/ voice of feral kid)

* * *

Post-apocalypse films offer an interesting look at what would happen to our planet if superpowers go to war, destroying the Earth and its resources in a war of attrition. The best thing going for filmmakers striving for that 'after the end of the world' authenticity was that there wouldn't be much left and the ruinous world would be considerably more primitive than the one we know and love today, and thus cheap to stage. If the apocalypse is now, then these films show what happened next.

A 1950s take on the post-apocalypse world was producer–director Roger Corman's misleadingly titled *Teenage Cave Man* (1958). Corman shot the movie as *Prehistoric World*, but his producers insisted on the 'teenage' title for their drive-in audience. It depicted a primitive clan of cave dwellers, blinkered in their beliefs and trust in 'The Law'. They never stray beyond the river to the forbidden fertile land beyond, which is inhabited by dinosaurs (stock footage from *One Million B.C.* [1940]). Robert Vaughn played an inquisitive cave teen who ventures beyond the river, where he faces 'The God That Gives Death with Its Touch', which is an old man in a radiation suit, signifying that these troglodytes are in fact nuclear-holocaust survivors. Campbell envisioned the old man's anti-radiation outfit as a space suit, but Corman acquired a beaky lizard costume from *Night of the Blood Beast* (1958) for $65. The film was shot in the caves at Bronson Canyon, the landscape of Iverson Ranch, Chatsworth, and the arboretum in Arcadia, for $70,000 in ten days. The final revelation, that the story 'happened a long time ago' before the Atomic Age, was reused in Antonio Margheriti's *Yor, the Hunter from the Future* (1983). Corman also made *The Last Woman on Earth* (1960), in which mobster Harold Gern (Antony Carbone), his wife Evelyn (Betsy Jones-Moreland) and Gern's lawyer, Martin ('Edward Wain'/Robert Towne) are the only survivors of an apocalypse while scuba diving off Puerto Rico. This results in a post-nuclear love triangle in which one of the men faces the ultimate rejection, by the last woman on Earth.

Richard Matheson's 1954 sci-fi horror novel *I Am Legend*, in which the population is decimated by a plague, has been adapted for the screen several times. The Italian-US *The Last Man on Earth* (1964), starring Vincent Price, plays more like a zombie movie than a sci-fi film. Boris Sagal's *The Ωmega Man* (1971) cast Charlton Heston as survivalist Colonel Robert Neville, in a post-plague-wracked 1977 Los Angeles. Neville cruises the streets by day in a convertible, systematically clearing the city of 'The Family', a mysterious society of cowled, monkish night-dwellers, with albino white skin, sores and sunglasses. By night Neville's barbed-wired, fortified residence is attacked by these brethren, led by former newsreader Jonathan Matthias (Anthony Zerbe). The scenes of the deserted, windblown, littered Los Angeles streets are the film's best. This oddball 1970s sci-fi has a good score by Ron Grainer and eccentric Neville, an 'Angel of Death', watches rockumentary concert film *Woodstock* (1970) alone in a deserted cinema – he's seen it so many times that he knows it word for word. *The Ωmega Man* lacks true horror and, despite occasionally arresting imagery and expansive Panavision cinematography by Russell Metty, it resembles a TV movie, complete with irritating zooms. *I Am Legend* (2007) starred Will Smith as Bob Marley fan Lieutenant Colonel Robert Neville, the lone avenger on behalf of the human race in a deserted, plague-wracked 2012 New York City. With his only companion, an Alsatian called Samantha, he hunts down plague victims, which are hideous, hairless, rodent-like scavengers (called haemocytes). Their affliction was caused in 2009 by KV (Krippin virus), a mutating measles virus that was genetically modified to cure cancer by Dr Alice Krippin (Emma Thompson). *I Am Legend* is part *The Last Man on Earth*, part *Buffy the Haemocyte Slayer*. The unconvincing CGI'd predators are the film's major failing. Their jerky movements more closely resemble computer-game graphics, though their wordless screams (created by Faith No More vocalist Mike Patton) are suitably blood-curdling. The film's greatest plus is its visuals of a long-abandoned New York, shot on location in New York City (much to the irritation of the current population), including such landmarks as the Brooklyn Bridge, Washington Square and the aircraft carrier *Intrepid*, which Robert uses as his golf driving range. Towering skyscrapers form concrete canyons, the metropolis returns to wilderness, weeds sprout on the sidewalks and roads, and lions hunt their deer prey in this urban jungle. *I Am Legend* was released to the box office with a tagline referencing Price's film: 'The Last Man on Earth is not Alone.'

George Miller's *Mad Max* (1979) redefined lean, mean action cinema in the late 1970s, with its combination of brutal action and a dramatic, tension-ratcheting score by Australian composer Brian May. 'A few years from now,' traffic cops the Main Force Patrol (MFP) are fighting an ongoing war with gangs of nomadic, motorcycle gangs. When renegade the Nightrider (Vince Gil) is killed during a police pursuit, his comrades swear vengeance. They capture cop Jim Goose (Steve Bisley) and burn him alive in a pickup wreck. His close friend and top cop Max Rockatansky (Mel Gibson) tries to resign from the force – the pressure is getting to him and he's starting to enjoy his job too much – but his superior, Fifi Macaffee (Roger Ward), tells him to take a vacation and reconsider. While Max, his wife Jessie (Joanne Samuel) and their little son Sprog (Brendan Heath) are enjoying a coastal touring holiday, the Nightrider's revengers strike.

Max was a star-making role for Mel Gibson and he successfully humanises what could have been a one-dimensional character. Already disillusioned with the force and haunted by nightmares of his hideously burnt friend, Goose, Max loses all that's dear to him in a horrific act of violence. Jessie – fleeing on foot with her babe in arms, with nowhere to hide along a long, open road – is mown down by the speeding biker gang. People may not believe in heroes any more, but as bruiser Fifi tells Max: 'We're gonna give 'em back their heroes.' Following the murders, Max dons his cop uniform and goes looking for revenge. The madcap psycho road punks are led by the cheerfully named Toecutter (Hugh Keays-Byrne), and his henchmen include Johnny the Boy (Tim Burns), Bubba Zanetti (Geoff Parry) and Cundalini (Paul Johnstone). They rape, rob and murder their way through the film and Miller often uses crows cawing on the soundtrack as a metaphor for these roadkill carrion. The Nightrider describes himself as a 'fuel-injected suicide machine' and, as a police radio operator notes, 'Nomad bikers, bulk trouble'. The MFP cops drive yellow police cars with red-and-blue striped livery (Max's is a supercharged black Ford V8 Interceptor) and wear biker boots and leather motorcycle gear, while the punks are kitted out in whatever was available in the dress-up box.

Mad Max was shot entirely on location in Victoria and Queensland, Australia, for A\$400,000, and it includes the most impressive, dangerous motorcycle and car-crash stunts of its era. The stunt co-ordinator was Grant Page. Cars and bikes smash through caravans, trucks or into each other and screech along long, straight roads. The flickering white line of the central reservation flashes by, tapering into a flat horizon, which is accentuated by David Eggby's widescreen cinematography. For killing his mate, his wife, his son, even his dog, Max exacts revenge. He runs the bikers off the road in his fuel-injected Interceptor,

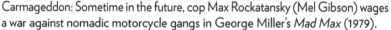

Carmageddon: Sometime in the future, cop Max Rockatansky (Mel Gibson) wages
a war against nomadic motorcycle gangs in George Miller's *Mad Max* (1979).

but in a desolate 'Prohibited Area' Max is ambushed. Bubba, Johnny and Toecutter shoot
him in the leg and then run over his right arm. Max shotguns Bubba, The Toecutter is
splattered across an oncoming truck, while Johnny is handcuffed by his ankle to a truck
wreck that Max rigs to explode, with his only option of escape to hacksaw through his
own leg. *Mad Max* is 89 minutes of comic-book mayhem – B-movie 'Ozploitation' of
the highest order. Posters bore the taglines 'When the gangs take over the highway…
Remember he's on your side' and 'Pray he's out there somewhere!'

If Miller's *Mad Max* had depicted Max's transformation from clean-cut cop to grim-
faced, limping avenger, by the start of *Mad Max 2* (1981), both society and Max have
further deteriorated. In the post-apocalypse desert wastelands – 'no place for man or

reptile' – desolate outposts cling onto survival against scavenging road gangs. Gasoline is the singularly most important commodity. Max, a lonely drifter in his V8, a mangy dog his only friend, learns from a gyrocopter pilot (Bruce Spence) that there are thousands of gallons of 'juice' in a ramshackle fortress-community compound huddled around a gasoline refinery. Unfortunately it's besieged by desert crazies, led by despotic the Humungus (Kjell Nilsson) and his psycho Mohawked henchman Wez (Vernon Wells). Max agrees to bring them a truck, to tow a tanker capable of carrying the fuel. The settlers plan to drive north, 2,000 miles, to a utopian place in the sun seen only in holiday postcards. Max fulfils his promise, but is later ambushed and badly injured by the Humungus's men. He's rescued by the gyro pilot, who takes him back to the fort, where Max recovers and drives the rig in the escape attempt. While the majority of the settlers head off in one direction, Max and a small contingent with the Mack tanker head on to the open desert highway, which for some will become their road to hell.

This sequel is set in an unrecognisably feudal post-industrial world. Over archive library footage of civil unrest, a prologue sets the scene, where a world powered by the 'black fuel' destroyed itself and the roads are now a 'white-line nightmare' battleground. Max is 'a burnt out, desolate man', the road warrior, in his battered police leathers, who lives on tins of 'Dinki-Di' dog food. Stubbly Gibson resembles Clint Eastwood and the film's style closely resembles Eastwood's spaghetti Westerns with Sergio Leone. Max packs a sawn-off shotgun stuffed in a holster, but it's not even loaded for the early part of the film (not that the bad guys know that). Max is a loner, dissuading a feral child at the compound (Emil Minty) from getting too close. His only friend is his dog, but as in the first film, man's best friend is slain – he's predestined to remain a loner. The feral child is revealed to be the tale's narrator and Max's heroism eventually reaches mythical proportions, though after the final confrontation they never see him again and 'He lives now only in my memories.'

A considerably bigger budget – A\$4 million as opposed to an estimated A\$400,000 for *Mad Max* – ensured that *Mad Max 2* is a 'bigger' film. The stunt work (co-ordinated by Max Aspin) and special effects (by Jeffrey Cliffords) far outstrip its predecessor. *Mad Max 2* is solely an action film, where emotion and human relationships are restricted to a glance or a couple of words. It was part of the Ozploitation cinema movement that is discussed in detail in Mark Hartley's excellent *Not Quite Hollywood: The Wild, Untold Story of Ozploitation* (2008). May returned to provide the score, in even more thundering, rumbling style in the manner of a gladiator epic, which adds to the robust, mythological atmosphere. It was photographed by Dean Semler in Panavision – like *Forbidden Planet, Planet of the Apes, 2001, Star Wars, Blade Runner* and *The Thing*, it must be seen in widescreen. The vivid blue sky and desert, complete with echoing coyote howls, is an arid landscape traversed by roads occasionally littered with car and truck wrecks, or roadkill kangaroos. This tarmac ribbon stretches into the distance to a flat, featureless, futureless horizon. Miller lensed the film in the orange sand, rock outcrops and plains at Broken

Hill, New South Wales. To the settlers at the refinery, Max is 'mercenary trash', a savage reflection of the burnt earth, but in this desolate frontier land, Max learns to live again.

Bruce Spence was excellent as the spindly, hot-footed, scampering gyrocopter pilot, wearing yellow leggings, pink sneakers, a flying helmet, goggles and a long leather coat. Mike Preston was patriarchal, almost Shakespearean, as the survivors' leader, Pappagallo. The wasteland is ruled by the Humungus, a sturdy chap in bondage pants and a hockey goalie's mask, but the film's real villain is his henchman, psychopathic Wez, the id, the Last of the Mohicans propelled into a nihilistic punk future. He's so crazy that Humungus keeps him leashed on a chain. Max Phipps played the Toadie, Humungus's sycophant, who wears a muskrat pelt as a hat. He attempts to catch the feral kid's razor-edged boomerang (the film's sole cultural concession to Australian 'outback' cinema), but loses a fistful of fingers instead. The film's future-punk style and Max's ragged biker gear were highly influential. The rest of the warriors of the wasteland – desert vermin who besiege the compound in the Valley of Death like angry ants – are dressed as punks, goths, pirates, bondage slaves and motorcycle cops, and speed along in a bizarre array of customised vehicles, including sports cars, 4x4s, jalopies, dragsters, jeeps, speedsters, motorbikes and sidecars. They roar though the wasteland, rolling thunder and dusty 'vapour trails' following in their wake.

Mad Max 2 is a futuristic movie where the hardware on display is actually inferior to what we have now – what might be termed 'regressive futurism'. The combatants are armed with all manner of oddball weaponry spanning the ages, including medieval maces, crossbows, knives, spears, bolt guns, tools, flame-throwers, petrol bombs, shotguns and Magnums. The film's violent content has been bridged for TV showings. *Mad Max 2* features some of the greatest vehicle stunts in cinema history, as stuntmen cartwheel through the air and impacting vehicles disintegrate into confetti. The film has a vaguely ecological message of 'saving the Earth', but on *Moviedrome* Alex Cox expressed concern as to what impact all that burning rubber and gasoline was having on the environment. Max's V8 is written off for good in a horrific smash from which Max barely emerges alive. In the climax, Max drives the gas rig, with Humungus's loonies in pursuit. Cars are dragged by grappling hooks and run off the road, bodies are stabbed, riddled or burnt, and Wez is splattered in a head-on collision with Humungus's fuel-injected jalopy. Eventually Max's truck skids, keels over and crashes, but the precious fuel is concealed in the settlers' convoy that left in the other direction – the truck was simply the most entertaining, action-packed decoy in movie history.

The original *Mad Max* was released in the US in 1980. Distributors AIP were concerned that American audiences wouldn't understand the cast's Australian accents, so American voices were dubbed on. Both the superior Australian dub and the American one are now available on DVD. *Mad Max* eventually earned $100 million worldwide, but it was *Mad Max 2* that broke the series in the US. Having been released in Australia in December 1981, it appeared in America in May 1982, retitled *The Road Warrior*, where it took over $11 million. It's also known in some territories as *Mad Max 2: The Road Warrior*. It won a Los Angeles critics' prize as Best Foreign Film. If *Mad Max* was a good film set in the near future, *Mad Max 2* is a near-perfect film set in the far future. Alongside Peter Weir's *Picnic at Hanging Rock* (1975) – its floaty, poetic antithesis – *Mad Max 2* is one of Australia's finest films. It remains the greatest ever 'car stunt' movie ever made and is a classic example of arthouse meets grindhouse. *Mad Max 2* was so far ahead of its time that it still hasn't aged.

The third 'Max' film, *Mad Max Beyond Thunderdome* (1985) was co-directed by Miller and George Ogilvie. Max wanders through the desert, his wagon-like vehicle drawn by a team of camels. When his rig is stolen by plane pilot-cum-trader Jedediah (Spence, playing a slightly different role to that in *Mad Max 2*) and Jed's little son (Adam Cockburn), Max arrives in the lawless Bartertown, a trading centre teeming with desert riff-raff. It's powered by methane manufactured in the Underworld factory from pig excrement. Local despot Aunty Entity (Tina Turner) hires Max to be her champion in the gladiatorial combat arena, the Thunderdome, to kill her main rival, the Blaster, but after Max's victory, Aunty betrays Max and exiles him to the wasteland. There he is saved by a primitive tribe of children, who take Max to be their messianic saviour.

Beyond Thunderdome has some interesting ideas and powerful imagery, including a passenger jet half buried in a sand dune. Made on a $12 million budget, it was shot on location in South Australia and New South Wales. This movie resembles Hollywood's idea of a *Mad Max* movie – it is more accessible, plot heavy and noticeably less violent than earlier instalments. The film loses its way when the children appear and turns into a combination of *The Emerald Forest*, *Lord of the Flies* and *The Ewok Adventure*, and tries to humanise and sentimentalise Max. For the Thunderdome arena combat, Gibson is on top form. In the arced, latticed arena, combatants are suspended from elasticated bungee cords and use any weapon they can lay their hands on, including clubs, spears, blades, mallets and chainsaws. 'I know you won't break the rules: there aren't any,' announces the emcee. The finale partially revisits *Mad Max 2*, as Max and some children (The Tribe Who Left) escape from Bartertown in a battletruck that runs on railway tracks, with Aunty Entity and her gang in pursuit in jalopies. Turner is good, though underused, as Aunty Entity, and crops up twice on the soundtrack, singing 'One of the Living' (accompanied by rock band Device) over the opening titles and 'We Don't Need Another Hero (Thunderdome)' during the end titles. Aunty's chief henchman, Ironbar, was played by Australian rock singer Angry Anderson. The Master Blaster, who runs the methane factory, consists of a midget, the Master (Angelo Rossitto), on the shoulders of the towering Blaster (Paul Larsson). Spence's pilot flies the children to a ruined city ('Tomorrow-morrow land') where they reboot civilisation amid the crumbled skyscrapers and elevate Max to mythological proportions through their storytelling, just as Miller had in his film series. Released in June 1985, *Beyond Thunderdome* took over $36 million in the US, making it the most successful, if not the best, of the series.

There followed innumerable copies, and predictably the Italians made the most imaginative *Mad Max* knock-off, in Enzo G. Castellari's *The New Barbarians* (1983; *Warriors of the Wasteland*). Roving loonies, the Templars, led by One (George Eastman), ramble the wasteland. Like *Mad Max 2*, this is a Western in futuristic garb, with Scorpion (Timothy Brent) wearing laser-proof armour under his poncho. The film remains unique in the action oeuvre as the only one where the hero is buggered by the villain. 'Martin Doleman'/ Sergio Martino's *2019, After the Fall of New York* (1983) managed to rip off *Mad Max 2*, *The Warriors*, *The Terminator*, *Escape from New York* and *Planet of the Apes* in its tale of a post-holocaust world which has been destroyed by the European Afro-Asian Confederation (EURAC). The heroes – daredevil mercenary Parsifal (Michael Sopkiw), Bronx (Vincent Scalondro), who has a mechanical pincer for a hand, and Ratchet (Romano Puppo), an acrobatic cyborg with an eyepatch and a deadly yo-yo – are dispatched to New York to rescue Melissa, civilisation's only fertile woman. As a post-apocalyptic busker (played by Ray Saunders) states: 'They baked the Big Apple', and the scum-infested ruins are a rat's domain. If not 'mad', Parsifal is certainly disgruntled. Further *Mad Max* rips from around the world include *Steel Dawn* (1987), *Steel Frontier* (1995), *Atlantis Interceptors* (1983), *Battletruck* (1982; aka *Warlords of the Twenty-First Century*), *The Exterminators of the Year 3000* (1983), *Rome 2033: The Fighter Centurions* (1984; *The New Gladiators*), *She* (1983), *Stryker* (1983), *Desert Warrior* (1988), *Land of Doom* (1986) and *Hell Comes to Frogtown* (1988).

Steve De Jarnatt's *Cherry 2000* (1988) was an eccentric pseudo-Western. In 2017 Anaheim, California, Sam Treadwell (David Andrews) loves his robotic, living doll playmate Cherry 2000 (Pamela Gidley) until she short-circuits. To replace the obsolete model, Sam travels into the deserty Zone 7 accompanied by his resourceful guide, E. Johnson (Melanie Griffith). They are pitted against renegade Lester (Tim Thomerson) and his dune-bike gang, and the film features some incredible stunts, including when E.'s Ford Mustang is suspended from a crane and dropped down a drain. Old-time John Fordsters Ben Johnson and Harry Carey Jr. steal their respective scenes as ferryman Six-Fingered Jake and crooked gas-station proprietor Snappy Tom, while icons Robbie the Robot and Gort make cameo appearances.

Jean-Claude Van Damme's starrer *Cyborg* (1989) was filmed with the leftovers from a proposed sequel to *Masters of the Universe* (1987). In a plague-ridden future New York, cyborg Pearl Prophet (Dayle Haddon) contains the information for a cure for the plague and must get back to a group of doctors, the Last Ones, in Atlanta. She is kidnapped by Pirates, led by Fender Tremolo (Vincent Klyn). Hard-ass, flashback-wracked Gibson 'Gibbs' Rickenbacker (Van Damme), whose family was murdered by Fender, sets off in pursuit. Most of the principal characters are named after equipment associated with rock bands, including Marshall Strat (Alex Daniels) and Furman Vox (Blaise Loong). It was followed by two sequels: *Cyborg 2* (1993), starring Angelina Jolie and Jack Palance, and the aptly-titled *Cyborg 3: The Recycler* (1995).

Though it was originally released in 1975, L.Q. Jones's *A Boy and His Dog* was reissued in 1982 with an added post-nuclear-war prologue. Based on a novella by Harlan Ellison, this is a very dark satirical comedy. It's AD 2024 and Vic (Don Johnson) travels the desert with Blood, a superintelligent ex-police dog, with whom he can communicate (Vic speaks aloud and the dog answers telepathically). Blood locates women and food for Vic and the bond between them is strong. When Vic meets Quilla June Holmes (Susanne Benton), she lures him into 'Down Under', leaving Blood to fend for himself. Down Under is an oddball subterranean society, with marching bands, tannoy announcements, parades and locals who wear strange white face make-up. The male population is sterile, so Vic is employed to impregnate the women, via a marriage-cum-insemination ritual. Jason Robards cropped up Down Under as Lew Craddock, a judge/preacher. Blood was played by 'Tiger' and voiced by Tim McIntire, who also sang the film's honky-tonk theme song. The desert's parched, littered visuals, the searing sunlight in the arid landscape and the scavengers' patched-up, make-do rags are close to *Mad Max 2*'s junkyard chic. Jones shot the desert scenes in Coyote Dry Lake, Yermo, California. The film is not to all tastes and the ending is rightly notorious. Vic, having escaped from Down Under with Quilla June, finds Blood in the desert in bad shape and near starving. To save Blood's life, the dog must eat soon, so Vic kills and cooks Quilla June and feeds her to him. 'She said she loved me,' said Vic. 'Well, I'd say she certainly had marvellous judgement... if not particularly good taste,' notes Blood, in the film's bleak punchline.

Perhaps the closest film in terms of visual style and production design to Miller's *Max* films, if not in results, was Kevin Reynolds' *Waterworld* (1995). The polar ice cap melts and in a flooded, post-land world, the survivors drift the oceans. The settlers' refinery outpost is now a floating, fortified harbour 'atoll', which is menaced by a gang called the Smokers, led by seaweedy despot Deacon (Dennis Hopper). The hero is Kevin Costner, the Mariner. A tattoo on orphan Enola's (Tina Majorino) back indicates the location of mythical 'Dryland', while the Smokers' HQ is rusting tanker *Exxon Valdez*. The Mariner's souped-up trimaran is a poor substitute for the Interceptor, and it's difficult to root for a hero with webbed feet and gills who drinks his own purified urine.

An Australian–US co-production, David Twohy's *Pitch Black* (1999) set frenetic alien action in *Mad Max 2*'s arid outback. It was shot on location in Queensland, Australia, and at New Deal Studios, Los Angeles. A merchant vessel en route to the Tangia System, with 40 commercial passengers on board, crashes on an inhospitable desert planet scorched by three suns. Twenty-two years ago, during an eclipse, a catastrophe befell the inhabitants and another tri-solar eclipse is imminent. When darkness falls, ferocious beasts attack from their subterranean lairs. The film divides neatly into two distinct visual styles: mellow yellow and pitch black. The first half is photographed in blinding yellowy desert hues, as those still alive explore the sunburnt wasteland, while, with the coming of the eclipse, the remainder of the action takes place in darkness. The protagonists include the ship's tough Captain Fry (Radha Mitchell), Imam (Keith David), Jack (Rhiana Griffith),

Shazza (Claudia Black), Zeke (John Moore), Owens (Simon Burke) and Paris (Lewis Fitz-Gerald), who are whittled down by the snapping monsters. Most memorable is convict Riddick (an excellently deadpan Vin Diesel) who is being escorted back to the slammer by cop Johns (Cole Hauser). Every time you think *Pitch Black* is going to take the easy, well-worn route, it lurches off in the opposite direction. The eventful story – as the survivors trek cross-country, dragging the power cells to repair a skiff – is punctuated by pitch-black humour and violence, as hundreds of the flying, screaming beasts attack, ripping victims to shreds. The film spawned a sequel, *The Chronicles of Riddick* (2004; directed by Twohy and starring Diesel) and an animated DVD *The Chronicles of Riddick: Dark Fury* (2004).

Thirty years after 'the Flash', when war has destroyed the Earth, Eli (Denzel Washington) – a roaming roadster and expert swordsman, given to quoting scripture and Johnny Cash – walks the unforgiving land, forever heading west in the Hughes Brothers' *The Book of Eli* (2010). Eli possesses the last remaining copy of the Bible. Shot in desaturated sepia tones in New Mexico for $80 million, there are also echoes of *Texas Chainsaw Massacre* and *Shogun Assassin* in this imaginatively staged, desiccated drama. Post-*Matrix*, everyone wears shades against the powerful sun. Local warlord Carnegie (Gary Oldman) realises the Bible will allow him control of the 'hearts and minds of the weak and desperate' and wants the volume at any price. Jennifer Beals played Carnegie's blind mistress, Claudia, and Mila Kunis was her daughter Solara. Eli escapes Carnegie's shanty town and Solara accompanies him. Eventually Eli and Solara arrive at Alcatraz, where scholars are rebuilding the world's library. Tom Waits played Carnegie's fix-it engineer and Ray Stevenson was henchman Redridge, who whistles Ennio Morricone's flute theme from *Once Upon a Time in America*. Frances de la Tour and Michael Gambon played genial, chilling cannibal couple Martha and George, who shelter the wanderers, if only to add them to the menu. Carnegie manages to take possession of the book, but discovers that it's in Braille. Eli, who is blind, dictates the book – chapter and verse – from memory, and scribe Lombardi (Malcolm McDowell) faithfully writes it all down as the seeds of a new world, built out of the social ruins, are sown.

16

'LIKE TEARS IN RAIN'

BLADE RUNNER (1982)

Director: Ridley Scott
Story: Philip K. Dick
Screenplay: Hampton Fancher and David Webb Peoples
Director of Photography: Jordan Cronenweth
Music: Vangelis
Panavision/Technicolor
A Michael Deeley–Ridley Scott/Ladd Company/Sir Run Run Shaw Production
Released by Warner Bros
114 minutes

Harrison Ford (Rick Deckard), Rutger Hauer (Roy Batty), Sean Young (Rachael), Edward James Olmos (Gaff), M. Emmet Walsh (Captain Harry Bryant), Daryl Hannah (Pris), William Sanderson (J.F. Sebastian), Brion James (Leon Kowalski), Joseph Turkel (Dr Eldon Tyrell), Joanna Cassidy (Zhora, alias Miss Salome), James Hong (Hannibal Chew), Morgan Paull (Holden), Kevin Thompson (Bear), John Edward Allen (Kaiser), Hy Pyke (Taffey Lewis), Robert Okazaki (Howie Lee), Ben Astar (Abdul Ben Hassan), Judith Burnett (Ming-Fa), Leo Gorcey Jr. (Louie, bartender)

❋ ❋ ❋

The landmark 1980s sci-fi film remains Ridley Scott's *Blade Runner*. In the early twenty-first century, the Tyrell Corporation is pioneering robotic evolution with replicants, the Nexus 6, which are almost impossible to tell apart from humans. They are used on off-world colonies as slave labour, but when a Nexus 6 combat team revolts, replicants are outlawed on Earth under penalty of death. Special police squads, so-called 'Blade Runner units', are dispatched to track them down and terminate them: 'This is not called execution. This is called retirement.' In Los Angeles in November 2019, ex-cop Rick Deckard (Harrison Ford) is recruited to track down the missing 'skin jobs' – Leon (Brion James), Zhora (Joanna Cassidy), Roy Batty (Rutger Hauer) and Pris (Daryl

Blade Runner: US poster for Ridley Scott's sci-fi manhunt movie, which has become one of the most popular science-fiction films of all time.

Hannah). The plot unfolds like a film-noir private-eye procedural (complete with voice-over narration), albeit one relocated to a vivid, glittering, neon-lit future city. Deckard learns there is an inbuilt fail-safe in the Nexus 6: they have been programmed with a four-year lifespan, to stop them developing emotions. He meets Rachael (Sean Young), a secretary at the Tyrell Corporation, whom he suspects is a replicant, but falls for her all the same. He tracks Zhora down to Taffey's Bar, where she's working as Miss Salome, an exotic snake dancer. Following a chase, he shoots her dead. 'The report read, "Routine retirement of a replicant", Deckard muses in voice-over. 'That didn't make me feel any better about shooting a woman in the back.' Deckard is subsequently attacked by Leon in the street and Rachael kills the robot. Meanwhile, Pris has taken shelter with genetic designer J.F. Sebastian (William Sanderson), who works for Tyrell, but whose hobby is making life-sized robotic mannequins and toys. Sebastian suffers from Methuselah syndrome: his glands grow old too fast and result in accelerated ageing. He lives in a vast, decaying hotel, the Bradbury building, where Pris's lover Roy shows up. He wants to meet the head of the Tyrell Corporation, Dr Eldon Tyrell (Joseph Turkel), and Sebastian engineers this, unwittingly taking Roy into the Tyrell HQ, where the replicant murders Tyrell, his 'father'. The police link Sebastian to the crime and Deckard is dispatched to the Bradbury to investigate. He is ambushed by Pris, whom he mistakes for a doll, and kills her. Roy, distraught at the death of Pris, attacks Deckard. Roy breaks two of Deckard's fingers on his gun hand and Deckard blows one of the replicant's ears off. Up on the roof, Deckard is left hanging precariously from a girder high above the street, and Roy saves Deckard's life, then expires, his four years up. Deckard returns to his apartment, expecting to find replicant Rachael dead, but she is 'special' and has no termination date. The two of them travel in a craft high above a spectacular wooded alpine landscape, as Deckard observes: 'I didn't know how long we'd have together... Who does?'

Blade Runner was based on Philip K. Dick's 1968 novel *Do Androids Dream of Electric Sheep?*, though Ridley Scott took inspiration for the title from an unrelated book (a credit thanks William S. Burroughs and Alan E. Nourse). Many changes were made to the novel for the screen adaptation. The original setting was San Francisco in 1992. In the novel Rick Deckard lives with his wife Iran and works as a bounty hunter of androids, or 'andys', for which he receives $1,000 per 'retirement'. In this post-apocalyptic society, animals and pets have added importance. Most animals have been wiped out in the apocalypse, termed World War Terminus. The Deckards had a sheep, but it died and they now have an electric sheep, which grazes, 'chomping away in simulated contentment'. Deckard uses some of his bounty money as a down payment on a real goat. The head of the Seattle-based Rosen Association (not the Tyrell Corporation) is Eldon Rosen, whose niece Rachael is Deckard's femme fatale, but Rachael also has a lookalike, Pris Stratton. Deckard has to kill six androids, two of which are Roy Baty and his wife Irmgard. Zhora was opera singer Luba Luft in the novel, J.F. Sebastian was J.R. Isidore, and there's a godlike character called Mercer who is exposed by TV show *Buster Friendly and His Friendly Friends* to be a drunkard B-movie actor. The book, while certainly futuristic with its hovercars and rogue androids, reads like a noirish detective novel and the action takes place during one day in Deckard's life.

Concieved under the working title *Dangerous Days*, *Blade Runner* was initially adapted by Hampton Fancher, with David Peoples also brought in for rewrites. Original casting choices for Deckard included Robert Mitchum, Sean Connery, Al Pacino, Burt Reynolds, Clint Eastwood and Dustin Hoffman. Harrison Ford was cast as he was perfect for the role and on the rise following the *Star Wars* films. Sean Young reminded Scott of Vivian Leigh and was preferred over Nina Axelrod, while Rutger Hauer, with his short-cropped blond hair, was evil personified, but also surprisingly engaging and charismatic. Edward James Olmos, as cop Gaff, invented his own 'city speak' for the film, from bits of Hungarian, French and German.

A budget that eventually topped $28 million was expended on location in Los Angeles and Burbank Studios, California, to create a glittering neo-noir neon LA that is one of the cinema's finest visions of the future. This exercise in style combined visuals with the score to create a sensory experience that some critics claim doesn't engage with the cold characters – the nighthawks who populate this bleak future. Visually and audibly, *Blade Runner* represents the art and craft of filmmaking at its most accomplished. Scott's personal vision is assured, from the Eastern bazaar atmosphere of Animoid Row, with its exotic animals, to the hubbub of rain-lashed Chinatown. *Blade Runner*'s world was created on the New York Street set at Warners, which was retrofitted to become an electric city of night. This necessitated filming taking place at night, with the set drenched with rain, which took its toll on cast and crew. Some of the signage was created from the neon Las Vegas set in *One from the Heart* (1982). The steamy, rain-slicked streets are busy with an array of people dressed in a multitude of styles, from Sid Vicious punks, strippers and geishas to cops and rabbis. The attention to detail even extends to the famous hovering police cars (called 'spinners'), Sebastian's truck and Deckard's sedan. Overhead, vast hovering billboard blimps advertise life 'off-world'.

The film's visual stylist was illustrator Syd Mead, who created this otherworldly location. There were no computer-generated images, with everything created by the multi-talented artisans who worked on the film using models, perspectival trickery and skilful matte paintings. The city becomes one of the protagonists and almost a distraction from the drama of the story. It utilised technologies developed for *Close Encounters of the Third Kind*, and scenes such as the searchlight-strobing blimp flying over the Bradbury atrium recall the exquisite beauty of Spielberg's sci-fi. But Scott's film is much darker, both in theme and style, in its depiction of the future. Flames leap high into the sky from oil cracking chimneys, and millions of tiny lights stretch into infinite, perpetual night, in the famed 'Hades landscape' of 2019 Los Angeles. The cityscape includes the glittering pyramidal Tyrell Corporation building (actually an immense scale model) and the police station precinct tower. Cars sweep past adverts for Atari, Pan Am and Coca Cola, and there are even little details such as parking meters. The vast interior of the waterlogged

Bradbury building in Los Angeles was utilised, the staircases and corridors cavernous and decrepit. The scene at Hannibal Chew's eye surgery was filmed in a refrigerated meat locker. The police station interior was Los Angeles's Union Station, while parts of Deckard's $175,000 apartment set were inspired by Frank Lloyd Wright's Ennis House. The Panavision cinematography was by Jordon Cronenweth. The film uses light, particularly strobing, light beams and lens flare, to create atmosphere. The special-effects team of *2001*'s Douglas Trumbull, Richard Yuricich and David Dryer were Oscar-nominated (they lost to *E.T.*). The film's troubled production, including Scott's time-consuming filmmaking style involving multiple takes, budget overruns and on-set tensions, is told in meticulous detail in *Dangerous Days: Making Blade Runner* (2007), which is over 90 minutes longer than the feature itself.

The glacial score, one of science-fiction cinema's finest, was by Vangelis. He composed some temp track themes, which Scott blasted out on the set to create atmosphere. Vangelis specialised in electronic scores, and his compositions, as delicate or deadly as fractured glass, are perfectly pitched for the material, from the tinkling piano of 'Memories of Green' and the smoochy purring neo-noir sax (played by Dick Morrisey) of 'Love Theme' to the soprano-led 'Rachel's Theme', the glistening synth of 'Blade Runner Blues' and the pulsing, soaring adrenalin of the end titles. Effects evoke yowling cats and throbbing engines, with Eastern stylings, wailing female vocals and dubby bass lines. It's a shimmering, eerily seductive accompaniment to this noir sci-fi mirage of shadows, neon and glitter.

The Voight-Kampff test is used by Blade Runners as an interrogation method to identify replicants in an attempt to elicit empathy and emotional response. The Nexus 6 are 'lifeforms' that possess superior strength and agility (and equal intelligence) to their creators. The colourful, robotic villain is so much more interesting and humanly emotional than the grumpy hero. Hauer steals the movie – his portrayal of the doomed antagonist is both convincing and moving. Leon is a thuggish killer, while Zhora, with her eight-year-old Burmese snake, is erotically exotic. Her death, smashing in slow motion through massive glass panes in a department store, was performed by stuntwoman Lee Pulford in a wig. Hannah based Pris's dark eye make-up on Klaus Kinski's sunken-eyed count in *Nosferatu*. Her gymnastic death, as she smashes into a wall, was doubled by a stuntman. Her doll-like demeanour, with blonde hair and goth chic, enables her to hide from Deckard among Sebastian's creations. Scott visualises some big theological ideas, as when Batty 'meets his maker' and then murders him, when he presses Tyrell for answers: 'The light that burns twice as bright burns half as long.' The replicants' incept dates are vital to understanding how much of the replicants' lifespans remain, but in the finale Batty saves Deckard's life and delivers one of the screen's great soliloquies: 'I've seen things you people wouldn't believe. Attack ships on fire off the shoulder of Orion. I've watched C-beams glitter in the dark near the Tannhauser Gate. All those moments will be lost in time, like tears in rain… Time to die.' In the eye of the storm, Batty clings onto life (a white dove) and finally lets life slip away (the dove flies), in one of sci-fi's greatest moments.

Blade Runner was premiered at the Directors Guild Theater, Sunset Boulevard, on 16 June 1982. Scott dedicated the film to Dick's memory, as he died a few weeks before the film opened. In a highly competitive year, against such films as *E.T.* and *Mad Max 2*, *Blade Runner* struggled to find an audience, taking only $15 million on its initial US release. The trailer touted an action movie in the *Star Wars* mould, but word of mouth soon established that this was more cerebral fare. The initial versions of *Blade Runner* were the US theatrical cut (running 112 minutes) and the more violent international theatrical cut, which includes some nasty business with bloody eye sockets during Roy's murder of Tyrell (who in an earlier draft script was a replicant), Pris sticking her fingers up Deckard's nostrils during a fight, Deckard shooting Pris three times (not two), and Roy piercing his hand with a nail. The 'happy ending' landscape was out-takes of Montana from *The Shining* (1980), with Ford and Young driving a car though Big Bear Lake, California. In post-production, Scott became deeply unhappy with some changes imposed on the film by his producers, in particular the voice-over narration to clarify plot points and the cheerful ending. In 1992, a director's cut surfaced. Out went the 'happy ending', with Deckard and Rachael entering the elevator to an ambiguous future. A dream sequence was inserted, with Deckard seeing a unicorn galloping through a misty wood (shot by Scott for *Legend*). This represents one of Deckard's memories, perhaps an implant. In 2007, Scott delivered 'the final cut', which is generally considered to be the finest version of all. Scott's 'work print' is even now available on DVD. It opens with a definition of a replicant, according to the 'New American Dictionary © 2016'. The voice-over version has its own merits, in the classic noir tradition, while later editions are more thoughtful and ambiguous, and perhaps more beautiful.

The most obvious and entertaining *Blade Runner* derivative was Charles Band's *Trancers* (1985; *Future Cop*), which sent twenty-third-century cop Trooper Jack Deth (Tim Thomerson) of the Angel City PD 300 years into the past (to Los Angeles during Christmas 1985), to track down master criminal Martin Whistler (Michael Stefani), who uses psychic power to turn the weak-willed into zombie-like minions called 'trancers'. In the past (or 'down the line'), Whistler impersonates Wiesling, an LAPD lieutenant. He is killing the ancestors of the future Angel City council, so Deth's personality is placed inside one of his own ancestors in 1985, journalist Philip Dethon. Deth is helped by Philip's girl, Leena (Helen Hunt). Their adventures in the past are entertaining, violent and humorous, as Deth comments on 1980s Los Angeles during his manhunt. This B-classic has a logic all of its own and a snappy script. It was shot on location in LA for $400,000. The film's production values are lifted by the Christmas setting and an ethereal score from Mark Ryder and Phil Davies, who deploy great swathes of shimmering, throbbing synths. Deth's habitation of his ancestor's body bears a resemblance to elements of *Avatar*, while the time-travelling cop is clearly *Terminator*-inspired. Deth is a great creation – part chain-smoking private eye, part hard-nosed Dirty Harry, he dispenses pithy observations and enjoys watching *Peter Gunn* on TV. He beats up hoodlums hassling him in a punk bar,

JACK DETH IS BACK... AND HE'S NEVER BEEN HERE BEFORE

HE'S A 23rd CENTURY CRIME-BUSTER, HEATING IT UP IN L.A. ... TODAY!

FUTURE COP ⓜ

Crime Time: Twenty-third-century cop Jack Deth (Tim Thomerson) time-travels back to Los Angeles in 1985 in the cult movie *Trancers*, under its alternative title *Future Cop*.

strikes matches on his teeth, drives a T-Bird like a maniac, wears a long mac and slicks back Philip's floppy 1980s hairstyle with the crack, 'Dry hair's for squids.' McNulty (Art LaFleur), Deth's boss in the twenty-third century, arrives in 1985 to bring Deth back, in the only relative they had available, a little girl (ten-year-old Alyson Croft). A trancer killed Deth's wife, so he tracks down the pallid zombies, submits them to a TSE (Trancer Suspect Examination) and 'scorches' them – when shot, trancers glow and leave only a scorched outline on the ground. Deth is armed with a 'period' .38 Special and deploys a device that can create a 'long second' (one second stretched to ten) which he uses to evade capture when cornered by Whistler and to save Leena's life when she plummets off a building. The film blurs the line between the noirish neon future world and modern Los Angeles. In the twenty-third century, the ruins of Los Angeles itself are underwater – Lost Angeles. Deth proved so resilient that he reappeared in a rash of sequels – *Trancers 2: The Return of Jack Deth* (1991), *Trancers 3: Deth Lives* (1992), *Trancers 4: Jack of Swords* (1994), *Trancers 5: Sudden Deth* (1994) and *Trancers 6* (2002).

Despite its title, Ringo Lam's *Replicant* (2001) is completely unrelated to *Blade Runner*. In this Jean-Claude Van Damme vehicle, serial killer Edward Garrotte (Van Damme), called 'the Torch' because he incinerates his victims, is hunted by retired cop Jake Riley (Michael Rooker). From a hair follicle containing Garrotte's DNA, the government grow a clone of the killer (Van Damme again), but the adult has a child's mind. Van Damme is convincing as the serial killer, but as the replicant it resembles a misjudged stab at Forrest Gump. Riley and the replicant team up in this buddy–cop thriller with a twist.

Dick's 1966 novel *We Can Remember It for You Wholesale* was adapted for the screen as Paul Verhoeven's *Total Recall* (1990), where Dick's subtle story was tumble-dried into an Arnold Schwarzenegger vehicle. On Earth in A D 2084, construction worker Doug Quaid (Douglas Quail in the book, played by Schwarzenegger) dreams of life on Mars, but can't convince his wife Lori (Sharon Stone). While commuting to work on the Metro train, Quaid sees a TV advertisement for Rekall Inc. and decides to have a memory implant of a two-week holiday living on Mars – an 'ego trip' that includes a role-play as a secret agent – where participants can 'take a vacation from themselves'. During the procedure, Quaid freaks out and the Rekall operatives realise there is a clash of personas (a 'schizoid embolism') as Quaid has already had his mind erased from a previous life. Quaid's idyllic eight-year marriage to Lori is a figment of his rewritten memory – she has been planted in his life to keep an eye on him. So begin Quaid's adventures, as he discovers he's a wanted man, an actual secret agent called 'Hauser', who has left Quaid a pre-recorded message instructing Quaid to travel to Mars. Quaid's mind holds secret information key to the Mars rebels, led by mind-reading mutant Kuato (Marshall Bell), to overthrow the planet's ruler Vilas Cohaagen (Ronny Cox), who is charging the population for the air they breathe, while raping the planet by mining mineral tribinium.

Though *Total Recall* is cleverly plotted and colourfully staged, and though the eye-popping Oscar-winning visual effects are brilliantly done, the film simply becomes a succession of action set pieces, car chases and shoot-outs, mopped up with gratuitous blood, profanity and wacky mutant make-up, thus reducing Dick's clever idea to a garish, sleazily surreal neon-lit world: a 'Dick-meets-Fellini' bullet-fest. Rachel Ticotin played Melina (Quaid/Hauser's ally on Mars), a prostitute who works the 'Last Resort' bar in 'Venusville', the Red Planet's red-light district. Michael Ironside was Cohaagen's henchman, Richter, Mel Johnson Jr. was taxi driver Benny, and Ray Baker played Rekall head, Bob McClane. *Total Recall* was shot in Mexico City at Estudios Churubusco Azteca, the Heroico Colegio Militar (military academy) and in the city's subway system. Jerry Goldsmith provided the score, and the Technicolor cinematography was by Jost Vacano. After much shooting, punching, stabbing and dismembering, Quaid wrestles a grinding mining machine and lowers a reactor into a glacier to oxygenate Mars. The Red Planet is transformed into a desert utopia of blue sky and mesas, resembling Arizona. The audience is left wondering if they have witnessed 'real' events, or Quaid's mind-bending experiences via Rekall Inc.'s implanted 'holiday'. *Total Recall* was remade by Len Wiseman, with Colin Farrell in the Schwarzenegger role, and released in 2012. Other Dick stories adapted for the screen include *Minority Report* (2002; also with Farrell) and sci-fi action thriller *Paycheck* (2003), which starred Uma Thurman and Aaron Eckhart, with Ben Affleck as a computer genius who is brought in by companies to solve their problems. His confidentiality is ensured, as after each job his memory is erased.

Another big slice of Schwarzenegger futurism was Paul Michael Glaser's *The Running Man* (1987), adapted from a novel by Stephen King (as 'Richard Bachman'). In 2017, the world economy has collapsed and TV is controlled by the state. The top-rated US show is the ICS network's *The Running Man*, where prisoners are let loose and chased by 'stalkers'. Ben Richards (Schwarzenegger) is wrongly accused of causing a civilian massacre (he's christened the 'butcher of Bakersfield') and is forced to take part in the show. As the film's trailer states, his choice is 'Hard Time or Prime Time'. A succession of stalkers are sent in pursuit: Subzero (armed with a razor-edged ice-hockey stick), Buzzsaw (armed with a chainsaw), Dynamo (who fires bolts of lightning from his hands), Fireball (played by Jim Brown), who tries his luck with his flame-thrower, and finally Captain Freedom (Jesse Ventura) comes out of retirement, as a last resort. Schwarzenegger handles himself well in the action scenes, despite being clad in a tight-fitting, unforgiving gold-and-silver jumpsuit. María Conchita Alonso played Richards's love interest, Amber Mendez, and the cast also included Dweezil Zappa (Frank's son) and the people's network of revolutionaries is led by Mic (Mick Fleetwood of Fleetwood Mac). The score was composed by Harold Faltermeyer, including the end-title song 'Running Away with You (Restless Heart)', sung by John Parr. *Running Man* is garishly photographed in comic-strip style by Thomas Del Ruth and its trump card is Richard Dawson as brash ratings-chasing presenter Damon Killian. The programme includes a baying 'Come on Down!' crowd, glitz, razzmatazz and dancing girls (choreographed by Paula Abdul). Before he's catapulted down a toboggan tube, which marks the beginning of the show, Richards assures Killian: 'I'll be back!', only to receive the reply: 'Only in a rerun.'

Not to be outdone in the future cop stakes, Schwarzenegger's big 1980s competition, Sylvester Stallone, starred as supercop Judge Dredd, a popular comic-book creation. In the third millennium, 'climate, nations, all were in upheaval'. Our planet is laid waste, a scorched 'cursed earth', with most of the population crammed into overcrowded, walled megacities. Mega-City One (formerly New York) is policed by 'the judges', and the most formidable is Judge Dredd. Arch-criminal Rico (Armand Assante) escapes from Aspen Penal Colony and frames Dredd for murder. Dredd is sentenced to a life term, but en route the prison shuttle is ambushed by scavenging cannibals, the Angel family. Dredd makes his way back to Mega-City One and faces Rico, who is his brother: they have the same DNA. They were the results of the genetically modified, top-secret Janus project. Rico creates an army of cloned Ricos (allowing Assante to utter: 'Send in the clones!') in an accelerated incubator, but Dredd, with help from petty criminal Fergie (Rob Schneider) and Judge Hershey (Diane Lane), manages to thwart Rico, evil scientist Ilsa (Joan Chen) and corrupt Judge Griffin (Jürgen Prochnow). Singer Ian Dury showed up as antiques dealer Geiger, and Max von Sydow was Judge Fargo.

Rico and his formidable ABC Robot cause havoc in Mega-City One, through acts of terrorism that decimate the judges in a series of attacks that result in revolt and chaos. The technology includes Dredd's voice-activated pistol sidearm, the Lawgiver Two gun, and the megacops ride Lawmaster bikes. Mean Machine (hulk Chris Adamson), one of the Manson-like Angel clan, is a horrific, Frankenstein creation, with one robotic arm. Dredd and cohorts break up a block war. Dredd mows down felons and then assures his colleagues: 'This room has been pacified.' Stallone is kitted out in a formidable armoured uniform and helmet designed by Gianni Versace, though he only wears it at the beginning and the end of the story. Dredd and Rico battle for supremacy in a lab hidden in the Statue of Liberty's head. Rico plummets to his death and Dredd decrees: 'Court's adjourned.' The futuristic streets, littered with neon advertisements and teeming with people and vehicles, were shot at Shepperton Studios, London, with exterior 'wasteland' scenes shot in Öræfi, Iceland. The end titles play out to The Cure's 'The Dredd Song' and Ryo Aska's 'Time'.

Like *Blade Runner*, Brett Leonard's *Virtuosity* (1995) was a sci-fi cop thriller that featured a manhunt for a killer who isn't all he seems. Parker Barnes (Denzel Washington), an ex-cop now in jail for murder, is released to track down Sid 6.7 (Russell Crowe). Sid is the newest version of a computer composite that incorporates almost 200 personality structures of the worst, most notorious murderers, serial killers and despots, including Charles Manson, Peter Sutcliffe, Saddam Hussein and Adolf Hitler. Sid 6.7 has been transferred into a humanoid 'synthetic organism' by rogue programmer Lindenmeyer (Stephen Spinella) and escapes into the real world, where he carries out copycat killings. In his colourful jackets, Sid looks like a demented game-show host, and Crowe gives a big, histrionic performance and a half, which is exactly what such material needs. When he takes over the Mediazone nightclub, Sid 6.7 creates a 'symphony' from the terrified patrons' screams, and for the finale he captures the nine-year-old daughter of criminal psychologist Madison Carter (Kelly Lynch) and engineers his own live TV broadcast (*Death TV*), with a phone-in vote ('life or death') to decide if she should be killed. Barnes has a score to settle with Sid, or at least part of him. One of Sid's multiple personalities is Matthew Grimes, a taunting, sadistic murderer who tricked Barnes into killing his own wife and daughter with a booby-trapped bomb. Barnes lost his left arm in the blast and it's now robotic. The film opens in an interesting computer simulation of the future world – where everyone dresses in bland grey suits – as Barnes tries to track down Sid 6.7 during 'virtual reality training' at the headquarters of LETAC (Law Enforcement Technology Advancement Center). Sid 6.7 is able to regenerate himself using tendrils to absorb glass. *Virtuosity* has some great ideas, but degenerates into a simple manhunt chase and explosive shoot-'em-up. Shaun Ryder's band Black Grape performs 'A Big Day in the North' as the film's theme tune.

The visual design of the future in *Blade Runner* has proved influential, not just in the production and settings of sci-fi cinema, but on pop culture in general. Such 'art' as TV adverts and pop videos exhibit an instantly recognisable influence, while the neon-lit streets of many cities now resemble the streets of *Blade Runner*'s Los Angeles. Bleak and beautiful, Scott's film was, is, and remains truly visionary.

17

'IT'S WEIRD AND PISSED OFF'

THE THING (1982)

Director: John Carpenter
Story: John W. Campbell Jr.
Screenplay: Bill Lancaster
Director of Photography: Dean Cundey
Music: Ennio Morricone
Technicolor/Panavision
A Turman-Foster Production
Released by Universal Pictures
104 minutes

Kurt Russell (R.J. MacReady, helicopter pilot), Wilford Brimley (Dr Blair), T.K. Carter (Nauls), David Clennon (Palmer), Keith David (Childs), Richard Dysart (Dr Copper), Charles Hallahan (Vance Norris), Peter Maloney (George Bennings), Richard Masur (Clark), Donald Moffat (Garry), Joel Polis (Fuchs), Thomas Waites (Windows, radio operator), Norbert Weisser (Norwegian), Larry Franco (Norwegian with rifle), Nate Irwin (helicopter pilot), William Zeman (pilot), Adrienne Barbeau (voice of Chess Wizard), John Carpenter (Norwegian in video footage), Jed (Dog Thing)

✻ ✻ ✻

Post-*Alien*, sci-fi horror entered an innovative era, gorily pitting its heroes against foes in a new breed of creature feature, and terrifying audiences with bloody, gut-twisting special effects and ultra-violence. If in space no one can hear you scream, then you can certainly hear screaming in these Earth-bound sci-fi horrors.

Their origins lay in 1950s sci-fi which depicted extraterrestrial creatures causing terrestrial mayhem. A good example is the early Steve McQueen starrer *The Blob* (1954), with teenagers battling an oozing mass in Valley Forge, Pennsylvania. There were space beings known only as 'It', as in Jack Arnold's brilliant sci-fi debut *It Came from Outer Space* (1953), an adaptation of Ray Bradbury's short story, 'The Meteor'. Aliens crash-land

Things to Come: John Carpenter's *The Thing* (1982) had its 12-man crew of US National Science Institute Station 4 trapped in their isolated research facility and menaced by who knows what, in a remake of the 1950s classic *The Thing from Another World* (1951).

in the Excelsior Mine in the Arizona desert and assume the personas of locals in Sand Rock while they repair their spacecraft. Astronomer John Putman (Richard Carlson) and schoolteacher Ellen Fields (Barbara Rush) are the voices of reason, until Ellen herself is overtaken by the beings, appearing as a prom-dressed zombie temptress to lure John into the mine, where John meets his own doppelgänger. This film anticipates *Invasion of the Body Snatchers* – the aliens take over human hosts, starting with two telephone-company workers, George (Russell Johnson) and Frank (Joe Sawyer). When the aliens manage to take off before an angry posse of vigilantes attacks them, John notes, 'They'll be back.' The smoky, bulbous-headed, one-eyed beasts are memorable and Arnold gives us an alien's-eye view of the world rendered in glorious fish-eyed bubble-vision (originally in 3-D in theatres). As trailers warned, 'It's Coming Right at You!' This classic from Universal–International, surely the most consistent 1950s Hollywood sci-fi studio, could be a parable of the personality-changing effects of drugs or alcohol, or of different races living together in harmony, but is most obviously another Red Scare movie about those damn Commies. The Arizona desert setting, a favourite Arnold location, harbours dangers that lurk eerily beside the long dusty highways, amid the tumbleweed and Joshua trees.

More extraterrestrial danger hurtled out of the sky in Nathan Juran's *20 Million Miles to Earth* (1957). US rocket XY-21 returns from its mission to Venus and crashes into the Mediterranean off the southern Sicilian fishing village of Gerra. The locals save two survivors: Bob Calder (William Hopper) and Dr Sharman (Arthur Space). Sharman is facially disfigured and dies shortly afterwards. Little Pepe (Bart Bradley) finds a jelly-like egg in a canister, which hatches a strange, reptilian Venusian creature with a tail that walks upright. It quickly grows to towering proportions and roams the pretty Italian country-side. Calder, with help from Marisa (Joan Taylor), the assistant to zoologist Dr Leonardo (Frank Puglia), manages to corral the beast at the sulphur beds at Mount Etna with an electrified net dropped from a helicopter. The creature eventually ends up in Rome Zoo, but it escapes, battles and kills an elephant and runs amok in the Eternal City, destroy-ing Sant'Angelo Bridge and careering through the Garden of Venus. The army deploy bazookas and flame-throwing tanks and it's finally trapped atop the Colosseum, where it plummets to its death. Called the Ymir, the Venusian was created in stop-motion by Ray Harryhausen, who also co-wrote the story. It was its creator's personal favourite among his gallery of beasts and Harryhausen also had a cameo as an elephant feeder. Shot on location in Italy, including Rome itself and the coast at Sperlonga, Latina, Lazio, this was an excellent monster-on-the-rampage movie from Columbia Pictures.

In Japan there was the imaginative thriller *The H-Man* (1958). People dissolve into thin air, leaving only their clothes, in this bizarre sci-fi movie that is part noir gangster flick, part Toho's take on *The Blob*. The cause is revealed to be an oozing slime that engulfs its victims. The film's best scenes depict a group of sailors finding the drifting ghost ship, *Ryūjin Maru*, which following H-bomb tests in the Pacific has created an amorphous liquid organism, a slime beast dubbed 'the liquid creature', with the mind of a human (an

H-Man), which turns its victims into green glowing slime monsters. In the finale, the blob is driven from Tokyo's sewers with burning gasoline and crisped with flame-throwers. The investigation is led by baffled Tokyo cop, Inspector Tominaga (Akihiko Hirata), Yumi Shirakawa played elegant nightclub singer Chikako Arai (whose gangster boyfriend Misaki, played by Hisaya Itō, dissolves in a rainstorm) and Kenji Sahara was biochemist boffin Dr Masada, who demonstrates the radiation's destructive power with an unpleasant dissolving experiment that resembles a froggy Alka-Seltzer. The English-language print is abridged at 79 minutes, but the uncut Japanese version, seven minutes longer, includes more of the police investigation of gangster drug dealers, gorier 'thing' special effects and more scantily clad exotic dancers at the Cabaret Homura. This beautiful-looking film, shot in TohoScope and Eastmancolor, has a great score by Masaru Satō, which incorporates torch songs, groovy jazz and a weird sonar-blip sound effect.

Honda's *Matango* (1963; *Fungus of Terror* or *Attack of the Mushroom People*) is often derided as one of the worst films ever made, when it's actually a beautifully shot, imaginative fantasy production. In the South Pacific, pleasure yacht *Aho Dori* is shipwrecked on an eerily deserted tropical paradise, where the seven passengers and crew find the beached wreck of a research ship. The survivors set up home in the ship and as their canned-food supply runs out, they eat anything (seaweed, turtle eggs, tubers) until their only option is to eat the large fungal mushrooms that grow in abundance on the island. But those who succumb go from marooned to 'shroomed, as they become shambling 'mushroom people'. Honda's film is both an entertaining sci-fi horror and an allegory for nuclear experimentation, hallucinatory drug use and pent-up sexual frustration. The research ship has been experimenting with atomic radiation and the fungal mutations resemble post-nuclear skin burns, while a large crate contains *matango*, a new genetic breed of mushroom (categorised by the trailer as not animal or plant, but a third life form). The survivors are assistant professor of psychology Kenji Murai (Akira Kubo), student Akiko Sōma (Miki Yashiro), radio and TV's 'first lady of song' Mami Sekiguchi (Kumi Mizuno, who sings in the movie), writer Etsurō Yoshida (Hiroshi Tachikawa) and the boat's wealthy owner Masafumi Kasai (Yoshio Tsuchiya). It is crewed by skipper Naoyuki Sakuta (Hiroshi Koizumi) and crewman Senzō Koyama (Kenji Sahara). There's splendid colour photography in saturated widescreen TohoScope by Hajime Koizumi and an atmospheric score from Sadao Bekku. Akiko is prim and virtuous, while Mami is a tease. While men who eat the mushrooms become 'atomic mushrooms', women who consume them become more beautiful, entrancing and seductive. The frightened mariners see half-man, half-fungi figures roaming the ship and are gradually overwhelmed by the mushroom crowd. The special effects included latex face make-up and an expanding Styrofoam mixture that created the illusion of the mushrooms growing quickly. The beached sailboat, with its tattered sails, resembles an eerie ghost galleon, while the tropical jungle, teeming with colourful fungi and predatory perambulating mushroom men, rings with cackling laughter. As Teruyoshi Nakano recalled of working on the special effects:

'It was normal to see monsters, people in samurai costumes and space aliens walking around the Toho lot during lunch.' The film is bookended by the party's lone survivor, a near-insane Kenji, in Tokyo Medical Centre, recounting his strange story.

In sci-fi, if it's not an it, a that, a *matango* or a blob, it's a thing. The archetypal 1950s Hollywood sci-fi horror, *The Thing from Another World* (1951) was co-directed by Christian Nyby, with uncredited help from Howard Hawks. A remote research station at the North Pole reports an air crash and an investigative party discover a flying saucer (which they inadvertently destroy) and an eight-foot-tall pilot, frozen in a block of ice. Back at the research station they accidentally thaw it out when Sergeant Barnes (William Self) covers the block with an electric blanket. The radioactive beast, billed as 'the Thing', resembles Frankenstein's monster and was played by six-foot-six-inch James Arness. It escapes into the snowy wastes, but has one of its arms ripped off when the outpost's dogs attack it. Scientists discover the arm is made of vegetable matter, though it is highly intelligent and thrives on blood. 'An intellectual carrot!' scoffs journalist Ned 'Scotty' Scott (Douglas Spencer), a hack desperate for a scoop. Dr Arthur Carrington (Robert Cornthwaite) wants to capture, examine and interrogate the beast, while Captain Pat Hendry (Kenneth Tobey) is determined to destroy it. The shadowy monochrome cinematography was by Russell Harlan, Dimitri Tiomkin composed the score and the special effects were by Don Steward and Linwood Dunn. Exteriors were filmed at Glacier National Park, Montana, with interiors at an ice and cold storage plant in Los Angeles.

The plot's a slow-burner that explodes in genuinely exciting confrontations between the outpost's defenders and the monster. At one point the Thing is doused in kerosene and set alight with a Very pistol. The Thing creeps into the facility's greenhouse and scientists are attacked and hung upside down, their throats cut. Carrington grows a selection of throbbing spores (which make a wailing noise similar to hungry babies), nourished with blood plasma. Hendry's love interest is Nikki Nicholson (Margaret Sheridan), one of Carrington's scientists. When the soldiers deliberate how to annihilate the 'super carrot', she suggests cooking it: 'Boil it, stew it, bake it, fry it.' As the temperature plummets and the survivors huddle in the generator room, the creature approaches and is fried alive via electrocution. Posters asked: 'Natural or Supernatural?' The trailer warned: 'Flames can't destroy the Thing, nor bullets kill it!' The film closes with one of the most memorable curtain lines in sci-fi movie history. Newsman Scotty broadcasts his report: 'Every one of you listening to my voice, tell the world. Tell this to everybody, wherever they are: "Watch the skies, everywhere. Keep looking, keep watching the skies!"'

In John Carpenter's 1982 remake, simply titled *The Thing*, it wasn't the skies that needed watching. Scripted by Bill Lancaster (actor Burt's son), this redo reversed the Poles, from Arctic to Antarctica, and set the action in US National Science Institute Station 4, an isolated facility a thousand miles from nowhere, with its 12-man crew. The story commences eerily with a helicopter chasing a husky across expansive snow meadows and vistas. A sniper on the chopper tries to kill the dog, but it manages to reach the safety of the US base. The helicopter and its crew are killed. They were Norwegians, the only survivors of a nearby research facility, where they have unearthed a fossilised 100,000 year-old monster, which thawed and wiped them out. The US team care for the dog, but when they investigate the Norwegian outpost, they bring some bloody, twisted, steaming remains back. But between the dog (which is carrying a Thing) and the remains (which aren't dead), the team is soon torn apart as the alien beast bursts from concealment within its hosts. The creature imitates other life forms, and when the Americans locate the site of the Norwegians' find, they also discover a spaceship in an ice crater. The Thing has arrived from another world and the big questions are: who has been infected, who hasn't, and how do they kill it? As helicopter pilot MacReady (Kurt Russell) surmises: 'If it takes us over, then it has no more enemies, nobody left to kill it, and then it's won.'

Like *Alien*, *The Thing* depended on its special effects and the capability, chemistry and charisma of its ensemble cast. Russell had just portrayed hissing antihero Snake Plissken in Carpenter's *Escape from New York* (1981) and had starred in Disney's sci-fi comedies *The Computer Wore Tennis Shoes* (1969), as Dexter, a kid who becomes super-intelligent when his brain absorbs a computer memory system, and the sequel *Now You See Him, Now You Don't* (1972), with invisibility as the gimmick. In *The Thing*, chopper pilot MacReady wears a full beard and a mane of black hair, a cowboy hat and shades. Russell may approach the role with all the cheerfulness of a man with an abscess, but his taciturn turn galvanises the outpost crew and the film. The rest of the eccentric, interesting cast includes roller-skating Nauls (T.K. Carter), George Bennings (Peter Maloney), dog-loving Clark (Richard Masur), Garry (Donald Moffat), Fuchs (Joel Polis) and radio operator Windows (Thomas Waites). David Clennon played smartass wacko Palmer, Keith David was Childs and Wilford Brimley played Dr Blair, who goes a little crazy and is locked in the tool shed, where he begins to assemble a spacecraft from chopper parts. Richard Dysart played Dr Copper, who loses his arms at the elbow when he attempts to cardio-jump-start Vance Morris (Charles Hallahan) and Morris's torso yawns open and transforms into a toothy beast.

Interiors were shot on the Universal Studios lot, using sound stages where the temperature was kept below freezing, while another unit worked at Universal–Hartland, lensing Rob Bottin's special effects. Exteriors were shot on the Taku Glacier on the Juneau Icefield, Alaska, situated in the Tongass National Forest, and the camp scenes were shot in the frozen wastes near Stewart, British Columbia. The filmmakers were billeted in Stewart itself, a played-out Gold Rush town. Station 4, the beleaguered outpost half buried in snow, was set against a magnificent alpine backdrop. After the US camp was torched and blown up for the film's finale (the Thing attempts to freeze itself again), the burnt-out ruin was used for the scenes at the Norwegian outpost.

Despite the considerable $15 million budget, Carpenter stayed close to the film's B-movie roots. Confinement, yet again, breeds terror as the monster stalks. The claustrophobic outpost, completely isolated when the radio and helicopter are destroyed by the Thing, was as effective a setting as *Nostromo*'s narrow corridors in *Alien*. The base's computer calculates the probability of one or more of the party being infected as 75 per cent, and if the organism reaches civilised areas the entire world's population would be infected 27,000 hours from first contact. This is a typically B-movie set-up. With the world's safety at stake, Earth is defended by a small, isolated group, locked in a battle to save humanity, armed with pistols, rifles, flame-throwers, kerosene, dynamite and flares. *The Thing* was photographed in Technicolor and Panavision by Dean Cundey. The visuals are bathed in blues and reds that flood the screen, like the vivid horror cinema of Mario Bava and Dario Argento, while the splatter-film horror effects recall Lucio Fulci at his most unrestrained. MacReady slugs J&B whisky, a blended Scotch with a distinctive yellow-and-red label, which was the favoured liquor in 1970s Italian cult movies.

The glacial score by Ennio Morricone is a vital component of the film. Carpenter often scored his own films, but here he employed the maestro of Italian cinema to provide one of the great horror sci-fi scores, its sparseness so simple and yet so effective in its relentless menace. The main theme is an ominous hum which develops into an ebbing synth fugue: the outpost's requiem. A flying saucer hurtles towards Earth and the title *The Thing*, ripped in searing white light, tears through the starscape. From the first twanging, repetitively insistent F♯ bass note of 'Humanity', low and resonant, as the helicopter pursues the infected husky, the score is an integral part of Carpenter's sound collage. This main theme is reprised for the fadeout – the throbbing bass, haunting synth and strings – which strips down to a bass 'heartbeat', before rising again.

From the moment the husky dashes across the snow wastes with the chopper in pursuit, *The Thing* grabs you around the throat and doesn't let go. *The Thing from Another World* and *The Thing* were both based on a 1938 sci-fi thriller story 'Who Goes There?', written by John W. Campbell Jr. as 'Don A. Stuart'. 'The Thing' in the story wasn't a biped monster (as in the 1951 movie), but a tentacled, three-eyed beast. Carpenter, Lancaster and Bottin recreated the new-look, shape-shifting parasite in the spirit of Campbell's original concept. Like *Invasion of the Body Snatchers*, there's an uneasy, paranoid untrustworthiness of 'Are you one?', though this is bodily assimilation rather than cloning. Even diehard fans of the movie aren't sure who's infected at which point in the movie. The crew decide on a blood test to find out who's who by dipping a hot wire into a plasma sample. When they test Palmer's, the blood leaps up, scatters on the floor and slithers for cover. Palmer begins to shudder and his head explodes, but he's tied to a couch with other terrified members of the crew, in the film's most blackly comic moment.

The Thing is renowned for a series of gross-out terror scenes that remain repulsively powerful today (it's rated 18 in the UK, R in the US). The special-visual-effects designer was Albert Whitlock, the special-effects supervisor was Roy Arbogast, dimensional animation effects were created by Randall William Cook, and the film thanks Stan Winston for his expert assistance. The extreme gore includes a bloody autopsy of the steaming creature, with a distorted, fused face and clutching hands, as well as several scenes where the Thing emerges from its hosts. The husky's face bursts, unpeeling like a banana, as the thrashing, tendrilled creature is unveiled. The distorted Norwegian bodily remains assault Bennings, who sprouts claw-like hands, so the crew douse him in kerosene and burn him alive with a flare. Fire is most effective and MacReady and others barbecue the Thing with flame-throwers, as in the scene when the creature grabs flailing Windows by the head. Hold onto your lunch for these nightmarish, strong images – creeping tendrils envelop victims, necks stretch, yellow gunk splatters, heads sprout legs and scuttle for cover, hands mutate into claws, tongues become lassos and the monstrous Thing is a butcher's-shop concoction of teeth, blood, slime and guts. After the carnage, the film's subdued, ambiguous finale is justly famous, with survivors MacReady and Childs huddling together and sharing a drink as they await the Thing's next appearance. In a seldom-seen, less ambiguous alternative ending, a husky dog escapes, pauses to look back at the smoking station and races off across into the arctic wastes.

The Thing was advertised as 'the ultimate in alien terror' where 'man is the warmest place to hide', and the trailer was a mayday radio call that builds in panic. Some TV broadcast versions cut the gore, and one version features a narration introducing the crew at the US research facility. The film was a relative failure, taking $19 million in the US, but its reputation has risen considerably and it is now regarded as a key science-fiction film of the 1980s. In 2011 it spawned a prequel, also called *The Thing*, recounting what happened at the Norwegian station. Directed by Matthijs van Heijningen and starring Mary Elizabeth Winstead, Joel Edgerton, Ulrich Thomsen, Eric Christian Olsen and Adewale Akinnuoye-Agbaje, it told the story of how the Thing came to be running towards US Station 4 disguised as a dog. The 1982 version remains Carpenter's favourite of all his films and is much loved by his fans.

One of many horrors where the monster thaws out, Eugenio Martín's *Horror Express* (1972) closely resembles 'Who Goes There?' and *The Thing from Another World*, despite being set in 1906 aboard the Trans-Siberian Express. It claims to be a true account of the discovery of a frozen 'fossil' in a Manchurian cave by the Royal Society's Professor Alexander Saxton (Christopher Lee), who transports the find by train though snowy wastes. When the creature thaws out, the hairy man-ape (Juan Olaguivel) with one glowing red eye attacks, causing bleeding eyes as it extracts its victims' memories. This alien from outer space has been on Earth for many millions of years and absorbs the brains of various victims (including the inventor of a high-strength steel and an engineer with knowledge of gravity) to construct a craft to take it home. It is also able to transfer from host to host. Martín's classic is very well mounted, with involute plotting and a knockout Euro-cult cast. The threatened passengers include Saxton's rival Dr Wells (Peter Cushing), Wells's assistant Miss Jones (Alice Reinheart), spy Natasha (Helga Line), engineer Yevtushenko (Ángel del Pozo), Inspector Mirov (Julio Peña), Count and Countess Petrovski (Jorge Rigaud and Silvia Tortosa), zealous spiritual adviser Father Pujardov (Alberto de Mendoza) and flamboyant Cossack Captain Kazan (Telly Savalas).

This UK–Spanish co-production was shot by Alejandro Ulloa in December 1971 near Madrid, with interiors (including one train carriage, which was redressed to play all the carriages) at Estudios Madrid 70 at Daganzo. The model train was reused from the Martin–Savalas Euro-Western *Pancho Villa* (1972) and the menacing score was composed by John Cacavas. The supporting cast included many familiar faces from Spanish genre cinema: José Jaspe, Victor Israel, Barta Barri, José Marco, José Canalejas and Vicente Rocca. *Horror Express* forges a 'missing link' between Gothic horror and science fiction – when anthropologists examine the monster's eye fluid under a microscope, they see an image of Earth as seen from space.

The Thing was one of several Earth-based gut-busting sci-fi horrors of the 1980s. In 'Lewis Coates'/Luigi Cozzi's *Alien Contamination* (1980; *Toxic Spawn* and *Contamination*), the freighter *Caribbean Lady* steams towards New York harbour. Its dead crew appear to have exploded from within. The ship's cargo of coffee crates contains large green pulsating eggs. When ripe, they explode and those splattered by the eggs' acid burst open from within, in graphic fountains of blood, guts and organs. The freighter is quarantined and the batch of eggs aboard the ship deep-frozen, while another clutch in an import–export warehouse in the Bronx is torched with flame-throwers. Colonel Stella Holmes ('Louise Monroe'/Louise Marleau) at Special Division 5 investigates the eggs' provenance. She teams up with New York cop Lieutenant Tony Aris (Marino Masé) and questions the astronaut, Commander Ian Hubbard (Ian McCulloch), who has returned from Mars with strange tales of alien eggs he found in a glacial snow cave on Mars's polar ice cap. His co-astronaut, Hamilton (Siegfried Rauch), was lost during the expedition and Hubbard is now a disgraced, drunken derelict. The trio are granted 72 hours by Washington to solve the case, so they fly to Colombia, where they infiltrate a coffee-processing factory run by Hamilton, who isn't dead but is being controlled by 'the cyclops', a giant Martian being which incubates the eggs for shipment around the world. The eggs are harvested by employees in white protective suits and gas masks, whom the locals call 'white zombies'. The monster swallows Tony whole, but Hubbard saves Stella and incinerates the cyclops with a flare gun. Studio work was done in Rome, with location scenes shot in New York, Florida and Colombia. Gisela Hahn cropped up as Hamilton's villainous cohort, Perla de la Cruz, and Goblin provided the throbbing, glistening synth score. Special effects – such as the egg bursts and anatomical eruptions – were staged bloodily by Giovanni Corridori. With the eggs destroyed in Colombia, Cozzi cuts to a bustling, rainy New York City street, where ripened eggs in a refuse bag explode. On its original release in the UK, it was dumped on the Video Nasty list, though it is now a 15 certificate on DVD. This uncut version, titled *Contamination*, runs 92 minutes, while the truncated US 83-minute print, *Alien Contamination*, is a better film – pacier and with less over-the-top gore.

Jack Sholder's *The Hidden* (1987) is a frantic, original amalgamation of sci-fi/horror and buddy–cop movie. World-weary LAPD detective Tom Beck (Michael Nouri) is teamed with FBI agent Lloyd Gallagher (Kyle MacLachlan). They investigate a murder, robbery and joyriding spree that is perpetrated by a slug-like alien able to take over human hosts. Its victims range from Brenda Lee Van Buren (Claudia Christian), a stripper from the 'Harem Room', to businessmen, a cop, a dog and finally a senator. It transpires that Gallagher is an alien too – an Altairian – and has tracked the creature from the planet where it killed Gallagher's wife, child and police partner. This violent movie has an impossible-to-predict plot and a great slug, which gorily orally transfers from one host to another until Gallagher immolates the senator with a flame-thrower and zaps the emerging slime with a laser gun. The strong supporting cast includes Ed O'Ross, Clu Gulager, Clarence Felder and Richard Brooks among the detectives, and the alien's penchant for rock music ensures a great soundtrack. A dreadful sequel, the sluggish *The Hidden II*, exposed itself in 1994.

The Italian–US co-production *Leviathan* (1989), directed by George Pan Cosmatos, had slimy, aquatic beasts by Stan Winston, and the mechanical effects co-coordinator was Giovanni Corridori. The story is set at a Tri-Oceanic mining operation, which is extracting silver and other precious metals 16,000 feet under the Atlantic Ocean. In Mining Shack No. 7, the eight-person crew nears the end of its 90-day shift when the wreck of Russian ship *Leviathan*, which appears to have been torpedoed, is discovered. The crew bring up the ship's safe and find a bottle of vodka. Whoever drinks the vodka (which is contaminated by a 'genetic alteration' virus) develops an itchy skin rash and the shivers and mutates into a tentacled, clawed fish-monster that seeks human blood. Unable to be evacuated – as Martin (Meg Foster), their boss back at HQ, claims there's a hurricane approaching – the crew appear condemned to watery graves. Under the command of geologist Steven Beck (Peter Weller), the crew includes posh Brit Elizabeth 'Willie' Williams (Amanda Pays, from *Max Headroom*), lecherous Buzz 'Sixpack' Parrish (Daniel Stern), Justin Jones (Ernie Hudson), Tony Rodero, known as 'DeJesus' (Michael Carmine), Bridget Bowman (Lisa Eilbacher), G.P. Cobb (Héctor Elizondo) and medic Dr Glen Thompson (Richard Crenna). The virus enables humans to breathe underwater (a new species dubbed *homo aquaticus*) and the *Leviathan* had been deliberately torpedoed and should never have been found. The spacious, convincing sets of the interiors of Mining Shack No. 7 and the excellent underwater scenes – especially as Williams makes her way towards the *Leviathan* through a tangled forest of giant tubeworms – are very effective. Bankrolled by MGM and Luigi and Aurelio De Laurentiis, *Leviathan* was shot at Cinecittà Studios, Rome, at Mediterranean Film Studios, Malta, and off the Gulf of Mexico. Jerry Goldsmith composed the score, which includes an orchestral theme augmented with whale noises. Sixpack and Bowman are both infected and their bodies are jettisoned, but a stray tentacle remains onboard. The crew are decimated by creatures that variously resemble a giant eel, a tentacle, a wobbly slab of slime, a bubbling boil, a severed arm and a walking, shrieking man-fish. Ridiculously plotted, this hokum is mounted with élan.

The Thing and other gory 1970s and 1980s horrors were key inspirations behind writer-director James Gunn's graphic *Slither* (2006), released by Universal. A meteorite lands in woodland near the town of Wheelsy, South Carolina (filmed in Vancouver, British Columbia), a Hicksville location if ever there was one, filled with slack-jawed lollygaggers. Grant Grant (Michael Rooker) is infected by an alien parasite and becomes grossly disfigured, as he feeds his appetite with animal corpses. He eventually grows into a huge slithering, squiddy creature, reminiscent of Carpenter's Thing, which terrorises the countryside. Grant's lover Brenda Gutierrez (Brenda James) also becomes infected, swells obesely, bursts and disgorges hundreds of wriggling slugs, which enter victims' mouths and turn them into zombies. There's a fine vein of humour running through the film, but its graphic violence stifles laughter. Local cop Bill Pardy (Nathan Fillion) leads a posse, including Grant's wife Starla (Elizabeth Banks), against the creatures, as the film mutates into a comedy–horror version of *Night of the Living Dead* and *The Thing*, with elements of David Cronenberg's films and the Troma stable. A lot of blood and guts are spilt, until Starla shoots the squiddy, tentacled creature that she once married 'for better or worse'. 'Much fuckin' worse,' comments a local.

Perhaps the best take on the action-packed 'rampaging alien on Earth' theme was John McTiernan's *Predator* (1987). Arnold Schwarzenegger starred as Major 'Dutch' Schaefer, the leader of a crack Special Forces commando unit dropped into the South American jungle. Supposedly there to rescue hostages held by rebels, the team end up being stalked and slashed by an agile, chameleon-like alien beast, capable of invisibility and carnage. Their foe resembles the *Creature from the Black Lagoon* or *The Horror of Party Beach*, with added weaponry, including laser guns and blades. Often seen as a rippling amorphous transparent presence rustling the jungle foliage, the alien was created by Stan Winston. Among the heavy hardware on display is the six-barrelled Minigun Gatling derivative, which reappeared in Schwarzenegger's *Terminator 2: Judgment Day* (1991). A hybrid of Vietnam jungle war movie and sci-fi creature feature, this straightforward idea, with its straightforward plot, is one of Schwarzenegger's finest films – his Austrian accent is passed off as Dutch. Wary scout Billy (Sonny Landham) reads the warning signs, and Elpidia Carrillo played Anna, a jungle rebel captured by commandos. The team, which is sent on the mission by General Phillips (R.G. Armstrong), features CIA agent Dillon (Carl Weathers) and commandos Mac (Bill Duke), Blain (Jesse Ventura), Poncho (Richard Chaves) and Hawkins (Shane Black). The squad's gory deaths include victims skinned alive, having arms ripped off, spines removed or brains blown out. Kevin Peter Hall played the seven-foot-tall alien Predator, which lands on Earth in a pod at the beginning of the film and oozes luminous green blood when shot. The movie was lensed at Puerto Vallarta, Jalisco and Palenque in Chiapas, Mexico, and was followed by two sequels – *Predator 2* (1990) and *Predators* (2010). The franchise, which includes video games, novels and comics, morphed with the *Alien* series, for *Alien vs. Predator* (2004). When the human opposition doesn't measure up, only beasts of comparable cine-mythical status will do. Keep watching the skies, or at least behind the bushes, and look out for *Alien (or Predator) vs. The Thing* at a multiplex near you.

18

'YOU HAVE NO CONCEPT OF TIME'

BACK TO THE FUTURE (1985)

Director: Robert Zemeckis
Screenplay: Robert Zemeckis and Bob Gale
Director of Photography: Dean Cundey
Music: Alan Silvestri
Panavision/Technicolor
An Amblin Entertainment/Universal Pictures Production
Released by Universal Pictures
111 minutes

Michael J. Fox (Marty McFly), Christopher Lloyd (Dr Emmett Brown), Lea Thompson (Lorraine Baines), Crispin Glover (George McFly), Thomas F. Wilson (Biff Tannen), Claudia Wells (Jennifer Parker), Marc McClure (Dave McFly), Wendie Jo Sperber (Linda McFly), George DiCenzo (Sam Baines), James Tolkan (Mr Strickland), Jeffrey Jay Cohen (Skinhead), Casey Siemaszko (3-D), Billy Zane (Match), Donald Fullilove (Goldie Wilson), Lisa Freeman (Babs), Cristen Kauffman (Betty), Buck Flower (Red Thomas), Harry Waters Jr. (Marvin Berry), Tommy Thomas, Granville 'Danny' Young, David Harold Brown, Lloyd L. Tolbert (The Starlighters), Paul Hanson, Lee Brownfield and Robert DeLapp (The Pinheads), Huey Lewis (high-school band audition judge)

* * *

I f H.G. Wells had owned a car when he wrote *The Time Machine* in 1895, he would surely have adapted it into a time-travelling craft. But if Wells's hero looked in wonderment at the future, then there were time travellers who strove to alter events and even tailor history for their own gain by disrupting the time continuum. This could result in an alternate or parallel future or in some cases a person's nonexistence. No films did time travel better than the *Back to the Future* trilogy, which began in 1985 and in its own way changed movie history.

Marty McFly (Michael J. Fox) lives in the peaceful Californian town of Hill Valley.

He dates pretty Jennifer Parker (Claudia Wells), and his father, George (Crispin Glover), is picked on by local bully Biff Tannen (Thomas F. Wilson). Doc Brown (Christopher Lloyd), an eccentric inventor with a patchy track record, invents a time machine installed in a DeLorean car: when the car reaches 88 mph, the vehicle warps through time and travels from 1985 to a preset destination, in the past or future. On 26 October 1985, Doc is demonstrating the car to Marty in the parking lot at Twin Pines Mall. Suddenly Libyan terrorists, whom Doc has duped in order to acquire the plutonium needed to create the nuclear reaction (to make the car's 'flux capacitor' facilitate space travel), appear and gun Doc down. Marty escapes in the DeLorean and travels to Hill Valley on Saturday 5 November 1955. The time machine's power runs down, so Marty locates Doc and explains what has happened. Doc – a hare-brained inventor even in his younger days – sets about devising a way of sending Marty back to the future. Marty knows that lightning will strike the town's clock tower at 10.04 p.m. next Saturday night. The bolt will be enough to provide the 1.21 GW of power needed to reactivate the flux capacitor. But Marty has to spend a week in 1955 and major problems arise when Marty's mother Lorraine Baines (Lea Thompson) falls in love with Marty rather than George. Marty must become matchmaker for his own parents, or else he'll never be born.

Budgeted at $19 million, *Back to the Future* was shot by Dean Cundey in Panavision and Technicolor. The film was partly shot at Universal Studios, on the standing 'Courthouse Square' backlot set at Universal Studios. Hill Valley's plaza was redressed to resemble both the 1980s and the 1950s. The exteriors of George, Biff and Lorraine's 1950s houses were on Bushnell Avenue, South Pasadena. Other location work included the exterior of Marty's 1985 house on Roslyndale Avenue, Pacoima, Los Angeles. School band auditions were shot in Burbank Community Center, the 'Enchantment under the Sea' school dance was filmed at the First United Methodist Church in Hollywood, and Hill Valley High School was Whittier High School, California. When Marty first arrives in 1955 he crashes into a scarecrow and barn on Twin Pines Ranch, which was filmed on Walt Disney's Golden Oak Ranch, Newhall, California. The interiors of Doc's 1950s mansion were filmed at the R.R. Blacker House, Hillcrest Avenue, Pasadena, while the exterior was the Gamble House, also in Pasadena. Puente Hills Mall, California, was the Twin Pines Mall parking lot where Doc is gunned down.

Twenty-four-year-old Canadian-born Michael J. Fox had become a TV star in the Emmy Award-winning sitcom *Family Ties* (1982–9). His easy charm and natural charisma, and aptitude for comedy, action and romance, made him perfect for bemused hero Marty, a disillusioned youngster with 'no future'. Christopher Lloyd was fittingly insane as madcap scientist Dr Emmett Brown, whose van bills him as 'Dr E. Brown Enterprises – 24 Hr Scientific Services'. With his wild Einstein-like hair and manic demeanour, Doc is one of cinema's great 'mad scientists'. Doc's companion is shaggy mutt Einstein, the world's first time-travelling dog. There's great chemistry between Lloyd and Fox: Doc's imagination

OUTATIME: Marty McFly (Michael J. Fox) checks his watch beside his time-travelling DeLorean DMC-12, with its gull-wing doors, in the US poster for Robert Zemeckis's *Back to the Future* (1985).

runs riot and makes flights of scientific fancy reality, while exasperated Marty follows. In the 1950s, Doc is even more manic as he tries to figure out a way of getting 'future boy' back home. When Doc sees a video recording of himself in the future, his first reaction is, 'Thank God I've still got my hair.' He enthuses, 'I finally invent something that works!', while Marty, assessing his predicament, mutters, 'Bet your ass it works.' Crispin Glover was ideal as nerdy punchbag George McFly, a walking sight gag incredibly low on self-confidence, who must learn to stand up for himself to win Lorraine (Lea Thompson). Lorraine tells her own daughter that it's 'not respectable' to chase boys, but is shameless in her pursuit of 'dreamboat' Calvin Klein (Marty's name according to his underwear) in 1955. Thomas F. Wilson played Biff Tannen, the thuggish high-school bully with a thick skull and an even thicker sense of humour. His Three Stooges henchmen, Skinhead,

Match and 3-D (with his 3-D specs) were played by Jeffrey Jay Cohen, Billy Zane and Casey Siemaszko. James Tolkan was slacker-hating school principal, Mr Strickland, in both 1955 and 1985. When Marty's band, The Pinheads, fail the school band auditions with a rock cover of 'The Power of Love', it's singer Huey Lewis as the judge who hollers through a megaphone: 'I'm afraid you're just too darn loud.'

Perhaps the souped-up DeLorean DMC-12 is the film's true star, with its gull-wing doors and iconic number plate 'OUTATIME'. Visual-effects shots were produced at Industrial Light & Magic, the special-effects supervisor was Kevin Pike and Ron Cobb is billed as 'Consultant: DeLorean Time Travel'. The film's principal special effects were the time-travelling scenes, as the DeLorean reaches 88 mph and zaps through time in a flash of light and a sonic boom, leaving only flaming tyre tracks in its wake. For the pyrotechnic finale, to send Marty back to 1985, Doc rigs a cable from the clock tower, which will feed the lightning down to a contact point, for the DeLorean to adrenalin-inject the flux capacitor. 'Don't worry,' assures Doc. 'As long as you hit that wire with the connecting hook at precisely 88 miles an hour the instant the lightning strikes the tower, everything will be fine.'

In this culture-clash comedy, the cultures come from different eras. At the Baineses' dinner, father Sam gets their first TV set fixed up. *The Honeymooners* is on and Marty comments that this is a great episode, but Lorraine's brother Milton says the show is brand new. Marty notes he must have seen a rerun. 'What's a rerun?' asks Milton. In 1985, Marty's uncle Joey is in jail; at the Baineses' in 1955, little Joey plays in his playpen: 'Better get used to these bars, kid,' suggests Marty. A cinema is exhibiting the 1954 RKO Western *Cattle Queen of Montana*, starring Barbara Stanwyck and Ronald Reagan: in 1985, Reagan was the US president. Marty conceals the DeLorean behind a 1955 sign promoting Lyon Estates (where Marty lives in 1985), with the promising tagline: 'Live in the Home of Tomorrow.' Viewed today, the 1980s scenes resemble a period setting as quaint as the 1950s-era scenes. But the film has a darker side too – for example, the fact that Doc deals with Libyan terrorists so he can carry on his research, having squandered his family fortune. There's some mild profanity ('son of a bitch'), Biff's rough assault on Lorraine is abridged in some TV prints, and one of the story's underlying themes is unwitting incest.

The middle section of the film plays as a 1950s 'flashback', with Marty as a character in his own life. The story also looks at how things we say and do, sometimes unwittingly, have future repercussions we are unaware of. It's an interesting narrative device and little details, such as a flyer for the clock-preservation fund, gain greater significance later in the story. In 1955 Marty tries to tell Doc that in 1985 he will be shot, but Doc doesn't want to know his destiny and rips up Marty's warning letter. But at the end of the film, Doc has read the letter and is wearing a bulletproof vest (a motif that is carried over into later films in the trilogy). As Doc survives, disrupting the space–time continuum and reshaping events, the end of the film creates a third time period, an alternative 1985. Now Biff waxes George's BMW and George is a successful sci-fi author.

The film also looks at wish-fulfilment fantasies and the triumph of the underdog. Strickland tells 'slacker' Marty that no McFly has ever amounted to anything: 'Yeah? Well history is gonna change.' In 1955 Marty knows everyone in Hill Valley's future. He knows that Goldie Wilson (Donald Fullilove), who is attending night school but sweeps floors in a café, will one day be Hill Valley mayor. In 1985 the town drunk, Red Thomas, sleeps on a bench, when in 1955 he was a mayoral candidate. At the 'Enchantment under the Sea' high-school dance, Marty stands in for Marvin Berry and the Starlighters' guitarist and jams the 1955 Chuck Berry number 'Johnny B. Goode' (though Fox's voice was dubbed by Mark Campbell). This musical number mutates into a litany of great guitar flourishes, referencing Pete Townshend's 'windmills', heavy metal, pomp-rock riffing, and a bit of Jimi Hendrix. Fox affects Berry's 'duck walk' across the stage and Marvin rushes to phone his cousin Chuck to tell him about a new sound. When the audience stop dancing to stare at Marty's performance, he notes: 'Guess you guys aren't ready for that yet… but your kids are gonna love it.'

Alan Silvestri composed the film's heroic, triumphant music, which was deployed in the time-travelling scenes and during a chase around the town plaza. In 1985 Marty commutes to school by skateboard, but in the 1955 scenes, when Biff and company chase him around the plaza in their car, Marty commandeers a kid's home-made wooden-crate scooter and converts it into a skateboard. The film features a great retro soundtrack, including The Four Aces' 'Mr Sandman' and Fess Parker's 'The Ballad of Davy Crockett' (young Milton Baines wears a coonskin hat, a sign that the Crockett craze was sweeping the country). Huey Lewis and the News had hits with 'Back in Time' and 'The Power of Love' due to the film. Marty dons a yellow radiation suit and plays George loud squalls of rock guitar (courtesy of Van Halen) through headphones, while pretending to be 'Darth Vader' from planet Vulcan, to scare sci-fi fan George into action. *Back to the Future* is old-fashioned entertainment in the classic Hollywood mould and also offers a clever twist on 1980s Hollywood nostalgia for the 1950s.

When it was released in the US in March 1985, *Back to the Future* was the year's biggest hit, taking over $210 million and over $350 million worldwide. It was rated PG in both the US and the UK, and its mild profanity has been redubbed for some TV showings. Posters, featuring Fox looking worriedly at his watch beside the DeLorean, had the tagline: 'He was never in time for his classes… He wasn't in time for his dinner… Then one day he wasn't in his time at all.' The film was followed by a 26-episode animated TV series of the same name, which ran in 1991–2 and included live-action guest appearances by Christopher Lloyd, with the cartoon Doc voiced by Dan Castellaneta. Marty's surname also inspired British pop band McFly.

Released in the same year as *Back to the Future*, Jonathan Betuel's *My Science Project* (1985) echoed Zemeckis's film and *Ghostbusters*. It was set in 1985 at Kit Carson High School (shot at Van Nuys High School, California). When petrolhead Michael Harlan (John Stockwell) tries to stage a knockout final-year project, he finds the power generator from a UFO that landed on Earth in 1957 in a USAF junkyard at Dawson Air Force Base. When he experiments with it, he discovers that it can transport him via a time and space warp. He is joined in his adventure by bookworm Ellie Sawyer (Danielle von Zerneck) and wisecracking, fast-talking Latino pop-culture vulture, Vinny Latello (Fisher Stevens). When his whacked-out yippie science teacher Bob Roberts (Dennis Hopper) plugs the gizmo into the national grid, it zaps him back to Woodstock. Later a massive time warp envelops the school, unleashing world history, from Neanderthal cavemen and a Tyrannosaurus rex (Rick Baker was the consultant on this monster), via Cleopatra and gladiators, to World War II Nazis, Vietcong fighters and futuristic post-apocalyptic mutants, which overrun the campus. The special effects – from the glowing purple static of the Tesla Globe UFO gizmo to the swirling clouds, strobe lightning and dry-ice destruction – are impressive for the period. The film is also partly a high-school comedy – with geeky Sherman (Raphael Sbarge) and a gang of bullies – and looks at the developing relationship between two opposites (car boy and book girl). It benefits from good performances from Stockwell and von Zerneck, and this kooky 1980s time capsule is well worth a look. Bizarrely, the film is still rated 15 in the UK for 'substance misuse', which amounts to a single shot of Hopper getting a hit by sucking on an oxygen canister. Strong stuff indeed from Disney.

Time travel also featured in TV movies such as *Time Stalkers* (1987), which took William Devane back in time to the Old West in search of Klaus Kinski. In TV film *When Time Expires* (1997), time traveller Travis Beck (Richard Grieco) has a watch fitted with a 'time flux continuum sensor' that beeps a warning if he's about to change the future, which would have been very useful for Marty McFly. It starts beeping, for example, when Travis passionately kisses waitress June Kelly (Cynthia Geary). This loony, low-budget sci-fi, which also features Mark Hamill, has Travis being trailed by assassins during his mission to feed a quarter into a parking meter before the parking 'time expires'.

Two *Back to the Future* sequels, made back to back by Zemeckis at $40 million apiece for Universal–Amblin, followed. Fox and Lloyd reprised their roles, ensuring continuity, though not all the original cast returned. *Back to the Future* ended with Doc, having zipped 30 years into the future, returning to 1985 in a flying DeLorean (which runs on garbage via a 'Mr Fusion Home Energy Reactor') to take Marty and Jennifer to 2015, where 'something's gotta be done about your kids'. In contrast to the first film's 'dreams coming true' scenario, *Back to the Future Part II* (1989) presents its flipside nightmare. *Part II* begins in October 1985, but with Elisabeth Shue now cast as Marty's girlfriend Jennifer. Doc whisks them to 2015, where the skyways are filled with hovercars, a cinema advertises *Jaws 19* and their son, Marty Jr. (Fox again), is to be jailed for 15 years for theft.

Part II lazily replays various scenes from the first film in a futuristic setting, as in the chase around the plaza, with Marty riding a hoverboard after a confrontation in the retro-themed Café 80s. In the future, Marty Jr.'s tormentors are Biff's son Griff (Wilson) and his cyberpunks, Data (Ricky Dean Logan), Spike (Darlene Vogel) and Whitey (Jason Scott Lee). In 2015, Jennifer has to be rescued by Doc and Marty when she is picked up by the police and taken 'home', where she comes face to face with the McFly family of the future, living in the rough 'hood' of Hill Dale. Jennifer sees Lorraine (Thompson) and George (Jeffrey Weissman replacing Glover), older Marty (Fox), his daughter Marlene (Fox again) and Jennifer herself.

In 2015, Marty buys a copy of *Gray's Sports Almanac*, which records the results of every important sporting event from 1950 to 2000, but Old Biff finds it, travels back in time to 1955 and gives the almanac to his younger self. When Doc, Marty and Jennifer return to 1985 they find an alternative future. Hill Valley is now an iniquitous den of gambling and the plaza is overrun with bikers and tanks, in the shadow of 'Biff's Pleasure Paradise', a glitteringly crass skyscraping hotel-cum-casino. Marty visits the Biff Tannen Museum and learns how 'Hill Valley's number one citizen and America's greatest folk hero' embarked on an extraordinarily lucky winning streak, which made him an overnight millionaire and founder of Biffco. In 1973 Biff married Lorraine Baines-McFly, and in the local cemetery Marty finds his father George's grave – he was murdered by Biff on 15 March 1973. The high school burnt down, Strickland (Tolkan) is a shotgun-toting vigilante, and Lyon Estates is a graffitied, littered ghetto. The seedy future world is rather depressing, with Marty's mother now a trashy, busty, silicone-enhanced drunk.

Biff's heavies are still Skinhead, 3-D and Match. Flea (bass player for the Red Hot Chili Peppers) played Needles, who coerces Marty Sr. into illegal activity at work which gets him fired. Marty and Doc have to go back to 1955 to prevent Biff receiving the almanac. *Part II* then revisits the first film, by interweaving the story of Marty trying to retrieve the almanac from Biff against the backdrop of the 'Enchantment under the Sea' dance, where there are two Docs and two Martys at large. Marty manages to retrieve the almanac from Biff but as the storm rages, the DeLorean is struck by lightning and vanishes with Doc driving it, leaving Marty trapped in 1955. A Western Union representative (Joe Flaherty) pulls up and hands Marty a letter from Doc they have been holding for 70 years, dated 1885. Marty rushes to Hill Valley, moments after Doc has sent Marty back to 1985 (the end of the first film is replayed) and when the other Marty shows up, Doc faints: 'Great Scott!' With plot threads dangling in mid-air, the film ends with the caption: 'To Be Concluded.'

Despite its shortcomings as a movie, ballyhoo ensured *Part II* still took over $118 million at the US box office when it was released in the US in November 1989. The poster artwork this time had both Fox and Lloyd in futuristic garb, looking at their watches beside a hovering DeLorean, with the strapline: 'Getting back was only the beginning.'

For *Back to the Future Part III* (1990), Marty travels back to the Wild West of 1885 to track down Doc, who is working as Hill Valley's blacksmith. With no such thing as electricity, let alone nuclear fusion, Doc must figure out an alternative way to accelerate the car to 88 mph. Meanwhile, Marty falls foul of local renegade Buford 'Mad Dog' Tannen (Wilson) and Doc falls for the town's new schoolteacher, Clara Clayton (Mary Steenburgen), as they share a love of sci-fi writer Jules Verne. Doc runs the DeLorean on railway tracks and powers it with a locomotive, which reaches 88 mph across a half-completed bridge, the other half of which Doc promises Marty will exist in 1985. The DeLorean once more goes back to the future, while Doc stays in the Old West to live with Clara.

The Wild West setting allows the filmmakers to have considerable fun. When he travels back in time from 1955, Marty is kitted out with a fringed dude-cowboy outfit. He introduces himself to Irish pioneers the McFlys, Seamus (Fox) and Maggie (Thompson), as 'Clint Eastwood'. In the alternative 1985 segment of *Part II*, Biff watches *A Fistful of Dollars*, and when Marty faces outlaw Mad Dog in *Part III* he uses a stove door as bulletproof protection beneath his poncho, as Eastwood did. To travel back in time, Marty drives the DeLorean at a drive-in screen in Monument Valley – as he arrives in the Old West, the Indians in the movie hoarding become real Indians being pursued by the US cavalry. Later the DeLorean is pulled through Monument Valley by six horses, like John Ford's *Stagecoach*. Chester, the Palace Saloon barman, is played by Western regular Matt Clark, and three grizzled patrons are beloved Western character actors Harry Carey Jr., Dub Taylor and Pat Buttran. Cinematographer Dean Cundey played a photographer who snaps Doc and Marty by the town clock. Richard Dysart played a barbed-wire salesman, Bill McKinney, a train engineer, Marvin J. McIntyre was the town's mortician, and Burton Gilliam played a Colt salesman who gives Marty a pistol. With his long hair and moustache, Marshal Strickland (Tolkan) resembles Wild Bill Hickok. Doc Brown (rather than Holiday) wears a long 'duster' coat and has a rifle with a futuristic-looking telescopic sight, and when a bad guy shoots at Marty's feet and yells, 'Dance!', Marty performs Michael Jackson's 'Moonwalk'. Beardy rockers ZZ Top appeared as a hoedown band and also played 'Doubleback' over the end titles. The poster artwork for *Part III* had Fox, Lloyd and Steenburgen in Western attire, looking at pocket watches, with the tagline: 'They've saved the best trip for last... but this time they may have gone too far.'

Part III winds up back in 1985, where Marty sees the DeLorean destroyed by a train, and at his family home at Lyon Estates all is well. At a stop light, Needles and his gang try to goad Marty and Jennifer (Shue) into racing them, but Marty doesn't rise to their taunt (Needles's radio is blasting out 'The Power of Love'). At the railway track, Jennifer and Marty witness a time-travelling locomotive arrive with Doc and Clara on board, plus their children Jules and Verne (Todd Cameron Brown and Dannel Evans). The film's final message is that the future is yet to be written, as Doc's time-travelling Victorian contraption takes to the sky.

As a trilogy, the 'Back to the Future' films have stood the test of time and remain immensely popular, via TV reruns and DVD releases. By transporting the characters and settings backwards and forwards, we see familiar protagonists in unfamiliar settings, with actors (particularly Fox) essaying multiple roles. The first two films' time jumps are a generation (30 years) while the third is a nostalgic history lesson. It's no surprise that *Back to the Future Part III* remains one of the most successful Westerns of all time, having taken almost $88 million since its release in May 1990. Even viewed today, with its 1980s fashions and attitudes, *Back to the Future* remains timeless.

19

'HASTA LA VISTA, BABY'

TERMINATOR 2: JUDGMENT DAY (1991)

Director: James Cameron
Story and Screenplay: James Cameron and William Wisher Jr.
Director of Photography: Adam Greenberg
Music: Brad Fiedel
Super 35/Technicolor
A Carolco/Pacific Western/Lightstorm Entertainment/Studio Canal Production
Released by TriStar Pictures
130 minutes

Arnold Schwarzenegger (T-800 Terminator), Linda Hamilton (Sarah Connor), Robert Patrick (T-1000 Terminator), Edward Furlong (John Connor), Earl Boen (Dr Silberman), Joe Morton (Miles Bennett Dyson), S. Epatha Merkerson (Tarissa Dyson), Cástulo Guerra (Enrique Salceda), Danny Cooksey (Tim), Jenette Goldstein and Xander Berkeley (Janelle and Todd Voight), Leslie Hamilton Gearren (twin Sarah in steel foundry), Ken Gibbel (Douglas), Pete Schrum (Lloyd), Michael Edwards (older John Connor), Ennalls Berl (Bryant), Don Lake (Mossberg), Richard Vidan (Weatherby), Don Stanton (Lewis the security guard), Dan Stanton (T-1000 as Lewis), DeVaughn Nixon (Danny Dyson), Diane Rodriguez (Jolanda Salceda), Robert Winley (cigar biker), Ron Young (pool-cue biker), Charles Robert Brown (tattoo biker), Dalton Abbott (infant John Connor), Abdul Salaam El Razzac (Gibbons, Cyberdyne desk guard)

* * *

In the 1980s' other great time-travelling movie, Kyle Reese (Michael Biehn), in 1984 Los Angeles, arrives back from the future. He's there to protect Sarah Connor from the T-800 Terminator, a cyborg assassin that has been dispatched from 2029 on a mission to kill her. Reese is also from 2029, where he was a sergeant in Tech-Com. In the future, the world is dominated by robots and war machines (such as the T-800 and the giant tracked laser cannons, the H-Ks, or hunter killers), following a nuclear fire that has

Back from the future: Half man, half machine, cybernetic organism and assassin T-800 targets Sarah Connor in 1984 Los Angeles. Arnold Schwarzenegger played the Cyberdyne Systems Model 101, as depicted in the Italian poster for *The Terminator* (1984).

decimated human society. Sarah is the mother of resistance leader John Connor and she has been 'targeted for termination'. The T-800 methodically works his way through the telephone book, killing two 'Sarah Connors', before tracking the real one to the Tech Noir disco bar. During a shoot-out, Reese intervenes and saves her. The two of them go on the run and the Terminator doggedly pursues them through the city by night, conducting his own running repairs on any damage done – he's a cybernetic organism, with human tissue over a robotic skeleton. Following a car chase, Sarah and Reese are arrested. In the West Hialeah Police Station, the Terminator carries out an indiscriminate massacre. Reese and Sarah escape and shelter in the Tiki Motel, preparing for the final showdown by making homemade nitroglycerin explosive Plastique. During a moment's respite they make love. The Terminator traces them to the motel and in the ensuing chase proves particularly difficult to kill.

Director James Cameron worked on the special effects of Roger Corman's *Battle beyond the Stars* (1980) and then directed *Piranha II: The Spawning* (1981; *Piranha II: the Flying Killers*) a gory Italian–US creature feature. *The Terminator* (1984) was made for approximately $6.4 million. It was shot in early 1984 on location in and around

Los Angeles. The 'Mexican' gas station where Sarah has her photograph taken at the film's close was in Sun Valley. Following its release, Cameron told Corman: 'We did the things we did when we were with you, but we had more money and we did them bigger.' It was co-written by Cameron, William Wisher Jr. and Gale Anne Hurd, another Corman alumna, who also acted as the film's producer. She was married to Cameron from 1985 to 1989. Linda Hamilton, who played Sarah, was also married to Cameron, from 1997 to 1999. The Alamo gunsmith, where the Terminator stocks up on hardware, was played by Corman regular Dick Miller. Uncredited sources for the story include the TV episode 'The Soldier', written by Harlan Ellison for the classic sci-fi series *The Outer Limits* (1963–5), and Franklin Adreon's *Cyborg 2087* (1966), which saw part man, part machine Garth A7 (Michael Rennie) sent back to 1966 to locate professor Sigmund Marx (Eduard Franz), with instructions to bring him back (so that future events can be altered) or kill him.

Austrian bodybuilder-turned-actor Arnold Schwarzenegger was perfectly cast as the relentless villain, a Cyberdyne Systems Model 101, most often referred to as the T-800. A former Mr Universe known as the 'Austrian Oak', Schwarzenegger transferred his slightly awkward, lumbering robotic screen presence into something altogether more chilling: an indestructible cyborg killing machine. He arrives one May night amid blinding light and lightning, naked, reborn on the littered streets of Los Angeles. Terminator builds his vocabulary throughout the film by listening to people. The film, rather like the Terminator, develops its own thundering momentum which is powered along by Brad Fiedel's industrial, shuddering industrial synthesiser score: an ominous, clanging steelworks symphony. The Terminator mercilessly mows down anyone who gets in his way or wanders into the crossfire, as when he opens fire in the crowded neon Tech Noir bar, spraying bullets from his Uzi and hitting several innocent bystanders (while Reese returns fire with a sawn-off shotgun), or when he opens up with a pump-action shotgun and a machine gun at the police station.

The Terminator is essentially a B-movie sci-fi noir, but one that is superbly staged and edited for maximum effect. Cameron provided an on-screen view of the Terminator's infrared vision panel, which would become a cliché of *Terminator* derivatives, as would the film's gun fetishism. Scenes depict the battle for Earth in AD 2029, as the caterpillar tracks crush human skulls and the H-Ks crush human resistance. The machines rose from the ashes of the nuclear fire, but the final battle for Earth wouldn't be fought amid the rubble of this post-apocalyptic world. An introductory blurb informs us: 'It would be fought here, in our present. Tonight.' The 'special Terminator effects' were created by Stan Winston and their effectiveness ensured the film's success.

For the show-stopping finale, Sarah and Reese manage to blow up the Terminator with a tanker truck. But as Reese and Sarah embrace, a robotic 'skeleton' rises from the flames of the blazing tanker – with its 'human' skin burnt away, all that remains is a glistening, demonic metallic framework. During a confrontation in a factory assembly line, Reese is killed, having blown the T-800 to smithereens, but the robot's torso and head crawl after Sarah, until she finally crushes the cyborg flat in a giant, vice-like hydraulic compressor. The Terminator was unstoppable at the box office, too. Rated 18 in the UK and R in the US, it has taken over $38 million in the US, plus a further $40 million worldwide. Since 2000 it has been re-rated 15 in the UK. The story ends with pregnant Sarah and her trusty Alsatian (dogs can sense the presence of cyborgs) heading south of the border, to seek refuge in the desert.

A sequel, *Terminator 2: Judgment Day* (1991), picked up the action in Los Angeles in AD 2029, during the war between the survivors of Judgement Day and the Skynet computer-controlled machines. A T-800 Terminator (Schwarzenegger) is sent back in time by resistance leader John Connor (Michael Edwards) to track down ten-year-old John Connor (Edward Furlong) in 1995 Los Angeles. When young John asks the Terminator who sent him, the Terminator replies: 'You did.' Unruly, troublesome John lives with foster parents, Janelle and Todd Voight (Jenette Goldstein and Xander Berkeley), as his mentally unbalanced mother Sarah (Hamilton) is incarcerated in Pescadero State Hospital for trying to blow up the Cyberdyne facility. Sarah breaks out and the T-800 helps Sarah and John evade an advanced-prototype shape-shifting T-1000 Terminator (Robert Patrick), which is on a mission to eliminate young John.

Terminator 2, sometimes abbreviated to *T2*, was budgeted at $102 million and lensed on location in California from October 1990 to March 1991 by Adam Greenberg in 2.35:1 ratio Super 35 and Technicolor. The Sherman Oaks Galleria was used for a shopping centre, when the T-1000 tracks down John to an amusement arcade. Other locations included Long Beach, San Jose and the Kaiser steelworks in Fontana (for the final show-down between the Terminators). Sites in Los Angeles included the distinctive concrete storm drain (seen during a truck-and-motorbike pursuit set piece) and Elysian Park, used for the flashback where Sarah sees herself and infant John (Dalton Abbott) killed on Judgement Day. The Lakeview Medical Center was used as Pescadero State Hospital and the Cyberdyne Systems Corporation building exterior was the Renco Investment Company in Fremont. Fiedel again composed the ominous score, which reprises the 'Terminator Theme'.

The chase narrative is expanded in this sequel, as the trio evade the T-1000 and head into the Mexican desert, where they shelter with rebel Enrique Salceda (Cástulo Guerra). At an underground weapons cache, Sarah and the T-800 arm themselves for the showdown. Earth's destruction on Judgement Day is due to occur on 29 August 1997, causing the deaths of 3 billion people in a nuclear fire. It was triggered by technology developed by Cyberdyne Systems: the Skynet defence system became self-aware and launched an attack causing the apocalypse. To try and outwit fate, Sarah aims to kill Miles Dyson (Joe Morton), the man responsible for developing the technology at Cyberdyne, technology that was based on original T-800 Terminator parts from the first film (a vault at Cyberdyne holds the Terminator's skeletal robotic

Arnold Schwarzenegger returned as the cyborg Terminator, now reinvented as a hero and saviour, in James Cameron's 1991 sequel, *Terminator 2: Judgment Day.*

arm and its CPU chip). Miles, Sarah, John and the Terminator infiltrate the Cyberdyne building and destroy the records of Dyson's research. In a final confrontation in a steelworks, the T-1000 is destroyed, but all elements of the futuristic cyborgs must be erased – the robotic arm, the chip and even the T-800 are destroyed. As distraught John looks on, Sarah lowers the T-800 (which cannot 'self terminate') into a vat of molten steel.

For reprising his role, Schwarzenegger received $15 million. He initially appears to be the villain again, until he assures Sarah: 'Come with me if you want to live.' This inversion of Schwarzenegger's character allows the actor to inject more 'humanity' into his portrayal of the killing machine. This is most obvious in his relationship with young

John, as the T-800 becomes a father figure to the boy. Their developing relationship and admiration is even more pronounced in Cameron's later 'special edition' extended cut, which further humanises the robot. In reference to John's later career as a rebel free-dom fighter, he wears a Public Enemy T-shirt throughout the film. John teaches T-800 a few essential slang phrases (including 'No problemo' and 'Hasta la vista, baby'). The Terminator is a bravura, grim-faced performance by Schwarzenegger, perhaps his career best. The T-800 cocks his sawn-off Winchester shotgun one-handed (like John Wayne in *Stagecoach*), wielding also a useful grenade-launcher, a gas-canister launcher and the film's most impressive weapon, a six-barrelled GE Minigun, which is a bullet-spewing Gatling gun – there's even more gun fetishism in this sequel. At the Corral biker bar, the T-800 commandeers an outfit from a cigar-smoking biker (Robert Winley). With his Terminator persona complete (Harley Davidson, biker boots, leather jacket, shades and a shotgun) Schwarzenegger embarks on his mission to the gravelly blues of 'Bad to the Bone', by the appropriately named George Thorogood and the Destroyers.

The formidable villain in the sequel was the T-1000. A motorcycle accident prevented rock singer Billy Idol from taking the role. Michael Biehn was also considered, before Robert Patrick was cast. Patrick had appeared in some budget action movies, including Cirio H. Santiano's US–Filipino *Future Hunters* (1988), which began as a post-apocalyptic *Mad Max* film, then morphed into an action thriller and martial-arts movie, before ending up in the jungle with tribes of pigmies and Amazons, in a search for the Spear of Longinus, from Christ's crucifixion, which enables time travel. Since the original *Terminator* film, special effects had improved dramatically and this new Skynet creation was a different breed of cyborg – sleek, shape-shifting, predatory, like a striking cobra – which takes on the guise of a police officer. The most impressive aspect of the T-1000 is its mercurial liquid-metal special effects, an incredible quicksilver 'morphing' effect. When it is shot, sliced or blown up, the cyborg automatically self-repairs, remoulding itself instantly. Industrial Light & Magic, supervised by Dennis Muren, created the computer graphics images and Stan Winston was responsible for special make-up and Terminator effects. The T-1000 can also run speedily and morph its arms into lethal sword-like blades or hooks, to dispatch victims or to cling to the trunk of a speeding car. The film opens with a nihilistic depiction of the future, as an army of skeletal Skynet Terminators and their spacecraft battle the human resistance. During a chase, the T-1000 drives a truck off a bridge into the open Los Angeles storm drain in pursuit of John, who rides a Honda motorbike. The T-800 gives chase on a Harley Davidson and saves John. There's also a mass shoot-out between the heavily-armed T-800 and the police and SWAT teams at the Cyberdyne building – the T-800 is still wanted by the police for the attack on the police station in 1984. In the finale, the T-1000 pursues its prey in a Cryoco (cryogenic-transport specialists) tanker truck carrying liquid nitrogen. Eventually the tanker smashes into a steel foundry, rupturing the tank, and the T-1000 is frozen in the dry ice. The T-800, deploying his newly learnt slang, dispatches the T-1000 into a million shards, with a well-aimed pistol bullet and the payoff, 'Hasta la vista, baby.' But in the furnace heat of the foundry, the mercurial villain rises again, setting up the final confrontation.

Pre-release trailers in the summer of 1991 featured a T-800 being assembled, with Arnie warning: 'I'll be back.' A second trailer implied that the T-800 was the villain ('The battle for tomorrow begins this summer'), while in a third it was clear that the T-800 is the hero, with the tagline 'Same make, same model, new mission.' *T2* was rated R in the US and 15 in the UK (after cuts were made). On home video in the UK the cut version was initially released in 1992, rated 15. A 1992 laserdisc re-release was uncut and rated 18. *T2* is now rated 15 even in its extended special-edition cut in the UK. It also won Oscars for make-up, sound mixing, sound effects and visual effects and has taken almost $520 million worldwide since its release in the US in July 1991. *T2* covered all bases: Guns N' Roses' 'You Could Be Mine' from their *Use Your Illusion II* album featured in the film, and audiences were encouraged to read the Bantam tie-in book and play the Nintendo game. Since the Terminator movies' original release, Cameron has tinkered with the two films via 'special editions', to enhance and converge the films' narrative threads – particularly the involvement of Cyberdyne and Skynet in the story, and the events of Judgement Day. The alterations to *The Terminator* were relatively minor, though the original theatrical release of the film is still the best version of the story. But for *T2*, the original 130-minute cut was beefed up to 147 minutes. In broadening the canvas, the narrative drive is decelerated and the plot now includes a dream sequence featuring Reese visiting Sarah. Though the 'special edition' is an interesting curio, the 130-minute cut of the film remains definitive and one of the finest action sci-fis of the 1990s.

Jonathan Mostow's *Terminator 3: Rise of the Machines* (2003) takes up John Connor's story in 2004. Having averted Judgement Day, Connor (Nick Stahl) is again the target of a Terminator: the formidable, heavily armed shape-shifting female TX (Kristanna Loken). The TX aims to erase from history Connor, his future wife Kate Brewster (Claire Danes) and six more 'priority targets' who will become involved in the human resistance against the machines. A technically obsolete Terminator T-800 (Schwarzenegger) is dispatched to deal with the TX. As a computer virus rampantly paralyses network systems, Earth's nuclear bases, governed by the Skynet Defence System, launch strikes worldwide, resulting in Judgement Day. The apocalypse cannot be averted, but John and Kate survive in a nuclear fallout bunker at Crystal Peak, in the Sierra Nevada. *Terminator 3* was the expected special-effects and stunt workout, with Industrial Light & Magic creating memorable action for the ongoing war between man and machine. Again, the story's main axis is a chase, with the heroes' deadly, beautiful blonde nemesis TX, a Terminatrix, packed into a figure-hugging red-leather outfit. In the film's best sequence, a searing vehicular pursuit, the TX wreaks havoc with a crane's swinging boom and the vehicle's extended stabilis-ers. Hamilton didn't reprise her role as Sarah Connor, who we learn died of leukaemia in 1997. We also learn that Arnie's T-800 is responsible for John Connor's death in the future. The T-800's arrival is a fine piece of self-parody by Schwarzenegger. He wanders naked into the *Desert Star* cowgirl roadhouse, where it's ladies' night, with male-stripper entertainment. The Terminator approaches a stripper (Jimmy Snyder) who is wearing a black-leather biker outfit and demands his clothes. As 'Macho Man' by the Village People rings in his ears, Terminator leaves the bar, reaches into the jacket pocket for some shades and dons a pair of red-tinted, silver-framed star-shaped sunglasses. Filmed for a reported $200 million on location in Los Angeles, the film was another huge success, grossing $433 million worldwide.

Sarah Connor's story was continued in the TV series, *Terminator: The Sarah Connor Chronicles* (2008–9). A fourth film instalment, *Terminator Salvation*, was released in 2009. In 2018, the human-versus-robot wars are ravaging the ruins of post-Judgement Day Los Angeles, where John Connor (Christian Bale) leads the resistance. Connor leads a raid on a Skynet facility and inadvertently releases Marcus Wright (Sam Worthington), a genetically modified criminal who had been put to death 15 years before in Longview Prison. Marcus had signed his body over to medical research and was subsequently experimented on by Cyberdyne's Dr Kogan (Helena Bonham Carter). He has been rebuilt and resurrected as a half human, half robot, with a hybrid nervous system and a beating human heart. Marcus is revealed to be an infiltrator prototype, designed to pass undetected among the resistance to bring in his target: John Connor. In the ongoing battle against Skynet, Kyle Reese (Anton Yelchin) is number one on their hit list, with Connor number two. Various examples of Skynet Terminator hardware – from man-sized to apartment-block-sized robots – menace the heroes. There are some tremendous, violent action sequences (this is a pretty full-on 12 certificate in the UK, a PG-13 in the US) and is a glorious shoot-'em-up. There's a motorcycle pursuit of a truck that is very reminiscent of *Mad Max 2*, the resistance's HQ is a submarine, and there are visual and thematic references to *The War of the Worlds*, *Blade Runner*, *The Great Escape*, *Apocalypse Now* and even echoes of US desert combat in Afghanistan. The resistance has attained a weapon that will confuse and disorient the Skynet forces, and the finale sees Connor attempting to extract Reese from Skynet Central – and the Terminator production line – before the all-out attack can commence. Moon Bloodgood played Blair Williams, a resistance jet-fighter pilot and Marcus's sassy love interest, and the pacy story is told with great reverence for the series. The iconic names 'Connor' and 'Reese' give even the blandest dialogue gravitas, but director McG does well to continue successfully a franchise that could have been past its sell-by date. There's a reprise of the lines 'I'll be back' and 'Come with me if you want to live' in unexpected circumstances, and even Schwarzenegger (or rather a computer-generated facsimile) makes a cameo. The film was dedicated to Stan Winston, who worked on the special effects, but who died during the film's making, in June 2008.

Like the Cyberdyne assembly line, many Terminator facsimiles have trooped in the original's wake. Perhaps the finest variation on the formula was Paul Verhoeven's inventive dystopian splatterfest *RoboCop* (1987), which featured a robot cop that combined the efficiency and indestructibility of *Dirty Harry* with the vigilante fervour of *Death Wish*. In futuristic Old Detroit, Omni Consumer Products (OCP) fund and run the police force. When ED-209, a galumphing robotic '24-hour cop' malfunctions, ambitious exec Bob Morton (Miguel Ferrer) steps in, promoting his newly developed RoboCop, a half man, half robot, which will eradicate crime to make way for OCP's construction project, Delta City. Officer Alex J. Murphy (Peter Weller) is murdered in a hailstorm of bullets by a gang of street hoods led by Clarence J. Boddicker (Kurtwood Smith) and is resurrected and reconstructed as RoboCop. He is assigned to Detroit Police Precinct Metro West (Murphy's old precinct) and comes into contact with Officer Anne Lewis (Nancy Allen), who recognises a tiny shred of humanity in RoboCop as the last remnants of Murphy. RoboCop proves highly successful at cleaning up the streets, but he also begins to recall his past, memories that trigger his revenge on Boddicker and his hoods. The cop killers are now mixed up with OCP divisional president Dick Jones (Ronny Cox).

Shot mostly on location in Dallas, Texas, for approximately $13 million, *RoboCop* showcases state-of-the-art special effects and extreme, bloody violence. Clint Eastwood's emotionless crook-wasting cop has become a literal machine, with a robotic, impenetrable exoskeleton and computerised brain. Weller was decked out in impressive full-body armour, designed and created by Rob Bottin, and twirls his gun like children's TV show hero *TJ Lazar*. Weller injects pathos and black humour into the difficult role and *RoboCop* is adult comic-strip action of the highest order, with a big, stirring score from Basil Poledouris. The giant robotic Enforcement Droid ED-209 – essentially weapons on legs – is a fine stop-motion creation by Phil Tippet. The film's satirical edge is highlighted by news links from *Mediabreak* fronted by Casey Wong (Mario Machado) and Jesse Perkins (Leeza Gibbons) – 'You give us three minutes and we'll give you the world' – and spoof TV adverts for artificial hearts, family board game *Nukem* and a top-of-the-range car, the 6000 SUX.

The murder of Murphy at the hands of the street gang in a steel mill (filmed in Pennsylvania) is the film's most graphic and controversial. Murphy's right hand is blown off and he is mercilessly shot to pieces by ferocious gunfire. It was rated R in the US and is still an 18 certificate in the UK. The extreme violence of the original 'theatrical version' is even more excessive in the unrated 'director's cut'. With its large-scale destruction and mayhem, the film is a carnival of broken glass, bullets and explosions, as RoboCop liquidates – and in some cases liquefies – street scum. RoboCop attacks a drugs factory and the final showdown sees him and Lewis versus Boddicker and his henchmen, in the steel mill where Murphy was 'killed'. Boddicker's bunch are armed with military weapons – the oversized Cobra Assault Cannon – but RoboCop emerges triumphant, as crook Emil Antonowsky (Paul McCrane) is mushily disintegrated when he drives his van into a vat of toxic waste and Boddicker himself is spiked through the neck by RoboCop. The film grossed $53 million in the US and resulted in various sequels – *RoboCop 2* (1990) being the best – a cartoon series, an arcade game, a Marvel comic book, a live-action TV series and even a theme park ride.

In Cullen Blaine's *R.O.T.O.R.* (1988) a Robotic Officer Tactical Operations Research policeman is unleashed by the Dallas PD when divisional commander Earl G. Buglar (Michael Hunter) demands results. Scientists accidentally activate robot motorcycle cop R.O.T.O.R., which proceeds to go forth 'to judge and execute'. It shoots Greg (James Cole) through the head for speeding and then relentlessly pursues his fiancée Sonya (Margaret Trigg). Captain Barrett C. Coldyron (Richard Gesswein) teams up with the combat chassis's inventor, Dr Steele (Jayne Smith), to track down and terminate the cop. Smith, a hunky skunk-haired bodybuilder, delivers some quality dialogue: 'I'm like a cemetery – I'll take anybody.' Coldyron surmises that R.O.T.O.R. loose is 'like a chainsaw set on *frappé*'. Coldyron tells Bulgar: 'You fire me and I'll make more noise than two skeletons making love in a tin coffin, brother.' And someone points out that this is 'How Terminator got started'. With his moustache and leathers, patrolman R.O.T.O.R. resembles a member of the Village People. R.O.T.O.R. is made from intelligent material ('The metal itself can learn, remember and teach itself') and this supposedly unstoppable cop's only weakness is loud noises.

Italian filmmakers tinkered with the Terminator formula, as in Nello Rosati's *Alien Terminator* (1989; *Top Line*) and Bruno Mattei's *Terminator II: Shocking Dark* (1990; *Alienator*). Sergio Martino's *Hands of Steel* (1986; *Atomic Cyborg* and *Return of the Terminator*) is the best example. A cyborg (Daniel Greene) is created by the Turner Foundation (headed by John Saxon) to assassinate prominent environmentalist Revd Arthur Mosley (Franco Fantasia). The cyborg has been created from Paco Queruak, a war veteran who was badly injured, had his limbs amputated, ended up in a deep coma and had 70 per cent of his body bionically reconstructed. Paco doesn't finish Mosley off and instead goes on the run towards Page, Arizona. He hides out at Champions Oasis in Marble Canyon, a motel run by Linda (Janet Agren), which is also the venue for arm-wrestling contests. George Eastman played sweary, sweaty Hispanic arm-wrestling trucker Raul Morales. Paco is pursued by European master hitman Peter Howell (Claudio Cassinelli) and the FBI. Forensics doctor Peckinpah (Amy Werba) deduces that Mosley's wound was caused by a robotic human hand. Among the film's many references, there's an acrobatic, karate-kicking android straight out of *Blade Runner*. Donal O'Brien played Professor Olster, who worked on Paco for the Turner Foundation – Turner's hitmen murder him and smash up his life's work, a lab that resembles a Chinese buffet. The film was shot in the red-rock deserts of Arizona, including the Grand Canyon and the futuristic eco-friendly town of Arcosanti. Martino stages some thumping action sequences (featuring lorries, cars and helicopters) accompanied by a score from Giorgio Simonetti that's as pumped-up as Paco. Pasta la vista, baby.

Craig R. Baxley's *Dark Angel* (1989; *I Come in Peace*) was a *Terminator*/buddy–cop action-movie hybrid, as indicated by its tagline 'A Totally Lethal Alien'. In the urban sci-fi hinterland of Houston, Texas, cop Jack Caine (Dolph Lundgren) is on the trail of yuppie heroin traffickers. But there's a new guy in town, the towering alien (Matthias Hues), who slits his victims' throats with a flying electromagnetic compact disc, or raises hell with an explosive fireball gun. With catastrophic destruction burning in his wake, he's walking napalm. This alien injects heroin into victims and extracts the resultant endorphins from their brain, which he harvests to take back to his planet. Caine romances coroner Diane (Betsy Brantley) and is partnered on the case with clean-cut FBI agent Arwood Smith (Brian Benben). There's an electronic synthesiser score by Jan Hammer and the expected 1980s cop-movie ingredients – car chases through malls, strip clubs, profanity, multiple shoot-outs and weaselly informants (Boner, played by cameoing Michael J. Pollard). Lundgren is great as the monosyllabic supercop and looks in magnificent shape (his gelled hair is credited to Alan R. Scott). There are some startling, gurning performances, particularly among the psychos. In the finale the witty byplay between the alien and Caine peaks. As they grapple for the precious phials of endorphin, the cocky alien predicts, 'I win.' 'Fuck you, spaceman,' Caine retorts, injecting a heroin overdose into the alien's neck and impaling him on a steel scaffolding pole. 'I come in peace,' says the alien (his misleading catchphrase throughout the movie), but Caine blasts him with the fireball gun: 'And you go in pieces, asshole.'

The UK shocker *Hardware* (1990) was directed by Richard Stanley and adapted by him from the comic story 'SHOK!' by Steve MacManus and Kevin O'Neill. The Nomad (Carl McCoy, frontman of Fields of the Nephilim) stalks the post-apocalyptic red desert (filmed in Morocco) and finds the remains of a cyborg. He sells it to Hard Mo Baxter (Dylan McDermott), who thinks it's just a harmless maintenance drone and gives it to his girlfriend Jill (Stacey Travis) for Christmas. She's an artist who creates metallic fusions of sculpture. Iggy Pop played WAR Radio DJ Angry Bob and Motorhead frontman Lemmy appeared as a water-taxi driver. This collision of punky stylistics and *Blade Runner* noir also includes nods to spaghetti Westerns, with 'Zone Tripper' the Nomad resembling Django. Things get interesting when the cyborg, which turns out to be a military prototype MARK-13, rebuilds itself and goes on a destructive rampage.

Roland Emmerich's *Universal Soldier* (1992) teamed Jean-Claude Van Damme, the Muscles from Brussels, with Swedish meatball Dolph Lundgren. During the Vietnam War in 1969, Luc Deveraux (Van Damme) and Sergeant Andrew Scott (Lundgren) shoot each other dead after Scott wipes out an innocent Vietnamese village. In the early 1990s they are resurrected as cyborg members of a clandestine crack commando unit, the Universal Soldiers or UniSols, which are controlled via headsets, in a project not officially sanctioned by the Pentagon. Despite having his memory erased, Deveraux recognises Scott as his nemesis and goes on the run with journalist Veronica 'Ronni' Roberts (Ally Walker), a yammering, chain-smoking, cynical journo who smells a story. *Universal Soldier* is a typical Van Damme vehicle, but the popcorn formula worked perfectly, resulting in a considerable worldwide hit. Van Damme enacts robotic confusion, as his memory fragments begin to crystallise, while Lundgren shoots people in the head and wears a necklace made of human ears. *Universal Soldier* was shot on location in Arizona and Nevada, and its stunt coordinator and assistant director was Vic Armstrong. A tense hostage situation is played out on the Hoover Dam, and there's a high-speed chase along dusty precipices at the Grand Canyon, with Deveraux and Veronica in a police bus and Scott pursing them in a truck. This violent, corpse-strewn film appropriately plays out to 'Body Count's in the House' by Ice-T's Body Count.

Even spin-offs of spin-offs wind up with mini-franchises, and *Universal Soldier* has so far spawned *Universal Soldier: The Return* (1999) and *Universal Soldier: Regeneration* (2009). Albert Pyun's *Nemesis* (1992) was followed by three straight-to-video sequels: *Nemesis 2: Nebula* (1995), *Nemesis III: Prey Harder* and *Nemesis 4: Death Angel* (both 1996). The original starred French kick-boxer-turned-actor Olivier Gruner as cyborg LAPD agent Alex Rane, who in AD 2097 is rebuilt, *RoboCop*-style, following a shoot-out. He is sent on a mission to Java against female villains Jared (Marjorie Monaghan) and Julian (Deborah Shelton), when the plans for a top-secret summit are stolen and are about to fall into the hands of terrorists, the Red Army Hammerheads. *Nemesis* borrows freely from *Blade Runner* (with a voice-over and predatory femmes fatales), the muscular superheroics of *Rambo*, *Escape from New York* (Alex has a ticking time bomb in his heart) and a stop-motion skeletal cyborg shows up for the final act. In one scene, Alex machine-guns through the wooden floors of a hotel, falling through each storey to make his escape. *Nemesis* is an entertaining B-movie that features action, nudity and profanity, hazy cinematography, heavy weaponry, long coats and sunglasses.

Blade Runner's script collaborator David Peoples wrote the '*Shane* in space meets *The Terminator*'-inspired *Soldier* (1998), with Kurt Russell as emotionless Todd, an outmoded, killing-machine soldier stranded on 'waste disposal planet' Arcadia 234. Richard Pepin's *CyberTracker* (1994) was a martial-arts take on *Terminator* and *RoboCop*, with secret-service agent Don 'The Dragon' Wilson framed for murder by the crooks running computerised justice system CyberCore, which dispatched unstoppable Cyber Trackers (all played by dome-headed hulk Jim Maniaci) to hunt him down. Deploying some impressive explosions and car crashes, this eventful B-movie is set in a future world that looks suspiciously like 1990s Los Angeles. The cyborg-soldier concept was developed in Norberto Barba's action-packed, Mexican-shot *Solo* (1996). Mario Van Peebles starred in the android title role. During a 'field test' to neutralise an airstrip held by rebels in a Latin American country, Solo overrides his directives when he establishes the distinction between soldiers and non-combatants and joins the local peasant villagers in their struggle against the rebels. Solo repairs himself by removing circuitry from the villagers' communal TV, ruining their viewing of *Earth vs. the Flying Saucers*. Solo Mk 2 is dispatched, which has no glitches of conscience, but does have a three-barrelled cannon for an arm. It confronts Solo for the explosive finale where they attempt to 'delete' each other for good. Solo is a 'perfect soldier', as 'no one will cry when Solo is gone'.

Based on the Dark Horse comic series, Peter Hyams' *Timecop* (1994) starred Jean-Claude Van Damme as Max Walker. In 2004 cop Walker works for the Time Enforcement Commission (TEC), policing criminals who are using time travel to alter history and gain advantages – a time-travelling highway robber with two machine guns steals a Confederate gold bullion shipment in 1863 Georgia, while another teleports into the Wall Street Crash of October 1929 and buys oil shares at rock bottom prices. US presidential candidate Senator Aaron McComb (Ron Silver) has risen to power by tipping off his younger self as to the economic importance of the microchip. Walker's expectant wife, Melissa (Mia Sara), was blown up by a bomb in 1994 by McComb's hoods, and Walker has the chance to save her. The blue-collar hero versus privileged, elitist politician is summed up when McComb tells Walker: 'You see, I'm an ambitious, Harvard-educated visionary who deserves to be the most powerful man the world. And you, you're a fucking idiot.' A sequel, *Timecop 2: The Berlin Decision* followed in 2003.

The robots again had the upper hand and upstaged the human cast in Michael Bay's action-packed *Transformers* (2009), a live-action update of Nelson Shin's 1986 animated film *Transformers: The Movie*, itself a spin-off from the cartoon TV series (1984–7) and Hasbro toy line. The Transformers are robots that can transform into vehicles, beasts or weapons. In Shin's *Transformers* cartoon, the monstrous killer planet Unicron (voiced by Orson Welles) cuts a swathe through the universe, devouring whole space stations and bases. Centred on the planet Cybertron, goodie transformers the Autobots battle bad guys the Decepticons for control of the Autobot Matrix. The Autobots are led by Optimus Prime, a robot that can transform into an articulated truck. The pumping, ominous score by Vince DiCola keeps things lively, and the juvenile mixture of rock songs and vivid explosions of colour proved popular. The theme song, performed by rockers Lion, handily outlined the Transformers' USP: 'Transformers! More than meets the eye! Transformers! Robots in disguise!' In addition to Welles, who must have wondered what the hell had happened to his career by this point, other vocal talent included Robert Stack, Leonard Nimoy, Eric Idle, Judd Nelson, Casey Kasem and Lionel Stander.

In Bay's revamp, teenager Sam Witwicky (Shia LaBeouf) buys a beaten-up yellow-and-black sports car, which he discovers is able to transform into Bumblebee, a robot from the planet Cybertron. The film depicts the conflict, now relocated from Cybertron to Earth, between the Autobots and Decepticons. Many years before, Megatron (voiced by Peter Cullen), the Decepticon's leader, travelled to Earth and was discovered by explorers, frozen in ice. With his cohorts Bonecrusher, Frenzy and Starscream, Megatron seeks the mystical Allspark, which can transform Earth's vehicles into a killer robot army. The good robots include Optimus Prime (an articulated lorry tractor, voiced by Hugo Weaving), Jazz, medical officer Ratchet and Ironside. In the final reckoning, the robots do bone-crushing battle in impressive, wantonly destructive action sequences. The transformations from trucks, police cars, jets and tanks, into towering, bandy-legged robots are impressively done. Megan Fox was Sam's love interest, Mikaela Banes, Josh

Duhamel played Captain William Lennox, Tyrese Gibson was USAF Tech Sergeant Epps, Rachael Taylor was computer expert Maggie Madsen, Jon Voight played Defence Secretary John Keller, and John Turturro was Simmons, a *Men in Black*-style 'Sector 7' agent, who is tracking these NBEs (Non-Biological Extraterrestrials). *Transformers* is a robot monster mash with a bit of teen romance churned into the mix. Considering the Hasbro Transformer toys are so popular with children, it is strange that this film is unsuitable for a pre-teen audience – it's a certificate 12 in the UK and PG-13 in the US. Bay followed this with *Transformers: Revenge of the Fallen* (2009), also starring LaBeouf, Fox, Duhamel, Gibson and Turturro.

These *Terminator* derivatives – either through robotics or time-travelling – all have good action, but their dialogue and acting sometimes let them down; though as long as there's plenty of robotic action, audiences seem happy. References to *Terminator*s appear in such unlikely places as the robotic dog in Wallace and Gromit's claymation adventure *A Close Shave* (1995). Cameron's creation and its unstoppable, nuts-and-bolts progeny won't be terminating anytime soon.

20

'HOUSTON, WE HAVE A PROBLEM'

APOLLO 13 (1995)

Director: Ron Howard
Story: James A. Lovell Jr. and Jeffrey Kluger
Screenplay: William Broyles Jr., John Sayles and Al Reinert
Director of Photography: Dean Cundey
Music: James Horner
Super 35/DeLuxe Color
An Imagine Entertainment Production
Released by Universal Pictures
134 minutes

Tom Hanks (Jim Lovell), Bill Paxton (Fred W. 'Freddo' Haise), Kevin Bacon (John L. 'Jack' Swigart), Gary Sinise (Ken Mattingly), Ed Harris (Gene Kranz), Kathleen Quinlan (Marilyn Lovell), Mary Kate Schellhardt (Barbara Lovell), Emily Ann Lloyd (Susan Lovell), Miko Hughes (Jeffrey Lovell), Max Elliott Slade (Jay Lovell), Jean Speegle Howard (Blanch Lovell), Tracy Reiner (Mary Haise), David Andrews (Pete Conrad), Michelle Little (Jane Conrad), Chris Ellis (Deke Slayton), Xander Berkeley (Henry Hurt), Joe Spano (NASA director), Rance Howard (reverend at Lovell's), Roger Corman (congressman), Jim Lovell (captain of USS Iwo Jima*)*

* * *

In the 1950s, world nations became obsessed with the Space Race, the expensive dash between the US and Soviet space programmes to put a man into space and later on the moon. Films depicting this race are what might be termed 'science fact', portraying actual space history, people and events. The Apollo programme was initiated by US President John F. Kennedy in May 1961. Its ultimate objective was to put a man on the Moon, which the National Aeronautics and Space Administration (NASA) managed on 20 July 1969, when Neil Armstrong took 'one small step for man, one giant leap for mankind' and set foot on the Moon. Edwin 'Buzz' Aldrin piloted the Lunar Module on this mission and was the second man on the Moon. True space adventure has given cinema some of its most memorable films, featuring events such as lunar landings and aborted space missions, with no sign of little green men, but occasional gremlins in the machinery.

Sci-fi filmmakers have always been fascinated by space missions. The earliest example of the genre was the lunar mission in Georges Méliès's *Le Voyage dans la Lune* (1902). Almost 20 years before the Apollo Moon landing, George Pal and his special-effects collaborators (including Lee Zavitz and artist and illustrator Chesley Bonestell) created a visit to the Moon with almost documentary-like realism – Irving Pichel's *Destination Moon* (1950) was based on the novel *Rocketship Galileo* by Robert A. Heinlein. Aircraft engineer Jim Barnes (John Archer) is approached by General Thayer (Tom Powers) to work on a rocket to the Moon. With Dr Charles Cargraves (Warner Anderson) they build a rocket ship, the *Luna*. Forced to launch having never tested the rocket, the intrepid untrained trio of Barnes, Thayer and wiseguy Joe Sweeney (Dick Wesson) undertake the 240,000-mile trip to the Moon, fearing they will become 'heroes or angels'.

It took 100 men and two months to construct the Moon crater set – a two-foot-high, 20-foot-long panorama – when *Luna* reaches its destination. Great pains were taken to ensure realism in the astronauts' weightless movements, as they explore the dusty, mountainous lunar surface, collect mineral samples and take photographs. In the post-World War II era of the Cold War, the Moon is seen as a way of controlling Earth, a launch site for missiles. The rocket is produced by resurgent 'American industry' and financiers are attracted by a promotional film, with Woody Woodpecker explaining the principles of space travel. In the tension-filled climax, the astronauts have to strip the rocket of all excess weight, to escape the Moon's gravitational pull. *Destination Moon* was a key sci-fi film that revitalised audience and critical interest in the genre and paved the way for further fantastical forays Moon-wards throughout the ensuing decade, including the Jules Verne-inspired *From the Earth to the Moon* (1958), starring Joseph Cotton, George Sanders and Debra Paget.

Kurt Neumann's *Rocketship X-M* (1950) was speedily put together during the making of *Destination Moon* and narrowly beat it to cinemas, making it the first post-World War II movie about space exploration. Accompanying Dr Karl Eckstrom (John Emery), a brilliant physicist, on the craft to the Moon were pilot Colonel Floyd Oldham (Lloyd Bridges), doctor of chemistry Lisa Van Horn (Osa Massen), engineer Major William Corrigan (Noah Beery Jr.) and Harry Chamberlain (Hugh O'Brian), an astronomer and the ship's navigator. The operation is overseen at mission control at White Sands, New Mexico, by Dr Fleming (Morris Ankrum). The rocket is accurately depicted in multistage sections, the cabin is detailed but cramped, and the film includes a meteorite storm, weightlessness and shots of planet Earth receding into the distance. The craft is knocked off course and the RX-M lands on Mars instead. The film switches from monochrome to a red tint for the scenes set in the Martian world (shot in Red Rock Canyon State Park, California). The astronauts explore the planet in oxygen masks and hiking gear. The

Heroes or Angels: The intrepid astronauts in Irving Pichel's *Destination Moon* (1950) were unsure what awaited them as they travelled moonward in space rocket *Luna*.

inhabitants are primitive, scarred, blind, cave people armed with axes and rocks, and though once highly advanced, an atomic blast has taken them back to the Stone Age. Decimated by the savages, the survivors take off. In the depressing ending, they run out of fuel and crash off Nova Scotia, but not before they have informed White Sands of the mistakes made on this mission. Asked by the press if the mission has been a failure, Dr Fleming is undiscouraged. It proves space travel is possible and tomorrow they will begin the construction of the RX-M2.

H.G. Wells' First Men in the Moon (1964), directed by Nathan Duran, is an unmistakably British science-fiction film, an adaptation of Wells's 1901 novel of Victorian space exploration. In the 1960s, a UN survey team land on the Moon, but the celebration is undermined by the discovery of a Union Jack flag and a document dated 1899, claiming the Moon for Britain. Journalists track down the Victorian party's sole survivor, Arnold Bedford (Edward Judd), to The Limes, a nursing home near Dymchurch in Kent. Bedford and his fiancée Kate Callender (Martha Hyer) became the financial backers of Professor Joseph Cavor (Lionel Jeffries), the inventor of 'Cavorite', a metallic paste based on helium that cuts off the force of gravity. Cavor coats his spaceship – a knobbly Heath Robinson steel sphere with portholes, which resembles a sea mine – with Cavorite, and Bedford, Kate and Cavor shoot off into space and land on the Moon. The spaceship rolls to a stop on the Moon like a bowling ball and the astronauts explore wearing diving suits as their space apparel (Cavor pops his head out of the ship and chirps, 'Hello Moon!') They are captured and interrogated by insectoid creatures, called Selenites. Bedford and Kate manage to escape, but Cavor, who is suffering from a cold, stays behind. The film was shot in Panavision, but released in West Germany in Cinerama. Subterranean caverns feature bubbling blue lava, massive mineral crystal formations and a bubbling 'oxygen generator', and they are menaced by giant caterpillars (in Ray Harryhausen's Dynamation), which the insectoids zap with lasers. The bulbous-headed head Moonman presides from inside a rippling orb and communicates in a quivering voice. The film ends with a twist similar to *The War of the Worlds*, as the UN team find that the Selenites have been wiped out by a virus. Bedford notes of Cavor, 'He did have such a terrible cold.' It's worth noting that that the space landing scenes of UN1, which open the film, are surprisingly accurate, compared to the actual Moon landing 5 years later.

The early years of the US and Russian space programmes were depicted in Philip Kaufman's *The Right Stuff* (1983), from supersonic jet flight through to the first manned space orbits. It was adapted from Tom Wolfe's book of the same name. In 1947 test pilots based in California's High Desert fly X-1 jets, trying to break the sound barrier and achieving speeds of Mach 1 and Mach 2, taking them from subsonic to supersonic. Top among these 'fighter jocks' is air-force pilot Chuck Yeager (Sam Shepard). But when the US government initiates its Project Mercury programme, Yeager and others are overlooked due to their lack of college education or military background. At Star City, the Russian space programme is way ahead of the US and in 1957 the Russians launch their first satellite, *Sputnik 1*. As part of the US government's programme, developed by US–German scientific know-how, 56 pilots are tested and the seven 'greatest pilots in America' become the first US astronauts. In April 1959 in Washington, DC, they are unveiled as Alan Shepard (Scott Glenn), John Glenn (Ed Harris), Gordon 'Hotdog' Cooper (Dennis Quaid), Gus Grissom (Fred Ward), Deke Slayton (Scott Paulin), Scott Carpenter (Charles Frank) and Wally Schirra (Lance Henriksen). In January 1961 a chimpanzee does the first US test flight, while Russian cosmonaut Yuri Gagarin completes the first orbit of the Earth on 12

April 1961. In May 1961 Shepard is launched into space, and on 20 February 1962 John Glenn in *Friendship 7* successfully orbits Earth three times, returning a national hero. The astronauts attend a ticker-tape parade and a huge reception in their honour in Houston, while in the desert Yeager continues to push the boundaries of supersonic flight on Earth. The story ends in May 1963, when Gordon takes off in a solo space flight to complete 22 orbits of the Earth and the Mercury programme comes to an end.

The Right Stuff is the great historical American space epic. It's perhaps overlong at 193 minutes, but is worth seeing for the tremendous colour NASA archive footage (depicting the disastrous rocket tests and successful launches) and the exhilarating aerial footage of supersonic jet flights (as Yeager and others scream through the air) and the first forays into outer space. Glenn's orbits of Earth are particularly well staged, as the *Friendship 7* capsule passes from day into Australian night and back to sunrise. In addition to the astronauts' stories, the film depicts the astronauts' wives and Yeager's pursuit of ever-more gravity-defying feats in supersonic jets. Donald Moffat played Lyndon B. Johnson, and Jeff Goldblum and Harry Shearer played the two government recruiters for a project whose financing dictates: 'No bucks, no Buck Rogers.' Kim Stanley played Pancho Barnes, the proprietor of Pancho's Happy Bottom Riding Club, the desert bar near Edwards Air Force Base used as a hang-out by the pilots, where the walls are decorated with portraits of deceased pilots. Royal Dano played the local minister who presides over their funerals, Barbara Hershey played Yeager's wife, Glennis, and Chuck Yeager himself played barman Fred. The test pilots had previously been depicted in Richard Donner's *X-15* (1961), starring Charles Bronson, David McLean, Ralph Taeger, Brad Dexter, Mary Tyler Moore and narrated by James Stewart. It is Yeager who emerges from *The Right Stuff* as an iconoclast hero of mythical proportions, even overshadowing the astronauts themselves, with his death-cheating obsession with speed.

The best film depicting the US space programme is Ron Howard's *Apollo 13* (1995). The Apollo 13 mission was to have been America's third moon landing. The drama became a resounding triumph of fortitude and ingenuity, which NASA snatched from the brink of disaster. On 11 April 1970, the Apollo 13 mission blasts off from Cape Kennedy, Florida, to general apathy from the American public. It can't even get airtime on US TV networks. During a routine procedure while stirring the oxygen tanks on day three of the mission (13 April) an explosion severely damages the tanks, there's a loss of power and the ship is 'bleeding to death'. 'Houston, we have a problem,' transmits Apollo 13. Plans for the Moon landing are abandoned as Mission Control at Houston try to get the astronauts safely back. For four days, Jim Lovell (Tom Hanks), Fred Haise (Bill Paxton) and Jack Swigart (Kevin Bacon) endure dwindling oxygen and water, CO_2 poisoning, extreme space cold, awful rations, sleep deprivation and the knowledge that their lives depend on others. The astronauts use the Lunar Module *Aquarius* as a lifeboat to conserve power in the Command Module, *Odyssey*. They navigate a 'slingshot' trajectory around the Moon, to fire themselves back towards Earth. Then they manually use the engine burners to bring the *Odyssey* back on course for re-entry. On day seven of the mission, as the world waits with breath drawn, the seconds agonisingly tick by until the capsule appears, its parachutes open (slowing it from 300 mph to 20 mph) and it splashes down in the South Pacific. On 17 April 1970, the astronauts are picked up by helicopters and taken to the USS *Iwo Jima* and then home, where they are greeted triumphantly as heroes for their 'successful failure'.

Apollo 13 was written by William Broyles Jr. and Al Reinert, based on the book *Lost Moon* by Lovell and Jeffrey Kluger. The end titles note: 'Although the film was based upon a true story, certain characters and events have been fictionalised for dramatic purposes.' A scene where friction between the astronauts boils over into an argument didn't happen. It had been Tom Hanks's childhood dream to be an astronaut, so it was wish fulfilment to play American national hero Lovell, another in Hanks's arsenal of 'extraordinary ordinary guys'.

Made for an estimated $62 million, *Apollo 13* was lensed on location in California, Texas and Florida, with interiors at Universal Studios. Howard didn't have to give any motivational speeches on set, as everyone was keen and up for the challenge. There were three principal settings. On the home front, Lovell's wife Marilyn and Haise's expectant wife Mary (Tracy Reiner) are condemned to fret on Earth while listening to news reports of their husbands' deepening predicament. An exact replica of the Houston control room was created for the film, where tiers of bespectacled space boffins, engineers, medical officers and number crunchers beaver away. Many cigarettes and pipes were smoked in those tense few days. The third setting was Apollo 13 itself; its command and Lunar Module interiors and the Apollo 13 spacesuits were replicated by Kansas Cosmosphere and Space Center. Some of the space-travel interior scenes were filmed in the KC-135, a Boeing jet that, when it goes into free fall, creates a zero-gravity 'weightless' atmosphere, which earned it the nickname the 'vomit comet'. The jet footage was combined with simulated 'weightlessness' footage shot in the studio. Actual astronauts and NASA officials who visited the set were impressed by the accuracy, with Howard and Hanks in particular dubbed 'the accuracy police' for their scrupulous attention to detail. The rocket launch footage was created by Digital Domain of Venice, California. Though it is partly based on NASA footage, it is entirely new material and includes such details as ice particles falling away as the rocket launches and shots from angles that wouldn't have been possible during the actual launch. This sequence fully captures the apprehension and exhilaration of setting off on a Moon flight.

Howard tells the astronauts' story and the drama provides the driving force. It is a tale of endurance and ingenuity, hope and deliverance, as in any story that is 'true-life drama'. Despite the fact that much of the action takes place within the cramped confines of the spacecraft, Dean Cundey imbues the film with a sense of epic scale and scope, shot in Super 35 widescreen. The filmmakers' deep reverence for the material is obvious, and Hanks stated in an interview that wearing the NASA space suit, entering the ship and taking the controls for the launch felt like 'performing a mass'. When the astronauts circle the dark side of the Moon they pass the spot where they were to have landed, and Howard depicts Lovell's (and Hanks's) fantasy imaginings of setting foot on the Moon. Lovell says at the end of the film, 'I look up at the Moon and wonder: "When will we be going back and who will that be?"'

Gary Sinise played Ken Mattingly, who was bumped from the mission two days before departure because there was a possibility he had measles, and was replaced by Swigart. He becomes the hero of the day, as he figures out how to use the minimum power during re-entry. Mattingly never did get the measles and later commanded Apollo 16 and piloted the Space Shuttle. Ed Harris was memorable as Gene Kranz, director of flight operations and the man who oversees the rescue operation: 'Failure is not an option.' Harris even sheds a tear at the successful conclusion of the mission. He earned a Best Supporting Actor nomination for his performance. For her performance as Marilyn Lovell, Kathleen Quinlan studied her subject (even staying at the Lovells' house) and she was nominated for a Best Supporting Actress Oscar. The scene when Marilyn loses her wedding ring down the shower plughole – surely the ultimate ill omen – was criticised by reviewers as Hollywood fiction, but did actually happen on the morning of the launch. There are also many cameos, including Howard's brother Clint as Sy Liebergot at Mission Control, Howard's wife Cheryl appeared in the launch site scene, and his father Rance played the priest at the Lovells'. Howard's mother Jean Speegle played Lovell's mother Blanch, who notes, 'If they could get a washing machine to fly, my Jimmy could land it.' Cult sci-fi director Roger Corman played a congressman and Lovell himself had a cameo as the captain of USS *Iwo Jima*.

Apollo 13 tells us more about the time in which it was made than the period it depicts. If the film has a theme, it is one of nostalgia for the 1960s and 1970s, when 'things were better'. This was a signature of many US and UK films of the 1990s and provided a ready-made soundtrack album to accompany the release. A period setting allowed the deployment of 'rock and roll' classics, an evocation of 'good times'. *Apollo 13*'s soundtrack includes 'Night Train' (James Brown), 'I Can See for Miles' (The Who), 'Somebody to Love' (Jefferson Airplane), 'Magic Carpet Ride' (Steppenwolf), 'Purple Haze' (Jimi Hendrix) and 'Spirit in the Sky' (Norman Greenbaum). James Horner's score included the soaring trumpet 'last post' main theme, a fitting salute for the golden age of space exploration. In place of contextualising the mission in the wider Cold War and turn-of-the-decade political tension, Howard offers rose-tinted, happy-days nostalgia.

Since its release in June 1995, *Apollo 13* has taken over $170 million in the US and in excess of $300 million worldwide. At the 1996 Academy Awards, it earned nine nominations (including Best Original Score and Best Picture), but only won Best Editing and Best Sound Mixing. In addition to the film itself, there's an excellent background 'making of' documentary, *Lost Moon: The Triumph of Apollo 13* (1996), which is essential viewing for anyone interested in the events. *Apollo 13* was re-released in IMAX in 2002 and remains the finest film to depict the 1960s and 1970s moon missions. It stands as both great entertainment and a living – and minor factual tweaks aside, largely accurate – historical document.

The year before the Apollo 13 mission, John Sturges's *Marooned* (1969; *Space Travellers*) predicted the ominous worst-case scenario. During a seven-month manned mission to the Saturn 4B orbital laboratory, three astronauts (Richard Crenna, Gene Hackman and James Franciscus) become marooned in orbit, 285 miles above Earth, in their Apollo *Ironman One* capsule when their retrofire rocket fails. Gregory Peck played Charles Keith, chief of manned space, who tried to figure out a way to save them, and David Janssen was senior astronaut Ted Dougherty, who is dispatched in a Red Arrow-like XRV through the eye of a raging hurricane to rescue them. Facing some tough choices as the 42 hours of oxygen runs out, one of the men makes the ultimate sacrifice and silently drifts off into space to save his buddies. Robie Robinson won an Oscar for Best Special Effects. The long-winded story isn't helped by the sparse score of humming electronica, which sounds like a washing machine. The film's most effective scenes are the comms hook-up conversations between the endangered astronauts and their wives (played by Lee Grant, Nancy Kovack and Mariette Hartley), where the men try to give the pretence of calmness. The Philco–Ford Corporation provided technical personnel for the film and constructed a convincing Houston Mission Control Center and the Air Force Launch Control Center interiors. Another realistic 'disaster in space' scenario unfolded in *Starflight One* (1983), with Lee Majors and others stranded on a jetliner in outer space, which has since been played for laughs in *Airplane II* (1982). And a lost in space 'shipwreck' scenario befalls George Clooney and Sandra Bullock in Alfonso Cuarón's 3-D hit sci-fi thriller *Gravity* (2013).

Harry Winer's *SpaceCamp* (1986) was a juvenile take on *Marooned*. A disparate group of kids who are spending a summer studying at NASA's Space Camp (filmed at US Space Camp, Huntsville, Alabama) are accidentally launched into orbit in space shuttle *Atlantis* with only 12 hours oxygen for a 14-hour trip, so they have to dock with satellite *Daedalus*. The kids were played by Lea Thompson, Tate Donovan, Kelly Preston, Larry B. Scott and Leaf (later Joaquin) Phoenix. They were accompanied by instructor and budding astronaut Andie Bergstrom (Kate Capshaw), whose husband Zach (Tom Skerritt) mans mission control. Cute robot friend JINX playfully hacks into NASA's master computer and engineers the launch. *SpaceCamp* is filled with awful 1980s fashions and an embarrassing profusion of sycophantic *Star Wars* references.

An interesting twist on the 'science fact' subgenre was Robert Wise's *The Andromeda Strain* (1970), which recounted events over a four-day 'biological crisis'. A crack team of scientists attempt to identify the extraterrestrial virus that has been brought back to Earth on an exploratory satellite, named Project Scoop. The scientists (played by Arthur Hill, David Wayne, Kate Reid and James Olsen) work in a secret laboratory in Flat Rock County, Nevada, codenamed Wildfire. The contaminated satellite has crashed near the desert town of Piedmont, New Mexico (filmed at the ghost town of Shafter, Texas), wiping out most of the inhabitants where they stand. Investigators in anti-contamination suits find the virus has caused the victims' blood to clot into powder, causing instant death.

Two survivors, a Hispanic baby and Jackson (George Mitchell), a crotchety local, are taken to Wildfire for examination. The film makes good use of split-screen within the Panavision frame and has an effective electronic score by Gil Mellé. Some of the desert scenes were filmed at Red Rock Canyon State Park (from *Rocketship X-M*). The ending has the scientists trying to deactivate an auto-destruct mechanism, protected in the central core by a laser defence system, which will feed the self-proliferating virus and disastrously disseminate it across the landscape (as in the *Quatermass* films, atomic energy will cause the organism to grow). The deadly organism, the 'Andromeda strain' consumes everything and wastes nothing. Based on Michael Crichton's 1969 bestselling novel, it was remade under the same title as a two-part TV miniseries in 2008.

Space Cowboys (2000) is both a nostalgic paean to the Apollo space programme and a spoof of such space operas. In 1958, four-man US Air Force team Daedalus, who test supersonic X-2 jets, are ready to fly into space, but have the chance snatched away when chimpanzee Mary-Ann is chosen as the first American to go into orbit. Over 40 years later, Ikon, a Soviet communications satellite, has suffered a total system failure and is dropping out of space towards Earth. Only Frank Corvin (director–star Clint Eastwood) is able to fix such obsolete technology and he agrees if his comrades from the 1958 project, long retired, are recruited too. Team Daedalus – Corvin plus navigator 'Tank' Sullivan (James Garner), structural engineer and designer Jerry O'Neill (Donald Sutherland) and ace pilot William 'the Hawk' Hawkins (Tommy Lee Jones) – is resurrected. When they reach the satellite in the Space Shuttle, they discover Russian nuclear missiles that are aimed at strategic installations in the US. Following a collision with the satellite, which damages the Shuttle, Hawkins pilots the satellite into deep space to its destruction, while Corvin brings the Shuttle, battered and low on fuel, safely back to Earth. Sequences were shot at Johnson Space Center (Houston, Texas) and at the Kennedy Space Center (Cape Canaveral, Florida). The Space Shuttle and Ikon interior, the flight simulator and the Mission Control were built at Warner Bros, and the special effects were staged by Industrial Light & Magic. *USA Today* runs a front-page article on aged team Daedalus headlined: 'The Ripe Stuff'.

Perhaps the most entertaining and imaginative of the 'science-fact' films is Peter Hyams' *Capricorn One* (1978). *Capricorn One* is due to set off on an expedition to land on Mars, but at the last moment, the three astronauts – Colonel Charles Brubaker (James Brolin), Peter Willis (Sam Waterston) and John Walker (O.J. Simpson) – are whisked to an army air base at Jackson, which has been closed since 12 December 1947. They are informed by Dr James Kelloway (Hal Holbrook) that the billion-dollar cost of the space programme is under scrutiny, amid public apathy. Through cost-cutting, *Capricorn One*'s life support system was faulty and they would have been dead in three weeks. A movie set has been built, with a lunar module and the surface of Mars, and the astronauts are persuaded to stage the Mars landing and to fake TV broadcasts and link-ups. The Mars landing is broadcast to the nation, but tech Elliot Whitter (Robert Walden) discovers that the mission's transmissions seem to be coming from 300 miles away. Whitter tells reporter Robert Caulfield (Elliott Gould) of his suspicions, but soon afterwards vanishes. When his own life is threatened, Caulfield starts digging.

A $5 million production from Sir Lew Grade, *Capricorn One* is partly a conspiracy-theory thriller, partly a cynical sci-fi satire. Before the world's media, *Capricorn One* burns up on re-entry and Kelloway has to announce the loss of the three astronauts. Now an even bigger problem arises and when the astronauts learn of their deaths, they realise that they too will have to be disposed of. They escape from the air-force base and steal a jet, but it is low on fuel and they crash in the desert (filmed in Imperial Valley and Red Rock Canyon State Park, California). Caulfield interviews Brubaker's wife, Kay (Brenda Vaccaro) and uncovers a vital clue, which is a reference to a Western movie set at Flat Rock, Arizona, where 'movie magic' fakery is made to look real. With help from Judy Drinkwater (Karen Black), Caulfield locates the disused air base, where he finds the remains of the Mars set. David Doyle was his long-suffering assignment editor, Walter Loughlin, and Telly Savalas played irascible crop-duster Albain, who whisks Brubaker to the Houston memorial service for the *Capricorn One* mission, which is being attended by the US president (Norman Bartold), Kelloway, various dignitaries and the astronauts' families. For once the triumphant and safe return of the astronauts from space isn't going to be greeted as good news, at least from the authorities' point of view.

21

'NOW THAT'S WHAT I CALL A CLOSE ENCOUNTER'

INDEPENDENCE DAY (1996)

Director: Roland Emmerich
Screenplay: Dean Devlin and Roland Emmerich
Director of Photography: Karl Walter Lindenlaub
Music: David Arnold
Panavision/DeLuxe
A Centropolis Entertainment Production
Released by Twentieth Century Fox
139 minutes

Will Smith (Captain Steven Hiller), Bill Pullman (President Thomas J. Whitmore), Jeff Goldblum (David Levinson), Mary McDonnell (Marilyn Whitmore), Judd Hirsch (Julius Levinson), Robert Loggia (General William Grey), Randy Quaid (Russell Casse), Margaret Colin (Constance 'Connie' Spano), Vivica A. Fox (Jasmine Dubrow), Ross Bagley (Dylan Dubrow), James Rebhorn (Albert Nimzicki), Harry Connick Jr. (Captain Jimmy Wilder), Kiersten Warren (Tiffany)

❉ ❉ ❉

Since the 1950s, alien-invasion flicks have continued to fascinate filmmakers and audiences, with each successive generation and nation getting their dose of invading flying saucers and little green men. In the US, Fred F. Sears's *Earth vs. the Flying Saucers* (1956; *Invasion of the Flying Saucers*) saw aliens from an unspecified world escaping their disintegrating solar system and seeking refuge on Earth. They attempt to contact Dr Russ Marvin (Hugh Marlowe) and his wife Carol (Joan Taylor), who are working on Operation Sky Hook, an observational-satellite launch programme, but their message is not translated in time. When UFOs arrive, it is construed as an attack. The aliens kidnap Carol's father, Gen John Hanley (Morris Ankrum), and extract the knowledge from his brain using 'an infinitely indexed memory bank', which puts his mind at their disposal. Earth is then given 56 days

Take Cover!: Fred F. Sears's *Earth vs. the Flying Saucers* (1956) saw aliens fleeing their own disintegrating solar system and arriving here to disintegrate ours.

to capitulate to the aliens, and when that threat fails they cause an explosion on the surface of the sun.

Earth vs. the Flying Saucers was shot on location in California, including the Hyperion Water Treatment Facility and Zuma Beach. The saucers were created by Ray Harryhausen, with the outer ring revolving around a stationary centre. When the aliens emerge from the vehicle, a force field protects them under the umbrella of the saucer. The aliens are rather nondescript, but the film does feature a strange, distorted alien language voiced by Paul Frees. When he's kidnapped, Hanley is informed matter-of-factly: 'You are in an interstellar conveyance.' Hanley becomes a zombie and is thrown out of the saucer, at altitude, into a forest fire. This pedestrian 1950s hokum is assured its place in sci-fi history for its finale, where ultrasonic cannons (invented by Russ) mounted on the back of trucks bring the saucers down. The spaceships plummet into various landmarks in Washington, DC, including the Potomac River, Union Station, the dome of the Capitol Building and, in the film's most famous image, the Washington Monument obelisk.

Japan released some of the greatest alien-invasion movies of the 1950s. Directed by genre master Ishirō Honda and with special effects by Eiji Tsuburaya, *The Mysterians* (1957) is the alien invasion of Earth, Toho-style. Near Mount Fuji, a lantern-light festival celebration is interrupted by a forest fire and later an entire village is swallowed by an earthquake. When the Fuji police investigate, a giant robotic bird (Mogera, which actually means 'mole') wreaks havoc. Scientist Ryōichi Shiraishi (Akihiko Hirata) goes missing, but leaves behind an incomplete dossier on a mysterious asteroid, Planet No. 5: the Mysteroid. Dr Adachi (Takashi Shimura) and his assistant Jōji Atsumi (Kenji Sahara) realise that the Mysterians are operating from a revolving space station on the far side of the Moon. Soon a large dome arises from beneath the ground near Fuji and the Mysterians want a small area of land, two miles in radius, and the right for Mysterian men to marry Earth women. Mysteroid was destroyed by a nuclear war and the survivors fled to Mars, where they hope to replenish their population. Any last-ditch use of H-bombs is more restrained than in US sci-fi cinema, while the Mysterians' heat ray contains strong gamma rays with a destructive power equal to 'the Great Japanese Earthquake of 1923' (commonly known as the Great Kantō Earthquake). Dr Adachi solemnly removes his glasses and intones: 'We must not use the H-bomb under any circumstances – it means our ruin.' The Mysterians contain strontium-90 in their bodies and 80 per cent of their children are abnormal: 'So we dispose of them.' The Mysterians claim they had H-bomb technology when Earth was in the Neolithic age and they have come to Earth to stop the planet destroying itself. Japan unites with the countries of the world to form the Defence Force of the Earth, a United Nations. Together they develop new technology – the marcalite ray guns (satellite dish contraptions which reflect the Mysterians' rays back at them), an Electron Gun and huge World Air Force aircraft to attack the dome, which is obliterated in a mushroom cloud. The film looks terrific in 2.35:1 ratio TohoScope and Eastmancolor. The Mysterians wear brightly coloured spacesuits, capes and helmets with tinted visors, and the interior of their dome is awash with flashing lights and buzzing electronica. The special-effects model work and miniatures are of a high standard and create some memorable set pieces, including the opening scenes of the forest fire and later a tidal wave that sweeps through a valley. Scientist Jōji discovers a stream flowing with dead fish and the heated ground near Fuji literally burns a jeep's tyres.

In Honda's sequel, *Battle in Outer Space* (1959), aliens from the planet Natal use the Moon as a base from which to launch attacks on Earth in 1965. They have an anti-gravity weapon, which lifts a railway trestle into mid-air, beaches a ship and floods Venice, but the United Nations of Earth stand firm. Akira Ifukube provided the *Godzilla*-esque score. Two rockets with multinational crews are dispatched into space. On the Moon, the astronauts attack the Natalians' base (in tracked moon cars that resemble sausage dogs) and destroy it. The Natalians attack Earth with space torpedoes. The special effects by Tsuburaya are a mixed bag, with the destruction of New York and San Francisco risible, although the anti-gravity attack on Tokyo is well done. Were such scenes as the destruction of the Golden Gate Bridge revenge by Japanese filmmakers for their country's bombing during the war? In the climax, jets take on the aliens' fighters and the mother ship in widescreen TohoScope. In some of these old prints it's difficult to tell if the vertical on-screen lines are scratches or suspension wires for the special effects.

Kōji Shima's *Warning from Space* (1956) had its alien invaders arriving to help Earth. Pairans are starfish-shaped aliens, with one cyclops eye. One of their number, Ginko, arrives on Earth transformed into popular Metropolitan Theatre singing star Hikari Aozora (Toyomi Karita). As in *When Worlds Collide*, a meteor is on a collision course with Earth. Ginko warns that Planet R will cause devastation. A nuclear strike from Earth fails to knock Planet R off course and finally Earth's scientists and the Pairans work together to save Earth, by building a missile capable of destroying Planet R, which the Pairans fire from their spaceship. The film ends with a literal New Dawn, with a positive post-World War II message of world amity.

In Antonio Margheriti's Italian sci-fi *Battle of the Worlds* (1961), a planet from another galaxy heads towards Earth. Professor Benson (Claude Rains) christens the planet 'The Outsider', and it begins to orbit the Earth and launches flying saucers in its defence. The professor discovers that the saucer fleet can be defeated with oscillating-sound-wave 'sonic warfare'. Earth is then swept with extreme weather conditions and the United Commission determine to destroy the planet, which Benson discovers is a survivors' 'raft' carrying 'fugitives from a dying world'. When he explores the red-hued bowls of the planet, he discovers a controlling electronic brain and strange, insect-like corpses in a grotto. Margheriti's sci-fi is notable for its B-movie special effects, where he deployed imagination rather than money to great success, creating swirls of space mist, glass-domed space stations and miniature spaceships with fiery thrusters. The musical score by Mario Migliardi includes extraordinary, oscillating avant-garde theme music, with a female vocalist wailing, 'The outsider is coming!'

Night of the Comet (1984), written and directed by Thom Eberhardt, was an offbeat depiction of invasion from outer space. At Christmas time, Earth is caught in the tail of 'the visitor', a comet that when it was last seen 65 million years ago coincided with the extinction of dinosaurs. Most of the population go out to look at the comet's light show and are either reduced to red calcium dust or transformed into flesh-eating 'comet zombies'.

Among the few survivors are 'El Rey' cinema usherette Regina Belmont (Catherine Mary Stewart), her airhead cheerleader sister, Samantha (Kelli Maroney) and trucker Hector (Robert Beltran). They and other survivors are closely observed by a sinister 'think tank' of scientists – including Dr Carter (Geoffrey Lewis), Audrey (Mary Woronov) and Oscar (John Achorn) – from their underground research facility in the desert. This is a low-budget movie, but the abandoned, post-apocalyptic streets and unsettlingly weird atmosphere work in the film's favour. The machine-gun-toting sisters and Hector decamp to a local radio station, where they attempt to contact other survivors via broadcasts. The garish 1980s decor, clothes, neon lights and fashions date the film, and the soundtrack is littered with pop and rock songs. Regina and Sam have fun in a department store, trying on clothes and performing an impromptu fashion show to 'Girls Just Want to Have Fun', sung by Tami Holbrook. Regina, Sam and Hector escape from the scientists' research facility with two surviving children, Sarah (Janice Kawaye) and Brian (Chance Boyer). In this new world, Regina and Hector become their 'parents' and create an archetypal middle-class American family.

Independence Day (1996) took *The War of the Worlds* and other invasion movies and remixed them into a massive Hollywood epic about nationhood, patriotism, valour and the defence of the American way. It also lifted much from *Battle of the Worlds*, switching 'The Outsider' to a mother ship. On 2 July SETI (Search for Extraterrestrial Intelligence Institute) in New Mexico detects a radio signal: a giant alien presence, 550 km in diameter, is approaching Earth, but it's not a meteor. It slows down and emits smaller craft, each 15 miles in diameter. They loom over the world's major cities, including New York, Washington, DC, and Los Angeles. Cable repairman and eco-friendly computer tech David Levinson (Jeff Goldblum) realises that the aliens are using the Earth's satellite system to coordinate their worldwide attack. Amid widespread panic, David travels with his father Julius (Judd Hirsch) to the White House, where his estranged wife Constance (Margaret Colin) works as the president's press officer, to try to warn US President Whitmore (Bill Pullman). When the attack begins, the aliens' powerful beams cause widespread destruction, levelling the three US cities, plus others worldwide. By 3 July a disparate group of survivors, refugees, scientists and military – including President Whitmore, his first lady, Marilyn (Mary McDonnell), David, Constance, jet pilot Captain Steve Hiller (Will Smith), Steve's lover Jasmine (Vivica A. Fox), strategist General William Grey (Robert Loggia) and washed-up pilot Russell Casse (Randy Quaid) – congregate at secret US base Area 51 in the Nevada desert. A team of scientists has been based there since the capture of a UFO and its three crew in the vicinity of Roswell, New Mexico in 1947. David formulates a strategy to destroy the aliens' impenetrable protective force field. He will upload a computer virus to the aliens' mother ship in space and their own signal will disseminate the 'cold'. Steve will pilot the UFO to deliver the virus. Following a failed nuclear strike, the plan is a success and, with the aliens' defences down, air forces worldwide launch a counterattack. The 4th of July becomes the day the world and mankind declare: 'We celebrate our independence.'

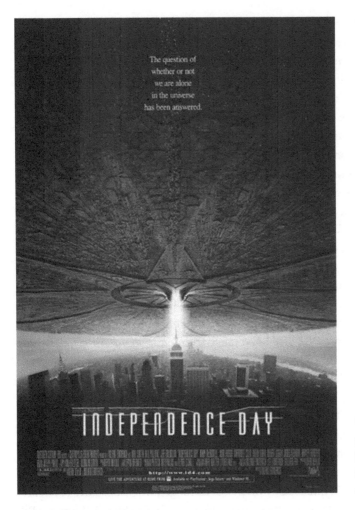

The question of
whether or not
we are alone
in the universe
has been answered.

INDEPENDENCE DAY

Vast alien space invaders target the Empire State Building in poster artwork for Roland Emmerich's *Independence Day* (1996).

As part of the large ensemble cast, Will Smith is a standout as US marine Captain Steven Hiller, a budding Space Shuttle astronaut who has just received a rejection from NASA. Smith gets to do what he does best, which is to wisecrack and mix it in the action. He's dubious that aliens have travelled 90 billion light years to 'start a fight and get all rowdy', but he enthuses that he's 'anxious to get up there and whop E.T.'s ass!' During an aerial dogfight he manages to down an alien fighter, which crashes in the desert. He approaches the craft and comes face to face with the tentacled alien pilot, so he punches it ('Welcome to Earth') and lights a cigar: 'Now that's what I call a close encounter.' The film is filled with heroes, from Steve's jet-pilot buddy, Captain Jimmy Wilder (Harry Connick Jr.), known as 'Raven' (in F-18 fighter squadron 'The Black Knights'), to redeemed drunk, alien-abductee and ex-Vietnam pilot Russell Casse (Randy Quaid), who lives in a trailer park in Imperial Valley and works as a crop-duster pilot. The aliens are moving from planet to planet, ravaging and exhausting each world's resources, like a plague of locusts. Judd Hirsch played David's hectoring father, Julius, a Yiddish everyman, and Margaret Colin played David's estranged wife, Constance, the president's press officer, who left him not because of lack of love, but his lack of ambition. Faced with the end of the world, she moans, 'Now he gets ambitious.' Jeff Goldblum's satellite-TV installer David Levinson is an unambitious underachiever, a computer whizz who is environmentally aware. Through cycling and recycling, he's always trying to save the planet: 'Here's my chance.'

For its faults in soap-opera plotting and acting, the film's hugeness, the epicness of this Hollywood juggernaut steamrollers all else with its scope and scale. It's the cinematic equivalent of 'never mind the quality, feel the width', photographed by Karl Walter Lindenlaub in Panavision and DeLuxe Color. The $75 million budget ensured *Independence Day* was filmed on a massive scale in a wide variety of shooting locations. David Arnold provided a fittingly stirring orchestral score, and cuts such as Link Ray's jangling classic 'Rumble' also featured. There were scenes filmed in the three principal US cities under attack (Los Angeles, New York and Washington, DC), with filming units based in Washington, DC, New York and Utah. Other locations included Georgia, Colorado, Texas, Oregon, Indiana and Pennsylvania. The most vivid location was the gypsum dune fields at White Sands, New Mexico, where Steve drags an extraterrestrial's smelly corpse in a parachute across the desert expanse and encounters a convoy of refugees. The alien creature effects were designed and supervised by Patrick Tatopoulos. White Sands is also the setting for the feel-good finale as Steve and David in their flight suits walk triumphantly back from the wreckage of the alien craft and enjoy a celebratory cigar, where other survivors are waiting. 'Happy fourth of July, daddy,' the president's little daughter Patricia (Mae Whitman) tells her father. 'Same to you, munchkin,' answers dad.

The production was monitored by the American Humane Society, which assured that 'no animal or alien was harmed in the making of this film'. Early in the story, a SETI radio playing 'It's the End of the World As We Know It' by REM establishes the light treatment afforded to the weighty subject matter. *Independence Day*'s special effects are among the greatest ever mounted and won the 1996 Academy Award for Best Visual Effects. Of note are the swooping, kinetic jet versus aliens aerial combat over the ruins of Los Angeles and the desert, the aliens' bombing raid on El Toro Air Base and Earth's jet attack on the alien craft in the climax. More impressive is the alien destruction of Earth's cities. Earth's 'Welcome Wagon' helicopters are disintegrated and the aliens unleash their mighty laser beam, which obliterates the Empire State Building, the White House and the US Bank Tower. The explosions radiate outwards, unstoppable tidal waves of fire and smoke, as cars are catapulted skywards and screaming, fleeing crowds burn up. Perhaps the film goes too far in this respect. The images of US cities enveloped and obliterated by orange, fiery plumes are truly horrific (the White House is literally blasted apart) in imagery which is every anti-American's dream. This slam-bang alien invasion film is as subtle as a 'Hammer the Gopher' fairground game.

Independence Day is patriotically right wing. It was made before the terrorist attacks on the World Trade Center in New York in 2001, and some scenes make uncomfortable viewing now. As the alien ships cruise in to menace world cities, the curious, awestruck population huddle around TV sets asking, 'Are you watching this?' and 'Can you believe this?' as events unfold, just as TV audiences watched in horror on 9/11. There are numerous references to the Gulf War and the Middle East, too – the US president is a Gulf War veteran and the first alien saucer appears in an ominous cloud of doom over the Northern Desert in Iraq. The president's rousing speech on the eve of battle, amid jets on the tarmac, before the largest aerial battle in history, is a jingoistic homage to *Henry V*. Running through its veins, the film has a pervading sense of America's confidence in the face of adversity, a sense of 'bring it on' – be it Saddam Hussein's Kuwait invaders or tentacled space invaders.

Independence Day remains one of the all-time box-office champions, taking a whopping $306 million on its original release in the US in 1996 alone – it was the year's biggest hit. Also known in promotional material as *ID4*, it was rated 12 in the UK and PG-13 in the US. The extended version of Emmerich's film, running 147 minutes in the UK, has eight minutes of 'restored footage', but the shorter, tighter version is the classic. BBC Radio 1 and Twentieth Century Fox co-produced a tie-in promotional radio show, *Independence Day UK*, which dramatised events in Britain during the alien invasion, with London overrun by aliens and the royal family escaping in a Radio 1 traffic-report helicopter.

With the success of *Independence Day*, Smith appeared in the hugely successful sci-fi action comedy *Men in Black* (1997; *MiB*), directed by Barry Sonnenfeld and executive-produced by Steven Spielberg. Smith also performed the title song and starred as NYPD cop James Darrel Edwards III, who is recruited by clandestine government department the Men in Black. It polices Earth's alien population (roughly 1,500 strong, located mainly on Manhattan) who appear to be human and live undetected among us. Rip Torn played MiB's boss, Zed, and Tommy Lee Jones was Agent Kay, Edwards's mentor. When Edwards becomes a Man in Black, his past life is erased and he is known as Agent Jay. The MiB discover that a bug-like alien has landed in a flaming meteor and taken over the body of farmer Edgar (Vincent D'Onofrio). The alien seeks to take control of a galaxy on Orion's Belt (which turns out to be a tiny galaxy in a pendant on the collar of a cat called Orion) which alien Arquillians demand to be returned, otherwise they will destroy the Earth.

MiB's vigorous narrative owes much to *Ghostbusters* – it's essentially 'Alien-busters' – and it was based on the Marvel comic by Lowell Cunningham. It's a daft, spoofy *X-Files*, with Smith playing the fool while Jones plays it cool. The Men in Black arrive at various alien occurrences, subdue the aliens and blank the minds of any human witnesses with a neuralyzer. They wear black suits, black ties and black shades – their sunglasses protect them against the neuralyzer's ray – and travel in a superfast Ford that transforms into a jet car. Edwards's love interest was morgue medical examiner Dr Laurel Weaver (Linda Fiorentino). In the surprisingly poignant ending, Agent Kay uses the neuralyzer on himself to retire to a normal, alien-free life. His return to society is announced by the headline: 'Medical Miracle! Man awakes from 35-year coma.' *Men in Black* boasts excellent alien special effects, particularly the scenes in MiB HQ, which resembles a hectic, interstellar airport arrivals lounge. The alien make-up won an Oscar for Rick Baker and David LeRoy Anderson. Zed notes that the MiB work on Centaurian Time, which involves 37-hour days: 'In a few months you'll get used to it, or you'll have a psychotic episode', and Kay assures that Elvis isn't dead, 'He just went home.' *MiB* was shot on location in New York and at Sony Pictures Studio, Culver City.

For the finale, the giant, insecty beast, which resembles an outsized dragonfly larvae, attempts to flee in a flying saucer that was disguised as a saucer-shaped observation tower at the 1964–5 New York World's Fair, but the alien craft is downed by Kay, Jay and some heavy artillery, and the saucer crashes through the Unisphere global sculpture in Flushing Meadows Park. *MiB* took $250 million in the US alone and sired several spin-offs, including official sequels *Men in Black II* (2002) and *Men in Black 3* (2012). In *Men in Black II*, Jay tracks down Kay, now working for the postal service, to tackle a multi-tentacled alien (sexy sadist Serleena, played by Lara Flynn Boyle), and her two-headed sidekick Scrad and Charlie (Johnny Knoxville). In the film's most memorable scene, the Statue of Liberty's torch becomes a citywide neuralyzer.

The importance of spectacular special effects above all else became the dumbed-down blight of late-1990s sci-fi and a film such as *Armageddon* (1998), from director Michael Bay and producer Jerry Bruckheimer, makes *Independence Day* look like nuanced arthouse cinema. A massive comet travelling at 224 mph will slam into and destroy Earth in 18 days, and so the race is on to blow it up. The chunk of rock is a 'global killer', capable of precipitating the end of mankind, including bacteria, via a three-mile-high impact tidal wave. Harry Stamper (Bruce Willis), 'the world's best deep-core driller', and his oil-rig crew of roughnecks (including Ben Affleck and Steve Buscemi) are enlisted to fly into space in shuttles named *Freedom* and *Independence*, land on the comet, drill a hole in it and place a nuke at its core. Billy Bob Thornton played NASA's executive director, Dan Truman; Liv Tyler played Stamper's daughter, Grace, who, against her father's wishes, is in love with Affleck; Tyler's real-life dad, Steven, and his band Aerosmith performed the film's tie-in single (appropriately a hit rock ballad) 'I Don't Want to Miss a Thing'. Pretty much the entire film is explosions and noise, with everyone either shouting or whispering their dialogue – all emotion is conveyed this way. Charlton Heston narrates *Armageddon*'s portentous intro, as a six-mile-wide rock causes the dinosaurs' extinction 65 million years ago: 'It happened before. It will happen again. It's just a question of when.' Space Shuttle *Atlantis* explodes in space when it is hit by a meteor, Shanghai and Paris are summarily demolished with barely a blink, and a meteor shower devastates New York. A cabby suspects it's a terrorist attack ('Saddam Hussein is bombing us') and there's an ominously prophetic shot of the damaged Twin Towers, one of which is missing its top floors and is on fire.

District 9 (2009), directed by Neill Blomkamp, is one of the most imaginative sci-fi movies of recent years, which melded the mutations of The Quatermass Xperiment with social commentary, action movie and satire. A vast alien ship arrived in Johannesburg, South Africa 20 years ago and the million aliens on board – derogatively nicknamed 'Prawns' by the locals due to their prawn-like facial features – are allowed to stay, ghettoised in a shanty town, designated District 9, in the shadow of their now inert, hovering mother ship. They are segregated and victimised by humans (there's 'Humans Only' signage), while Multi-National United (MNU) carry out genetic experiments on them. Following the discovery of alien arms caches and alien rioting in the scavenger colony, the 'Prawns' are to be relocated to Sanctuary Park, a ring-fenced site 200 km outside the city which resembles a concentration camp. The relocation is to be carried out by heavily armed private military contractors. MNU employee Wikus Van De Merwe (Sharlto Copley) serves notices of eviction, but he comes into contact with a black, viral substance in a metallic tube, which is alien in origin, and becomes severely ill. He begins to metamorphose into an alien, his fingernails fall out and his hand mutates into a claw. Only aliens can fire their sophisticated weaponry and under test conditions MNU realise that Wikus is able to operate them too. He becomes 'the most valuable business artefact on Earth'. As MNU prepares to extract his heart, Wikus escapes and takes refuge in District 9. His wife Tania (Vanessa Haywood) is turned against him by her father, MNU executive Piet Smit (Louis Minnaar), and news stories are circulated that Wikus has engaged in sexual activity with aliens. Wikus hides out with alien Christopher Johnson (Jason Cope) and his little son, who explain that the alien fluid is needed to operate a spacecraft they have concealed under their shack. They plan to use the craft to access their mother ship and return to their own planet.

This US–New Zealand co-production was shot in pseudo-documentary style by Trent Opaloch at Stone Street Studios, Wellington, New Zealand, and on location in Soweto, Johannesburg. There are talking-head experts and participants commenting on the action, and TV-news reportage inserts. The aliens' weaponry literally obliterates their enemies into showers of blood and chunks of meat. Like Victor Carroon, Wikus is a half-human, half-alien fugitive. At one point he's caught by Nigerian gangsters led by wheelchair-using warlord Obesandjo (Eugene Khumbanyiwa), who profiteer from the aliens (they sell them overpriced cat food in exchange for weapons) and devour alien body parts in an effort to become part alien. Operating a giant robot, Wikus helps Christopher and his son to flee. Christopher promises to come back in three years and Wikus is left behind to transform fully and assimilate into the ghetto. District 9 is torn down after the 2.5 million aliens are successfully relocated to their new home in District 10. Made for $30 million, District 9 was a hit, taking over $200 million worldwide. It was also nominated for Best Picture, Special Effects, Editing and Adapted Screenplay at the Oscars and is a good example of how to mix splatter action, impressive special effects and social commentary to box office success.

Jonathan Liebesman's *Battle: Los Angeles* (2011; *Battle: LA* and *World Invasion: Battle Los Angeles*) depicted a worldwide invasion of 20 cities in August 2011, through the actions of a US Marine Corps platoon. The film focuses in particular on Staff Sergeant Michael Nantz (Aaron Eckhart), whose foul-up cost his men's lives on a previous action, and his battle to earn his men's respect, including Corporal Jason Lockett (Cory Hardrict), the brother of one of those killed. The film is filled with familiar old-school war-movie stereotypes – the veteran on the cusp of retirement, rookies, family men and old hands – plus new action-movie archetypes, such as the 'sassy babe', in the shape of Michelle Rodriguez (from *Avatar*) as US Air Force sergeant Elena Santos. Meteor showers off the Santa Monica coast are revealed to extraterrestrial craft when an alien army emerges from the sea and sweeps all before it, aided by pilotless 'drones'. Nantz's marines are ordered to West Los Angeles Police Station, to save civilians trapped there. They undertake this against the clock, as a massive bomb strike is due to obliterate Santa Monica. This is a familiarly gung-ho World War II movie (there's even a John Wayne reference), reimagined as an alien invasion flick. Eventually the bomb strike doesn't materialise – US forces have been routed – and it's up to Nantz and his crew's heroics to destroy the aliens' massive command and control centre, neutralising the drones. Not for the first time in a post-9/11 American movie have the heroes ended up standing triumphantly amid rubble. Between the relentless explosive action, the film's human drama is beefed up by Brian Tyler's epic score. Cinema's alien invaders of the 1950s had been little green men in flying saucers; by the 1970s they had pacified to 'come in peace' to make contact with earthlings. In *Independence Day*, the little green men of the 1950s now travelled in much-improved special effects, but by 2011, the alien invasion of Earth took on a contemporary, realistic edge, with Los Angeles closely resembling the streets of Baghdad.

22

'WELCOME TO THE REAL WORLD'

THE MATRIX (1999)

Director: Larry and Andy Wachowski
Producer: Joel Silver
Screenplay: Larry and Andy Wachowski
Director of Photography: Bill Pope
Music: Don Davis
Panavision/Technicolor
A Village Roadshow/Silver Pictures Production
Released by Warner Bros
136 minutes

Keanu Reeves (Thomas A. Anderson, alias Neo), Laurence Fishburne (Morpheus), Carrie-Anne Moss (Trinity), Joe Pantoliano (Cypher, alias Mr Regan), Hugo Weaving (Agent Smith), Belinda McClory (Switch), Julian Arahanga (Apoc), Marcus Chong (Tank), Robert Taylor (Agent Jones), Matt Doran (Mouse), Gloria Foster (Oracle)

✳ ✳ ✳

The Earth worlds of science fiction provide limitless opportunities for invention and creation. There are futuristic worlds, worlds past and eerily present, parallel worlds and make-believe 'virtual reality' worlds that conform to or manifest our fears or desires. There have been dystopian societies and alternate realities. In the future, will we all be living on hovering cloud cities, or in space bases on the Moon or in labyrinthine subterranea, or on Soylent Green? Whatever the outcome, as special effects develop and improve, so too do these spectacular settings.

Periodically in cinema, there are special-effects milestones – from the parting of the Red Sea in *The Ten Commandments,* to the liquid metal T-1000 in *Terminator 2* and the bullet-time acrobatics of *The Matrix.* In the 1980s, one of the most significant sci-fi developments was the computer-generated world of Steven Lisberger's *Tron* (1982), a $17 million Walt Disney release, which strove to depict the mainframe of a computer system in a visually exciting, engaging way. Kevin Flynn (Jeff Bridges), a software programmer for ENCOM, has invented various video games, including 'Space Paranoids', but his boss Ed Dillinger (David Warner) has taken the credit and reaped the financial rewards. Flynn seeks evidence of Dillinger's wrongdoing and when he attempts to hack the ENROM computer, he is zapped via a 'matter transfer' into the computer's Master Control Programme (MCP). There, in the Gaming Grid, his avatar Clu (Bridges again) battles with Sark (Warner again) for control of the computer. The garish tech visuals are a feast for the eyes, the comic-book futurism rendered in angular video images. The characters in the Gaming Grid are the personifications of computer programmes and data, who wear glowing data 'armour' and take part in gladiatorial combat against other video warrior 'conscripts' – so Flynn is menaced by his own programme creations. Clu is helped in his efforts to outwit the MCP by Tron (Bruce Boxleitner) and Yori (Cindy Morgan), who are the avatars of his ENCOM colleagues Alan Bradley and Lora. At the film's conclusion, in the 'real world' Flynn is now ENCOM's boss, having proved that Dillinger stole Flynn's ideas. The film's most memorable images are those of the 'light cycle' race, where avatars on superfast bikes trail solid 'walls' of colour in their wake, causing the confines of the gaming arena to become smaller (as in *Snake*). For all its flash, in Super Panavision 70, *Tron* is essentially *Fantastic Voyage* relocated into a machine. It's also a fascinating time capsule of the early days of video-gaming – even Pac-Man makes a cameo appearance.

In Roland Emmerich's *Stargate* (1994), a portal to another world is discovered in 1928 at the pyramids at Giza. In the present day, a recon party – including Egyptologist Dr Daniel Jackson (James Spader) and soldier Colonel Jack O'Neil (Kurt Russell) – is sent from Earth to investigate. They travel through the 'stargate' to a faraway planet, which with its endless sand dunes, shaggy camel–bison hybrids and pyramids resembles Ancient Egypt. But the sun god Ra that the ragged locals serve, worship and are oppressed by is in fact an alien from another galaxy. Ra (Jaye Davidson) and his godlike henchmen, Anubis (Carlos Lauchu) and Horus (Djimon), are determined to destroy the Earth by sending a bomb though the Stargate ('I created your civilisation… now I will destroy it'), so the Earth visitors stir up a slave revolt. *Stargate* – which spawned various spin-offs, including the TV series *Stargate SG-1* (1997–2007) – was a US–Canadian co-production shot on location in Yuma (Arizona), Long Beach (California) and at Santa Clarita Film Studios. Among the ancients are valorous Skaara (Alexis Cruz) and Jackson's love interest Sha'uri (Mili Avital). The godhead Ra, with his laser guns, resembles the Predator and the film includes disparate elements from *Lawrence of Arabia*, *The Lion King*, cast-of-thousands biblical epics, Gulf War desert combat and *Indiana Jones* movies. The concept that Earth's ancients were aliens derives from Erich von Däniken's *Chariots of the Gods?* and other such tomes.

Director–producer–writer Alex Proyas created the memorable *Dark City* (1998), which surreally tangles future-fiction and darkest noir. John Murdoch (Rufus Sewell) wakes up in a bath in a strange hotel room and discovers a woman's corpse. He's suffering from amnesia, but seems to be the perpetrator of a series of killings. He also has the ability to make things happen by will alone, a gift known as 'tuning'. Discovering he has a wife, torch singer Emma (Jennifer Connelly), Murdoch is pursued by the police, led by embittered Inspector Frank Bumstead (William Hurt), and by a gang of *Nosferatu*-like agents, the Strangers. Chief among them are Mr Hand (Richard O'Brien), Mr Book (Ian Richardson) and Mr Wall (Bruce Spence). Proyas, who also made *The Crow* (1994), blends *Blade Runner*, *The Cabinet of Dr Caligari*, murder mysteries, old film noirs, Gothic horror and thriller-chiller, with elements of Philip K. Dick's work (such as *We Can Remember It for You Wholesale*), to create a completely original sci-fi experience, lensed in shadowy widescreen Super 35 by Dariusz Wolski. The future city and some of the cast's costumery anticipates *The Matrix*, which was shot at Fox Studios Australia the following year, reputedly on some of this film's sets. Every 12 hours, the population fall asleep en masse at twelve o'clock, in this city of endless night where the sun never shines, and the buildings mutate and restructure to create a new cityscape. This is an immense experiment by the Strangers on the human population of this free-drifting city in space. People are injected with new personalities and wake up new people, as the Strangers revise and refine their construction to discover what makes them human. The interesting cast included Kiefer Sutherland as Dr Daniel Schreber, who injects the population with new, individually formulated personalities. The film's visual imagination is exhilarating and the future city resembles those of *Metropolis* and *Brazil*, where fantasy meets reality in jarring, delightful ways. *Dark City* performed badly at the box office, but has since been reassessed and has gained a sizeable cult following.

The innovations in special-effects technology throughout the 1990s culminated in Larry and Andy Wachowski's mind-blowing *The Matrix* (1999), which spawned a saga and reinvented science-fiction action cinema. It also managed to be a cerebral discourse on the reality/fantasy of the 'real world' and a dystopian thriller that blended shoot-'em-up thrills with philosophy and religion, in a story that became curiouser and curiouser.

Thomas A. Anderson (Keanu Reeves) leads a double life. His public face is as a computer-program writer at the Metacortex software company, but Anderson is also master computer hacker Neo. He is approached by Trinity (Carrie-Anne Moss) to join a group of dissidents led by the mysterious Morpheus (Laurence Fishburne), who travel on their hovercraft the *Nebuchadnezzar*. They deem Neo 'The One' who will free mankind from servitude in a computer created 'Matrix', which has been formulated as a 'prison of the mind'. Since a war between robots and humans, the Matrix is a computer-generated dream world where humans are kept under control. Neo is told this is no longer 1999, but nearer 2199. In preparation for his fight to destroy this artificial world, Neo is plugged into a neural interactive simulation, where he is schooled in intense combat techniques, including martial arts. These skills are downloaded straight into his mind – he becomes a human vessel that can simply have information inserted into its brain, with no learning involved. This is echoed in the blank-white screen of 'the Construct', where any-thing can be loaded onto it: an entire landscape, living environment or society. Soon Neo – who as Anderson was scared of heights – has freed his mind and is leaping buildings and engaging in martial arts at superfast speeds.

A US–Australian co-production, *The Matrix* was filmed on location in Sydney, Australia, and at Fox's Australian studio, in sleek Panavision and Technicolor by Bill Pope. Like *Dark City*, the world of the Matrix is one of perpetual night – in the battle between humans and robots, the humans have tried to blot out the

EVERYTHING THAT HAS A BEGINNING HAS AN END

MATRIX
REVOLUTIONS
NOVEMBER 5

Keanu Reeves reprised his role as Neo in *The Matrix Revolutions* (2003), the second sequel to *The Matrix* (1999).

sun, as the robots are solar powered. A comic-book style permeates the setting of Zion, the last human city, and most noticeably the costumes. Morpheus wears a long black leather coat, while his cohorts model a cool, futurist look of latex, boots and leather – walking arsenals, en route to a fetish club. The government agents that police and enforce the Matrix and pursue Neo are black-suited, with commonplace names such as Smith and Jones. And even though it's night-time, everyone wears sunglasses. Fishburne was excel-lent as Neo's mentor, Morpheus, and Hugo Weaving was also excellent as his nemesis, delving government agent Smith. Morpheus's ensemble include Carrie-Anne Moss as Trinity, Belinda Mcclory as white-clad Switch, Julian Arahanga as Apoc, Marcus Chong as Tank, Anthony Ray Parker as Dozer, and Matt Doran as programmer Mouse. Joe Pantoliano played traitorous Cypher, alias Mr Regan, who tries to sell Neo, Morpheus et al. to the agents, in an effort to get the access codes to the Zion mainframe, known only by Morpheus.

There's a rainy, faded, crumbling grandeur to the city, backed by a pumping score by Don Davis. Tracks are culled from the usual suspects (Massive Attack, Rob Zombie, Prodigy, Propellerheads, Marilyn Manson, Rage Against the Machine) and some surprises (Duke Ellington and gypsy jazzman Django Reinhardt). On a $63 million budget, the special effects are tremendous. At the 1999 Oscars, *The Matrix* won several statuettes, including Best Sound and Best Sound Effects Editing. Zach Staenberg's jaw-dropping editing won, and John Gaeta, Janek Sirrs, Steven Courtley and Jon Thum were rewarded for their visual effects. The combat sequences are a barrage of tightly edited set-ups, involving cutting-edge trickery, which results in impossible acrobatics and chasmic leaps. Neo is able to limbo under flying bullets or mystically and harmlessly halt them in mid-air. Trinity and Neo try to save Morpheus from the agents, resulting in a cataclysmic shoot-out, amid hails of whizzing bullets and shattering, atomised masonry. This superheroism has since found its way into the acrobatic lightsabre duels of the later *Star Wars* films. Within this construct, physical rules (such as gravity and speed) can be bent or broken. Thus fighters can run up walls, hover, pivot and spin in mid-air and perform martial arts at fantastical, quicker-than-the-eye speed. Anderson's body sits in a chair, wired up to the software, while Neo spars with Morpheus or battles Agent Smith in the Matrix. This arrangement influenced *Avatar*, in that the hero is represented elsewhere while his body is hooked up to this virtual world, though the world Jake inhabits as a Na'vitar is a real one.

The Matrix complexly blends martial-arts movies, Hong Kong action flicks and *The Wizard of Oz* with mysticism, theology and Greek mythology. At one point Neo meets seer the Oracle (Gloria Foster), presented here as a housewife baking cookies in her kitchen, to discover if he is indeed 'The One'. There are explicit references to Lewis Carroll's *Alice's Adventures in Wonderland* (1865) and its sequel *Through the Looking-Glass* (1872). Morpheus offers Neo, who doesn't believe in fate, a choice between taking two pills – one the path to adventure, one not. If he takes the blue pill, the story ends and he returns to his normal, mundane existence, but take the red and he gets to stay in Wonderland, to see 'how deep the rabbit hole goes'. The virtual 'rabbit hole' Neo finds himself in is revealed to be the Matrix, a virtual reality that conceals the truth. Humans are slaves, in a prison of the mind, a mind that makes the Matrix real. If you die within it, your body dies also, as the body cannot live without the mind. The Matrix itself appears on-screen as green encoded lines of data, like Marshall McLuhan's 'the medium is the message' TV appearances. This construct – to infinity and beyond – is part zoo, part computer program, part society, part reality, part surreality. Eventually Neo defeats Smith, realises that he is the One and causes a computer systems failure. Reborn into a world where anything is possible, Neo flies off into the sky.

The Matrix was a resounding hit – tapping in as it did to the computer-generated imagery of video games, sci-fi action movies and the infinite possibilities of the ever-expanding internet. It was rated 15 in the UK and R in the US, where it took $171 million. A poster campaign featured stylishly attired protagonists Neo, Morpheus, Trinity and Cypher, amid stuttering vertical lines of data, falling like Zion rain. The original was followed by two sequels and an animated series, *The Animatrix* (2003). *The Matrix Reloaded* (2003) and *The Matrix Revolutions* (also 2003) were also directed by the Wachowskis, with the leading players reprising their roles and the machines on the attack. *Reloaded* begins with cascading 'data rain', but is a shadow of its innovative predecessor. Zion, the human bastion, is threatened by a gathering army of machines, and Neo, Morpheus and crew must defend it. The narrative is more linearly conventional, with diversions to domestic dramas and for Neo and Trinity to get emotionally and physically involved. There's much shades-and-leathers posturing and Neo's long, tailored coat makes Reeves resemble a flying martial-artist priest. The settings and the metropolis of Zion as a backdrop are excellent, but it's the action of two grand set pieces that stand out – an extended hand-to-hand mêlée between Neo and dozens of Agent Smiths in a plaza, and a mind- and fender-bending, physics-defying car chase.

In Disney's post-*Matrix Tron* sequel, *Tron: Legacy* (2010), Jeff Bridges reprised his role as Kevin Flynn, who, following the death of his wife in 1985, disappeared in 1989. Kevin's son Sam (Garrett Hedlund) goes in search of his father and is transported into a significantly more visually impressive Grid, a search that encompasses spectacular aerial combat, martial arts and 'light cycle' action, a kinetic blur of liquid light and sound. Scenes in the Grid are in 1.85:1 screen ratio, while off-Grid events are shot in 2.35:1. Sam encounters his father, now an old man, and also Clu, who hasn't aged and is a digital recreation of Bridges's younger self. Clu is now the villain and this 'inside world' is amassing an army that will open up a portal and attack the outside world, which father and son must prevent. Their principle ally is Quorra (Olivia Wilde), Bruce Boxleitner recreated his role as ENCOM's Alan Bradley, and Michael Sheen appeared as David-Bowie-meets-John-Inman villain Zuse. Directed by Joseph Kosinski, *Tron: Legacy* has high energy levels and a fantastic score by Daft Punk, but is rather like watching someone else playing a video game.

Spectacular special effects weren't the only way forward for sci-fi worlds, and there have been many different depictions of life on Earth. George Lucas's movie debut *THX 1138* (1970) was based on a story by Lucas and was an expansion of his 20-minute UCLA student film *THX 2238 4EB*. The film presents a bleak dystopian police state, where sex is illegal and shiftless drones toil in a sterilised subterranean world. Everyone is shaven-headed, wears white clothes, takes libidinal suppressants and, as in the TV series *The Prisoner* (1967), is identified by numbers. THX 1138 (Robert Duvall) makes love with LUH 3417 (Maggie McOmie), who becomes pregnant. In detention THX is tortured with sound and electronic cattle prods, and fellow prisoner SEN 5241 (Donald Pleasence) suggests that THX escapes. Lucas's vision is striking, with the environment's white interiors, often with no discerning features or furniture, patrolled by chrome-faced enforcers. Lalo

Schifrin provided the oppressive score for this society, with its automated confessional booths and masturbation machines. This is a different kind of futurism, with few flashy special effects, which goes baldly where no sci-fi has gone before. The executive producer was Francis Ford Coppola and Lucas shot the film at American Zoetrope Studios, San Francisco and on location in California. Low-key for the most part, *THX* ends with an exciting tunnel chase, as THX speeds away from motorcycle cops in a sleek car. In a fine joke about budget moviemaking, the authorities terminate the chase, as their resource budget for the pursuit runs out. *THX* was re-edited by Warner Bros for its original release, but in 2004 Lucas reworked the film as a 'director's cut' (its added nudity resulted in a re-rating, to R from PG) and overlaid CGI enhancements. The presence of Johnny Weissmuller Jr., the son of celebrated vine-swinger Johnny Weissmuller, as a chrome robo-cop, brings to mind Jean-Luc Godard's original title for *Alphaville*, *Tarzan vs IMB*.

According to Richard Fleischer's *Soylent Green* (1973), the New York City of 2022 will have a population of 40 million people, be vastly overcrowded and they will queue for government handouts of synthetic foodstuffs, including Soylent Green. During his investigation of the murder of industrialist William Morris Simonson (Joseph Cotton), 14th Precinct detective Thorn (Charlton Heston) begins to suspect that Simonson's bodyguard Tab Fielding (Chuck Connors) is responsible. Simonson was one of the directors of the Soylent company, which provides half the world's food supply. Thorn is helped in his inquiries by call girl Shirl (Leigh Taylor-Young) and his roommate Sol Roth (Edward G. Robinson, in his 101st and final screen role). Thorn discovers a widespread cover-up, which involves state governor Santini (Whit Bissell). Trailing the Sanitation Squad of garbage trucks, Thorn sees them being filled with corpses which are then taken to a food-processing plant, where they are recycled. Thorn realises that 'Soylent Green is people!' – the next step will be breeding people like cattle, solely for food. A plodding police procedural, *Soylent Green* comes alive when it concentrates on the Green itself. During a food riot, demonstrators are tackled by Riot Control units, which scoop them up and throw them into the back of mechanical trucks. *Soylent Green* was adapted for the screen by Stanley R. Greenberg from Harry Harrison's 1966 novel *Make Room! Make Room!*, but like several high-profile 1970s movies, *Soylent Green* also has an unpleasant undertone of misogyny, as women are often slapped around and call girls are referred to as 'furniture'.

In *Logan's Run* (1976), futuristic police of the twenty-third century, known as Sandmen, track down and terminate anyone who tries to escape the domed city. The survivors of a post-catastrophe world live in this utopia only for pleasure, but everyone dies by the age of 30. They live in hope of being 'reborn' by the bizarre 'fiery ritual of the Carrousel', but this is a myth. Those wishing to avoid the 'last day', when the flashing red crystal in the palm of their hand dulls to black, try to reach the outside world, becoming 'runners' in search of sanctuary. Sandman Logan 5 (Michael York) is assigned by the central computer to find the sanctuary. He goes on the run with Jessica 6 (Jenny Agutter) and is pursued by his friend, fellow Sandman Francis 7 (Richard Jordan). Directed by Michael Anderson, *Logan's Run* won the Best Visual Effects Oscar for 1976. The presence of Farrah Fawcett as beautician Holly, in her radiant *Charlie's Angels* period, reinforces the 1970s kitsch. The 'Arcade' of the future doesn't look that dissimilar to a shopping centre today (barring the orgasmic 'Love Shop'), while the floaty multicoloured costuming makes this future appear to be the world's biggest toga party. The film was shot mostly in Texas, including the Dallas Market Center, the Arlington National Health Studio and the cascades at Fort Worth Water Gardens. Emerging into the outside world, Logan and Jessica set eyes on the sun for the first time, enjoying a fleeting Eden moment, before discovering the vegetation-engulfed ruins of Washington, DC, where they encounter an eccentric old man (Peter Ustinov) and his cats, who tells them of old age. Realising there is no sanctuary, they return with the old man to the bubble of the Domed City, to reveal the truth to its inhabitants. *Logan's Run* boasts an interesting Jerry Goldsmith score, and it later became a popular but short-lived TV series, running to 14 episodes in 1977–8, with Gregory Harrison as Logan, Heather Menzies as Jessica and Randy Powell as Francis.

In writer–director Michael Crichton's *Westworld* (1973), tourists pay $1,000 a day to stay in the resort of Delos, which features three self-contained themed 'worlds': the thirteenth-century 'Medievalworld', the Pompeian 'Romanworld' and the 1880s Wild West town of 'Westworld'. The worlds where 'nothing can go wrong' are populated by realistic-looking robots, which act out the tourists' adventures. Eerie scenes depict the staff carting the robot 'corpses' by night to 'central repair'. Billed as 'The Vacation of the Future – Today!', the holiday of a lifetime turns sour when the robots malfunction, turn on the tourists and murder them. Peter Martin (Richard Benjamin) and John Blane (James Brolin) are two city boys who enjoy the responsibility-free vicarious thrills of the cow town (shot on the 'Laramie' Western street at Warner Bros), bedding the robot 'saloon gals' and gunning down rival shootists in can't-lose pre-programmed showdowns. Yul Brynner was the ice-cold gunfighter who is repeatedly shot by Benjamin or Brolin until a power outage in the robots' control centre and a contagious computer virus, a 'disease of machines', allows him to fight back. The killer gunfighter chases Martin into the surrounding desert (Red Rock Canyon, California), through Romanworld (the gardens of Harold Lloyd's Greenacres estate), the scene of a terrible tourist massacre, and on to Medievalworld (a sound stage at MGM), until Martin manages to blind the robot with acid and immolate it.

The neighbouring 'worlds' allow a merging of genres – one minute the film is a medieval adventure, the next a Western – with the scientists controlling the scenarios that unfold like stage managers. When Martin flees into the desert, the scenes resemble a Western manhunt, until the spell is broken when he encounters a technician attempting to repair his buggy in the arid waste, who is gunned down at long range by Brynner's rifle. Crichton revisited this 'world gone mad' scenario with the *Jurassic Park*

Westworld: Yul Brynner stars as the robotic gunslinger at the tourist resort Delos, where visitors can enjoy 'The Vacation of the Future – Today!'

films. *Westworld* was followed by a very brief TV series *Beyond Westworld* (1980) and the sequel feature, *Futureworld* (1976) from AIP, with Peter Fonda and Blythe Danner as reporters, and Brynner reprising his role as the gunslinger in a reopened Delos. Another stone-faced killer cowboy, Jack Palance, got in on the act with Peter Sasdy's *Welcome to Blood City* (1977). Western town Blood City is part of a social experiment staged by scientists as a 'survival of the fittest'. The inhabitants have been taken from the real world and had their memories wiped. Awards and social advancement are totally reliant on killing. Starting off as slaves, inmates can become respectable citizens who wear black outfits with red crosses on the front and back – they become literal walking targets. Palance played the town sheriff, Frendlander, who because of his 20 kills is now deemed an immortal. Keir Dullea played Lewis, a new arrival to whom scientist Katherine (Samantha Eggar) takes a shine and attempts to help him climb the ladder by programming herself into the 'game'.

Other societies see the 'games' become violent entertainment as a norm. These include Elio Petri's *The 10th Victim* (1965) and Gary Ross's *The Hunger Games* (2012). Paul Bartel's *Death Race 2000* (1975) depicts the 20th Transcontinental Road Race, a three-day coast-to-coaster from New York Memorial Raceway to New LA, in which five contestants and their navigators attempt to score points for running down pedestrians en route. Women are worth ten points, teenagers 40, children under twelve 70 points, and anyone over the age of seventy-five 100 points. The contestants include Frankenstein (David Carradine), a bionic man with a mechanical arm, who wears a cape, mask and gimp suit, and whose toothed, spiky car is called 'the Monster'; Chicago gangster 'Machine Gun' Joe Viterbo (Sylvester Stallone), 'loved by thousands, hated by millions', who runs over his own pit crew; gladiator Ray 'Nero the Hero' Lonnegan (Martin Kove) and his sexy navigator Cleopatra (Leslie McRay); cowgirl 'Calamity' Jane Kelly (Mary Woronov); and 'swastika sweetheart' Matilda the Hun (Roberta Collins) and her navigator 'Herman the German' Fox Boch (Fred Grandy) in a 'buzz bomb' car with Nazi livery. Mounted by producer Roger Corman, this is blackly comic satire played for macabre laughs. The widow of the race's 'first score' wins an apartment in Acapulco. The film includes mock news bulletins from overenthusiastic on-the-spot reporters such as Junior Bruce (The Real Don Steele) and Grace Panda (Joyce Jameson). The poster tagline was: 'In the year 2000, hit and run driving is no longer a felony. It's the national sport!' The action features passers-by being levelled in gory head-squashing, groin-cleaving action, a sort of 'hacky races'. The deadly racing cars were designed by James Powers and constructed by Dean Jefferies, and for a film set in the filmmaker's future (now our past), *Death Race 2000* looks oddly dated. The 2008 remake, Paul W.S. Anderson's *Death Race*, starred Jason Statham, which itself sired a 2011 sequel, *Death Race 2*.

Co-produced and co-written by Luc Besson, *District 13* (2004; originally *Banlieue 13* and also known as *District B13*) imagined a Paris that by 2010 had become so run-down and riddled with crime and grime that the borough of the title has been surrounded by a wall, à la *Escape from New York*. Director Pierre Morel kept the pace breakneck, to the accompaniment of propellant, thumping grooves from Da Octopusss, in this imaginative, entertaining take on future society where the big crooks are the government officials and cops. District 13 resident Leito (David Belle), a criminal, teams up with *un flic*, Captain Damien Tomaso (Cyril Raffaelli), who goes undercover in the district to find an experimental radioactive bomb that has been stolen by crime lord Taha Bemamud (Larbi Naceri). With only 24 hours until the device detonates, the duo have to negotiate the crime-plagued district. For Laito it's personal: Taha has Laito's sister Lola (Dany Verissimo) prisoner and has turned her into a drug addict, in revenge for Laito destroying a drug shipment. Taha has his own private, heavily armed army led by 2K (Tony D'Amario). This super-stylish non-stop action movie oozes *la classe* and presents highly stylised urban degradation. But the best reason for seeing the film is the springing, death-defying martial arts and leaping, daredevil acrobatic parkour displays by Belle and Raffaelli, which outdo even *The Matrix* for thrills. It is also a highly political film, with Damien's secret mission to recover the bomb revealed to be a scheme by the government to obliterate District 13 and solve the city's social problems at the touch of a button. The sequel, Patrick Alessandrin's *District 13: Ultimatum* (2009), which teamed Belle and Raffaelli against corrupt cops who murder their own to foment trouble in the district in order to destroy and redevelop it, was almost as good.

In Chris Wedge's animated *Robots* (2005), in Rivet Town, which is populated by robots, son of a dishwasher, Rodney Copperbottom (voiced by Ewan McGregor), dreams of being an inventor and travels to Robot City to visit his idol, the inventor Mr Bigweld (Mel Brooks). Bigweld has been abducted and his company, now under nefarious control, is to discontinue making spare parts, making all existing robots 'outmodes' that will need replacing with new models. Every cliché is wheeled out, from the 'follow your dream' story to the tiresome oddball assemblage of kooky robots that Rodney gathers to locate Bigweld. The film's world looks suitably futuristic and fantastic (as designed by children's author–illustrator William Joyce), with intricate, technical visuals, but it's a fine example of cute not automatically guaranteeing audience appeal. It's technically brilliant, but less than riveting.

If the future looked bleak in America, France and Rivet Town, Britain too has little to look forward to, if the thuggish Droogs of Kubrick's *A Clockwork Orange* (1971) and the drudgery of Big Brother society in *Nineteen Eighty-Four* (1984) are any indication. In *Children of Men* (2006) the action begins on 16 November 2027 in fascist Britain. The government plants bombs and blames dissidents, order has broken down and immigrants are rounded up and held in containment centres. All women are infertile and the last baby was born 18 years ago. The death of 'Baby Diego', at 18 the youngest person on the planet, is mourned worldwide. Theories as to why women are infertile range from genetic experiments to gamma rays and pollution. In a sorrowful, hostile, but still recognisable London, ex-political activist Theo Faron (Clive Owen) is contacted by resistance cell the Fishes to obtain transit papers for a woman to Bexhill on the south coast. One of the Fishes' leaders, Julian Taylor (Julianne Moore), is Theo's one-time lover, with whom he had a son, Dylan. A flu epidemic in 2008 killed Dylan and they haven't seen each other for almost 20 years. Theo can only obtain a joint paper and so has to accompany the woman, Kee (Clare-Hope Ashitey), who is pregnant. She is to be taken to the coast, where they will rendezvous with a ship, the *Tomorrow*, which will convey her to the 'Human project' – scientists striving to cure infertility from their base on an island in the Azores. Accompanied by midwife Miriam (Pam Ferris), Julian and dissident Luke (Chiwetel Ejiofor), they head towards Canterbury, but Julian is killed by renegades and Luke shoots two police officers. Theo discovers that the Fishes engineered Julian's death and want to use Kee and her child as political bargaining chips. Theo, Kee and Miriam escape and hide out with Theo's friend, Jasper, an old ganja-smoking hippy (played by Michael Caine with more than a whiff of John Lennon and Richard Harris). The Fishes track them to Jasper's and they flee to Bexhill Refugee Camp. As an uprising overtakes the compound, Kee gives birth to a daughter and amid the street fighting, they make it to a rowing boat with help from contact Marichka (Oana Pellea). Heading out to the sea, they watch as an air strike hits the Bexhill compound. Waiting in the foggy stillness near a buoy for the rendezvous, wounded Theo dies as *Tomorrow* comes.

Directed and co-written by Alfonso Cuarón, and inspired by a story by P.D. James, *Children of Men* is a nihilistic 'real world' vision of future Britain as a fascist state. It was shot on location in London (the ministry building is the Tate Britain), Hertfordshire, Surrey, Hampshire and East Sussex. The squalor and poverty, the ruins of a civilisation in its death throes, were filmed with unflinching grit or else bathed in the pale hopeful glow of Dickensian lamplight by cinematographer Emmanuel Lubezki. Memorable moments include the opening scene (as Theo buys a coffee, a terrorist bomb rips through a London street) and a scene where Theo frantically tries to bump-start a car as it freewheels away from a farm, with fanatical Fishes in pursuit. *Children of Men* is a powerful film, made with considerable skill, and it develops into a chase that doesn't let up. Owen, in perhaps his finest performance, is the hard-drinking cynic involuntarily drawn back to political activism, who is rewarded for his selfless heroism when Kee names her daughter Dylan.

If life on Earth in the future is going to be rubbish, then it's lucky WALL·E is on hand to tidy up. Andrew Stanton's *WALL·E* (2008) was an excellent example of how to imbue animated robotic characters with personalities, and it explores themes of sustainability and ecology. This Disney–Pixar venture, in widescreen Pixarvision, won the Best Animated Feature Academy Award. Many years in the future (some time beyond 2775), Earth is a huge refuse dump, a wasteland strewn with piles of junk, rusting hulks and detritus, the remnants of a wrecked consumer society which is incapable of sustaining life. WALL·E (Waste Allocation Load Lifter Earth-Class) is a solar-powered robotic trash compactor which roams this dust-storm ravaged landscape, squashing the rubbish into cubes that are then neatly stacked into tower blocks as part of 'Operation Clean-up'. His only companion is a cricket-like insect, until the arrival of a spaceship, which drops off a probe, EVE (Extraterrestrial Vegetation Evaluator). EVE proceeds to analyse life on Earth and when she finds a green shoot, a sign that Earth is once again arable, she returns to space, with her admirer WALL·E in tow. In deep space, people live on executive starliner *Axiom*, which is celebrating the 700th anniversary of its five-year pleasure cruise. It's run by Buy 'n' Large (BnL), a super-corporation responsible for Earth's state via homogenised consumerism. Human civilisation in its entirety has become blubbery, self-satisfied and lazy, floating around on hovering easy chairs. The *Axiom* periodically sends out probes such as EVE in an attempt to find life on Earth. When EVE returns, like the biblical dove to the Ark, the ship's computer puts the programme 'Operation Re-colonise' into practice, which takes the *Axiom* back home.

It's a simple narrative. A creation story of the rebirth of Earth. WALL·E is an engaging, appealing protagonist, a haphazard creation with tracked wheels, a square 'trash compactor' body, two pincer arms, a neck and binocular head. His wooing of EVE and his relationship with the chirruping cricket are the film's best. WALL·E was voiced by Ben Burtt, who also voiced fastidiously tidying *Axiom* robot M-O, forever scrubbing 'foreign contaminants' in WALL·E's wake. The svelte white hovering probe EVE (voiced by Elissa Knight) is angelic but also destructive (she has a blaster fitted to her arm), and the *Axiom*'s computer was voiced by Sigourney Weaver. AUTO, the *Axiom*'s Autopilot, resembles disingenuous master computer HAL, and when *Axiom*'s lethargic, tubby captain takes his first steps of exercise for many years, *Thus Spake Zarathustra* booms on the soundtrack. When EVE's spacecraft breaks through Earth's atmosphere, it smashes through a layer of old satellites and obsolete space junk, the unseen, celestial legacy of consumerism. *WALL·E* has a nostalgic feel and the choreography of the robot's life compacting owes much to silent comedy. 'Put on Your Sunday Clothes' and 'It Only Takes a Moment' from *Hello, Dolly!* (1969) play as WALL·E repeatedly watches the film on videotape and records the soundtrack onto audio cassette. During his clean-up operation of Earth, WALL·E has hoarded retro artefacts, from Rubik's cubes and Zippos to tele-tennis video games and bubble wrap. *WALL·E* cost $180 million, but has taken over $500 million. In an era where sustainability, waste disposal and power generation are buzzwords, it was fitting that for this 'reboot' of Earth, the green shoot of recovery that proves life can survive and plants photosynthesise is kept in an old boot.

Just as data streams created the Matrix, they have created art too. *WALL·E*, a beautifully realised computer-animated film, was created and produced at Pixar Animation in Emeryville, California. The studio has also produced such hits as the *Toy Story* films, with its astronaut hero Buzz Lightyear. No one knows what the future holds for us earthlings, but so far the options are less than inspiring.

23

'BY GRABTHAR'S HAMMER!'

GALAXY QUEST (1999)

Director: Dean Parisot
Story: David Howard and Robert Gordon
Screenplay: Robert Gordon
Director of Photography: Jerzy Zielinski
Music: David Newman
Panavision/Technicolor
A Mark Johnson Production
Released by DreamWorks SKG
97 minutes

Tim Allen (Jason Nesmith), Sigourney Weaver (Gwen DeMarco), Alan Rickman (Alexander Dane), Tony Shalhoub (Fred Kwan), Sam Rockwell (Guy Fleegman), Daryl Mitchell (Tommy Webber), Enrico Colantoni (Mathesar), Robin Sachs (Sarris), Patrick Breen (Quellek), Missi Pyle (Laliari), Jed Rees (Teb), Justin Long (Brandon), Jeremy Howard (Kyle), Kaitlin Cullum (Katelyn), Jonathan Feyer (Hollister), Corbin Bleu (Tommy Webber, aged 9), Wayne Pére (Lathe), Heidi Swedberg (Brandon's mum), Samuel Lloyd (Neru), Rainn Wilson (Lahnk), Joe Frank (voice of the NSEA Protector's computer)

✻ ✻ ✻

There are two types of science-fiction comedy films – the intentionally funny and the unintentionally funny. The former includes satires such as *Dark Star* and *Demolition Man*, the slapstick sci-fi of *Sleeper* and the broad comedy of *Spaceballs*, *My Favourite Martian* and *Morons from Outer Space*. The second includes low-budget B-movies where the filmmakers' ineptitude is exposed, in such entries as *Santa Claus Conquers the Martians*, *Teenagers from Outer Space* and *Robot Monster*. Other intentional comedies include many outings from Disney, such as *The Computer Wore Tennis Shoes* (1970) and *The Cat from Outer* Space (1978), British comedies such as *Man in the Moon* (1960; with Kenneth More) and *The Mouse on the Moon* (1963; with Margaret Rutherford,

245

Ron Moody, Bernard Cribbins and Terry Thomas) and oddball spoof star vehicles like *The Three Stooges in Orbit* (1962), Jerry Lewis's *Way... Way Out* (1966) and Don Knott's *The Reluctant Astronaut* (1967). Sci-fi comedy has given us some great titles, including *Mutant on the Bounty* (1989), *The Creature Wasn't Nice* (1981) and *My Stepmother is an Alien* (1988), which was billed as 'Barbarella goes shopping'.

Woody Allen directed and starred in one of the most consistent sci-fi spoofs: *Sleeper* (1973). Miles Monroe (Allen) is frozen in 1973 when he visits St Vincent's Hospital for routine exploration of a minor peptic ulcer. Two hundred years later his capsule is found in woods in the Central Parallel of the American Federation and he's reawakened by dissident scientists. As Miles has no Citizen's Record, they hope to use him to infiltrate the Western District and discover what the top-secret Aries project entails. A hundred years ago, a nuclear war ravaged the US and the country is now a fascist state, the Federation, presided over by the Great Leader. In 1973, 35-year-old Miles was part-owner of the Happy Carrot health-food restaurant and a clarinettist in the Ragtime Rascals. In 2073, he's public enemy number one. Ten months ago the Great Leader was blown up by the rebels and on Aries Day the Federation plans to clone another Great Leader from his nose, before Aries Phase 2 exterminates all dissident factions.

Sleeper is an almost non-stop barrage of verbal and sight gags, with much of the humour inspired by slapstick silent comedy, and is accompanied by ragtime jazz. The automated Domesticon home-help robot servants are Chaplinesque, and Allen includes chases, a pie-in-the-face gag and a slippery banana peel. Miles impersonates Milo, a robot, and battles an out-of-control instant pudding with a broom. He steals outsized genetically modified fruit and veg, including a banana the size of a canoe, beats a man senseless with a giant strawberry and flees a giant chicken. Miles also bounces around like a human spacehopper and speeds to safety in an inflatable hydrovac suit. Allen had included a creature-feature parody in 'Are the Findings of Doctors and Clinics Who Do Sexual Research Accurate?', the sixth segment of *Everything You Always Wanted to Know about Sex* (*But Were Afraid to Ask)* (1972). Sinister Doctor Bernardo conducts suspect experiments and when his lab explodes, it unleashes a 40-foot-high breast and a plethora of gags ('They usually travel in pairs', 'We're up against a very clever tit', 'Don't worry, I know how to handle tits'), until it's corralled by an X-cup brassiere.

Sleeper was shot on location in California and Colorado and created an authentic, simple sci-fi *mise-en-scène* though lighting, suggestion and some well-chosen buildings. Dr Melik's house, where Miles is thawed out from cryogenic immersion, was designed by architect Charles Deaton. The domed space cars look like the ones in *The Wild, Wild Planet* and Miles finds a 200-year-old, built-to-last VW Beetle in Bronson Caves. Diane Keaton appeared as neurotic, flakily dense New Age poet and greetings-card writer Luna Schlosser, who falls in with the underground, where's she's turned into 'Miss Pseudo-Intellectual' by the rebels' hunky leader, Erno Windt (John Beck). In the future, fatty, unhealthy foods and smoking are deemed good for you, lovemaking has been replaced by a walk-in cubicle called the Orgasmatron, and 'the Orb', a handheld steel globe, provides tactile satiation. The golden arches of McDonald's are still on the high street. During the operation to remake the Great Leader at the Lexitron Hospital, Miles and Luna impersonate doctors and plan to clone him straight into his suit. The voice of the operation's computer (the Biocentral Computer 2100 Series G) is voiced by Douglas Rain, the voice of HAL in *2001*.

John Carpenter's *Dark Star* (1973) was a rambling, stoner space oddity that followed the mission of the scout ship *Dark Star*, which is clearing space for colonisation by destroying unstable planets with talking bombs. The crew resemble beardy-weirdy college dropouts, and their dilapidated quarters resemble a college squat. They have an onboard alien mascot, a squawking beach-ball with clawed feet. This whacked-out sci-fi movie was shot for $60,000 over a three-year period, and in the memorable finale the crew have to talk bomb No. 20 out of exploding, by engaging it in a philosophical discussion. Cookie Knapp provided the alluring voice of the ship's computer. *Airplane II: The Sequel* (1982) depicted lunar colonisation. Disaster strikes as lunar shuttle *Mayflower 1* makes its maiden voyage, when the onboard computer sets course for the Sun. The spoofs include a great turn by William Shatner as Buck Murdock, the commander of lunar base Alpha Beta, where the crew make the 'shhhh' noise to operate the voice-activated doors.

In W.D. Richter's offbeat space spoof *Buckaroo Banzai* (1984), Peter Weller played the title role as the surgeon, racing driver and rock-'n'-roll singer, who with his backing band, the Hong Kong Cavaliers – featuring Rawhide (Clancy Brown), Reno Nevada (Pepe Serna), Perfect Tony (Lewis Smith) and New Jersey (Jeff Goldblum) – saves the world from aliens from Planet 10. The surreal material drew eccentric performances from Christopher Lloyd, Matt Clark and John Lithgow (as Dr Lizardo). The film's alternative title, *The Adventures of Buckaroo Banzai Across the 8th Dimension*, clued audiences in to what to expect, in a film that featured as a plot point the fact that Orson Welles's *The War of the Worlds* radio broadcast was in fact real and he was hypnotised by aliens into saying it was a hoax.

Another spoof, *My Stepmother is an Alien* (1988), starred Kim Basinger in an eccentric performance as alien visitor Celeste Martin, who, along with her talking purse, moves in with scientist Dr Steven Mills (Dan Aykroyd). A pre-*Buffy the Vampire Slayer* Alyson Hannigan was Mills's daughter Jesse, and her *Buffy* love interest Seth Green also plays her beau here. The film has a fine sense of the bizarre, but seems unduly obsessed with Princess Stephanie of Monaco and Jimmy Durante.

In John Badham's kid-friendly comedy sci-fi *Short Circuit* (1986), Nova Robotics has developed five laser-firing robot weapons for the US government. But Number 5 is struck by lightning and short-circuits. He then escapes and is sheltered by food vendor Stephanie Speck (Ally Sheedy). Number 5 learns to talk in an irritating voice (provided by Tim Blaney) and absorbs US culture via TV. He imitates John Wayne, George Raft and John Travolta's *Saturday Night Fever* dancing. He also reprograms three of the other government robots sent to apprehend him to enact a Three Stooges routine. With a $25,000 reward on his metallic head, Number 5 reprograms and rewires itself to become human ('Number 5 is alive'). Steve Guttenberg played the robots' inventor, Newton Crosby, and Fisher Stevens was Newton's sidekick, Ben Jabituya. The incompetent government troops in pursuit of Number 5 are commanded by Skroeder (G.W. Bailey). At Vasquez Rocks Natural Park Area, California, a military helicopter obliterates Number 5 with a missile, but the destroyed robot is revealed to be an impersonator built by Number 5. It was followed by *Short Circuit 2* (1988), with Fisher now Number 5's companion.

All things to all fans, *Galaxy Quest* was a post-modern satire of sci-fi fandom, a B-movie send-up, a laugh-out-loud comedy and even a bona fide sci-fi film. It follows the adventures of the cast of a now defunct 1980s US TV show, also called *Galaxy Quest*, which travelled through space in the NSEA *Protector*. The regular cast members, Jason Nesmith (Tim Allen), Gwen DeMarco (Sigourney Weaver), Alexander Dane (Alan Rickman), Fred Kwan (Tony Shalhoub) and Tommy Webber (Daryl Mitchell), eke out a living making personal appearances at *Galaxy Quest* fan conventions and opening supermarkets in the guises of their characters: Commander Peter Quincy Taggart, Lieutenant Tawny Madison, Dr Lazarus, Tech sergeant Chen and pilot Laredo. When Jason is approached at 'Galaxy Quest Convention 18' by a group of Thermians from the Klaatu Nebula, he thinks it's another gig. But they are real aliens who have based their entire technology on 'historical documents', which are actually TV shows such as *Galaxy Quest* and *Gilligan's Island* ('Those poor people,' fret the Thermians). Jason manages to convince the rest of the cast, plus extra Guy Fleegman (Sam Rockwell), to travel to the Thermians' ship, the *Protector 2*, to save the Thermians from their oppressor, Sarris.

The film is brilliantly cast, with the sci-fi actors unhappily fulfilling their obligation to fans, more through poverty than dedication. Allan was good as egomaniac Jason, the star of the show and a star of the convention circuit who is also a heavy drinker. If Peter Quincy Taggart is Captain Kirk from *Star Trek*, then Tawny, as played by Sigourney Weaver, is his Uhura. Gwen bemoans the fact that Tawny didn't really have any personality or character. She was cast, in her partially unzipped, figure-hugging spacesuit, as set decoration, whose *TV Guide* interview was six paragraphs 'about my boobs and how they fit into my suit'. Her job on the *Protector* is 'to repeat the computer' and she rigorously carries out her duty, to hilarious effect. Rickman is ideal as seething, grouchy thespian Alexander Dane, who is sick to death of Dr Lazarus (the Mr Spock character), with his finned skull, piercing gaze and detested catchphrase: 'By Grabthar's hammer... you shall be avenged!' Tony Shalhoub was laid-back engineer Fred Kwan (the Scotty character), who stays calm regardless of the situation, and Daryl Mitchell was disbelieving pilot Laredo, who in the original series was only nine years old. 'My, how you've grown,' marvel the Thermians when they meet Tommy now. Guy Rockwell is also excellent as bit-part actor Guy Fleegman, who has been trading on his brief moment in the spotlight ever

Dr Lazarus, Lieutenant Tawny Madison and Commander Peter Quincy Taggart, the heroes of TV show *Galaxy Quest*, as played by Alexander Dane (Alan Rickman), Gwen DeMarco (Sigourney Weaver) and Jason Nesmith (Tim Allen).

since 1982, where his character, 'crewman number six', is killed by a lava monster before the first ad break. Enrico Colantoni played Mathesar, the Thermians' leader, who has an oddly oscillating voice. The Thermians are tentacled beings, but in their humanoid form they are rather odd creatures, with their silvery suits, severe, jet-black haircuts, and mannerisms and communications akin to dolphins and seals.

Galaxy Quest was shot at Culver Studios, Culver City, California, and on location in Los Angeles, including at the Hollywood Palladium (for the *Galaxy Quest* convention). The alien make-up and creature effects were created by Stan Winston, with Sarris himself (Robin Sachs) a convincingly armoured green insectoid alien. The effects are so good that the film feels like a real sci-fi movie, not a spoof. This in contrast to the budget clips of TV show *Galaxy Quest*. The film begins with a convention screening of lost *Galaxy Quest* episode 92, a two-parter, unseen since its original broadcast in 1982, which culminates with Taggart ordering: 'Activate the Omega 13.' When the *Protector 2* narrowly outruns Sarris's ship, their Beryllium Sphere fractures, so Jason and his crew beam down to a mining facility, where they are chased by a giant rock monster made up of individual sandstone boulders (shot in the weird desert rocks of Goblin Valley State Park, Utah).

As they battle Sarris, the cast morph into their on-screen personas and believe the show's corny motto: 'Never give up, never surrender.' Sarris forces the actors to admit to the ever-trusting Thermians that they lied, but the crew redeem themselves and save the Thermians, who are being slowly suffocated in a chamber by Sarris. Jason performs selfless heroics, while Gwen ends up with her clothes shredded, crawling through ducts ('Why's it always ducts?' she moans, an in-joke reference to Weaver's Ripley and the duct-stalking *Alien*). They also encounter real hazards from old episodes of the show and must remember what they did to surmount these challenges on TV, including a succession of crushing, metallic 'chompers'. In the final battle, Commander Taggart defeats the villain by ordering 'Activate the Omega 13', a time-warping device. Fred is befriended by Laliari, a Thermian (a reference to TV series' passing love interest for characters) and Dr Lazarus, his disintegrating finned cranium make-up gradually becoming more tattered, eventually believes he's Dr Lazarus. When Thermian Quellek, who sees the doctor as a father figure, is killed, Alexander promises him, totally convincingly, 'By Grabthar's hammer… you shall be avenged.'

The film also looks at science-fiction fandom, through the fan-club members that cram into the convention to see their heroes and to secure their autographs. But when Jason overhears some non-believers ridiculing the sci-fi convention fans and its has-been stars, he loses his temper with his geeky fans, including Brandon (Justin Long) and his sincere cohorts, and blasts them with the awful truth: there was no ship, it was a set, the show's not real. Later Commander Taggart contacts fans of the show on Earth (including Brandon), who help them defeat Sarris. The *Protector 2* crashes through a car park and onto the convention-hall stage. As each of the cast emerge from the wreckage, the emcee announces them to the cheering crowd, and when Sarris emerges also, Jason shoots him. The film ends with news that 18 years since it was last broadcast, a new series has been commissioned – *The New Adventures of Galaxy Quest: The Journey Continues*. The actors reprise their roles, with two new additions. Chen is now assisted by Laliari (played by an actress billed as Jane Doe) and Guy Fleegman has earned his stripes and is now billed as 'Introducing Guy Fleegman as Security Chief Roc Ingersol'. This entertainingly daft movie doubled its money – it cost $45 million and took $90 million.

Donald Petrie's *My Favourite Martian* (1999) updated the 1960s series, where Tim O'Hara (Bill Bixby) had passed off his Martian house guest as 'Uncle Martin' (Ray Walston). In the retread, Tim (Jeff Daniels), a Santa Barbara TV-news producer, is lumbered with Martian Martin, barnstormingly played by Christopher Lloyd. The farcical plot revisits *Back to the Future*, with Martin attempting to repair his ship's electron accelerator for the vortex generator so he can return home. Elizabeth Hurley played spoilt brat news reporter Brace Channing, Daryl Hannah was camerawoman Lizzie and special effects include an animated polymorphic silver space suit (energetically voiced by Wayne Knight) called Zoot. The level of humour is illustrated by the scene where a fat man is blasted off his toilet seat by a de-miniaturising car, to the strains of *Thus Spake Zarathustra*. The film's best moment is the opening scene. A Mars probe trundles across the red planet, taking rock samples. The camera cranes over the horizon, just out of sight of the probe, to reveal a vast, futuristic space city, as the controllers on Earth congratulate themselves that their Mars mission was five years and $3 trillion well spent. *Martians Go Home* (1989) saw Mark Devereaux (Randy Quaid), a composer of TV theme tunes, asked to compose a 'beautiful greeting', a 'universal handshake between the worlds' for his latest project, a Paramount sci-fi epic in the manner of *Close Encounters*. Mark summons Martians to Earth when the score is accidentally broadcast by a radio station. If the premise is promising, the hideous execution makes for an excruciating film experience, due to the irritating, yammering Martians. Mike Nichols's *What Planet Are You From?* (2000) cast Garry Shandling as emotionless alien H-1449-6, from a male-only planet whose inhabitants' sexual organs have withered and who survive by cloning. He is dispatched to Earth to find a mate and conceive an alien–human baby. This is another sci-fi movie that's really about human interaction and relationships. Shandling's alien blunders his way through the female population with a barrage of astonishingly crass, sexist chat-up lines that eventually pay off when he pulls vulnerable, recovering alcoholic and bad-man magnet Susan Hart (Annette Bening).

Mike Judge's hilariously dumb-ass *Idiocracy* (2006) begins in 2005, with the inauguration of the US government's Human Hibernation Project (the HHP). The first guinea pigs are 'Average Joe' soldier Joe Bauers (Luke Wilson) and, representing the private sector, hooker Rita (Maya Rudolph). But Joe and Rita wake up 500 years in the future and natural selection has favoured the imbecile. Cities are ruinously littered with mountains of garbage, causing avalanches, and water is only found in toilet bowls, as everyone drinks fizzy drink 'Brawndo: The Thirst Mutilator'. Joe is suddenly 'the smartest guy in history' and is appointed by champion wrestler, porn superstar and President of the USA Dwayne Elizondo Mountain Dew Herbert Camacho (Terry Alan Crews) as secretary of the interior. The English language has degenerated into a hybrid of hillbilly, Valley Girl, inner-city slang and various grunts. Dax Shepard was excellent as Joe's idiot lawyer, Frito, who spends his days watching *Ow! My Balls* on the Violence Channel. The movie is crammed with sight gags, such as the town's clock tower, which has a digital display that flashes on 12.00, because no one knows how to reset it. Starbucks is now a brothel, as society's driving forces are money and pornography. In the finale, Joe finds himself chained to a rock in a vast arena, for a monster truck rally where his opponents are the 'correctional vehicles' Dildozer and Assblaster, and superstar he-man Beef Supreme, armed with a flame-thrower. Joe triumphs and the president announces: 'This guy just got his ass a pardon!'

British comedians Mel Smith and Griff Rhys Jones starred in a scattershot sci-fi spoof *Morons from Outer Space* (1985; originally titled *Illegal Aliens*). Humanoid extraterrestrials from the planet Blob, 14 million light years away, land on Earth and are revealed to be complete idiots, who come in peace 'to do a bit of shopping'. Rhys Jones played UKBC TV reporter Graham Sweetley, who becomes the aliens' manager on their rise to fame, first as media darlings and later as rock stars. The aliens are dipsomaniac Desmond Brock (Jimmy Nail), his bimbo wife Sandra (Joanne Pearce) and their fellow moron, Julian Tope (Paul Bown). In a spectacular set piece, their craft crash-lands on the M1 south of Luton and the government cover up the incident, claiming the mysterious craft was a 'prototype seven-storey helium-driven hovercraft' being tested on the Solent. Meanwhile the aliens' cohort Bernard (Mel Smith), whom they left stranded in space, crash-lands in Arizona. Smith's odyssey provides the film with its best moments, whether Bernard is trying to communicate with a litter bin or orchestrating a breakout of the asylum he is confined in, in a hilarious spoof of *One Flew over the Cuckoo's Nest*. The *Close Encounters* parody that ends the film has a space-podule agent arriving to say that their vehicle rental is well overdue. Director Mike Hodges noted that *Morons* received his favourite review of all his films: 'Die before you see this film.'

Mel Brooks's *Spaceballs* (1987) depicted the evil title race, who live in orb-like pods and covet the peace-loving, fairy-tale planet Druidia's clean, fresh air. The Spaceballs are led by pint-sized Lord Dark Helmet (Rick Moranis). With his Spaceball crew, including Colonel Sandurz and Major Asshole, Dark Helmet aims to kidnap Druidia's Princess Vespa (Daphne Zuniga) so he can steal 10,000 years of fresh air. Vespa is saved by Lone Starr (Bill Pullman) and his half-man, half-dog, wholly unamusing sidekick Barf the Mawg (John Candy wearing furry ears and with a wagging tail), who delivers one of the most embarrassing comedy performances in cinema history. Starr drives an intergalactic Winnebago with the bumper sticker 'I ♥ Uranus', and the heroes crash-land on a moon of Vega where they encounter the Dinks (who resemble Jawas) and Yoda-like Yogurt (Mel Brooks), a Yiddish mystic who extols: 'May the Schwartz be with you!' Other characters include Pizza the Hutt (Dom DeLuise) and droid Dot Matrix (a C-3PO clone), gratingly voiced by Joan 'Can we talk?' Rivers. The parodies range from *The Bridge on the River Kwai* and *The Wizard of Oz* to *Star Trek*, *Planet of the Apes*, *Jaws* and *Snow White and the Seven Dwarfs*. That thudding sound you can hear throughout the movie is joke after joke falling flat. In a rare moment of amusement, the heroes evade capture, but their stunt doubles do not, and an alien bursts from John Hurt's chest ('Oh no, not again!') and performs a song-and-dance number. The Spinners perform the Jellybean-produced title song 'Spaceballs' and there's a credit for Rick Lazzarini for 'Barf Ear Animatronics'.

Julian Temple's *Earth Girls Are Easy* (1988) was garish Day-Glo sci-fi, with three furry, multicoloured aliens – Mac (Jeff Goldblum), Wiploc (Jim Carrey) and Zebo (Damon Wayans) – landing their spacecraft in the swimming pool of Valley Girl manicurist Valerie (Geena Davis). A *Saturday Night Live* skit expanded to feature length, Steve Barron's *Coneheads* (1993) starred Dan Aykroyd and Jane Curtin (later of sci-fi spoof TV series *3rd Rock from the Sun*) as the prominently cone-headed aliens Beldar and Prymatt from the planet Remulak. They crash-land in New Jersey and assimilate into American life among the 'blunt skulls', until immigration control officers Gorman Seedling (Michael McKean) and Eli Turnbull (David Spade) track them down. This nutty comedy is consistently funny, and the winning performances by Aykroyd, Curtin and Michelle Burke, as their Earth-born daughter Connie, are great. Check out their motorbike bumper sticker: 'Helmet Laws Suck'. A very different take on alien visitors was John Sayles's *The Brother from Another Planet* (1984). Mute Brother (Joe Morton) arrives at the Ellis Island Immigration Center and attempts to blend into Harlem life, even though he is a three-toed alien with a mystical gift for healing and repair. This simple, brilliantly observed low-key satirical fable was shot by writer–director Sayles for $200,000 on location in New York.

On paper, *Evolution* (2001) must have looked a sure thing, with *Ghostbusters* director Ivan Reitman delivering a wacky sci-fi story set near Page, Arizona. College professors Ira Kane (David Duchovny) and Harry Block (Orlando Jones) investigate a meteor oozing gunk that rapidly grows into multi-cellular creatures, flatworms, plants, insectoid beasts, ape-like primates and oxygen-breathing flying dinosaurs, before eventually regressing into a giant, destructive blob (staged by Phil Tippett). Duchovny is clearly out to send up his *X-Files* persona, via his teaming with cold-facts scientist Allison Reed (Julianne Moore). The film's marketing campaign featured a yellow 'Smiley' face logo with three eyes. If you stick around for the climax, you'll witness Earth's saviours defeating the behemoth blob with a 'Head & Shoulders' shampoo enema administered with a fire-truck hose. Ron Underwood's *Pluto Nash* (2002; *The Adventures of Pluto Nash*) isn't quite as bad as its bomb-like reputation and box-office performance suggests. It has a good score by John Powell, grand lunar city settings as 'Little America' and an interesting cast, which includes Rosario Dawson, Burt Young, Randy Quaid, Peter Boyle, Victor Varnado, John Cleese and Pam Grier. In 2087, former smuggler Pluto Nash (Eddie Murphy) runs a nightclub, 'Club Pluto', which is the subject of an attempted takeover by underworld kingpin Rex Crater (Murphy again). It only scraped back $7 million of its reported $100 million budget, and looking at the scant 95 minutes, you've got to wonder where the money went.

Sci-fi satire is more difficult to pull off than outright spoof. Marco Brambilla's *Demolition Man* (1993) was a clever sci-fi satire masquerading as a Sylvester Stallone action vehicle. Having apprehended hijacker Simon Phoenix (Wesley Snipes) in 1996 Los Angeles, destructive police sergeant John Spartan (Stallone) is placed in 'cryo prison' when he accidentally incinerates Phoenix's hostages. In 2032, Spartan is thawed out to catch Phoenix, who has escaped to commit Murder Death Kill (MDK) in the city now known as 'San Angeles'. Society is peacefully ultra-polite, with no crime, and the police force, the SAPD, are woefully under-equipped to tackle Phoenix, now a super killer. Spartan meanwhile has been rehabilitated and is now fond of knitting. He's helped on the case by Lieutenant Lenina Huxley (Sandra Bullock) and finds that this new society's Machiavellian patriarch Dr Raymond Cocteau (Nigel Hawthorne) has released Phoenix to kill Edgar Friendly (Denis Leary), a free-thinking freedom fighter. *Demolition Man* is one of Stallone's finest roles and he's well at home amid the film's satire, while Bullock is very good as his foil, who constantly misquotes idioms and is a collector of retro chic – she's learnt martial arts by watching old Jackie Chan movies. Snipes is excellent as the villain ('a blast from the past'), who in a memorable scene breaks into a museum's 'Hall of Violence' armoury exhibit to arm himself, so he and Spartan shoot it out with a variety of retro 'period' weaponry. All things perceived as being bad for you (alcohol, smoking, sex, salt, meat, spicy food

Memorable poster artwork for Phil Tucker's *Robot Monster* (1953) tells audiences all they need to know about this sci-fi movie shot in Bronson Canyon, Griffith Park in Los Angeles, which has been used as the setting for many low-budget sci-fi movies.

and contact sports) are banned, and Spartan and Huxley have virtual, non-contact 'sex' via headsets, in a scene that could have appeared in a 1970s Italian B-movie. Profanity is illegal and every time Spartan and Phoenix swear, a buzzer sounds and a machine issues a verbal dressing-down and spot fine. Every restaurant is a Taco Bell (the victors of the Franchise Wars), radio stations play nothing but jingles, and San Angeles has the 'Schwarzenegger Presidential Library', as the actor was once US president.

The Fifth Element (1997) was an eye-popping French comic-strip satire directed by Luc Besson, with over-the-top costume design by Jean-Paul Gaultier. The film begins in Egypt in 1914, with the discovery of a 'fifth element', capable of saving the world from catastrophe. Three hundred years later, a huge fireball planet, 1,200 miles in diameter, is hurtling towards Earth and the only thing that can save mankind is the super weapon, the 'fifth element', in the form of beautiful 'supreme being' Leeloo (Milla Jovovich). The fifth element and the four stones (representing fire, water, wind and earth) are also the target for despot Zorg (Gary Oldman), who with his weird black parted hair and outré apparel resembles a futuristic hybrid of Ming the Merciless and Hitler. Leeloo falls in with Korben Dallas (Bruce Willis), ex-US elite special-forces major, now driving a New York cab, and the pair go on the run. This Eurotrash starcrash of ideas has *Blade Runner*-style flying cars and a shoot-out climax at a celebrity ball and gala opera concert on the paradisiacal interplanetary luxury liner, The Fhloston Paradise Hotel. Bizarre sights include Zorg's baby-elephant-like pet, Zorg's minions (the shape-shifting pig-eared Mangalores) and the Mondoshawan, which resemble lumbering, metallic badgers. Zorg's weapon is the ZF1, an all-purpose machine-gun-cum-flame-thrower that also fires arrows, a net, a deep-freezing icer and rockets. *The Fifth Element* also features a great French-flavoured score by Eric Serra that incorporates grand opera, dance music, reggae, African house and an accordion. Amid all this surrealism, the film's sticking point is camp, irritating radio-talk-show host Ruby Rhod, played by Chris Tucker, a preening, prancing, quivering, blabbering Prince clone, who is unfortunately given his head towards the end of the film. British trip-hop artist Tricky appeared as Zorg henchman Right Arm, and Lee Evans played Fhloston Paradise crewman, Fog. Jovovich is captivating as Leeloo and Willis sends up his macho action-man image (he's constantly being harassed by phone calls from his mother) in this utterly bizarre satire that's wholly successful on its own insane terms. Besson and company's unfettered imaginations result in garish, Felliniesque oddness.

And so to the unintentionally hilarious – what might be termed the best of the worst. Phil Tucker's *Robot Monster* (1953) featured an alien that was a gorilla in a deep-sea diving helmet. In Bronson Canyon, sci-fi mad Johnny (Gregory Moffett) plays spacemen with his sister Carla (Pamela Paulson). They are there with their elder sister Alice (Claudia Barrett) and mother (Selena Royale). Johnny meets a German professor (John Mylong) and Roy (George Nader), who are exploring the caves. After their picnic, Johnny and his family nap. Johnny then investigates the caves and encounters the alien, called Ro-Man XJ-2.

Both Ro-Man and his leader, Great Guidance, were played by George Barrows, who was hired because he owned his own gorilla suit and charged $40 a day. Both Ro-Men were dubbed by John Brown. There is no reason given as to why Ro-Man has an Automatic Billion Bubble Machine in the cave, nor why Great Guidance's rod of office is a violin bow. *Robot Monster* was shot on location in Bronson Canyon and Carson's Canyon, California, in four days for $16,000. It appears that the humans are Earth's last defenders, as Ro-Man has wiped out humanity with the Calcinator Beam, a death ray. But Ro-Man fails in his mission when he falls in love with Alice. Ordered to kill her, Ro-man wrestles with his conscience: 'I cannot, yet I must. How do you calculate that? At what point on the graph do must and cannot meet? Yet I must, but I cannot.' The Great Guidance spares him the decision when he zaps Ro-Man and uses the cosmic tube ray to materialise prehistoric reptiles (stock footage from *One Million B.C.* [1940]) and cyclonic vibrations to cause an earthquake. The film's nonsensical plot is revealed to be Johnny's dream. As a result of being the first sci-fi film with stereophonic sound and in 3-D, it took $1 million in the US. A favourite with 'bad movie' buffs, *Robot Monster* is actually a rather clever little film: exactly what you'd expect of the fantastical product of a napping, comic-book-obsessed child's overactive imagination.

W. Lee Wilder (Billy's lesser-known brother) directed *Phantom from Space* (1953). A UFO crashes in Santa Monica and the authorities track radio interference, which emanates from a murderous, tall space-suited alien. It is termed an 'X-man saboteur' and 'Mr X', and the signal is emanating from the radioactive suit. This incompetent film is almost of Ed Wood proportions, from its *Dragnet*-style voice-over to its wooden performances and inept special effects. When the X-man removes his helmet and suit, he's invisible (hence the film's ghostly title). He's often just a helmet hovering in the air, or more frequently the only evidence of his presence is opening or closing doors, sliding chairs and twitching curtains. Revealed in ultraviolet light, the alien suffocates as its oxygen runs out. The Frankenstein-like alien was played by towering Dick Sands, who also played in Wilder's yeti adventure *The Snow Creature* (1953).

Teenagers from Outer Space (1959) was the responsibility of one-man-band Tom Graeff, who wrote, produced, photographed, edited, created the special effects for and directed this sci-fi atrocity. Graeff also played Los Angeles newspaper reporter Joe Rogers, under the pseudonym 'Tom Lockyear', who is investigating strange goings-on following the arrival of a flying saucer. Location scenes were shot in Bronson Canyon and around Los Angeles. Visitors from another planet arrive with a 'gargon specimen' (a lobster) and plan to use Earth as a breeding ground. The gargons grow to immense size and herds of them will graze on Earth and provide the aliens with sustenance. Rebellious space teen Derek (David Love) doesn't want to destroy civilisation, and runs away to suburban Los Angeles. He's allowed by teenage earthling Betty Morgan (Dawn Anderson) to stay in the house she shares with her grandfather (Harvey B. Dunn), presuming Derek is just another misunderstood teenager. Teen alien Thor (Bryan Grant) is dispatched with a ray gun to apprehend Derek. Meanwhile, the gargon grows to gigantic proportions and threatens Los Angeles. This special effect is simply the shadow of a lobster held in silhouette in front of a projector. The film also features some awful acting, hairstyles and teeth. The alien teens speak in a very old-fashioned way – when Thor is shot by a cop, he orders Derek: 'You will take me to a man of surgery to remove the metal pellets from my flesh.' Thor's weapon, the focusing disintegrator ray 'blasts flesh right off the bone', instantaneously reducing its victims to skeletons. For the human victims, a science-lab skeleton is used, which has clearly visible metal riveted joints.

In Nicholas Webster's *Santa Claus Conquers the Martians* (1964), Martian children are bored and the Martian leader, Kimar (Leonard Hicks), consults 800-year-old wise man Chochem (Carl Don), who decrees that although it is 'September' on Mars, on Earth it is nearly time for 'the Christmas'. Earth children are visited by Santa Claus (John Call), so Kimar and his Martian cohorts – including baddie Voldar (Vincent Beck), comedy relief imbecile Dropo (Bill McCutcheon) and Torg, a robot of the 'tinfoil-covered cardboard box' variety – travel to Santa's workshop at the North Pole and kidnap him. This children's sci-fi fantasy is an assault on the senses in every sense of the word.

As is often said during the movie: Wowee! Pick out a strong beer to accompany this one, or better yet, a crate. Marvel at the colourfully awful effects (Mars resembles a paint-splattered ping-pong ball) and Santa's workshop is populated by elf helpers such as Winky (Ivor Bodin). The Martians wear green greasepaint make-up, capes, near-indecent leotards and helmets with antennae and mug handles attached. The film begins with the irritatingly catchy, infuriatingly unforgettable 'Hooray for Santy Claus', performed squeakingly out-of-tune by the Little Eskimos, and the score is by Milton DeLugg. Unfettered by logic, the plot stumbles blindly, and Call's irritating performance as the bespectacled, ruddy-faced, beardy tub of cheerfulness invites kidnapping. But there's something sinister going on here. Martian children, such as Bomar (Chris North) and Girmar (Pia Zadora), never laugh and are given 'sleep spray' every night by their mother, Lady Momar (Leila Martin). These emotionless, bored kids, who spend all day in front of the TV, are contrasted with lively Earth children Betty and Billy Foster (Donna Conforti and Victor Stiles). Eventually Santa's release is negotiated and Dropo dons Santa's mantle on Mars, becoming Dropo Claus. The movie was shot for $200,000 at 'Michael Myorborg Studios', New York (actually a converted aircraft hangar at Roosevelt Field, Long Island). Producer Paul Jacobson made it because he detected a gap in the Christmas market. It was only Disney films that were decent children's entertainment in cinemas at Christmas time. After the release of Jacobson's brainchild, that gap in the market remained, though *Santa Claus* did show up for years every Yuletide on TV, a big fat turkey amid the festive schedule. This comedy should come with a public elf warning.

Minority Report: Murder is a thing of the past, thanks to the Precrime Division. But its infallibility is called into question when the department's captain, John Anderton (Tom Cruise), is named and framed as a killer.

24

'WE SEE WHAT THEY SEE'

MINORITY REPORT (2002)

Director: Steven Spielberg
Story: Philip K. Dick
Screenplay: Scott Frank and Jon Cohen
Director of Photography: Janusz Kamiński
Music: John Williams
Panavision/Technicolor
A Cruise/Wagner/Blue Tulip/Ronald Shusett/Gary Goldman Production
Released by Twentieth Century Fox and DreamWorks SKG
139 minutes

Tom Cruise (Captain John Anderton, DCPD), Max von Sydow (Director Lamar Burgess), Colin Farrell (FBI agent Danny Witwer), Samantha Morton (Agatha Lively, pre-cog), Daniel London (Wally), Lois Smith (Dr Iris Hineman), Tim Blake Wilson (Gideon, sentry at the Department of Containment), George Wallace (Chief Justice Pollard), Ann Ryerson (Dr Katherine James), Kathryn Morris (Lara Clarke), Tyler Patrick Jones (older Sean), Dominic Scott Kay (younger Sean), Michael and Arthur Dickman (Arthur and Dashiell, pre-cogs), Steve Harris (Jad), Neal McDonough (Fletcher), Patrick Kilpatrick (Knott), Jessica Capshaw (Evanna), Arye Gross (Howard Marks), Ashley Crow (Sarah Marks), Mike Binder (Leo Crow), Joel Gretsch (Donald Dubin), Jessica Harper (Anne Lively, Agatha's mother), Bertell Lawrence (John Doe), Jason Antoon (Rufus T. Riley, at Cyber Parlour)

* * *

Future crime takes many forms, from the kidnapping 'galaxy criminals' of *The Wild, Wild Planet* (1965) to the tracking of renegade replicants in *Blade Runner* and the paranoid conspiracy theories of *The X-Files*. Just as sci-fi has cross-bred with the action-movie genre, or horror, so too have crime scenarios. These sometimes take the form of US police investigations, procedurals that could just as easily take place on the streets of present-day Los Angeles, New York or San Francisco, but instead are dressed up in sci-fi costume, or murder mystery sci-fi, where bemused protagonists ponder through plots as unfathomable as a black hole.

The French New Wave's Jean-Luc Godard wrote and directed *Alphaville* (1965), starring Eddie Constantine as secret agent Lemmy Caution. Godard melded 1940s-style film noir to mystery, espionage, philosophy and science fiction. Caution, Agent 003, arrives in the metropolis of Alphaville from the 'Lands Without', under the guise of Ivan Johnson, a journalist for *Figaro-Pravda*. His mission is to find Professor von Braun, also called Leonard Nosferatu (Howard Vernon), a fugitive from the 'Lands Without', who now operates Alpha 60, a supercomputer that rules the city. Caution must bring von Braun back alive to the Lands Without, or liquidate him.

Godard presents the fantastical in the everyday. The film was shot in monochrome by Raoul Coutard on location in Paris, a Paris that appears as a futuristic concrete-and-glass labyrinth, illuminated by artificial lighting, neon signs, flickering bulbs and glittering lights. Caution's car, a Ford Galaxy, is his 'spaceship'; a fan, flashing lamps and microphones represent Alpha 60. When dissidents are executed for 'behaving illogically', they are machine-gunned from a diving board into a swimming pool, where their corpses are recovered by women wearing bathing suits. Caution's fistfights with Alphaville heavies and a car chase play close to spoof. Anna Karina was Natasha, von Braun's daughter, who has forgotten – like all in Alphaville – the meaning of words such as 'conscious' and 'love'. Akim Tamiroff was Henri Dickson, alias Agent X21, one of Caution's predecessors. Caution finds him hiding out in the seedy Red Star Hotel. The abrasive soundtrack makes the film very harsh on the ear, from Alpha 60's deep, gravelly voice to the intrusive, self-consciously dramatic bursts of music by Paul Misraki. Caution, dressed like a 1940s private eye, spits terse, hardboiled noir dialogue and sparks cigarettes with a flick of his Zippo. He photographs each character he meets, ostensibly for his 'news story' on von Braun, but really for police records. Caution later shoots von Braun and leaves Alphaville with Natasha as the abstract world is destroyed by Alpha 60. *Alphaville* won the Golden Bear at the 1965 Berlin Film Festival and was originally to have been called *Tarzan vs IBM*. Godard had previously dabbled in sci-fi in the 20-minute 'The New World' segment of the portmanteau film *RoGoPaG* (1962), where an atomic super-explosion 120,000 metres above Paris causes a barely discernible change in people and places. The population begins popping pills, 'a mysterious, sullen hysteria' settles on the city and Alessandra (Alexandra Stewart) begins an affair at a swimming pool and tells her former lover (Jean-Marc Bory), 'I ex-love you.'

Perhaps the most famous work of sci-fi mystery was Andrei Tarkovsky's *Solaris* (1972; original title *Solyaris*), based on the 1961 novel by Stanisław Lem and scripted by Tarkovsky and Fridrikh Gorenshtein. Psychologist Dr Kris Kelvin (Donatas Banionis) travels to the planet Solaris to investigate strange phenomena at a space station manned by astrobiologist Dr Sartorious (Anatoly Solonitsyn), cybernetics expert Dr Snaut (in some prints Snow, played by Jüri Järvet) and physiologist Dr Gibarian (Sos Sargsyan).

Kelvin discovers the men are suffering from psychological imbalances and hallucinations, which has led to Gibarian's suicide. Solaris Ocean, the liquid mass perpetually wreathed in drifting fog, is an intelligent, giant, brainy life form capable of influencing and extracting human knowledge, and it's also able to think. It conjures up physical manifestations of loved ones from deep within the scientists' psyches. For Kelvin, it's his wife Hari (Natalya Bondarchuk), who died ten years ago. Kelvin has been warned to expect the unexpected. In the film's introduction, when Kelvin is visited at his parents' country house by search-and-rescue pilot Henri Berton (André Burton in some prints, played by Vladislav Dvorzhetsky), who testified at an inquiry about the weird goings-on on Solaris. The inquiry concluded they bore 'almost no relation to reality'. Kelvin fires the first apparition of Hari into space in a rocket, but while he sleeps, another Hari manifests herself. The film is filled with strange, eerie imagery, made eerier by the humming, ominous electronic score from Eduard Artemyev, which resembles distant, indiscernible machines. The titles play in to the gloomy organ of Bach's Chorale Prelude in F Minor, which sets the film's tone.

Tarkovsky's film is often terrific, but at 165 minutes it is also terrifically slow. The film will not be hurried, keeping a serene pace, with imagery steeped in memory, half memory, nostalgia and dream. The early part of the film is Kelvin's sad goodbyes in his final days on Earth to his father (Nikolai Grinko) and mother (Olga Barnet), at their wintry country estate. This melancholy opening, during which Kelvin realises he probably won't see his father alive again, such is the length of the mission, is gently poetic and deeply sad. He burns many mementos of his life on a bonfire. The film was shot in long, static compositions, portraits of strange tableau, by Vadim Yusov in widescreen Sovscope and Sovcolor. The film switches from monochrome to colour, and the natural poetry of the scenes in the country contrast with the cold, unsettling interiors of the space station, where fluttering strips of paper attached to the ventilators imitate rustling leaves. The countryside scenes were shot near Zvenigorod, an old town near Moscow, with Solaris interiors at Mosfilm Studios, Moscow. There is artful use of light bursts and Kelvin's journey to Solaris is depicted largely through suggestion and lights. Special effects were by A. Klimenko and V. Sevostyanov. This space trip is contrasted with Berton's long car journey with his son, along endless flyovers and tunnels, filmed in Osaka and Tokyo. To banish the oppressive visions of the dark subconscious, hauntings from the id, the Solaris scientists deliberate their course of action: to expose the oceanic plasma to intense radiation. Kelvin's childhood memories conjure up visions that become more numerous, and his mother and his dog appear on Solaris. When the 'visitors' eventually vanish, islands begin to appear in the maelstrom of Solaris – islands of memory in the open sea – and the film's final image is worth sticking around for. Kelvin returns to his parents' house and sees his father, but the camera cranes upward, away through the fog bank, to reveal the house standing on a tiny island in Solaris Ocean. As in so much arthouse cinema, this mystery offers no conventional solution.

Steven Soderbergh nobly had a bash at Lem's novel in a Hollywood version of *Solaris* (2002). Kelvin (George Clooney) arrives at the Solaris station and is haunted by a facsimile of his dead wife, Rheya (Natascha McElhone), a suicide. Jeremy Davis played Snow, while Viola Davis was a stoic Dr Gordon. Planet Solaris is drifting coloured fog, like in a Mario Bava movie. The station interiors and space sequences are *2001*-ish, and the film stirs in Dylan Thomas's poetry, arty cinematography and dinner-party discussions about the existence of God, but it's all so smug and low-key to the point of stasis. Clooney does his usual suave, Cary Grant thing, which works fine for Danny Ocean, but not for Solaris Ocean. With its visits to bookshops, walks in the rain, love scenes and naked noodle-eating, it's more *Saturn 3* than *Solaris*. Kelvin's first reaction to his resurrected wife lying beside him (he jumps out of bed, runs across the room and shouts, 'God dammit!') may be more realistic, but it is much less poetic than Tarkovsky's interpretation.

Both *Solaris* films demonstrate the flexibility of the genre. If filmmakers can resist the compulsion to fill their future worlds with spaceships, predatory robots and laser guns, the results can often be much more effective. Writer–director Andrew Niccol's *Gattaca* (1997) is one of the most brilliantly original science-fiction films and certainly one that repays multiple viewings. In the not too distant future, people can choose to conceive children naturally, with all the imperfections and health defects inherent in natural births, or with the aid of scientists they can selectively genetically engineer perfect specimens. Vincent Freeman (Ethan Hawke) is an 'in-valid', a natural birth who has a heart defect, poor eyesight and a reduced life expectancy, while his younger brother Anton is a genetically perfect 'valid'. To realise his dream of travelling into space as an astronaut, Vincent becomes a janitor at Gattaca, a facility that operates a space-launch programme run by Commander Josef (Gore Vidal). Vincent infiltrates Gattaca and becomes one of the elites working there by buying a valid's identity, becoming a 'borrowed ladder'. Following an accident, Jerome Morrow (Jude Law), a swimming silver medallist, has a broken back and is confined to a wheelchair. Jerome will become 'Eugene' and Vincent 'Jerome', for 25 per cent of Vincent's earnings. To pass for Jerome, Vincent must be able to provide blood and urine samples, to prove his elite provenance. This he does by carrying blood samples concealed on his thumb and a urine sample bag strapped to his thigh. He achieves the rank of navigator first class and is chosen to be part of a year-long space mission to Titan. But when the mission's commander is found murdered, the police investigation indicates that an in-valid has infiltrated Gattaca.

In terms of plotting and characterisation, *Gattaca* is streets ahead of most science fiction. Niccol's brilliantly imaginative story, his directorial debut, takes place in a setting where cold futurism meets retro 1930s gangster decor. The employees at Gattaca wear formal suits and Detective Hugo (Alan Arkin) resembles a Bogart-era gumshoe. Even the future's eco-friendly cars have a retro look (French Citroëns and British Rover 2000s), despite emitting a strange whining noise and no exhaust fumes. Parts of the Gattaca complex were filmed at Frank Lloyd Wright's Marin County Civic Center, California, while the exterior of Jerome and Vincent's house was the CLA Building at California Polytechnic University. Ernest Borgnine played Gattaca's head janitor, Caesar, Tony Shalhoub was the mysterious 'German' who facilitates Vincent and Jerome's 'business arrangement', and Xander Berkeley was Gattaca's Dr Lamar, who identifies Vincent's in-valid status, but keeps the secret. The story's emotional drive is complemented by Michael Nyman's magnificent tidal score and the relationship between Vincent and Jerome, and Jerome and Eugene, is well played by Hawke and Law, both of whom are admirable in difficult roles. Uma Thurman is classy as demure Irene Cassini, a Gattaca employee with whom Vincent falls in love, as Hawke did on set. A stray eyelash in Gattaca can lead to an enquiry, and the investigating officers include Vincent's brother, Anton (Loren Dean). The film has much to say about inherent inherited privilege, fate and love, but is never self-righteous and always absorbing, surprising and moving. Jerome tells Vincent that he only lent him his body, but Vincent lent Jerome 'his dream' – while in his wheelchair, it is valid Jerome that is an invalid. In a terrific denouement, Vincent seems to have failed, but although he does take the space launch to Titan, *Gattaca* doesn't have an entirely happy ending.

King of 1990s sci-fi TV was Chris Carter's memorable cult series *The X-Files* (1993–2002), which blended sci-fi and supernatural investigations with conspiracy theories, the unsolved and the unexplained. David Duchovny jumped to stardom as Special Agent Fox Mulder, called Spooky by his FBI colleagues, who is teamed with sceptical realist Special Agent Dana Scully (Gillian Anderson), the voice of reason, to investigate various obscure, baffling or downright weird occurrences that are filed under 'X'. With its haunting theme tune by Mark Snow and strong stories, it became a massive hit for Twentieth Century Fox. Series regulars included their exasperated boss, Walter Skinner (Mitch Pileggi), and shadowy, noirish, desiccated 'cigarette-smoking man' Spender (William B. Davis), while Robert Patrick and Annabeth Gish joined late on as Agents John Doggett and Monica Reyes. But the series eventually imploded after nine seasons under its own convolution. At its height, such was the series' popularity that Welsh indie rock band Catatonia had a hit single with 'Mulder and Scully' and even minor characters, über-conspiracy theorists the Lone Gunmen – Ringo Langley (Dean Haglund), Melvin Frohike (Tom Braidwood) and John Byers (Bruce Harwood) – got their own short-lived series in 2001. *The X-Files'* tagline was 'the truth is out there', and Mulder's ongoing quest was to prove conclusively the existence of extraterrestrials. Mulder's sister Samantha was an alien abductee, which became a thread of the series, as his investigations opened then closed doors, and he was continually left without concrete evidence.

A 1998 film spin-off directed by Rob Bowman expanded on the 'trust no one' para-noia, with the bombing of a Federal building in Dallas being used as a cover-up for the disposal of people who have come into contact with a deadly extraterrestrial virus. The scenario thrust Mulder and Scully into a broader canvas than normal, with large-scale action sequences and chases, as the government is apparently cultivating the virus – in cornfields and silo domes in the desert – to be disseminated by bees. Mulder has to save

Scully when she is stung by one of the infected bees, and Martin Landau from cult TV series *Space: 1999* (1975–7) played Mulder's informant Dr Alvin Kurtzweil, who puts the agent on the right track by suggesting the people killed in the explosion (a boy and two firemen) were dead already. The chemistry between Duchovny and Anderson, the series' trump card, is more than in evidence – they almost kiss – as is the series' mischievous sense of humour. At one point, Mulder relieves himself on an *Independence Day* poster in a back alley. The film plays much better today, distanced from the series, as a superior piece of conspiracy theory. A further cinema spin-off, *The X-Files: I Want to Believe*, followed in 2008.

Part of the ongoing appeal of sci-fi cinema is its perpetual evolution. A genre that can create *Solaris* and *Gattaca* can also craft a film that blends nuance, mystery, murder and narrative intelligence, and still deliver pulsating action sequences. Steven Spielberg's *Minority Report* (2002) was an influential intellectual sci-fi that fused the world of Philip K. Dick and conspiracy theories with the flamboyance and death-defying deeds of Tom Cruise's *Mission: Impossible* films.

In 2054 in the District of Columbia murder is a thing of the past. The Precrime Division has achieved this by using three 'pre-cogs', seers able to foretell slayings before they occur. Captain John Anderton (Cruise) commands the unit, under the directorship of Lamarr Burgess (Max von Sydow). Anderton is driven by the loss of his son Sean, who went missing from a public swimming pool in Baltimore six years ago. There's a public vote imminent to decide if Precrime should 'go national' and the unit is under observation by the FBI's Danny Witwer (Colin Farrell). The three pre-cogs are Agatha, the strongest of the seers, and twins Arthur and Dashiell. When Agatha has flashbacks to a crime that has already been solved, Anderton finds that it was the murder of Anne Lively by a killer of unknown identity, a 'John Doe'. On the latest murder inquiry, Anderton is named as the killer who will strike in 36 hours. He's been framed, goes on the run and visits Precrime pioneer Dr Iris Hineman, who tells him that pre-cogs are not infallible. There's an 'insignificant variable', which means that all three pre-cogs need not agree on the culprit. The 'minority report' is ignored and the majority observed. Anderton begins to suspect he's put innocent people away.

Minority Report was based on the 1956 short story by Philip K. Dick. In the short story, the Precrime department is in New York City and John Allison Anderton is the Commissioner of Police, with Ed Witwer his assistant. Three pre-cog mutants predict criminal actions that 'boldly and successfully abolished the post-crime punitive system of jails and fines'. Would-be criminals are imprisoned before they can carry out the murders. Anderton is implicated in the murder of Leopold Kaplan, General of the Army of the Federated Westbloc Alliance, and Anderton's wife Lisa is part of a plot to frame him. Anderton goes on the run as unemployed electrician Ernest Temple. The pre-cogs are Jerry, Donna and Mike. Anderton assassinates Kaplan at an army rally, fulfilling the majority report prophecy – Anderton and Lisa are exiled and Precrime continues unquestioned. The film versions of Dick's books take ideas, moments and moods from his work, rather than entire plots and characters. Dick wrote confused, rushed narratives during amphetamine-fuelled writing sessions and he died of a stroke, aged 54.

Though this is darker sci-fi than Spielberg's family-friendly 1970s and 1980s releases, *Minority Report* is closer to conventional Hollywood action movies than, for example, *Blade Runner*. This is telegraphed by the casting of Tom Cruise as Anderton. Max von Sydow played the sinister head of Precrime, while Colin Farrell was at his most slick and buttoned-down as FBI investigator Witwer. Anderton heads into the 'Sprawl', a grimy urban ghetto, to score drugs ('clarity') and Witwer plans to bust Anderton for this. It would have been interesting to have seen the two leads' casting reversed, as Farrell is an edgier actor than Cruise and more interesting to watch. Samantha Morton was excellent as the frail, shaven-headed seer Agatha, and Daniel London was her sympathetic carer, Wally. Lois Smith, as Dr Hineman, tells Anderton: 'Sometimes in order to see the light, you have to risk the dark.' Tim Blake Wilson plays Gideon, the sentry at the Department of Containment jail facility, who warns Anderton: 'Careful, chief – you dig up the past, all you get is dirty.' Anderton's estranged wife Lara was played by Kathryn Morris, and Steve Harris and Neal McDonough were Precrime's Jad and Fletcher, formerly Anderton's colleagues, now his hunters. Jason Antoon portrayed Rufus T. Riley, the proprietor of a cyber parlour where fantasies – whether a lap dance or a murder – can be experienced in holographic form. Peter Stormare was Dr Solomon Eddie, the surgeon who performs Anderton's eye transplant. In 2054, the DC population is ID'd at every turn by retinal scan. Anderton has a new set of eyes fitted, so that he can make his way through the metropolis undetected, and he carries his own eyes in a plastic bag, enabling him to access Precrime HQ. Anne Lively, revealed to be Agatha's mother and the key to the mystery, was played by Jessica Harper, from Dario Argento's *Suspiria* (1977).

Minority Report was filmed for an estimated $102 million budget, on studio interiors and exteriors at Infinite Horizon, Twentieth Century Fox, Universal Studios and Warner Bros Studios, and on location in Los Angeles, Washington, DC, and in Virginia. The score was composed by John Williams, but the soundtrack also features compositions by Schubert, Tchaikovsky, Haydn and Bach ('Jesu, Joy of Man's Desiring'). The story is rendered in a muted, steely colour palette, photographed by Janusz Kamiński in Panavision and Technicolor, often with brightly filtered, haloed light. The grainy, jumpy 'prevision sequences' show the murderous premonitions, visions of death experienced by the pre-cogs: 'We see what they see.' Their crime projections are projected onto screens, and the names of the perpetrator and victim or victims appear etched onto grained balls, like a bizarre bingo-ball machine. In Precrime HQ, Anderton is depicted literally 'conducting' the investigation to classical music, as image files and data are moved across screens by Anderton's fingertips.

Visual highlights include the *Metropolis*-like cityscapes, the sleek futuristic vehicles gliding along multi-lane highways, the deified pre-cogs' rippling azure 'temple' and the

Department of Containment, lined with hundreds of immobilised felons. The commercials, infomercials and interactive billboards around DC were used by Spielberg as both clever product placement and a commentary on futuristic consumerism. These retina-activated adverts target customers as they walk by, in a variation on 'direct marketing'. In 2054, newspapers are interactive – when Anderton flees on a metro train, an issue of *USA Today* automatically updates its headline: 'Precrime hunts its own! Captain John Anderton, DCPD, Prime Target in Citywide Precrime Manhunt (More as Story Unfolds)'. At home, tormented, guilt-ridden Anderton watches 3-D holographic images of Sean, which enable him to 'interact' with his son.

The film's initially edgy atmosphere is gradually dispersed by increasingly flamboyant action set pieces, as all eyes are on wanted Anderton. Cops are armed with pacifying 'halos' and 'sick sticks' (batons that make their victims vomit) and their sawn-off-shotgun-like sidearms blast out sonic waves. When the police sweep the ghetto tenements, where Anderton is recovering from his eye transplant, they send in spiders: scuttling tripod retinal scanners. An impressively choreographed scene has Anderton and Agatha escape from the Precrime squad through a mall, with Agatha using her seer abilities to plot their course in advance.

Witwer discovers that the pre-cogs sometimes see the same murder more than once, an 'echo', or pre-cog déjà vu. But in Anne's case, someone has gone to the trouble of staging the murder, having a fall-guy convicted – a John Doe with 'new eyes' (Bertell Lawrence) – and then restaged the killing for real. There are tangled Machiavellian forces at work behind Precrime's success story and Witwer is murdered. Eventually, the foundation stone of Precrime is revealed to be deeply flawed. In 2054, the Precrime experiment is abandoned and convicted felons are pardoned and released. John and Lara are reunited (with her expecting a baby) and the pre-cogs live in an undisclosed, idyllic rural location: 'A place where they could find relief from the gifts, a place where they could live out their lives in peace.'

Minority Report premiered in June 2002, taking $132 million in the US and a further $196 million worldwide. Some poster artwork featured Cruise wearing eye bandages; some concentrated on the film's chase, with the tagline 'This Year Everyone Runs'. It was rated PG-13 in the US and 12 in the UK. Dick's short story was reprinted with Cruise on the cover as a tie-in, as though the story was the entire book. In reality, it's only the first chapter, with the remainder padded out with unrelated Dick short stories.

Terry Gilliam's *Twelve Monkeys* (1995) dealt with time travel and the Cassandra complex – of foreknowledge without the ability to change future events. A UK–US co-production, it was set in 2035, where the Earth is barely habitable and a deadly virus has wiped out billions of people. Animals once again rule the surface of the Earth and the one per cent of the population that has survived live underground. James Cole (Bruce Willis) is supposed to be sent back to 1996, before the virus strikes, but instead arrives in 1990, where he is deemed a lunatic and incarcerated in a mental institute. He meets Jeffrey

Goines (Brad Pitt), the activist son of prominent vivisectionist Dr Goines (Christopher Plummer), who in the future will be the leader of the Army of the Twelve Monkeys, those supposedly responsible for the virus's release. Madeleine Stowe played Cole's psychiatrist, Dr Kathryn Railly, and Frank Gorshin (the Riddler in TV's *Batman*) played the head of the asylum, Dr Fletcher. Cole tries again and arrives in 1996 Baltimore, where he contacts Railly to help him locate the Twelve Monkeys, but Cole begins to doubt their responsibility. *Twelve Monkeys* was partly inspired by Chris Marker's half-hour French short *La Jetée* (1962), a stylish monochrome film made almost entirely of still images, which was released on a double bill with *Alphaville*. Pitt was nominated for a Best Supporting Actor Oscar for his twitchy, jabbering performance.

There were other ways of dealing with a rising crime rate, however, as displayed in John Carpenter's *Escape from New York* (1981). In 1980 the US crime rate has risen by

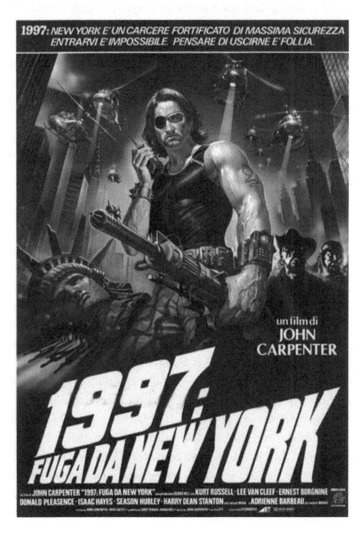

In 1997 Snake Plissken (Kurt Russell) ventures into the maximum-security prison on Manhattan Island to rescue the US president (Donald Pleasence). Italian poster for John Carpenter's *Escape from New York* (1981).

400 per cent and Manhattan Island has been ringed by a 50-foot containment wall and turned into a maximum-security prison, where the country's scum are left to their own devices. In 1997 criminal Snake Plissken (Kurt Russell) is dispatched by police commissioner Bob Hauk (Lee Van Cleef) in a glider, which lands on the roof of the World Trade Center, to rescue the US president (Donald Pleasence), who has been kidnapped by the National Liberation Front of America. Plissken must complete his mission against the clock, as Hauk has implanted tiny explosive devices that will open up arteries in Plissken's neck. In the graffitied ghettos of a city that is literally 'chock full o' nuts', Plissken evades scuttling shadows, runs the pelted gauntlet of Broadway, fights sewer-dwelling crazies and finds himself up against the king of the urban jungle, warlord the Duke of New York (Isaac Hayes). Ernest Borgnine played partisan Yellow Cab Co. driver Cabby, Harry Dean Stanton was rattish boffin Brains, and beautiful Adrienne Barbeau displayed avarice, marksmanship and spectacular cleavage as Brain's cohort Maggie. Frank Doubleday, who played psycho henchman Romero, looked like a cross between Klaus Kinski and a fox caught in a wind tunnel. The climax has Plissken and company escaping across the mined 69th Street Bridge. Carpenter followed it with *Escape from LA* (1996), where Russell reprised his role and was surrounded by another interesting cast, including A.J. Langer, Steve Buscemi, Stacy Keach, Pam Grier, Peter Fonda and Cliff Robertson (as the US president). With Walter Hill's *The Warriors* (1979), *New York* inspired a slew of Italian imitators throughout the 1980s. The combination of urban wrack-and-ruin, anything-goes costumery and ultraviolence was a winning one in such films as *1990: The Bronx Warriors* (1982) and *2019: After the Fall of New York* (1983).

Alex Proyas's *I, Robot* (2004) shares *Minority Report*'s chromium cinematography and themes of conspiracy theory and corruption in high places. In Chicago in 2035, Detective Del Spooner (Smith) is called to the apparent suicide of his friend Dr Alfred Lanning (James Cromwell), who works for US Robotics (USR), headed by Lawrence Robertson (Bruce Greenwood). Lanning plummeted to his death from his office window into the lobby of USR. In 2035 robots live alongside humans and perform menial jobs, governed by the 'three laws', which ensure they will never harm humans. Spooner suspects that Lanning was murdered and there's a conspiracy and cover-up masterminded by Robertson. Spooner's boss, Lieutenant Bergin (Chi McBride), thinks Spooner is paranoid, bumping him off the force. Spooner is led by Lanning's holographic message on a trail of clues. Robot Sonny, who exhibits human-like emotions and insubordination, holds the key to the mystery. Spooner continues his unofficial investigation with USR developer Dr Calvin (Bridget Moynahan), and when USR launch a new NS-5 domestic robot the machines rise and take over the city. The ghosts in the machine Lanning has warned about have murder on their mind. The revolt's master is USR's mainframe computer VIKI, so Spooner destroys her Positronic brain with nanotechnology (nanites) and immobilises the robot army. The film was inspired by short story collection *I, Robot* (1950) by Russian-born American author and scientist Isaac Asimov, who coined the word 'robotics'. Spooner is part robot, as he lost his left arm in a car accident and had it replaced by a mechanical one in USR's cybernetics programme. It could have resulted in understated sci-fi, but instead careers out of control as an action vehicle, complete with car chases, fist fights and Oscar-nominated special effects, including scores of rampaging robots and a scene where a 'demobot' demolishes Lanning's house.

Sci-crime has now begun to examine contemporary threats, such as terrorism. In Tony Scott's *Déjà Vu* (2006), produced by Jerry Bruckheimer, a bomb sinks the Algiers ferry in New Orleans during Mardi Gras. The Bureau of Alcohol, Tobacco, Firearms and Explosives (ATF) agent Doug Carlin (Denzel Washington) finds that a dead woman washed up after the event was actually burnt and killed beforehand, her murder made to appear part of the ferry disaster (as in the first *X-Files* film). Carlin joins a new investigative unit, headed by Agent Pryzwarra (Val Kilmer), using ultra-complex new technologies, dubbed the Snow White programme. This video viewing system collates information relayed from four satellites to recreate a complete picture of past events from four days ago. It is a digital recreation through multiple angles, a single trailing moment in the past that cannot be rewound, presenting events via 'time windows'. The technology resembles a very sophisticated Google Earth, which creates a visual timeline portmanteau like a non-reversible DVD. The team watch the murder victim, Claire Kuchever (Paula Patton), in her home and see her last movements – she becomes inadvertently embroiled in the tragedy when the bomber, Carroll Oerstadt (Jim Caviezel), a psychologically wobbly 'patriot' who has failed in his attempts to join the military and is now an anti-government loner, buys her Bronco to use as a car bomb. Having established Oerstadt's guilt, Carlin travels back in time to save Claire and prevent the bombing. The plot is contrived, but finely constructed and skilfully executed, with the cast convincing. Aboard the ferry, Carlin and Claire fight it out with Oerstadt, and Carlin drives the car bomb into the Mississippi. Having been killed in the blast, the 'present day' Carlin reappears on the dock to investigate the bombing and is 'reunited' with Claire, despite the fact that he hasn't yet met her. The film plays on the American consciousness's need for closure – the opening ferry sinking is suitably hellish – but it is also a love story, as Carlin begins to care about Claire and her plight as much as (if not more than) the hundreds of ferry passengers about to die.

But amid such flights of fantasy, Precrime and the anticipation of future events are already here. In 2012, the Los Angeles Police Department announced it was using a computer program called 'predictive policing', which mapped 'boxed' areas that identified where crimes were likely to happen. Based on data collated from earlier felonies, these crime hotspots are areas where burglary and vehicle theft are likely to occur. The LAPD predictive policing model has convinced its detractors – such as older, set-in-their ways policemen – and succeeded in driving down the crime rate by anticipating where crimes will occur, or rather recur.

Star Trek: Uhura (Zoë Saldana), James T. Kirk (Chris Pine) and Spock (Zachary Quinto) in J.J. Abrams's highly successful 2009 reboot of the TV and movie franchise.

25

'LIVE LONG AND PROSPER'

STAR TREK (2009)

Director: J.J. Abrams
Producers: J.J. Abrams and Damon Lindelof
Story and Screenplay: Roberto Orci, Alex Kurtzman and Gene Roddenberry
Director of Photography: Dan Mindel
Music: Michael Giacchino
Panavision/DeLuxe
A Spyglass/Bad Robot Production
Released by Paramount Pictures
126 minutes

Chris Pine (James T. Kirk), Zachary Quinto (Spock), Leonard Nimoy (Spock Prime), Eric Bana (Nero), Bruce Greenwood (Captain Christopher Pike), Karl Urban (Dr Leonard 'Bones' McCoy), Zoë Saldana (Uhura), Simon Pegg (Montgomery 'Scotty' Scott), John Cho (Hikaru Sulu), Anton Yelchin (Pavel Chekov), Ben Cross (Sarek), Winona Ryder (Amanda Grayson), Clifton Collins Jr. (Ayel), Chris Hemsworth (Lieutenant George Kirk), Jennifer Morrison (Winona Kirk), Faran Tahir (Captain Robau), Jacob Kogan (young Spock), Jimmy Bennett (young James T. Kirk)

* * *

The *Star Trek* franchise – a snowballing enigma of TV series and movie spin-offs – actually began with a single TV pilot, 'The Cage', starring Jeffrey Hunter as Captain Christopher Pike. The subsequent cult TV series ran for 79 hour-long episodes over three seasons on NBC, from 1966 to 1969, with Captain James T. Kirk replacing Pike at the helm of the starship USS *Enterprise*. The series was created by Gene Roddenberry and made household names of its cast regulars – William Shatner played Kirk, Leonard Nimoy was half-human, half-Vulcan science officer Mr Spock and DeForest Kelley played medic Dr Leonard 'Bones' McCoy. The adventures pitted them against a roster of bad guys, assorted allies, love entanglements and monsters in far-off galaxies and time frames, with the concept behind the series 'Wagon Train in space'. Its trademarks included the opening captain's log narration and stardate time frame, the iconic uniforms, phaser weapons that can be set to 'stun', the white starship USS Enterprise (armed with photon torpedoes) and galloping 'Telstar'-style theme-tune music by Alexander Courage. Viewed today the series retains its retro charm and in the intervening years it has built up a strong, loyal fan base through TV repeats, both in the US and UK – the so-called Trekkers.

As Nimoy recalled, when he went to see Star Wars in 1977 and witnessed the audience's reaction, he knew it wouldn't be long before Paramount contacted him about a Star Trek spin-off movie. He was contacted within days of Star Wars' success. Star Trek: The Motion Picture (1979) was helmed by Robert Wise, the director of The Day the Earth Stood Still. The TV-series regulars returned for this outing and the screenplay was a contraction of two episodes from the series, 'The Changeling' and 'The Doomsday Machine'. In the twenty-third century, Earth is menaced by a noxious blue cloud, which heads through space, obliterating everything in its path. The film opens with three Imperial Klingon cruisers being disintegrated with plasma energy. Having been away from command for two and a half years, Admiral James T. Kirk (Shatner) manages to regain command of the Enterprise, at the United Federation of Planets' Starfleet Headquarters in San Francisco. The Enterprise has undergone a revamp and a refit, and its present commander, Willard Decker (Stephen Collins), stays on as the ship's executive officer. The ship's chief engineer is Commander Montgomery 'Scotty' Scott (James Doohan). Other familiar faces present included Sulu (George Takei), Uhura (meaning 'freedom' in Swahili, played by Nichelle Nichols), Pavel Chekov (Walter Koenig) and Dr Christine Chapel (Majel Barrett). 'Bones' McCoy (Kelley) arrives grumpily, as he's only present because he's been drafted. When a Vulcan science officer, Commander Sonak (Jon Rashad Kamal), is killed in a teleportation accident, Spock (Nimoy) beams up from Vulcan to be installed in his place.

Star Trek: The Motion Picture, while successful on its own terms, exhibits remarkable reverence for the series, and Jerry Goldsmith's majestic score and the widescreen Panavision cinematography by Richard H. Cline combine to excellent effect. The extended scene when Kirk is reunited with the Enterprise, circling his old craft and admiring her, is scored as a romantic love scene, while the drifting blue malevolence has a jarring chord as its ominous leitmotif. There's great beauty to the visuals here, almost at the expense of action and story. The visual and special effects, some of which were overseen by Douglas Trumbull and John Dykstra, stage 2001-like planets and starfields and graceful, gliding spacecraft. The instantly recognisable Enterprise NCC 1701 with its sleek design is retained for the movie, looking rather like an elegant airship. As to be expected, the craft's sets are a huge leap forward in interior decoration, with the iconic bridge considerably improved for this widescreen outing. When the ship encounters turbulence, or undergoes attack, the crew are thrown from side to side (the camera tilting to accentuate the motion) and cling on to the furniture, as though tossed upon a raging sea. They also 'beam up' in the teleporter, just like in the series.

When the *Enterprise* is drawn deep into the intruder cloud's interior by a tractor beam, the evil force takes over the ship's Delton navigator, Ilia (Persis Khambatta). Earlier there had been a whiff of romance between her and Decker. Now reprogrammed by the entity, named V'Ger, she demands to be taken by these 'carbon-based units' (humans) to its creator on Earth. At the centre of the vast cloudy mass, Kirk and company find the wreck of NASA's *Voyager 6*, an Earth exploratory spacecraft launched over 300 years ago, which was thought lost in a black hole. The craft has been drifting through space, accumulating so much knowledge that it has become a living entity. The romance between Decker and Ilia is consummated when they kiss, as they are united 'in flux', a melding that results in the intruder's destruction and the salvation of Earth. In this way, rather like an episode of the TV series, parity is restored, and the old familiar crew is ready to embark on future adventures. Uhura asks Kirk for a heading. 'Out there', points Kirk into space, 'thataway' – as the *Enterprise* zooms off at warp one and a caption announces: 'The human adventure is just beginning.'

Though *Star Trek: The Motion Picture*'s special-effects schedule was rushed, its budget ballooned from $15 million to $45 million and critics dubbed it 'the motionless picture', it still took $56 million in the US on its release in 1979. A ready-made audience of Trekkers ensured the film's success. As Nimoy recalled of the franchise's success and his close association with Mr Spock, he was never short of work. But he remains forever associated with his distinctive creation, with his arched eyebrows, pointed ears, emotion-less logical demeanour of dark mystery and the ability to immobilise enemies with his Vulcan 'nerve pinch'.

Nicholas Meyer's *Star Trek II: The Wrath of Khan* (1982) was a sequel to the TV episode 'Space Seed' (from February 1967), which featured despot Khan Noonien Singh (Ricardo Montalbán). When the starship USS *Reliant*, commanded by Captain Terrell (Paul Winfield) and Chekov (Koenig), investigate lifeless Ceti Alpha V, they are captured by Khan and other survivors of a prison colony, who have been stranded there for 15 years. Khan seeks revenge on Kirk for the death of his wife. The neighbouring planet Ceti Alpha VI exploded shortly after their arrival and the devastation laid waste to Ceti Alpha V. Khan and his clan take over the *Reliant* and seek out Kirk, who is on a routine training exercise with an *Enterprise* crew largely consisting of untried space cadets. Spock, Bones, Uhura and Sulu are present, plus Vulcan cadet Saavik (Kirstie Alley). Khan attacks the laboratory on Regula 1, where they torture and wipe out most of the researchers. Dr Carol Marcus (Bibi Besch), Kirk's old flame, manages to escape, but her Genesis project, a device capable of creating planetary life, falls into Khan's possession.

This second instalment is rated by many fans as the best and the crew have new, dark-crimson uniforms. Kirk ponders philosophically about ageing and the film also examines his relationship with David Marcus (Merritt Butrick), his son with Carol. Montalbán is wonderful, leading his barbarian brigands like a white-haired Apache war chief. Noteworthy moments include when the *Enterprise* and the *Reliant* stalk each other through the shifting blue-and-magenta clouds of nebula before the showdown. The space academy practice exercise, the attempted rescue of spacecraft *Kobayashi Maru*, is played out for real in the finale, with a solution found to this no-win quandary. The film's biggest shock comes with the death of Spock, who gives his life to re-energise the *Enterprise*'s power circuits. This enables the craft to outrun the explosion caused when Khan goes out in a blaze of glory, by detonating the Genesis device aboard the *Reliant*. Spock shares a few last words with Kirk, performs his familiar Vulcan hand salute and utters his credo one final time: 'Live long and prosper.' His casket is jettisoned into space, where it comes to rest amid the lush woodland of the planet created in the wake of the Genesis explosion. Thus the sacrifice of the few, or the one, for the greater good of many, gives new life to old.

Star Trek II, which took $97 million from a tightly reined budget of $11 million, was deemed a great success. *Star Trek III: The Search for Spock* (1984) was directed by Spock himself, Nimoy. Spock was a two-hour make-up job, but thankfully he was on screen very little. The *Enterprise* is to be decommissioned. Colonel Morrow (Robert Hooks) refuses Kirk permission to go in search of Spock, when the Vulcan contacts him via Bones and reveals that he is on Genesis. Before his demise, Spock mind-melded with Bones and the doc is now the keeper of the Vulcan's soul. Kirk, Bones, Sulu, Chekov and Scotty steal the *Enterprise* and head for Genesis. Meanwhile David Marcus (Butrick) and Saavik (Robin Curtis) are exploring the planet, where Spock has regenerated as a young boy. As a result of the accelerating Genesis effect, the planet and Spock are maturing at an alarming rate, with the planet set to destroy itself within hours. In this instalment, the villains are the Klingons, in their first prominent appearance for a big-screen outing. They covet the Genesis, which they plan to use as a weapon. They are led by Kruge (Christopher Lloyd) and he and his men speak their own language, devised by linguist Marc Okrand. The Klingons fly a Romulan starship, with an invisibility 'cloaking device'. They kill Kirk's son, destroy the USS *Grissom* and even the *Enterprise* is sacrificed, going down in a blaze of glory, so that Kirk can rescue Spock. With the *Enterprise* crew safely aboard the hijacked Klingon vessel, Kirk settles his score with Kruge with a good old-fashioned brawl as Genesis volcanically ruptures. The rapidly maturing Spocks on Genesis were played by Carl Steven, Vadia Potenza, Stephen Manley and Joe W. Davis. Sexy space warrior Valkris (Cathie Shirriff) makes an early appearance, but is swiftly obliterated by the Klingons. In the finale, Kirk and company rendezvous with Uhura on Vulcan and in a ceremony on Mount Selena, Spock's soul is restored in a ritual presided over by Spock's father, Ambassador Sarek (Mark Lenard) and the High Priestess (Dame Judith Anderson). In saving his friend above all else, Kirk has proved with this episode that now the needs of the one have outweighed the needs of the many.

Star Trek IV: The Voyage Home (1986) was again directed by Nimoy and began with Kirk, Spock, Bones, Scotty, Sulu, Chekov and Uhura leaving Vulcan to return to Earth. Our planet is facing destruction from a vast approaching probe that is emitting a message that's revealed to be the song of the humpback whale, a species that has been extinct on Earth since the twenty-first century. Travelling in their purloined Klingon ship, now dubbed *HMS Bounty*, the crew travel through a time warp and back to the US west coast, circa 1986, to locate a whale and take it back to the twenty-third century to save Earth from obliteration. This $26 million epic was shot on the Paramount lot and on location in California, including San Francisco Bay and Monterey Bay Aquarium, Monterey. The heroes land their invisible 'Bird of Prey' craft in Golden Gate Park and proceed to scour San Francisco for three vital components: humpback whales, nuclear photons to recharge the Klingon craft's dilithium crystals and a tank to transport the mammals to the twenty-third century. Scotty and Bones visit a Plexiglas company to acquire a floatation tank, Uhura and Chekov attract the attention of a cop when they enquire where nuclear weapons are stowed (they eventually drain power from aircraft carrier *Enterprise*, actually played by USS *Ranger*). Shatner and Nimoy forge an unlikely odd couple double act – Kirk in his crimson tunic, Spock in flowing white robes and a headband. Having located two humpback whales at the Sausalito Cetacean Institute, they enlist the help of whale biologist Dr Gillian Taylor (Catherine Hicks), who asks why wacko Spock keeps addressing Kirk as 'Admiral'. Kirk romances Gillian in some well-played scenes – if *The Wrath of Khan* was Nimoy's finest acting hour, then this may be Shatner's. The film's noble ecological, anti-whaling message (a hunt to extinction) is almost lost amid the fast pace and comedy. The film begins with a 'story so far' segment, like a TV episode, and is dedicated to the men and women of spaceship *Challenger*, a reference to the Space Shuttle disaster of January 1986, when seven astronauts died as their craft disintegrated on take-off. Back in the twenty-third century, the whales' song answers the cylindrical probe, which is neutralised. Kirk et al. are exonerated of stealing the *Enterprise*, though for disobeying orders Kirk is demoted to captain and he and his crew are assigned a new ship, the *Enterprise NCC 1701-A*.

The original crew soldiered on through two more adventures. *Star Trek V: The Final Frontier* (1989) had the *Enterprise* investigating the kidnapping of three dignitaries – including Klingon St John Talbot (David Warner) – on Nimbus III in the Neutral Zone. The culprit, zealot Sybok (Laurence Luckinbill), who is also Spock's half-brother, wants to use the starship *Enterprise* to travel to the centre of the galaxy to confront God himself. Fittingly for a film directed and co-scripted by Shatner, the focus is on Kirk. The movie opens with him tackling El Capitan in Yosemite National Park, and the central axis for much of the action is the trio of Kirk, Spock and Bones.

This was followed by the superior *Star Trek VI: The Undiscovered Country* (1991), directed by Nicholas Meyer. The Klingons' moon, Praxis, explodes from over-mining, resulting in Klingon society having only 50 years left. The Klingons proffer peace with the United Federation of Planets and a new unity in the 'undiscovered country' (the future) which will mothball Starfleet. During a peace-mission rendezvous, the *Enterprise* defiles the fragile truce, fires on the Klingon vessel *Kronos 1* and assassins murder Chancellor

Korkon (David Warner) of the Klingon high council. Kirk and his crew have been framed and the actual shots were fired from a prototype Klingon ship that can fire when cloaked in invisibility. Kirk and Bones are sentenced to life imprisonment in a dilithium mine on snow-swept asteroid 'Aliens' Graveyard', while Spock and crew attempt to solve the chancellor's murder. Christopher Plummer played Klingon General Chang, the Shakespearean eye-patch-wearing villain of the piece, and Kim Cattrall donned pointed ears as a Vulcan helmsman. Iman was shape-shifting convict Martia, who at one point transforms into Kirk for some Shatner-vs-Shatner action (the first bout since the spaghetti Western *White Comanche* in 1968). Sulu is now captain of his own craft, the *Excelsior*. The film displays interesting themes of diplomacy and reconciliation, and some good tension throughout the story. This one begins with the dedication 'For Gene Roddenberry', who died in 1991. On stardate 6525.1, the *Enterprise* is informed that it is to be decommissioned and the crew retired. The regular cast's names appear as signatures against the starfield, in tribute to the end of their voyage.

During *Star Trek*'s big-screen era, the TV series *Star Trek: The Next Generation* (1987–94), ran for 178 hour-long episodes. A highly successful sci-fi series in its own right, it depicted the adventures of the USS *Enterprise NCC-1701-D*, captained by Jean-Luc Picard (Patrick Stewart). His crew included first officer Commander William T. Ryker (Jonathan Frakes), android Data (Brent Spiner), Geordi La Forge (LeVar Burton), Dr Beverly Crusher (Gates McFadden), Deanna Troi (Marina Sirtis) and Lieutenant Worf (Michael Dorn), a Klingon who gave the Federation starship insider knowledge of their enemies. It was natural for this series too to transfer to the big screen, and in David Carson's *Star Trek: Generations* (1994) the Kirk era met the Picard era in a story that threw everything at the audience – from warmongering Klingons to the holodeck, a feature of the *Next Generation*. Malcolm McDowell played Dr Soran, who has plans to live for eternity in the utopian Nexus. It is up to Picard and co. to stop him, but when he pursues Soran through an energy ribbon into the Nexus, Picard encounters Kirk, who was thought to have been killed in space 78 years ago. Kirk, Chekov and Scotty had been special guests on the *NCC-1701-B*'s maiden voyage, but during a rescue mission Kirk was lost. Later, as the two captains unite to fight Soran, Kirk is killed.

The *Next Generation* cast then continued the film series with *Star Trek: First Contact* (1996) and *Star Trek: Insurrection* (1998), both of which were directed by Jonathan Frakes, and Stuart Baird's *Star Trek: Nemesis* (2002). By far the best aspect of *The Next Generation* was the commanding performance from Stewart as Captain Picard, who gave the material gravitas with his meditative wisdom, indomitable spirit and gently encouraging catchphrase: 'Make it so.' In addition there were two further spin-off TV series. *Star Trek: Deep Space Nine* (1993–9) was set on the Federation space station of the title, with Avery Brooks as Captain Benjamin Sisko, and regulars including René Auberjonois, Nana Visitor, Colm Meaney, Cirroc Lofton and Armin Shimerman. *Star Trek: Voyager* (1995–2001) followed the starship on its return journey to Earth through the Delta Quadrant. Kate Mulgrew played Captain Kathryn Janeway, and the cast included Robert Beltran, Tim Russ, Robert Duncan McNeill, Roxann Dawson, Robert Picardo, Ethan Phillips, Garrett Wang and Jennifer Lien, with Jeri Ryan as sexy Borg Seven of Nine.

In 2009, the *Star Trek* cinema franchise was rebooted by Paramount. Titled simply *Star Trek*, J.J. Abrams's film went back to look at how all the characters met. The USS *Kelvin* is under attack from Romulan ship the *Narada*, which has travelled from the future. When the *Kelvin*'s commander Captain Robau (Faran Tahir) is killed, Lieutenant George Kirk (Chris Hemsworth) takes the helm, while his pregnant wife Winona (Jennifer Morrison) manages to escape the attack. She gives birth to a son, whom she names James (after her father) Tiberius (after his father), while George is killed by the Romulans. Tearaway James T. Kirk (Chris Pine) grows up in Iowa and speeds along deserty roads to 'Sabotage' by the Beastie Boys. Following encouragement from Captain Christopher Pike (Bruce Greenwood), he follows in his father's footsteps and enrols in Starfleet Academy. Although he has been accepted into the Vulcan Science Academy, half-human, half-Vulcan Spock (Zachary Quinto) also enrols at Starfleet.

Three years later headstrong Kirk is accused of cheating on his *Kobayashi Maru* test by Spock. An attack on Vulcan by a Romulan ship leads to the Starfleet cadets being deployed in action aboard the *Enterprise*. The Romulans bore into the planet with a core drill and destroy Vulcan with 'red matter'. When Kirk becomes stranded on Delta Vega, he meets Ambassador Spock (Leonard Nimoy) in the future, who informs him that the Romulan's commander, war criminal Nero (Eric Bana), blames Spock for the destruction of Romulus. Beamed back aboard the *Enterprise*, Kirk takes command, leads a surprise attack on the *Narada* and eventually manages to destroy the Romulan vessel before the core drill can bore into the Earth. Pike is promoted to Admiral and Kirk is made captain of the *Enterprise*.

This reboot was made with great reverence for its subject matter. A measure of this reverence and attention to detail is that the *Enterprise*'s Starfleet computer was voiced by Majel Barrett Roddenberry, the series creator's wife, who had voiced the computer on TV. Nimoy also made a reappearance, as Spock Prime, who appears in a time-travelling alternate reality created by the Romulans. Thus continuity with elements of the original franchise was established. Key ingredients and dialogue also surface, such as the Vulcan nerve pinch and 'set phasers to stun'. The well-paced, eventful story was written by Robert Orci and Alex Kurtzman. Throughout the story, familiar characters appear, including 'Bones' McCoy (Karl Urban), Uhura (Zoë Saldana), Hakira Sulu (John Cho) and Anton Yelchin (Pavel Chekov). Simon Pegg played Montgomery 'Scotty' Scott, who delivers such familiar lines as 'I'm giving her all she's got, Captain.' Ben Cross and Winona Ryder played Spock's parents, while Captain Pike forged links with the very first TV pilot, 'The Cage'. The film's trump card is Zachary Quinto as Spock. He is perfect as the pointy-eared human–Vulcan hybrid. Quinto had risen to prominence in the sci-fi series *Heroes* as killer Sylar, which also featured George Takei in a supporting role.

Abrams's *Star Trek* was filmed for $140 million, on location in California, Vermont, Utah and at Paramount Studios. Locations included Vasquez Rocks (Agua Dulce) and San Rafael Swell (Utah) as Vulcan, and California State University, Northridge, Los Angeles, as Starfleet Academy. The special effects look splendid in Panavision and it was also exhibited in IMAX. There's a real sense of cinematic artistry to the visuals, of colour and space, in Dan Mindel's cinematography, and there's also good use of lens flare – that sunbeam sunburst effect first associated with acid trip movies such as *Easy Rider*. It's glorious to see the *Enterprise* back in action, and the scenes of combat and action, a swirl of colour, flash, speed and noise, are handled masterfully. Michael Giacchino composed an original, triumphant score, but also incorporated references to Courage's TV theme. The film's sign-off, with the *Enterprise* now manned by the classic *Star Trek* crew, features Nimoy intoning: 'Space, the final frontier. These are the voyages of the starship *Enterprise*.'

Star Trek was a hit at the box office when released in May 2009 and was received positively by Star Trek fans, film critics and general filmgoers. It has taken almost $400 million worldwide. The film was known in some territories as *Star Trek: The Future Begins* and trailers depicted the *Enterprise* under construction. It was a PG-13 in the US, a 12 certificate in the UK, and was nominated for four Oscars in 2010 (including Sound Editing, Sound Mixing and Visual Effects), though it only won Best Make-up for Barney Burman, Mindy Hall and Joel Harlow. The billing of 'not your father's *Star Trek*, but your father will probably love it anyway' telegraphed that the reboot was pitched at the current young generation of filmgoers. That it was so successful across all generations of sci-fi fans is testament to the filmmakers' skill. This resounding reboot was a welcome return for one of the most popular franchises in motion pictures – one built on mythology, fan loyalty, great characters and catchphrases, and stories that created, fed and grew the *Star Trek* cult. It is a myth that continues to thrive with fans and looks set to live long and prosper into a new millennium. With the cast in place and settled into their characters, Abrams returned to the franchise in 2013 for *Star Trek Into Darkness*. Pine, Quinto, Urban, Saldana, Cho, Yelchin, Pegg and Greenwood reprised their respective roles from the first film as the *Enterprise*'s crew, as did Nimoy as Spock Prime. New additions included Benedict Cumberbatch as villain Khan, Alice Eve as Dr Carol Marcus and Robocop himself, Peter Weller, as Carol's father. The film's huge grosses – over $450 million worldwide – ensured that the franchise's reboot was full of dilithium and not a doomed enterprise.

26

'I SEE YOU'

AVATAR (2009)

Director: James Cameron
Story and Screenplay: James Cameron
Director of Photography: Mauro Fiore
Music: James Horner
3-D HD Widescreen/DeLuxe Color
A James Cameron Film
Released by Twentieth Century Fox
155 minutes

Sam Worthington (Corporal Jake Sully), Zoë Saldana (Neytiri), Sigourney Weaver (Dr Grace Augustine), Stephen Lang (Colonel Miles Quaritch), Michelle Rodriguez (Trudy Chacón, Tiltrotor pilot), Giovanni Ribisi (Parker Selfridge), Joel David Moore (Dr Norm Spellman), Carol Christine Hilaria Pounder (Mo'at, Na'vi shaman and Neytiri's mother), Wes Studi (Eytukan, Omaticaya clan leader and Neytiri's father), Laz Alonso (Tsu'tey), Dileep Rao (Dr Max Patel), Scott Lawrence (ISV Venture Star Crew chief), James Pitt (Valkyrie Shuttle pilot), Peter Mensah (Horse clan leader), Alicia Vela-Bailey (Ikran clan leader), Jahnel Curfman and Ilram Choi (basketball avatars)

* * *

Having established himself as one of the foremost sci-fi directors of his generation, James Cameron's next foray into science fiction, produced again by Gale Anne Hurd, was very different to the action adventure of *The Terminator* and *Aliens*. *The Abyss* (1989) is essentially a sci-fi epic set underwater. Nuclear submarine USS *Montana* is sunk with all hands, following a mysterious close encounter in the deep. A salvage operation is launched from underwater rig *Deepcore*, 2,000 feet below the sea. The ocean floor landscapes, murkily lit by the salvagers' lamps, are lunar in their appearance. The salvagers' craft glide across the screen like spaceships, and their diving suits resemble space suits as they drift weightlessly through the azure world. This undersea kingdom as 'outer space' reappears at the beginning of Cameron's *Titanic* (1997), with salvagers exploring the sunken title vessel in futuristic-looking submersibles. In *The Abyss*, Cameron also looked at the tensions between an estranged couple – salvage-team leader Bud Brigman (Ed Harris) and engineer Lindsey Brigman (Mary Elizabeth Mastrantonio). Michael Biehn played Lieutenant Coffey, the jittery leader of a party of SEALs that is to recover the submarine's nuclear warheads. Other salvagers were played by Kimberly Scott (Lisa 'One Night' Standing) and John Bedford Lloyd ('Jammer' Willis). While Hurricane Fredrick rages on the surface, the crew of *Deepcore* detect an extrater-restrial presence. Coffey activates one of the warheads to explode, which then falls into a deep-water trench, so Bud must dive into the abyss to disarm it. There he encounters a massive spacecraft crewed by fluttering neon aliens, angelic in appearance and peaceful in intent. The alien spacecraft rises to the surface, saving Bud and the *Deepcore* rig, and beaching the operation's control ship, *Benthic Explorer*, on its vast hull. Alan Silvestri injected a massive dose of the biblicals with his heavenly score, but despite the hi-tech distractions, there's no avoiding that this is really an old-fashioned Hollywood love story of Bud and Lindsey's reconciliation. Nominated for several Oscars, *The Abyss* won only for Best Visual Effects.

In 1992 Cameron prepared a 171-minute 'special edition', which added approximately 28 minutes of footage. This begins with a quote from Friedrich Nietzsche: 'When you look into an abyss, the abyss also looks into you.' It fleshed out the salvage crews' personalities and drastically altered the climax. When Bud is taken inside the alien ship, he is now shown news footage of a massive tsunami about to engulf New York. Aliens can control water, which explains the long sequence in the original version with a water snake, which mimics the salvagers' faces (this effect was reputedly Cameron's try-out for the special effect used as the quicksilver cop in *Terminator 2*). The aliens tell Bud that if we continue to develop ever more powerful nuclear weapons, the aliens will intervene. The tsunami, at the point of destruction, freezes and then subsides. It was a warning, a demonstration of power, a message that Earth must heed or risk itself plunging into the abyss.

Barry Levinson's *Sphere* (1998) was Cameron-inspired aquatic sci-fi, with a team of specialists – including psychologist Dr Norman Goodman (Dustin Hoffman), his estranged lover, biochemist Dr Beth Halperin (Sharon Stone), and mathematician Harry Adams (Samuel L. Jackson) – investigating what they are told is a Pacific Ocean plane crash but is actually a spacecraft buried in coral since 1709. These aquanauts detect the presence of a ULF (unknown life form) and discover English language data screens and humanoid corpses. They surmise that this is a 300-year-old American spaceship, from a time when there weren't even Americans, let alone spaceships. A storm on the surface traps them below and audiences will empathise with the order, 'Break out your five-day deodorant pads – we're here for the duration.' Aboard the spaceship is a rippling gold sphere and the edgy narrative develops into a familiar aquanauts-in-jeopardy scenario, as the alien entity preys on their innermost fears.

Avatar (2009) was James Cameron's return to the genre with which he'd made his name. Some 15 years in gestation and making, its release in 3-D became the movie event of winter 2009–10, continuing Cameron's interest in fantastical, blue-hued other worlds. On the distant planet of Pandora, one of the moons of Polyphemus, 4.4 light years from Earth, the Research Development Administration (RDA) is mining valuable mineral unobtanium. The mining company, headed by ruthless Parker Selfridge, plan to relocate the native Na'vi population by diplomacy or force, out of their tropical jungle. The hub of the Na'vis' settlement, Hometree, sits on the unobtanium mother lode. Humans disguised as Na'vi – inhabiting avatars, or cloned Na'vi humanoid life forms – infiltrate the Na'vi settlement. The head of the Avatar programme, Dr Grace Augustine (Sigourney Weaver), plans to contact the Na'vi and study them. Corporal Jake Sully (Sam Worthington), a paraplegic Marine veteran, replaces his murdered brother Tommy on the project. Jake, in avatar form now able to walk, ingratiates himself with the Na'vi and is schooled in their ways by Neytiri (Zoë Saldana), the chief and shaman's daughter. Jake eventually gains their acceptance, trust and Neytiri's love, even though Neytiri is betrothed to Tsu'tey, the next clan leader (Laz Alonso), and is destined to become clan shaman. Jake has an ulterior motive: Colonel Miles Quaritch (Stephen Lang), the RDA's head of security, has promised Jake will undergo an operation enabling him to walk again if he reports all intelligence concerning the Na'vi to the RDA. Jake realises he cannot betray the Na'vi and their culture, but the RDA decide they have waited long enough for diplomacy to take its course and set about taking the Na'vi homeland with force.

Avatar's budget was an estimated $237 million. Though Cameron had conceived the film in 1994, filmmaking techniques simply weren't up to par for his vision. The project resumed in 2006. Prior to shooting, Cameron took his actors to Hawaii, to live like the Na'vi, to give them a sense of the jungle atmosphere, as there would be no physical sets for them to perform in back at the studio. Actors enacted scenes shot by motion-capture cameras at Hughes Aircraft Hangar in California and were then digitally enhanced. The film was shot in Stone Street Studios, Wellington, New Zealand, and in Los Angeles, with computer-generated landscapes combined with miniature work and other visual effects to create the wonderland of Pandora and its inhabitants. Special effects were created by, among others, Weta Digital, Stan Winston Studio and Weta Workshop. The film was imaged in 3-D with the Pace/Cameron Fusion Camera System, with colour by DeLuxe. Filming took place in April–December 2007, with Cameron meticulously designing every detail of the film, including providing the Na'vi with their own vocabulary.

The heroes and villains are drawn in broad, unsubtle strokes, resulting in two-dimensional characterisations, even in 3-D. But Cameron understands cinema and its visual possibilities. Avatar is a breathtaking cinematic experience – viewed ideally in a 3-D cinema with a large appreciative audience – and its real power lies not in its words but in its look and sound. The cinematography by Mauro Fiore renders Pandora in a pageant of imagination and colour, an exotic kaleidoscope of fauna and flora. This

When Worlds Collide: Na'vi Neytiri (Zoë Saldana) and soldier Jake Sully (Sam Worthington) meet and fall in love on the fantastical planet of Pandora. Poster artwork for James Cameron's all-time box-office champion, *Avatar* (2009).

includes the *Fungimonium giganteum* (giant neon toxic mushrooms), *Helicoradium spirale* (spiralled umbrellas that retract into the ground when touched) and the luminous, fluttering, jellyfish-like wood sprites. The film is infused with the bioluminescence that imbues the flora of Pandora with its lush, pulsating glow. This tropical tendril paradise, of mossy trees, crawling insects, tree-trunk bridges, the glowing Tree of Souls, waterfalls and vines, harbours great danger. Cameron fills his primordial world with pseudo-prehistoric beasts, such as the rhino-like charging hammerhead titanothere, the winged mountain banshees and the great leonopteryx, the so-called 'flying king lion'. To be avoided are the viperwolves, which hunt in packs by night, while the direhorses are the Na'vi's horse-like steeds.

The Na'vi avatars that the key protagonists inhabit and animate were created on Earth and allowed to grow naturally during the six-year journey to Pandora on the Interstellar Vehicle (ISV) *Venture Star*. Jake is placed in a pod from which he controls his avatar via sensors.

Such virtual-reality technology was nothing new to sci-fi. In *Alien Intruder* (1992), four lifers (including Maxwell Caulfield) from New Alcatraz maximum-security prison in AD 2022 are recruited for a salvage operation in the uncharted G-Sector on salvage spaceship USS *Presley*. As their weekend relaxation they use the Aphrodite programme – they enter pods (as in *Avatar*) and inhabit virtual-reality worlds: the Wild West, a 1950s biker scenario, a *Casablanca*-style film noir and a beach surfing idyll, where they enjoy sexual encounters. Into each fantasy, Ariel (Tracy Scoggins), a mysterious, sexy woman invades, seducing each convict. Eventually revealed to be the manifestation of an alien virus, she breaks out of their fantasies and into reality, as the convicts and Commander Skyler (Billy Dee Williams) jealously fight over her among themselves. In *Avatar*, injured Jake can now enjoy the sensory sensation of walking. When he sleeps, his avatar lives and vice versa. 'Out there is the true world, in here is the dream,' he surmises. The Na'vi call avatars Uniltirantokx: 'dreamwalker body'. After the RDA has been defeated in a climactic Battle of Pandora, which owes much to C.S. Lewis's *The Last Battle* and the battle for Naboo in *Star Wars Episode I: The Phantom Menace*, Jake is reborn as an avatar, setting up the inevitable sequels.

Just as filmmakers stopped shooting 'Injuns' in 1950s Westerns when they became 'Native Americans', so too have aliens become the goodies and it is we who are bad. The native population of Pandora is the Na'vi, blue humanoid creatures whose culture and tribal motifs resemble Native American Indians. Though their physical characteristics are human – two arms, two legs, one head, hands and feet, and the females of the species have breasts – their bodily features are almost feline, and they have pointed ears and long tails. The principal focus for the film is the Omaticaya clan, though when the tribes gather we are made aware of the wider Na'vi population – the Horse clan of the Plains, the Ikran people of the Eastern Sea. Their society is Neolithic and Carol Christine Hilaria Pounder played Mo'at, the clan's shamanic spiritual leader, a key player in Native American tribal custom, here called a *tsahik*, 'the one who interprets the will of Eywa' (the Na'vis' god). Wes Studi, who played Omaticaya clan leader Eytukan, was a full-blooded Cherokee from Oklahoma who has portrayed several iconic Native American roles on-screen, including Red Cloud, Wovoka, Black Kettle and Geronimo. The Na'vi's costuming and ornaments (including the warbonnet ferns), bows and arrows, knives and war paint closely resemble Native American culture, and when they are riding their direhorse steeds in full flight, they look like whooping 'Blueskins'. Critics christened Cameron's film 'Dances with Smurfs', for the plot's resemblance to the Oscar-winning Western *Dances with Wolves* (1990), where a soldier befriends and integrates into Sioux society. Bizarrely, the film *Avatar* most closely resembles is Antonio Margheriti's ecologically themed Italian action movie, *Indio* (1989). Francisco Quinn starred as half-Indian US marine Daniel Morell, who saves the rainforest and its inhabitants from ruthless developer Brian Dennehy, in a scenario that is equal parts *Rambo: First Blood Part II*, *Navajo Joe* and *The Mission*.

Avatar's ecological message, with the destruction of the Pandoran landscape by goliath RDA bulldozers which tear through the pretty undergrowth, is writ loud and clear. All the trees on Pandora are connected, creating a network of neurological connections greater than the human brain, while the chanted 'Hometree Songs', like Native American tribal rituals, fuse the inhabitants with their land. *Avatar* also references the endurance Western *A Man Called Horse* (1970), where Richard Harris's English lord is captured by the Sioux and learns their customs and way of life, eventually becoming accepted as one of their clan. Cameron's got everyone watching Westerns again, even if they don't realise it. In *Avatar*, Jake takes part in trials to become one of the clan, as when he treks into the Hallelujah Mountains – visually stunning stone-monolith outcrops, teeming with vegetation, that hover thousands of metres in the air – and creates a bond (*tsaheylu*) with an Ikran (a mountain banshee) to become a hunter (*taronyu*), as Jake finally becomes a 'son of Omaticaya'. Also referenced is *Stargate*, which featured a love story between an Egyptologist from another world, Dr Jackson (James Spader), and maiden Sha'uri (Mili Avital). The Na'vi have their own language, presented with on-screen subtitles (as do the natives of *Stargate*), and for some reason subtitled films always have added gravitas and meaning, even when fielding the most banal dialogue.

Within the scenario of Jake's dual relationship with the Na'vi and Neytiri, *Avatar* also looks at American politics and history in simple terms. Marine Jake is seen by the scientists as just 'another dumb grunt' and the military, the heroes of Cameron's *Aliens*, are the imperialist villains, who talk about winning over the 'hearts and minds' of the natives. The RDA military hardware – the C-21 Dragon Gunship, the looming, explosive-laden Valkyrie Shuttle and the AT-99 Scorpion Gunships – wouldn't look that out of place in Afghanistan. There's plenty of heavy artillery on display to please the shoot-'em-up fans – from the outsized S-9 Wasp revolvers and the hefty Gau 90 30-mm cannon, to the MK-6 Amplified Mobility Platform (the four-metre high robotic AMP Suits, with its enclosed cab and built-in-breathing system, or BIBS). When the Na'vi clans unite to fight for their vanishing world, the coming together of tribes resembles the Plains Indians uniting prior to the Battle of the Little Bighorn, while Quaritch resembles foolhardy Custer, here a muscle-bound bastard Rambo gone bad. 'Killing the indigenous looks bad', but if the Na'vi can't be persuaded to move off their land, 'it's gonna have to be all stick' (that is, military intervention). The scenes of destruction are shockingly realised within the fantasy sci-fi format. The felling of the hub of the Na'vi society, Hometree, devastatingly enacted on-screen with its cascading white ash and the fire imagery of which Cameron is so fond, is the Na'vis' 9/11. The final battle, where nature fights back and the Pandoran animals charge in to help out (like elephants in a Tarzan movie) may be contrived, but works brilliantly as spectacle. Particularly effective is James Horner's score, one of his finest, which combines indigenous tribal drums, flute blasts and primeval chanting with the tremendously moving, ebbing orchestral theme, powerfully rising and falling like an immense, unstoppable wave during the action scenes. The end titles are accompanied by 'I See You (Theme from *Avatar*)' performed by UK *X Factor* winner Leona Lewis.

Avatar was released in three formats – the 2K 3-D version, in a screen ratio of 1.78:1, which was also shown in the giant IMAX format, and a flat 2-D version in 2.35:1 wide-screen ratio. It was rated 12A in the UK (since re-rated 12 on DVD) and PG-13 in the US. DVD releases have included a 'Family Audio Track', which removes all 'objectionable language' for a home-video audience, though not the scenes of smoking, which are so frowned upon in media nowadays. Critics were generally favourable, with some jeering at the by-the-numbers plot and flimsy characterisation, but even if it had been universally slated, nothing would have suppressed the hype surrounding this movie, nor slowed the tsunami of filmgoers from heading towards cinemas. I saw it in 3-D in a packed house on its opening night on general release in the UK on Thursday, 16 December 2009, and it went down very well. Soon afterwards Sam Worthington starred as Perseus in *Clash of the Titans* (2010), which, following the huge box office of *Avatar*, was also released in 3-D. With a worldwide take by 31 January 2010 of $2 billion, *Avatar* rapidly became the biggest-grossing film in the history of cinema, wresting the honour from Cameron's own *Titanic* – though it was helped by the higher prices for 3-D and IMAX screenings. By November 2010 it had taken $760 million in the US. At the Oscars, it won awards for Cinematography, Art Direction and obviously Visual Effects, though it missed out on Best Picture, Best Director and Original Screenplay. *Avatar: Special Edition*, which features extra footage and runs 163 minutes, was released in cinemas in August 2010 and reaped further revenue. For DVD, a 'collector's extended cut' further enhanced the Pandoran environment and Jake's backstory, running 170 minutes. From the blue-hued cryo-cells aboard the ISV *Venture Star* to the incandescent bioluminescence and the scantily-clad Na'vi themselves, *Avatar* is one blue movie the whole family can enjoy.

At the turn of the new millennium, there was another sci-fi epic that gave everyone the blues. If *Avatar* was a costly gamble that paid off, *Battlefield Earth: A Saga of the Year*

3000 (2000) was one that didn't. In AD 3000, Earth is ruled by a race of cruel, opportunist aliens, the Psychlos, who mine Earth's valuable metals (notably gold) and teleport it to their home planet, Psychlo. Humans are reduced to cave-dwelling primitives, or else slaves in the Psychlo mines. Tyler (Barry Pepper), a troglodyte 'Greener', is captured and experimented on by the Psychlos to see if 'man animals' can be made intelligent enough to operate machinery in the gold mines. Via a laser-beam mind machine, Tyler acquires great scientific and mathematical knowledge, which he uses to lead a slave revolt that manages to rout the Psychlos and destroy their home planet. *Battlefield Earth* was directed by Roger Christian and was based on a 1982 novel by L. Ron Hubbard, the founder of the Church of Scientology. The plot is sound, but this ludicrous film is crippled by some of the most ridiculous visuals and ugliest make-up in cinema history. The endangered remnants of human society are *Captain Caveman* types: Tyler resembles the dreadlocked bass player from a swamp rock band and his cavegirl, Chrissy (Sabine Karsenti), is from the Raquel Welch school of troglodytes. The Psychlos feature amazing hairstyles (braids, dreadlocks, quiffs – often simultaneously), clawed hands and prominent eyebrows, and there's weird breathing apparatus that consists of a nasal clip and two tubular nose-danglers. Terl, the Psychlo security chief on Earth, was played by John Travolta, a Scientologist who as co-producer was instrumental in bringing Hubbard's book to the screen. He jovially overacts throughout, while delivering nonsense. Forest Whitaker appeared as Terl's Psychlo sidekick Ker, who resembles the Cowardly Lion in *The Wizard of Oz*, and other actors unfortunate enough to be involved include Kim Coates, Richard Tyson, Michael MacRae and Kelly Preston. The film keeps slipping into slow motion, and for the big, noisy, ramshackle finale Tyler teaches the humans how to fly US jet fighters (which they call 'flying spears') to defeat the Psychlos. This $44 million epic only managed to scratch back a fraction of its cost.

Like *Avatar*, Duncan Jones's *Source Code* (2011) had an injured protagonist who was 'existing' via a bodily vessel. The story, played out in eight-minute segments, depicted the frantic search for a bomb (and the passenger who planted it) on a CRR train bound for Chicago's Union Station. Captain Colter Stevens (Jake Gyllenhaal), a helicopter pilot in the 17th Airborne who last remembers being in Afghanistan, carries out the search. Each time he fails, the train blows up and he finds himself in a capsule, communicating via a visual-monitor screen with Coleen Goodwin (Vera Farmiga) and Dr Rutledge (Jeffrey Wright). They are part of the Source Code project, which allows a past real event to be 'reset' and their subject to relive the last eight minutes, an example not of time travel, but of time reassignment. Colter is 'a hand on a clock', which can be rewound to replay the event until the bomber is caught. The train attack is the first of a series – the train's demise is predestined, but the next attack, a dirty bomb to be detonated in downtown Chicago, can be averted. Through conversations with Coleen, Colter realises that he was killed in Afghanistan two months ago and his mutilated remains (critically his brain) have been kept alive. This experiment is not a simulation and real lives are at stake.

Colter's personality inhabits the body of passenger Sean Fentress, who is the avatar allowing him to carry out his investigation. Successive 'visits' to the train allow Colter to construct a picture of events, enabling him to deactivate the cellphone-activated train device (in the vent of the restroom) and locate the next bomb (in a van in a car park). Once his mission is completed, Colter is to be kept alive by Dr Rutledge as part of the Source Code project, even though the doctor promised to allow him to rest in peace. Colter is helped by Sean's work colleague, Christina Warren (Michelle Monaghan) and the bomber is eventually identified as Derek Frost (Michael Arden). The film also charts the developing relationship between Colter and Christina – it's *Groundhog Day* with a ticking bomb instead of Punxsutawney Phil. Chris Bacon provided the big Hitchcockian score. During phone conversations, Colter's father was voiced by Scott Bakula from the time-travelling TV show *Quantum Leap*. Shot in Montreal, Canada, and Chicago for $32 million, this brilliantly written tale by Ben Ripley has taken over $120 million worldwide and reinforced Jones's reputation for twisty sci-fi. In its simplicity, it's accessible, superior sci-fi; topically the successful deployment of the Source Code will now be a powerful weapon in the 'war on terror'.

If *Avatar* depicted an imaginary world that within the film's fantasy appeared to exist and *Source Code* a real world that could be manipulated, then Christopher Nolan went further in the creation of synthetic cinematic environments. A wholly original alternate take on alternate reality, Nolan's massively successful *Inception* (2010) took sci-fi film concepts to another plane. This intricate, literate, multilayered story featured thief Dom Cobb (Leonard DiCaprio), who infiltrates and inveigles the minds of his victims. His violations of people's minds – termed extractions – are engineered by his backup team, played by Joseph Gordon-Levitt, Ellen Page, Tom Hardy and Dileep Rao. His latest contract is one of corporate espionage. Cobb is employed by Mr Saito (Ken Watanabe) to plant the seed of an idea, an inception, into the subconscious mind of Robert Fischer (Cillian Murphy), son and heir of an energy empire currently run by his ailing father, Maurice (Pete Postlethwaite), with the aim of splitting up and weakening their empire.

The film unfolds in scenes of reality and unreality, of dreams within dreams, via a stream of unconsciousness where nothing has to make sense or add up. Cobb and his team traverse the spaces of Robert's mind, delving deeper and deeper, peeling back the onion layers of his subconscious dreams, which allows director Nolan free narrative rein. At one point the movie turns into a snowbound gun battle, like a James Bond movie; in another a train careers down a city street with no tracks. In the vividly realised moment of spatial disorientation, an incredible special effect renders the streets of Paris to fold over on themselves. Marion Cotillard played Cobb's deceased wife Mal, who continually manifests herself during the mission, jeopardising its success, and her ghostly presence is a memory Dom can't control or erase – like the ghosts of *Solaris*. The film's ambition is admirable, visually impressive and the narrative impressively complex, and Hans Zimmer's score to these imaginary dreamscapes is excellent. Nolan's cinematic syntax is bold, mesmerising filmmaking, but as is often the case with cerebral sci-fi – *Minority Report* for example – it often takes the easy, action set-piece way out, which distracts from something more interesting going on elsewhere. Films such as *Inception* are often over-praised for their complexity and ingenuity, the filmmakers safe in the knowledge that their work doesn't really have to hold together, unravel, sustain scrutiny or make sense. They're a dream, a fantasy, an unreality where the impossible and unimaginable are commonplace. As technologies continue to evolve and the cinema experience becomes ever more immersive, these science-fiction worlds will become ever more convincing – and the line between the real world and science fiction, between our space, outer space and cyberspace, will continue to blur.

BIBLIOGRAPHY AND SOURCES

Adams, Mark, *Mike Hodges* (Pocket Essentials, 2000)

Atkinson, John, *The Oscars* (Pocket Essentials, 2001)

Clarke, Arthur C., *2001: A Space Odyssey* (Hutchinson, 1968)

Cox, Alex and Nick Jones, *Moviedrome: The Guide* (Broadcasting Support Services, 1990)

Duncan, Paul, *Stanley Kubrick* (Pocket Essentials, 1999)

Eames, John Douglas, *The MGM Story* (Octopus, 1977)

——, *The Paramount Story* (Octopus, 1985)

Everman, Welch, *Cult Science Fiction Films* (Citadel Press, 1995)

Fane-Saunders, Kilmeny (ed.), *Radio Times Guide to Science Fiction* (BBC Worldwide, 2001)

Fitzgerald, Martin, *Orson Welles* (Pocket Essentials, 2000)

Fox, Keith and Maitland McDonagh, *The Tenth Virgin Film Guide* (Virgin, 2001)

Frank, Alan, *The Films of Roger Corman* (Batsford, 1998)

Gray, Beverly, *Roger Corman* (Renaissance Books, 2000)

Hardy, Phil (ed.), *The Aurum Encyclopedia of Science Fiction Movies* (Aurum, 1984)

——, *The Aurum Encyclopedia of Horror* (Aurum, 1985)

Hirschhorn, Clive, *The Warner Bros. Story* (Octopus, 1983)

Howarth, Troy, *The Haunted World of Mario Bava* (FAB Press, 2002)

Jewell, Richard B. and Vernon Harbin, *The RKO Story* (Octopus, 1982)

Kaminsky, Stuart M., *Don Siegel: Director* (Curtis, 1974)

Katz, Ephraim, *The Macmillan International Film Encyclopedia* (HarperCollins, 1998)

Lloyd, Ann (ed.), *Movies of the Fifties* (Orbis, 1982)

——, *Movies of the Sixties* (Orbis, 1983)

——, *Movies of the Seventies* (Orbis, 1984)

Lloyd, Ann, and Graham Fuller (eds), *The Illustrated Who's Who of the Cinema* (Orbis, 1983)

Luck, Steve (ed.), *Philip's Compact Encyclopedia* (Chancellor Press, 1999)

Maltin, Leonard (ed.), *2011 Movie Guide* (Signet, 2010)

Medved, Harry and Michael, *The Fifty Worst Films of All Time (And How They Got That Way)* (Angus & Robertson, 1978)

——, *Son of Golden Turkey Awards: The Best of the Worst from Hollywood* (Angus & Robertson, 1986)

Müller, Jürgen, *Movies of the 60s* (Taschen, 2004)

Newman, Kim, *Apocalypse Movies: End of the World Cinema* (St Martin's Griffin, 2000)

——, *Nightmare Movies: Horror on Screen since the 1960s* (Bloomsbury, 2011)

Nourmand, Tony and Graham Marsh, *Film Posters: Science Fiction* (Evergreen, 2006)

Ross, Jonathan, *The Incredibly Strange Film Book: An Alternative History of Cinema* (Simon & Schuster, 1993)

Rovin, Jeff, *A Pictorial History of Science Fiction Films* (Citadel Press, 1975)

Russell, Jamie, *Generation Xbox: How Video Games Invaded Hollywood* (Yellow Ant, 2012)

Scalzi, John, *The Rough Guide to Sci-Fi Movies* (Rough Guides, 2005)

Scheuer, Steven H. (ed.), *Movies on TV* (Bantam Books, 1977)

Siegel, Don, *A Siegel Film* (Faber and Faber, 1993)

Weldon, Michael J., *The Psychotronic Video Guide* (St Martin's Griffin, 1996)

Wells, H.G., *The Time Machine* (Penguin, 2005)

———, *The War of the Worlds* (Penguin, 2005)

Whitehead, Mark, *Roger Corman* (Pocket Essentials, 2003)

INTERNET SOURCES

The Internet Movie Database (www.imdb.com)

The British Board of Film Classification (www.bbfc.co.uk)

Amazon UK (www.amazon.co.uk)

Amazon US (www.amazon.com)

Box Office Mojo (www.boxofficemojo.com)

YouTube (www.youtube.com)

The Internet Archive (http://archive.org/details/moviesandfilms)

The Motion Picture Association of America (www.mpaa.org)

INDEX OF FILM TITLES

Productions listed where possible by their best known English language title, with alternative titles in parenthesis. TV = made-for-TV movie, series or miniseries, as indicated. Numbers in bold indicate illustrations. Titles in bold indicate chapter devoted to film.